INDUSTRIAL ENVIRONMENTAL MANAGEMENT
A PRACTICAL HANDBOOK

Jack E. Daugherty

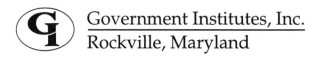

Government Institutes, Inc.
Rockville, Maryland

Government Institutes, Inc., 4 Research Place, Rockville, Maryland 20850, USA.

99 98 97 96   5   4   3   2

Library of Congress Cataloging-in-Publication Data

Daugherty, Jack E.

       Industrial environmental management: a practical handbook / by Jack E. Daugherty.
           p.   cm.
      Includes index.
      ISBN: 0-86587-515-4
      1. Industrial management--Environmental aspects. 2. Environmental management. I. Title
      HD30.255.D38   1996
      658.4' 08--dc20

                        95-48415
                        CIP

Printed in the United States of America

SUMMARY OF CONTENTS

TABLE OF CONTENTS

LIST OF FIGURES

PREFACE

Manufacturing plants, especially small to medium-sized ones, typically assign environmental compliance responsibilities to an overworked individual who is talented in his or her field, but a complete novice in environmental management. These *nonexpert generalists* may be personnel managers, plant engineers, maintenance superintendents, purchasing agents, etc. Often, they are not even technically oriented though some, such as plant engineers, do have a technical background.

A smaller group of plant environmental managers are professionals with immense responsibilities but slight authority and budget, until something goes wrong. Then they get a blank check to fix the problem. A few of these *expert generalists* work on small but effective teams of environmental professionals with adequate line authority and budget. Such teams report directly to the plant manager or a vice-president. Typically, each team member specializes in a compliance area (air, water, hazardous waste) but is not a specialist.

True *specialists* focus on only one aspect of a compliance area and are typically not found in industry, which can ill afford them, but in consulting firms, which hire them out at considerable cost to those who need their services.

This book is written for nonexpert generalists, but I hope that expert generalists and brand new specialists will gain from it, too. The idea for the book came from a roundtable meeting I established a few years ago. I was interested in developing sound source reduction plans, but information from pollution prevention clearinghouses had limited value. So I called some colleagues and started a monthly meeting at my plant to discuss compliance problems, source reduction difficulties, and success stories.

The meetings were fruitful, but it was clear that the nonexpert generalists worked under tremendous stress. One might say under duress. These colleagues were particularly stressed by complex regulations about which they were ignorant.

As a result of the roundtables, I became a mentor to several nonexpert compliance managers. Being a mentor is not the same as being a consultant. It is closer to being a father confessor or spiritual director who walks with you on a particular path but neither pushes or pulls, neither cajoles nor nags, neither laughs at nor tattles on. The mentor encourages the learner to think a problem through for himself or herself once all the facts are available.

Mentoring led to this practical, how-to book. Don't other books do that already? No. Indeed, many environmental management books are on the market, but none of them do what I hope I have accomplished herein. I place the books in four categories and, for the record, I endorse all of them and none of them. I am not naming favorites here.

Academic books are invaluable for professional environmental compliance managers, but nonexpert generalists often find their technical discussions, mathematical derivations, and formal voice to be intimidating. Academic books that specialize in one major compliance area are particularly invaluable for a deeper understanding of scientific and technical issues and solutions.

The books written in *regulatory* voice discuss laws and regulations by essentially repeating them word-for-word. This is important: the more viewpoints you have available on any given law or regulation, the quicker you can understand them and arrive at a sound compliance strategy for your plant. For persons intimidated by laws and regulations, these books do little to alleviate that fear. Nonexpert generalists may buy them, but they hardly ever read them, based on my own informal polling.

The *advanced* book, written by an experienced specialist for others in the field, is mostly over the heads of all but a chosen few and one generally has infrequent cause to consult them. Conference proceedings are in this category, but specialist books can be found in every major book publisher's current catalog.

Finally, *checklists*, written by veterans, are excellent tools when used by experts or specialists, or as an introduction to a topic. But nonexpert generalists have been known to get into trouble following checklists when they do not fully understand when and how to use them.

Each type of book is important. Each has its use. *Industrial Environmental Management* is one book that I hope you can use immediately with little experience or training, but one which will spark the learning process within you.

Do not treat this (or any) book as a free consulting service. An author can only describe problems in terms of generalities. Even if a particular example seems to exactly fit your problem or situation, factors not considered in the book may be crucial in your case. Do not treat a book as a source of legal advice. If you do, are you ever in trouble! First, I am not a lawyer. Second, discussions of laws and regulations herein are from the viewpoint of a regulated person, not of a regulator or legal expert. Third, even if I were a legal expert, there may be factors in your situation that would result in a dramatically different legal opinion than a case study may suggest.

Caveats notwithstanding, I hope this book helps you in your job.

Jack E. Daugherty
Jackson, MS

ABOUT THE AUTHOR

The effects of explosive, nuclear, biological and chemical agents on the human body that he studied during eleven years in the United States Navy inspired **Jack E. Daugherty** to pursue a career in environmental safety and health engineering when he left the service in 1977.

Since then, his professional experience in EH&S has ranged from studying sedimentation rates and implementing chemical safety procedures and training at Engelhard Minerals and Chemicals and process-orienting environmental safety and health affairs with Mississippi Chemical Corporation to managing clients' air, water, hazardous waste, pesticide, PCB, remediation, and closure projects while at Environmental Protection Systems and his current duties as environmental and safety engineer for Vickers Inc., where he has worked since 1987.

Jack holds Master's and Bachelor's degrees in Chemical Engineering from the University of Mississippi and Auburn University, respectively. He is a Certified Industrial Hygienist, Certified Hazardous Materials Manager, and a professional engineer licensed in the state of Mississippi. He is a member of the American Society of Safety Engineers' Mississippi Chapter, the American Industrial Hygiene Association, the American Academy of Industrial Hygiene, and the Academy of Certified Hazardous Materials Managers.

Jack's articles on environmental and occupational safety and health topics have appeared in several trade journals including *Occupational Hazards* and *Industrial Safety and Hygiene News*. He is listed in *Who's Who in the South*.

A native of Tennessee, Jack lives and works in Jackson, MS. He is married to the former Carolyn Anne Guidry of New Orleans. They are the parents of Scott Daugherty and Rayne Mabus (wife of Barry) and grandparents of Joshua, Zachery, and Andrew Mabus.

ACKNOWLEDGMENTS

I wish to acknowledge and thank the staff of Government Institutes, Inc., for their patience and assistance. Never in my wildest dreams did I imagine that such a work as this would be easy, but it would have been far more difficult, if not impossible, without expert advice about book crafting. Special thanks to Alex Padro who believed in my project and to Terry Fischer for his assistance.

How far can a person go with an encouraging, affirming spouse? As far as he or she wants. I think that such a person has no boundaries, so I wish to express my gratitude and love for my wife. She is a gift of joy.

To my soul brothers Skip Wilson, Mike Booth, Michael Denham, and David Hagan, many thanks for their belief in me, their affirming brotherhood, and especially for their persistent prayer for me. Skip, this is my tao.

To my inspiration, my life—Pepper

1

Understanding Environmental Hazards

The challenges of managing pollution in the next century, and solving environmental problems left over from this century, have their roots in the past. An increase in the sensible management of environmental hazards has occurred despite much inertia and lack of leadership. Now, at least, compliance management has become a distinct profession.

Hazardous residuals of human endeavor have been around for a long time. Even when people occupied themselves mostly with hunting game or gathering seeds and nuts, residuals bearing natural poisons had to be dealt with in order for the nascent human race to survive. An encounter with an unknown species of plant or animal meant taking a gamble; the stakes could be life or death. Primitive people accepted such hazards as evidence of the capricious nature of their gods.

Today, we know more about environmental hazards and people are not as willing to accept these risks as they once were. Acceptance of risk is a paradox in modern society. Modern people voluntarily accept risk, but do not accept imposed risk. Good citizens will not accept a hazardous waste management facility in their community (imposed risk), but they will smoke, drive faster than the speed limit, drive without lap and shoulder restraints, and drive while intoxicated (voluntary risks). A lesson for environmental compliance managers is that, no matter how comfortable you feel around your waste materials, other people do not necessarily feel safe when they are exposed to the same potential hazards. Modern society expects science and technology to continually improve the standard of living, yet progress has its price, a price which is becoming dearer.

Some people are disillusioned with science and technology. It is up to industrial environmental compliance managers—as well as scientists and policy makers—to restore faith in human achievement. Three types of compliance managers can be found in industry: nonexpert generalists, expert generalists, and specialists. The generalist has the task of keeping an industrial plant in compliance with all sorts of tough, confusing laws and regulations. The nonexpert generalist must perform these same tasks while also performing unrelated duties which are his or her principal responsibilities. The stress of establishing and maintaining compliance—often with unfamiliar rules and technical and legal issues which he or she does not understand—can be overwhelming. Sometimes environmental compliance management seems like a monolithic structure of infinite proportions. One would just like to know where to start.

A general familiarity with the rules is quite feasible: technical and legal issues do have a logical basis. The compliance management monolith can be broken down into basic building blocks which can be more readily digested. Let us start by examining pollution and its effects in each media of the environment of human beings: Earth with its atmosphere and water and soils and human society.

AIR POLLUTION

Air pollution has been a problem since the dawn of time. Nature has always polluted the air in titanic proportions by means of volcanic eruptions, cyclonic storms, and forest fires. Humanity and the polluted residuals of its progress has been a relatively recent atmospheric annoyance. To understand humanity's atmospheric impact, we must first look at the anatomy of the atmosphere which has four chief components: the troposphere, stratosphere, mesosphere, and thermosphere.

From the surface of the earth to just over nine miles high is the troposphere. This is the area where clouds form, convective currents (winds) occur, and air temperature decreases with altitude. Falling temperatures create vertical mixing in the rigorous troposphere. The decrease of temperature with altitude ceases at the tropopause, a transition zone between the troposphere and the stratosphere.

The air temperature begins to increase again with altitude in the stratosphere, which is the component from the tropopause to about thirty miles high at the next transition zone, the stratopause. Very little vertical mixing occurs in the stratosphere. From thirty to fifty miles high we find the mesosphere, where temperatures again decrease with altitude and vertical mixing occurs. The mesopause divides the mesosphere and thermosphere. The major portion of the stratosphere, the mesosphere and the lower part of the thermosphere are called the chemosphere. The thermosphere is located from about fifty to seventy-plus miles out into space.

The transitional locations within this layered atmospheric system vary with latitude, season, and time. Mostly we have tried to protect the troposphere, where we live, but in recent years we have found the need for concern about other levels of the atmosphere as well.

Though natural phenomena can contribute huge amounts of pollution to the atmosphere, humankind also has had an increasingly ill effect on this atmospheric system. Anthropogenic (human-made) air pollution is not a new phenomenon. In the twelfth century, for instance, Spanish philosopher and physician Moses Maimonides wrote about air pollution problems in Spanish cities.

Often, not only has the growth of human endeavor had a negative impact on the environment, but also the environment has been affected by our economic choices. In the thirteenth century in London, for instance, coal replaced wood as the fuel of choice in fireplace and factory alike, causing the London air to become so repugnant that, in 1257, Eleanor, queen of Henry III, felt obliged to move from Nottingham for the protection of her health.

The first known pollution abatement law, passed by the English parliament in 1273, prohibited smoke because it was detrimental to public health. In 1307, the King proclaimed the burning of coal to be illegal in London. The need for heat and power meant these laws were unenforceable, and smog in London was just as prevalent some three hundred years later.

Air pollution as a public policy and health problem worsened with the rapid industrial expansion experienced during the Industrial Revolution. People unmistakably became seriously ill as a result of exposure to air pollution. Then, in 1930, emissions from steel mills in the Meuse River valley in eastern Belgium resulted in sixty confirmed deaths over a six day period. Air pollution was no longer just a nuisance; it had turned lethal.

Injury to vegetation from air pollution was first reported in Los Angeles County, California, in 1944. Los Angeles is plagued with petrochemical pollution which comes not only from factories, of which

Los Angeles has plenty, but also from unburned hydrocarbons in the exhaust of automobile engines. Los Angeles freeways are the epitome of the modern superhighway; perhaps Greater Los Angeles has more vehicles in one air pollution basin than any other place on earth.

Emissions from heavy industries in the Monangahela River Valley, in southwest Pennsylvania, combined to form a lethal gas which caused twenty deaths and 6,000 illnesses in the town of Donora, which is located on a hill overlooking the polluting mills. Roughly forty-five percent of the population of Donora became ill during the episode, which lasted from October 30 to 31, 1948—Donora's Halloween of Death.

In London, fog, sulfur dioxide emissions from factories, and particulates from fireplaces combined to cause 3,000 to 5,000 deaths more than normal during a two-week period in 1952. This lethal combination came to be known as *smog*, short for "smoke and fog." The temperature inversion, which existed over London during these episodes, was at such a low altitude that tall smokestacks could be seen in clear air above the smog.

On Thanksgiving Day in 1966, a three day temperature inversion over New York City trapped particulate matter, hydrocarbons, ozone, sulfur dioxide and carbon monoxide at ground level. Between 150 and 175 people were confirmed to have died as a result of the episode.

In early 1973, 50,000 people were told to wear gas masks in Marghera, a port town near Venice, Italy. Industrial emissions were so voluminous and concentrated in Marghera that at least one worker had to be hospitalized each day due to breathing the noxious cloud of pollution that hung in the factory yards and buildings. As late as 1976, fourteen people in Marghera died during an air pollution emergency.

Around 1970, atmospheric scientists determined that acid precipitation, airborne toxics, and other anthropogenic air pollution were linked in one continuous cycle with the chemistry of the pristine troposphere. This discovery raised the stakes of uncontrolled air pollution to apocalyptic portions and meant that even the future of the human race could be at risk. About half of today's world-wide urban population—over one billion people—breathes unacceptable levels of sulfur dioxide. Atmospheric levels of sulfur dioxide and other pollutants (such as particulate matter (PM), nitrogen oxides, and carbon monoxide) have been reduced when considered overall, but these reductions just have not benefitted the urban populations. Along with unchecked development of the earth's surface, more fuel burners are in use, including vehicles with internal combustion engines. Even though these wonderful machines are intended to make the lives of modern people easier, freer, and more fun, they emit an ever increasing pollution load into the air.

Air pollution is emerging as the critical international issue for the twenty-first century. To assign a low priority to the problem verges on criminal negligence, and, in fact, our government as well as other governments have declared air pollution to be a high priority by legislation and treaty. To overreact and prohibit further development is to dictate austere living conditions for much of the world. Modern people want a pristine planet yet are unwilling to give up their late-twentieth century luxuries. Today, nations are discussing the concept of sustainable development (discussed below), a process which, in theory, allows both the population of this planet and industrial progress to double or triple in the next century while improving living conditions for much of the human race.

Smog/Tropospheric Ozone

The principal ingredient of urban smog is ozone. While beneficial in the stratosphere, where it filters out harmful ultraviolet radiation, ozone is a pollutant in the troposphere. The air pollution that is usually referred to as smog is actually a photochemical reaction in which hydrocarbons, and oxides of nitrogen, are driven by the energy in sunlight to react to form ozone and other pollutants, which are collectively known as smog.

Primary Pollutants

Materials directly emitted into the air from factories are primary pollutants. This is not a regulatory term, but a scientific one. Ozone is a secondary pollutant, since it is a product of primary pollutants, which have reacted with each other in the presence of sunlight. Primary air pollutants include particulate matter (such as dust and fibers), sulfur dioxide, oxides of nitrogen, carbon monoxide, and organics such as volatile organics, non-methane hydrocarbons, and hazardous air pollutants

(HAPs). Other toxics (such as lead, mercury, silver, and beryllium) are also primary air pollutants.

Acid Precipitation

The issue of acid precipitation (acid deposition or acid rain) is a major international environmental issue which is second only to stratospheric ozone depletion in importance. The reason for all the attention is that acid precipitation threatens agriculture, forests, fisheries, and wildlife across international borders. The dieback of about thirty-five percent of the great forests of Europe has been cited as evidence of the destructive power of acid precipitation.

In 1987, the Convention on Long-range Transboundary Air Pollution developed its "Protocol on Reduction of Sulfur Emissions or Their Transboundary Fluxes" calling for a thirty percent reduction from 1980 emission levels of sulfur dioxide by 1993. The Convention also passed a "Protocol on The Control of Emissions of Nitrogen Oxides and Their Transboundary Fluxes" which calls for a freeze on 1987 emission levels of nitrogen oxides until 1994. Further discussions are scheduled in 1996 to achieve nitrogen oxide emission reductions.

The European Community (EC), in November 1988, issued a directive for its member countries to lower emissions of sulfur dioxides from 1980 levels to fifty-seven percent of those levels by 2003. The same directive calls for the reduction of nitrogen oxide emissions by thirty percent by 1998.

Global Warming

Certain gases trap solar energy between the earth's surface and their accumulated mass in the troposphere, thus preventing energy absorbed by Earth during the day from being completely reradiated to space during the night. Entrapment of energy by atmospheric gases (called the "greenhouse effect") is necessary, because without it Earth would be uninhabitably frigid—about 90°F colder than it is today. The beneficial effects of greenhouse gases are known, but the usual warming of Earth caused by carbon dioxide and water vapor may be spiraling out of control as the result of human activities. For instance, the burning of fossil fuels (including forest debris) releases vast quantities of carbon dioxide into the atmosphere.

Some scientists believe that humanity's effects on this greenhouse phenomena may lead to increased global warming with potentially serious consequences for the inhabitants of Earth. Concerned scientists expect a change in sea level causing much coastal flooding, due to the partial melting of the polar ice caps, and the frequency and intensity of storms may also increase. Soil moisture, precipitation patterns, and periods of drought are predicted to change for the worse in many areas, but change for the better in others.

The negative effects of global warming may therefore be partially offset by some positive effects, but no country wants to sacrifice its coastal cities so that people in colder climates may have a longer crop year. So far, meteorologists and other scientists have not shown conclusively that increased anthropogenic greenhouse gases are causing harm. Such proof will take years to collect and verify.

Greenhouse gases, however, are clearly accumulating at an alarming rate in the atmosphere. Human activity presently puts twice the quantity of carbon dioxide into the atmosphere that natural sources do, making the total gas volume three times the volume without human impact. As more forest area is cut from the surface of the earth, the greenhouse gas imbalance has more significance for life on earth. The concentration of carbon dioxide in the troposphere is now twenty-five percent higher than in pre-industrial times, and each year the concentration of carbon dioxide increases by 0.5 percent. Methane in the troposphere increases at a rate of one percent each year; nitrous oxide increases at the rate of 0.3 percent per year. Global warming gases such as chlorofluorocarbons are made only by humans and do not occur in nature. Fortunately, the largest contributor to the greenhouse effect is water vapor which occurs so voluminously in nature that human activities have little impact on its overall concentration in the atmosphere. Humanity's largest contribution comes from carbon dioxide generated from combustion processes.

The effect of industrial pollution on global warming is very complicated, not well understood, and therefore a controversial subject. Chlorofluorocarbons (CFCs) act as greenhouse gases in the troposphere, but destroy ozone in the stratosphere. Ozone depletion, in turn, cools the climate, which offsets the warming effect of CFCs (but not the effect of the other gases). Dust, from volcanoes, also has a cooling effect on the climate by absorbing and reflecting radiation. Volcanic dust, though, has a much shorter half-life in the atmosphere than greenhouse gases do, especially the human-made ones.

The Intergovernmental Panel on Climate Change (IPCC) has extensively studied the greenhouse effect, tracking gases such as carbon dioxide, methane, nitrous oxides, and CFCs. A global warming trend of three to eight degrees Fahrenheit has been predicted to occur over the next one hundred years, a change unprecedented in the past 10,000 years. The Second World Climate Conference, in 1990, considered the IPCC studies and began negotiations to take action to control greenhouse gases, other than CFCs (which are already banned for other reasons).

The Japanese—more sensitive than other peoples are about global warming because so much of Japan's land mass borders the ocean—propose to reduce atmospheric carbon dioxide by pumping it into the ocean. *Shinkai*, a Japanese expression for "deep-sea," is a project designed to pump carbon dioxide nearly 10,000 feet under the sea where it will not dissolve in the cold sea water, but will instead remain in suspension there as a large bubble of gas trapped in a clathrate, or protective membrane. Critics claim the Shinkai project will acidify the sea, if it ever leaks. The Japanese counter that highly alkaline mollusks on the sea floor will neutralize any leaking carbon dioxide while also minimizing damage to benthic (bottom-living) animals.

Other schemes to limit carbon dioxide include isolating it from stack gases and diverting it into any of several storage arrangements. In one such scheme, carbon dioxide would be injected into the ground for enhanced oil recovery. Another plan would inject the gas into the ground, where it could be made to undergo unphotosynthesized biofixation, resulting in a reusable carbon dioxide-based fuel.

The concept of global warming is most controversial in the United States, where the primary anthropogenic source of greenhouse gas is the combustion of fossil fuels in automobiles, boilers, electric power generating plants, and residential fireplaces. Another greenhouse gas, methane, is produced by municipal landfills which Americans fill at astonishing rates. CFCs have no natural counterparts and account for about twenty-five percent of the warming effect. They are used extensively in America for refrigeration and cleaning (though they are being forced out of production at the end of 1995 due to their lop-sided contribution to the depletion of ozone in the upper atmosphere). Americans are not getting on the global warming bandwagon without a fuss. In 1990, ninety-eight U.S. cities were in violation of standards for pollutants caused mostly by combustion of fuel. In 1994, the list was shortened by only a handful.

President George Bush proposed a global climate treaty at the June 1992 U.N. Environmental Summit in Brazil in which he called on all nations to develop national climate action plans. For the U.S., he proposed a National Energy Strategy to restrain greenhouse gas emissions without sacrificing economic growth. In a speech to Congress, Bush stated, "Restraining electricity demand cuts emissions of carbon dioxide and acid rain precursors, lowers energy bills for homeowners and businesses, and limits the need for new powerplant construction." Since then, the EPA has successfully implemented, though piecemeal, the Green Lights Program, as the Bush proposal is called. Unfortunately, state-level plans to control greenhouse pollutants in the U.S. are lacking, according to a report by the National Research Council. The Clinton Administration continued this effort.

A notable signal-processing researcher has taken a completely fresh look at the problem by detailed consideration of particular climate-watching sites with long, historical records. He tracked the annual cycle of seasons at these sites, from the seventeenth century to present. After allowing for any changes caused by the switch from the Julian calendar to the Gregorian calendar in 1752, he found that the seasonal cycle shifts gradually, by just over 24 hours each century, until about 50 years ago when a pronounced anomaly in the timing of seasonal temperature shifts occurred in the Northern Hemisphere.

This temperature shift results from the competition between direct solar or radiative heating, and transport of heat from other parts of the globe. The evidence uncovered shows a definite shift, in the Northern Hemisphere, from transport to radiative heating, consistent with a global warming scenario.

One way or another, government leaders may soon be forced to make some difficult and unpopular policy decisions concerning greenhouse pollutants. Recent studies claim, amidst controversy, that another carbon dioxide global warming signal has already been detected.

Stratospheric Ozone

Since the industrial revolution, chemists have synthesized more and more chlorinated and fluorinated organic compounds (CFCs) thus providing countless benefits to modern society. Many of their CFC inventions have been overwhelmingly positive in their effect on the quality of our lives. Refrigeration compounds allow us to watch movies in cool comfort, have comfortable homes on the hottest summer days, preserve food in freezers, and preserve unstable medicinal compounds. Other CFCs are used to clean industrial parts for refrigerators, ranges, washers, dryers, automobiles, lawn mowers, and all manner of products that improve the quality of human life.

In 1974, two scientists at the University of California at Irvine, Sherwood Rowland and Mario Molina, announced a theory that chlorofluorocarbons (CFCs) in the stratosphere cause depletion of the ozone located there. This stratospheric ozone layer is important to life on earth because it filters out much of the ultraviolet (UV) spectrum in the sun's rays, thus reducing the incidence of skin cancer, cataracts, and other UV-induced health problems.

The ozone depletion theory slowly gained acceptance, but quantitative data to verify the predictions was elusive at first. In spite of lacking physical proof, the EPA moved to ban nonessential uses of CFCs in aerosol spray cans in 1978.

In 1985, the presence of an ozone "hole" over Antarctica was predicted, verified, and announced. The World Meteorological Organization promptly suggested that unrestricted use of CFCs would eventually lead to total destruction of the ozone layer. Ozone monitoring stations in Antarctica detected ozone losses of thirty to forty percent over that region in the Spring. At some altitudes, the loss totals as much as ninety-five percent.

In 1988, NASA found that the ozone layer was actually depleting faster than predicted by Rowland and Molina. A three to five percent depletion showed up over Antarctica in 1988, compared to levels NASA measured in 1969. The public became alarmed in 1992 when NASA unexpectedly discovered a hole over North America in the summer months of 1991 and also discovered that CFC levels over North America were at the highest level ever recorded anywhere in the world.

Anthropogenic chlorine has increased in the stratosphere to a level where verifiable damage is being done to the ozone layer. The ozone protects human and animal inhabitants of Earth from harmful doses of UV-B radiation from the sun. The more UV-B that reaches the surface of the earth, the more skin cancer, cataracts, and immune system disorders that occur in the exposed population. Plant growth is stunted by too much UV-B, which also kills the tiny organisms forming the base of the marine food chain. A single molecule of chlorine in the stratosphere destroys up to 100,000 molecules of ozone over a period of years.

NASA studies, as recently as 1993, verify that the depletion of the ozone layer over North America is proceeding, but at more than twice the destruction rate predicted earlier. The total destruction from the Arctic Circle to the Antarctic Circle averages 0.26 percent per year. North of latitude 35° North (where Memphis, Crete, and Kyoto are located), springtime ozone depletion runs three to five percent. At 45° North (where Ottawa and Belgrade are), winter depletion reaches up to nine percent. Unfortunately, chlorine from CFCs will remain in the stratosphere for perhaps hundreds of years, taking part in many ozone consuming photochemical reactions.

Unless CFC emissions are reduced soon, the ozone layer could deplete by as much as three percent over the next seventy years. Each one percent of ozone reduction amounts to about a two percent increase in UV-B radiation. Globally, this means about 100,000 more people will go blind each year due to cataracts. An extra 50,000 cases of non-melanoma skin cancer will occur. Melanoma, the deadliest skin cancer, may also increase because of additional UV-B.

The 1987 Montreal Protocol on Substances That Deplete The Ozone Layer was a precedent setting international agreement that strengthened and coordinated action underway by individual countries, such as the U.S. At a London meeting in 1990, the Montreal Protocol countries agreed to phase out CFCs and related compound production by the year 2000. Methyl chloroform was to have been phased out in 2003. In February 1992, President George Bush announced that the U.S. would phase out production of these chemicals altogether, which ended in 1995.

Recently, however, scientists have implicated oxides of hydrogen and nitrogen as causing the unaccounted for depletion over the mid-latitudes. These compounds, in fact, account for over fifty percent of the depletion below twelve miles high, where supersonic airplanes fly and leave behind the ozone destroying chemicals. Can the planes fly higher and avoid the ozone situation? Nitrogen oxides are also the most important of the ozone depleting compounds over eighteen miles high.

The stratospheric ozone layer is depleting at the polar regions and at northern mid-latitudes (USA and Europe) at alarming rates. How this phenomena will affect life in the twenty-first century depends a great deal on effective and prompt response to current regulations.

Hazardous Air Pollutants

Several hundred chemicals, only recently manufactured, also enter into the air pollution picture. Some are volatile organic compounds (VOCs). Strictly of concern in indoor air quality until very recently, the EPA and its international counterparts are starting to regulate the presence of VOCs in the atmosphere. A VOC is any compound of carbon which reacts in the atmosphere. Many solvents, used in paints and other top coatings, are reactive in the presence of sunlight. Other VOCs include cleaning materials used by industry. Unburned hydrocarbons from internal combustion engines are also considered VOCs. Reacting with nitrogen oxide and sunlight, VOCs produce ozone in the troposphere where it damages lung tissue and other biological tissues and cells. People with asthma and other respiratory function impairments are most susceptible to this pollution.

A more generic category of such air contamination has been dubbed *hazardous air pollutants* (HAPs) which includes the VOC category. HAPs are compounds that can cause serious or irreversible health effects. Before the 1990 amendments to the Clean Air Act, only eight HAPs were regulated by the EPA: arsenic, asbestos, benzene, beryllium, coke oven emissions, mercury, radionuclides, and vinyl chloride. Since 1990, the most protective air pollution law ever is expected to reduce HAPs by ninety percent when fully implemented at the turn of the century.

HAPs defined by the Clean Air Act Amendments are given in Figure 1.1.

Figure 1.1
Hazardous Air Pollutants

Acetaldehyde
Acetonitrile
Acetophone
2-Acetylaminofluorene
Acrolein
Acrylamide
Acrylic Acid
Acrylonitrile
Allyl Chloride
4-Aminodiphenyl
Aniline
(ortho-)Anisidine
Antimony Compounds
Arsenic Compounds
Asbestos
Benzene
Benzidine
Benzotrichloride
Benzyl Chloride
Beryllium Compounds
Biphenyl
Bis(2-ethylhexyl)phthalate
(DEHP) (Dioctyl Phthalate)
Bromoform
1,3-Butadiene
Cadmium Compounds
Calcium Cyanamide
Caprolactam
Captan
Carbaryl
Carbon Disulfide

Carbon Tetrachloride
Carbonyl Sulfide
Catechol
Chloramben
Chlordane
Chlorine
Chloracetic Acid
2-Chloroacetophone
Chlorobenzene
Chlorobenzinate
Chloroform
Chloroprene (Neoprene; 2-Acetamide
    Chloro-1,3-Butadiene)
Chromium (VI) Compounds
Cobalt Carbonyl
Cobalt Compounds
Cobalt Hydrocarbonyl
Coke Oven Emissions
Cresols/Cresylic Acid
(meta-)Cresol
(ortho-)Cresol
(para-)Cresol
Cumene (Isopropylbenzene)
Cyanide Compounds[1]
DDE
Diazomethane
Dibenzofurans
1,3-Dibromo-3-chloropropane
Dibutylphthalate
1,4-Dichloro-para-benzene
3,3'-Dichlorobenzidene

Figure 1.1 *(cont'd)*

Dichloroethyl Ether (Bis (2-chloroethyl)ether)
Ethylene Oxide
Ethylene Thiourea
1,3-Dichloropropene
Ethylidene Dichloride (1,1-Dichloroethane)
Dichlorvos
Diethanolamine
Formaldehyde
N,N'-Diethyl Aniline
Glycol Ethers[2]
Diethyl Sulfate
Heptachlor
3,3'-Dimethoxybenzidine
Hexachlorobenzene
4-Dimethyl Aminoazobenzene
Hexachlorocyclopentadiene
3,3'-Dimethyl Benzidine
Hexachloroethane
Dimethyl Carbamoyl Chloride
Hexamethylene-1,6-Diisocyanate
Dimethyl Formamide
Hexamethylphosphoramide
1,1-Dimethyl Hydrazine
Hexane
Dimethyl Phthalate
Hydrazine
Dimethyl Sulfate
Hydrochloric Acid
4,6-Dinitro-ortho-cresol (salts)
Hydrogen Fluoride (Hydrofluoric
2,4-Dinitrophenol
Acid)
2,4-Dinitrotoluene
Hydroquinone
1,4-Dioxane (1,4-Diethylene-oxide)
1,2-Diphenylhydrazine
Isophorone
2,4-D (also salts and esters)
Lead Compounds
Epichlorohydrin (1-Chloro-2, 3-epoxypropane)
Lindane
1,2-Epoxybutane (1,2-Butylene Oxide)
Maleic Anhydride
Manganese Compounds
Mercury Compounds
Ethyl Acrylate
Methanol
Ethyl Benzene
Metoxychlor
Ethyl Carbamate (Urethane)
Methyl Bromide (Bromomethane)
Ethyl Chloride (Chlorethane)
Methyl Chloride (Chloromethane)
Ethylene Dibromide (1,2-Dibromoethane)
Methyl Chloroform (1,1,1-Trichloroethane)
Ethylene Dichloride (1,2-Dichloroethane)
Methyl Ethyl Ketone (2-Butanone) (MEK)
Ethylene Glycol
Methyl Hydrazine
Ethylene Imine (Azridine)
Methyl Iodide (Iodomethane)

Figure 1.1 *(cont'd)*

Methyl Isobutyl Ketone (Hexone)
Methyl Isocyanate
Methyl Methacrylate
Methyl tert-Butyl Ether
4,4'-Methylene bis(chloroaniline) (MOCA)
Methylene Chloride (Dichloro-methane)
Methylene Diphenyl Diisocyanate (MDI)
4,4'-Methylenedianiline
Mineral Fibers[3] (respirable)
Naphthalene
Nickel Compounds
Nickel refinery dust
Nickel subsulfide
Nitrobenzene
4-Nitrodiphenyl
4-Nitrophenol
2-Nitropropane
N-Nitrosodimethylamine (Dimethylnitrosoamine)
N-Nitrosomorpholine
N-Nitroso-N-Methylurea
Parathion
Pentachloronitrobenzene
Pentachlorophenol
Phenol
(para-)Phenylenediamine
Phosgene
Phosphine
Phosphorus
Phthalic Anhydride
Polychlorinated Biphenyls

Polycyclic Organic Matter[4]
1,3-Propanesultone
beta-Propiolactone
Propionaldehyde
Propoxur
Propylene Dichloride (1,2-Dichloropropane)
1,2-Propylene Imine (2-Methyl Aziridine)
Propylene Oxide
Quinoline
Quinone (1,4-Cyclohexadienedione)
Radionuclides
Selenium Compounds
Styrene
Styrene Oxide
2,3,7,8-Tetrachlorodibenzo-para-dioxin) (TCDD) (Dioxin)
1,1,2,2-Tetrachloroethane
Tetrachloroethylene (Perchloroethylene)
Titanium Tetrachloride
Toluene
2,4-Toluene Diamine (2,4-Diaminotoluene)
2,4-Toluene Diisocyanate
(ortho-)Toluidine
Toxaphene (Chlorinated Camphene)
1,2,4-Trichlorobenzene
1,1,2-Trichloroethane
Trichloroethylene
2,4,5-Trichlorophenol
2,4,6-Trichlorophenol
Triethylamine
Trifluralin

Figure 1.1 *(cont'd)*

2,2,4-Trimethylpentane	Xylenes (mixed isomers)
Vinyl Chloride	(meta-)Xylene
Vinyl Acetate	(ortho-)Xylene
Vinyl Bromide	(para-)Xylene
Vinyl Chloride	
Vinylidene Chloride (1,1-Di-chloroethylene)	

Notes:

1. X'CN where X = H' or any other group where a formal dissociation may occur, for example: KCN or $Ca(CN)_2$.
2. Includes mono- and di-ethers of ethylene glycol, diethylene glycol and triethylene glycol $R-(OCH_2CH_2)_n-OR'$ where:

   n = 1, 2, or 3

   R = alkyl or aryl groups

   R' = R, H or a group which when removed yields glycol ether with the structure $R-(OCH_2CH_2)_n-OH$.

   Polymers are excluded from this category.
3. Includes glass microfibers, glass wool fibers, rock wool fibers, and slag wool fibers, each characterized as "respirable" (fiber diameter less than 3.5 micrometers) and possessing an aspect ratio (fiber length divided by fiber diameter) greater than 3.
4. Organic compounds with more than one benzene ring and have a boiling point greater than or equal to 100°C.

CAUSES AND EFFECTS OF AIR POLLUTION

Air pollution has a profound effect on the quality of human life, with an intensity that is directly related to the density of population and industrial activity. Some pollutant sources have counterparts in nature, but anthropogenic pollution has long since outpaced what nature does to itself. Many anthropogenic air pollution sources have no natural counterparts and are persistent and cumulative in their effects, unlike natural pollutants which maintain a balance to which various species of life can adapt.

You may have heard that volcanos pump more pollution into the atmosphere in a day than human endeavors can in a year. Like all myths, this one has a grain of truth. The facts that are being ignored by people who cling to this myth are 1) the volcano activity endures only for a limited time, it is not ongoing; and 2) once the natural pollution generating activity is finished, the natural pollutants disperse quickly, and pristine atmospheric conditions are soon restored. Nature dampens natural pollution, so that its long-term effect is barely noticeable. Anthropogenic air pollution has a documented history of accumulating in the atmosphere, with persistent chemicals reacting at several hundred percent of the strength of natural pollutants. Nature is also attempting to dampen anthropogenic pollution, but is being overwhelmed in the short term. Nature's short term is many tens of thousand years longer than human life. Notwithstanding our previous discussions, what causes air pollution and what effect does it have on people and their environment?

Sources and Nature of Pollutants

Look at where and how fuel is burned and you will find the source of most human induced pollution. When human impact was negligible, natural pollutants maintained a balance. Now, anthropogenic pollution overwhelms the natural equilibrium. Volcanos cause particulate matter and sulfur dioxide to peak in the atmosphere periodically, but after only a few months, everything is back to normal, with the exception of the interim increase in anthropogenic particulate matter and sulfur dioxide. Those anthropogenic increases have yet to peak, nor have they shown signs of lessening. Natural pollution, then, is of little long-term consequence, except that it forms a baseline below which we cannot abate and, therefore, it defines pristine conditions.

Natural particulate matter comes from volcanos, natural sources of radiation, and forest fires. Particulate matter is also introduced by many human activities such as excavation of soil, building roads, farming, mining, mineral processing, and fuel burning. The latter source is particularly true of wood burning activities, such as land clearing and residential fire places. Smoke is a very fine particulate matter called an aerosol.

Sulfur dioxide is another pollutant which comes mainly from fuel combustion, especially the burning of coal. Petroleum refining, sulfuric acid manufacturing, and metal smelting especially copper also produce sulfur dioxide.

The oxides of nitrogen are produced principally by burning fossil fuels. Whenever air is heated to combustion temperature, some amount of nitrogen oxides are produced.

Carbon monoxide is produced almost exclusively from inefficient combustion of fuel.

Ozone, mentioned above, is a secondary pollutant formed by reaction in sunlight of non-methane hydrocarbons, most of which come from factories. VOCs and HAPs are almost exclusively anthropogenic. Organic compounds, such as CFCs, have no natural sources. Some naturally generated particulate matter includes inorganic HAP constituents, but these sources are minor compared to the human generated inorganic HAP sources.

Effects of Sources

Very fine dusts and aerosols often escape being removed from breathing air by nasal hair and cilia (tiny, hair-like cells which move trapped fibers and particles back into the upper respiratory system, nasal passages, and mouth for expulsion from the body). Fine PM causes irritation and upper respiratory tract inflammation. Fine PM trapped in the lower respiratory passages and alveoli can eventually block the efficient exchange of oxygen between the lungs and the blood stream. Toxic and carcinogenic substances can also use fine PM as a vehicle for entering the lungs. For fine PM, then, the chief effect is the impairment of human health.

Because it is water soluble, sulfur dioxide (SO_2) combines with moisture in the upper respiratory passages to make sulfuric acid, which leads to tissue irritation and damage. Bronchial asthma, a condition exacerbated by SO_2, has been implicated in many of the deaths during the air pollution episodes of the 1950s and 1960s. SO_2 is also a major pollutant in acid rain.

The oxides of nitrogen (NO_x) react with hydrocarbons in the presence of sunlight to form ozone, which reacts to form photochemical smog, an irritant to the respiratory passages of humans which contributes to chronic diseases such as emphysema and asthma. NO_x is also one of the precursors responsible for acid deposition.

Carbon monoxide (CO) asphyxiation prevents blood from being oxygenated. Even though CO concentrations as a pollutant are rarely high enough for asphyxiation, concentrations can reach levels where the efficiency of blood oxygenation is impaired, thus exacerbating cardiovascular diseases such as angina and peripheral vascular disease. Temporary nervous system impairment is also caused by mild CO concentrations.

The effects of inorganic air toxics have been documented since ancient times. Lead, often used in building materials and paints, accumulates in blood, bone, and soft tissue and also affects the kidneys, liver, nervous system, and hemopoietic (blood-forming) organs. Fetuses, infants, and small children are particularly susceptible to lead exposure which can cause seizures, mental retardation, and behavioral disorders. Mercury, beryllium, chromium, silver, and other metals have similarly been identified as sources of serious health problems among humans, and these effects have been noted as long ago as pre-Christian time.

VOCs react with NO_x to form ozone, which forms photochemical smog. Ozone breaks down biological tissues and cells, especially in the respiratory system. Several billions of dollars of crops are lost annually due to tropospheric ozone, mostly formed from anthropogenic VOC sources. Organic HAPs also cause a variety of health problems in humans and some are harmful to crops as well.

Acid precipitation kills vegetation, as experienced in the forests of northern Europe, and also affects life in ponds and lakes (some lakes in northern European, New York state, and eastern Canada have been "killed" due to acid precipitation). However, we have to use caution in blaming acid rain for every dead body of water, because scientists have found by studying sediments that some lakes in Sweden were far more acidic four hundred years ago than they are now. That means that acid precipitation from power plants and factories is only one factor in making surface water acidic. However, we know that acid rain does "kill" lakes and ponds and its effects on aquatic life are well documented. We also know that acid precipitation damages concrete structures. Therefore, we must not fail to act just because we do not yet understand all the factors involved in how acid precipitation affects the environment.

Global warming will affect agriculture around the world. Climate patterns affect when and how much water is available in the growing season for crops, and these patterns will undoubtedly change due to global warming. Some agricultural areas will lose growing season length while others will gain. Some coastal lands now available to humans for development will be lost due to the rising ocean level.

The loss of stratospheric ozone, as mentioned above, will affect the lives of millions of people by causing more skin cancers, more cataracts, and more incidents of immune deficiencies. Depletion of stratospheric ozone may also affect animals and vegetation but that issue is still being studied and the effects of UV-B on animals and plants are not well understood.

Air Quality Requirements

Uncontrolled air quality is directly proportional to the density of population and amount of heavy industry. This is especially recognizable in areas where many people own internal combustion engines. Public policy should control air pollution at levels which do not adversely affect humans based on current scientific understanding. We need to decide, both as a nation and as a global community, what economic cost is acceptable. Legislation and concomitant regulations should neither result in unreasonable economic consequences nor be so lax as to be detrimental to the environment.

WATER POLLUTION

Rachel Carson warned about destruction of water resources in her book *Silent Spring*, published in 1962. She was concerned about pesticides and agricultural chemicals that accumulate in the environment instead of breaking down into simpler, relatively harmless compounds. Before World War II, pesticides were manufactured from naturally occurring poisons such as arsenic, copper, lead, manganese, zinc, and other minerals which were common poisons for insects, mammalian pests, and weeds. Other natural poisons include nicotine sulfate (from tobacco), pyrethrum (from chrysanthemums) and rotenone (from East Indian legumes).

After World War II, insecticides became more potent and deadly. Modern insecticides are either chlorinated hydrocarbons or organophosphates. These new synthesized poisons are fat soluble and therefore accumulate in the body organs that tend to store fat, such as the liver, kidneys, mesentery tissue, adrenal glands, testes, and thyroid. Stored poisons are dormant but can act on the body at a future time, when their source may not even be traceable. Chlorinated poisons include DDT, chlordane, heptachlor, dieldrin, aldrin, and endrin. The organophosphates include parathion and malathion.

A few years ago, the most environmentally progressive farm bill ever addressed, among other issues, pesticide use and water quality. Both are serious environmental problems. In some areas, pesticide pollution is of an order-of-magnitude greater than that of industrial environmental pollution. Nitrates from agricultural sources have been found in the groundwaters of nearly every state. The U.S. Geological Survey has been tracking well water quality for over twenty-five years and the problem has worsened to the point where over twenty percent of wells tested have elevated nitrate levels. Six percent of all wells tested show nitrate levels greater than EPA allows for drinking water.

Agricultural stress in the form of excess nutrients, pesticides, and sediment is responsible for fifty-eight percent of impaired lakes, fifty-five percent of impaired stream miles, and twenty-one percent of impaired estuarine systems. The Science Advisory Board, in a 1990 report to the EPA, identified high risk agricultural problems including habitat alteration and destruction. Draining and degrading wetlands clearly leads to habitat destruction and so do soil erosion and deforestation, which are common agricultural activities. Farmers need cleared land to grow plants or animals, but agricultural activities also cause environmental problems, such as species extinction, which in turn, affects the number of genetic permutations available in the future.

After agricultural chemicals, underground disposal of industrial wastes are the greatest threat to water supplies. In 1972, several scientists urged the government to carefully study the practice of disposing of wastes by deep well injection. One such well spewed 150,000 gallons of dioxin-bearing paper mill waste into Lake Erie. Although that is a tiny amount compared to the total volume of the lake, even small quantities of dioxin are undesirable in fishing and recreational waters, much less drinking water. A succession of minor earthquakes near Denver in the early seventies turned out to have been caused by the Army Corps of Engineers, as they pumped waste into a well two miles deep. The full implications of deep well injection are poorly understood and Congress has required EPA to ban the practice except for a few, primarily nonhazardous waste streams.

Water quality is also affected by wastes stored in the ground or discharged at surface level. During the 1970s, a cleanup was started at the Stringfellow Acid Pits, a hazardous waste landfill located near Glen Avon, California. Leachate from the site contaminated the Chino Basin Aquifer, which once provided about a half million people with drinking water. The Stringfellow landfill is frequently cited as a classic example of improper siting and disposal techniques for hazardous waste and the impact on the environment.

In 1974, Life Sciences Products, a small business owned by former Allied Chemical employees operating out of a former gas station in Hopewell, Virginia, contracted with Allied Chemical to produce the pesticide Kepone. An investigation by OSHA, EPA, and the Virginia Water Control Board revealed that Life Sciences and Allied Chemical had not only exposed employees to safety hazards, but had also discharged Kepone into the James River—untreated and without a permit to do so—for sixteen months. Kepone, a cumulative poison, causes cancer in mice and rats.

In 1976, fishing was banned in the Hudson River and also in rivers and lakes in South Carolina and Georgia due to contamination by polychlorinated biphenyls (PCBs), another persistent toxic chemical. Human-made water pollution affects not only drinking water, but the water used for recreation as well.

More than seventy percent of the surface of the earth is covered by oceans, the most complex and diverse ecosystems on the planet. Coastal zones account for only ten percent of the total area of oceans, but account for more than half of the oceans' productivity. Sixty percent of the population of the world lives within sixty miles of a sea coast! Pollution of oceans includes runoff from agriculture, industrial discharges, pavement runoff from cities, and contamination from ships. Pollution generated by a coastal country may circulate for great distances, due to ocean currents. Deterioration of coastal waters remains particularly severe in many countries where oil, raw sewage, medical waste, and household garbage are just some of the forms of pollution being dumped into the ocean.

The U.S. has declared a moratorium on offshore oil and gas development until after 2000 for ninety percent of the California coast. The same moratorium has been declared for the entire sea coasts of Washington, Oregon, New England, and the southern coast of Florida. Over 300 million dollars has been secured for improving sewage treatment in key coastal cities. The ocean dumping of sewage has been prohibited since 1992. A system for tracking the disposal of medical waste was devised after syringes and other used medical devices washed up on a New Jersey shore.

Another effort to protect oceans was an international protocol to strengthen laws governing oil transport. The Oil Spill Prevention Act of 1990 requires the phase-in of double-hulled oil tankers. This law also increases the liability of those responsible for oil spills.

The 1980s was named the International Drinking Water Supply and Sanitation Decade, the goal of which was to provide all people with clean water supplies and adequate sanitation by 1990. Although the goal was not met, the activities of the decade provided about 1.4 billion additional people in developing countries with safe drinking water supplies and about 1.5 billion people with new sanitation services. Another 1.2 billion still lack safe drinking water and 1.8 billion still do not have adequate sanitation. Population growth directly affects water supplies and sanitation.

Only a tiny fraction of the earth's unprocessed water is useful to humanity. Ninety-four percent of the water on earth is salt water. Ninety-nine percent of the remainder is tied up in glaciers, ice caps, or is deep underground. Only 0.06 percent of the earth's water supply is readily available for drinking. Over the last forty years, fresh water consumption has tripled. Agricultural uses account for sixty-nine percent of usable water, industry uses another twenty-three percent, and domestic usage is merely eight percent.

Many drinking water resources are shared by more than one country and this poses another problem. About fifty countries have seventy-five percent or more of their total area in international river basins. Furthermore, about 35-40 percent of the world's population lives in these international river basins.

Oxygen Balance

A body of water requires oxygen to support life, with the exception of anaerobic bacteria. In deep, stagnant bodies of water, oxygen is typically depleted on the bottom where significant levels of iron and manganese are deposited. Concentration gradients of increasing oxygen and decreasing iron and manganese are usually found from the bottom to the surface. Flowing streams have more dissolved oxygen available for life than deep, stagnant pools.

Bacteria that need oxygen and give off carbon dioxide as a waste are called *aerobic*. *Anaerobic* bacteria, on the other hand, do not need oxygen and give off carbon dioxide, methane, hydrogen, ammonia, and hydrogen sulfide in the process of fermentation. Facultative microorganisms can adapt to either oxygen enriched or oxygen depleted water.

The oxygen balance in a body of water strongly affects the animal and plant life forms that live in it. Besides bacteria, plants such as algae help maintain the oxygen balance, although the presence of too much algae, called an algae bloom, can strip the water of oxygen. Chemicals discharged from factories also consume oxygen, thus competing with aquatic life. This depletion of oxygen due to chemical reaction is referred to as chemical oxygen demand (COD). Decomposing organic matter can place a biological oxygen demand (BOD) on a body of water.

Modeling Techniques

Early techniques for modeling the effects of pollution on streams were highly dependent on the dissolved oxygen balance. The latest water quality models consider the BOD load of the stream as well as dissolved oxygen. These models analyze *point sources* (industrial discharge) or *distributed sources* (agricultural and municipal storm runoff). Steady-state (unchanging) flow conditions are assumed during the period of time under analysis. Nitrification and photosynthesis are assumed to be negligible. Most models do not consider dispersion in tidal estuaries although some private models do. In any case, EPA and the states do not measure dilution in considering water quality. Finally, water quality models consider a uniform reach (a hypothetical section of the stream assumed to have constant cross-sectional area, velocity, and depth) which is rarely the case in real life.

Assimilative Capacity of Receiving Streams

Water, especially flowing water, assimilates a certain amount of contamination without ill effect. Beyond that amount, the contaminant becomes a pollutant. Regulation writers at EPA generally use the latest toxicological information about a contaminant's effect on human health or aquatic life to set water quality criteria by.

Eutrophication

The slow death of a body of surface water due to demands on oxygen by excessive nutrients, algae blooms, decaying organics, and chemicals is called *eutrophication*. The flip side is *oligotrophic* water which has too little plant nutrient yet has abundant oxygen. The eutrophication of a lake can be retarded by restricting nutrient input. Phosphorus and nitrogen compounds and carbon dioxide must be removed from incoming waters. Many authorities believe that phosphorus reduction is the key to restoring advanced eutrophic lakes but the process of eutrophication is difficult to eliminate once begun. Years of treatment may be needed to restore an eutrophic lake to support aquatic life again.

Thermal Pollution

Discharging heated water into streams causes several problems, too. Variations in temperature make wastewater treatment difficult, as temperature figures into the efficiency of several treatment operations. If the temperature of a stream is raised, it has that much less value as a coolant to an industry downstream. Thermal stratification occurs when warm water is added to surface water, since warm water is lighter than cold water. In thermally stratified streams, fish and other wildlife seek the bottom, where the water is cooler but contains less dissolved oxygen. Finally, since bacteria activity increases with temperature, oxygen depletion is accelerated as bacteria competes for it.

CAUSES AND EFFECTS OF WATER POLLUTION

No water in nature is entirely pure but a water contaminant is not a pollutant unless it affects human health or aquatic life in water intended to be drinkable—called *potable* water—or else destroys its recreational or aesthetic value. Pollution degrades a body of water, either by killing desirable aquatic life or by exacerbating eutrophication.

Dissolved oxygen (DO) content of the water is the first measure of the effect of pollution on a given body of water. Without knowing a specific pollutant, one can identify a wastewater discharge by measuring DO. Immediately downstream of the discharge of any pollutant, a dip in DO concentration will be observed. A graph of DO verse location on the stream is called a DO sag curve and is evidence of pollutant discharge. Typically, as DO decreases, the amount of degradable waste (BOD) increases. When the two measurements correlate, BINGO! Pollution! This knowledge is how enforcement agents find midnight wastewater discharges.

Sources and Nature of Pollutants

BOD is an effect caused by dissolved and suspended (colloidal) organic material on the biological treatment units of wastewater treatment plants (POTW or Publicly Owned Treatment Works). In streams, BOD depletes DO and sets up septic conditions in deep pools. Suspended solids cause silting, odors from decomposition, and oxygen depletion in streams. Inorganic solids also hinder the sludge digestion process at the POTW.

Acids and bases affect the pH of streams which must be maintained between 4.5 and 9.5 for fish. Extremely low pH (acidic water) can destroy concrete in the POTW and either low or high pH will interfere with the POTW's biological treatment operations. Toxic chemicals can kill fish and other aquatic life as well as stop the biological processes in the POTW. Some toxic chemicals are hard to remove and remain in the water throughout the purification process for making drinking water. For instance, heavy metals (cadmium, chromium, copper, lead, mercury, nickel, selenium, silver, zinc) can be removed but POTWs are not equipped to do so. Removal of heavy metals and toxic chemicals is the responsibility of industries, which are required to pretreat before discharging to public sewers.

Conventional Pollutants

The conventional pollutants are those that have been studied since before the Federal Water Pollution Control Act was enacted. Most of these pollutants are tracked by measuring BOD including organic waste, nutrients, bacteria, viruses, and fecal coliform. These are sometimes measured individually. Other conventional pollutants, or pollutant indicators, are sediment, oil and grease, suspended solids, pH, temperature and, in some areas, color.

Water Toxics

Some chemicals are toxic to aquatic life in very low concentrations such as insecticides, herbicides, and rodenticides. Industrial chemicals, such as the highly complex synthetic molecules used to manufacture fibers, are also toxic. Inorganic salts are typically toxic to aquatic life. Toxic metal ions tie up enzymes needed to oxidize organic matter and thus interfere with biological oxidation. Even small amounts of such metals hinder sludge digestion. Water toxics, called Priority Pollutants, are listed in Figure 1.2.

Effects of Pollutants on Aquatic Life

Pollutants upset the aquatic food chain. If pollution makes the water murky (increasing turbidity), sunlight is blocked and plant growth is either stunted or killed. In contrast, some pollutants provide nutrients to aquatic plants and then a bloom occurs. This is an especially disastrous situation in stagnant or low turnover lakes. Several industrial wastes kill fish directly, either by shifting the pH of water or by toxicity. The latter pollutants can be passed up the food chain to herbivores, larger fish, and finally to humans. Toxic pollutants bioaccumulate in tissue, such as fat cells, and are passed on when the host tissue is eaten by a predator.

Figure 1.2
Priority Pollutants

Aldrin	Endrin	Tetrachlorinated Ethanes
Antimony	Ethylbenzene	1,2,4,5-Tetrachlorobenzene
Arsenic	Fluoranthene	1,1,2,2-Tetrachloroethane
Asbestos	Haloethers	Tetrachloroethylene
Benzene	Halomethanes	2,3,5,6-Tetrachlorophenol
Cadmium	Heptachlor	Thallium
Carbon Tetrachloride	Hexachlorobenzene	Toluene
Chlordane	Hexachlorobutadiene	Toxaphene
Chlorinated Benzenes	Hexachlorocyclohexane	Trichlorinated Ethanes
Chloroform	(Lindane)	1,1,1-Trichloroethane
Chromium (hexavalent)	Hexachlorocyclo-	1,1,2-Trichloroethane
Copper	pentadiene	Trichloroethylene
Cyanide	Isophorone	2,4,6-Trichlorophenol
DDT	Lead	Vinyl Chloride
DDE (DDT metabolite)	Mercury	Zinc
Demeton	Monochlorobenzene	
Di-2-ethylhexylphthalate	Naphthalene	
Dichlorobenzenes	Nickel	
Dichlorobenzidine	Nitrobenzene	
1,2-Dichloroethane	Nitrophenols	
Dichloroethylene	Nitrosamines	
Dichloropropane	Nitrosobutylamine N	
Dichloropropene	Nitrosodiethylamine N	
Dieldrin	Nitrosodipentylamine N	
Diethylphthalate	Nitrosopyrrolidine	
2,4-Dimethylphenol	PCB's	
Dimethylphthalate	Phenol	
Dioxin (2,3,7,8-TCDD)	Phthalate Esters	
1,2-Diphenylhydrazine	Polynuclear Aromatic	
2,4-Dinitro-o-cresol	Hydrocarbons (PAHs)	
2,4-Dinitrotoluene	Selenium	
Endosulfan	Silver	

Sanitary wastes from municipalities, farms, and large industrial plants can pollute streams with water borne disease. A common indicator of the presence of sewage in water is the *Escherichia coli* bacteria, found in large quantities in human intestines. Although *E. coli* is harmless in the bowels of humans, its presence in water means that untreated sanitary waste—sewage—is also present. The intestinal tracts of humans also contain viruses and harmful bacteria which are passed into raw sewage.

Water Quality Requirements

Two methods are used to maintain water quality: effluent standards and stream standards. Effluent standards are devised for specific industries and all such plants must remove contaminants to the same degree before discharging. Knowing and understanding suitable types of treatment schemes allows the standard developers to choose discharge limits representing efficient removal of pollution. However, a very large plant discharges more of the same contaminants than a very small plant does, yet has the same standard of discharge to meet. Under the stream standard method, each industry is assigned a certain portion of the stream's assimilative capacity based on computer modeling. The larger plant does not necessarily get the lion's share as in the effluent standard method.

Water laws and wastewater regulations are aimed at protecting surface waters for recreation and drinking. Not every stream or body of water must be preserved for both uses and sometimes water does not need to serve either need. As population grows, untreated wastewater can be tolerated less and less. Surface water standards define the quality of water acceptable for recreation or drinking water, or both. Groundwater standards define drinking water quality except for some irrigation needs. Wastewater standards define the quality of water discharged (effluent) from industrial plants directly into surface water bodies or indirectly via sewage treatment plants. As it becomes more difficult to maintain the standards set for recreation and drinking water, effluent limitations will become more restrictive.

WETLANDS

The issue of wetlands is seldom neutral. Real estate developers and industrialists typically have no use for wetlands; nevertheless, funds for research and protection of wetlands have increased to record levels.

Wetlands are transitional areas that exist between high and dry land and open water. Sometimes they are almost dry and at other times they are almost pond, but they are never totally dry land or pond. These areas have frequently been drained and filled for farmland, shopping centers, industrial parks, and subdivisions.

Part of the reason people get so emotional about wetlands is that, until recently, they were considered unusable, unwanted land. If someone came along and developed the area, he was often somewhat of a local hero. Wetlands, however, are not only extremely valuable but also very productive ecosystems, home to many rare and beautiful species. Actually, wetlands are the home of many species of animals and plants with recreational and commercial value—so productive that only tropical rain forests are more productive, according to EPA literature. Leaves and stems from plants biodegrading in the water of a wetlands cell can generate nutrients that support the production of many shell fish, fish, and wildlife.

Some wetlands contain the overflow of rivers during seasonal flooding. Other wetlands collect natural runoff during storms. In either case, wetlands filter sediment and debris from the water before returning it to a river and stream or allowing it to evaporate. Wetlands are a much more efficient flood barrier than dams and dikes. But, of course, people do not want to live near a river that regularly overflows its normal banks.

Another value of wetlands is that they protect shorelines of rivers and streams from erosion. They bind soil, dampen wave action, and reduce current velocity by friction. By intercepting surface water runoff before it reaches open water, wetlands maintain and improve water quality. Nutrients are removed, for one thing. Without removal of nutrients, the receiving river or lake would bloom with algae and weeds which would grow out of control. Oxygen depletion and fish kills follow when algae blooms decompose. Organic wastes are also processed by wetlands and sediments are reduced, as mentioned earlier.

The populations of game ducks have steadily declined since 1955, which correlates exactly to simultaneous losses of vast areas of wetlands. Some of the earliest proponents of saving wetlands were, in fact, duck hunting U.S. Congressmen, who frequently hunted at naval gunfire training facilities along the Chesapeake Bay and its connecting rivers on weekends while congress was in session.

Another sign of wetlands degradation is the appearance of deformed species. This problem is especially notable at Kesterson National Wildlife Refuge in California, where water birds are hatching fewer chicks, and more and more of those that do hatch are deformed from selenium exposure.

Fifty-three percent of wetlands in the U.S. were lost during the period beginning in the late eighteenth century until the late twentieth century. From the mid-1970s to mid-1980s, 290,000 acres of wetlands were lost per year! Eighty percent of breeding bird populations require bottomland hardwood systems, which are wooded swamps located mostly in the Southeast. Over-logging of mature bottomland hardwood forests has reduced many of these breeding species considerably and has probably led to the demise of the largest woodpecker species, the Ivory-Billed Woodpecker.

Twenty-two states have lost more than fifty percent of original wetlands. California, Indiana, Illinois, Iowa, Kentucky, Missouri, and Ohio have lost more than eighty percent of their original wetlands. Despite anti-progress horror stories told by developers, fewer than 2.5 percent of requests to build on wetlands were denied by the Army Corps of Engineers in 1992. In twenty-one years, the EPA vetoed only eleven permits to build on wetlands.

Recently, EPA announced a new policy, developed in cooperation with eight other federal government agencies, in an attempt to simplify the federal requirements for preservation of wetlands. Perhaps the new policy will balance nature and development. Landowners will now be able to seek review of permit decisions without going to court. A loophole that allowed certain destructive activities to continue has been closed. Farmers will be able to contribute to wetlands restoration by selling easements to the government in a new wetlands reserve program. Deadlines and additional guidance are aimed at speeding up the permitting process, and state, local, and tribal governments will be brought more into the procedure for reviewing permits. If a wetlands involves farm lands, the Soil Conservation Service of the USDA will be the lead agency, hopefully preventing duplication and inconsistency, which have been characteristics of past permitting.

HAZARDOUS WASTE

Public Concerns

While hazardous waste regulations proliferate, permitted hazardous waste management facilities continue to present serious cleanup problems when they go bankrupt. Does this indicate that financial audits of hazardous waste facility owners are more important than compliance audits of facility operators? Financial health is at least as important as regulatory compliance.

Hazardous waste, as a threat to the quality of the environment, will not go away anytime soon. Unfortunately, EPA overregulates hazardous waste in some cases and underregulates in others. Some hazardous waste facilities still operate under interim permits without meeting financial assurance requirements. Bankruptcy of hazardous waste facilities leads to a greater public health risk than does noncompliance with regulatory minutiae.

What makes waste hazardous? Some wastes, hazardous by edict, do not seem to be so hazardous in the environment. Other wastes, defined as nonhazardous, may be riskier than first thought, such as used oil. EPA dreads regulating used oil, for example, but evidence continues to stack up against its safety. Debris and other waste material that once had contact with a listed waste and is therefore hazardous by definition may have no real hazardous characteristics of its own. Precious hazardous waste landfill space is being filled up with debris, which could safely be sent to a nonhazardous landfill meeting minimal design standards. One-third of hazardous waste landfills will be closed by 1997 due to having reached their capacity, yet EPA keeps adding to the hazardous waste list.

Another problem is that industry continues to generate hazardous waste despite the fact that generation and management of hazardous waste depletes the bottom line. Pollution prevention is slowly catching on, but, at any speed, only so much can be done. Too many people are counting on the success of pollution prevention. On-site treatment with permits, similar to NPDES or Title V air permits, will one day be needed by relatively small industrial operations in order to send the residue off-site. Right now, the onerous task of submitting a RCRA Part B application discourages on-site treatment. Fortunately, any pollution prevented is a step in the right direction. The only worthwhile environmental goal for any company is zero waste discharge, but, in the meantime, one hundred percent conformance to regulatory compliance requirements is the goal.

Some tough questions need to be addressed by planners for the twenty-first century. Corporate planners need to ask, "How can we continue to produce goods for an ever increasing population, while limiting the amount of hazardous waste we pour into the environment?" More often these days, companies ask this question of themselves. Public policy planners need to ask, "Is there a system of incentives based on public image, economics, tax, or a combination of these which would be more effective than regulations?" The current conservative congress seems to be asking such questions. The question asked at every Superfund or RCRA corrective action site is, "How clean is clean?" Put another way, "Do these planned actions protect the public health and welfare at a cost we can afford?" Are we going far enough with cleanups? Or are we going too far? Industry claims EPA is too severe in its demands and exaggerates threats to human health. On the other hand, environmentalists charge that Superfund has never been given a chance to prove itself and that EPA should therefore hold the line on—or even toughen—cleanliness standards. Given the amount of money being spent, and the potential for health impairment, both sides deserve an answer to these questions.

Current actions tend to be reactions and dialogue tends to be unproductive opportunities to accuse the other side of intransigence. For instance, Barry Commoner's book about toxic and radioactive substances, *Science and Survival*, raised a number of professional eyebrows in 1966 but received keen attention from environmentalists. More specifically, in 1972, vinyl chloride was identified as causing a rare and fatal form of liver cancer in laboratory rats. In 1974, thirty American workers were determined to be dying each year due to vinyl chloride exposure. Widespread concern around Cleveland, Ohio, and in three Ohio counties where vinyl chloride factories were located led to studies by both OSHA and EPA. OSHA lowered the Permissible Exposure Limit (PEL) for vinyl chloride to 1 ppm, in order to increase protection for workers, but EPA concluded that vinyl chloride was not an environmental hazard. Nevertheless, even today, widespread fears about the risk of vinyl chloride in the environment prevails and industrial companies must report it on annual community right-to-know reports. Such public issues need to be put to rest, notwithstanding new evidence to the contrary.

Public paranoia about chemicals, "chemophobia," has a painfully bitter history. Around noon on Saturday, July 10, 1976, a trichlorophenol reactor overheated and ruptured, spewing a cloud containing 1 kg (2.2 pounds) of dioxin (the deadliest chemical to rodents ever synthesized) over the towns of Seveso and Meda, Italy. The cloud eventually spread toward metropolitan Milano. The plant, Industrie Chemiche Meda Societa Aromia (ICMESA), was a subsidiary of Swiss pharmaceutical giant, Hoffman-La Roche. The accident was the worst chemical disaster ever recorded at the time. John G. Fuller told a poignant story from the viewpoint of Seveso townspeople, who suffered terribly from the accident because of early misinformation from Hoffman-La Roche to the Italian federal and town governments.

Dioxin is a generic term for polychlorinated dibenzodioxins, the most toxic of which is 2,3,7,8-tetrachlorodibenzo-p-dioxin or 2,3,7,8-TCDD. Contact with TCDD gives an ugly skin rash called chloracne, which may take weeks after exposure to develop, but which may persist for months. That is the least of the worries, if exposed. TCDD causes tumors in several organs of the body and promotes cancer. The median lethal dose to TCDD for guinea pigs is 600 nanograms per kg of body weight, making dioxin the most potent poison known.

The cleanup of Seveso and neighboring area cost Hoffman-La Roche over $200 million and the chemical industry lost much credibility because of miscommunication and mishandling of the accident. Hand-wringing and the hiding or withholding of facts makes corporate officers appear as villains rather than co-victims.

The Love Canal Incident

In 1978, President Jimmy Carter took an unprecedented measure and declared a federal emergency at a blue-collar neighborhood in Niagara Falls, New York. The subdivision, known as Love Canal, was built over an old canal of that name. Even today, whenever some chemical disaster occurs, the media inevitably reminisces about Love Canal. As Gerald B. Silverman says, "...the words 'Love Canal' have become so widely known that they are virtually synonymous with toxic waste...[and] have also come to symbolize corporate irresponsibility, government myopia, and the high human and environmental costs of living in an industrial society."

Love Canal was not so much a technical problem as a public policy problem and the crisis was actually about the frustration caused when government and industry leaders reached an indecisive deadlock about what to do about poor decisions made in the past. Housewife Lois Marie Gibbs, President of the Love Canal Homeowners Association, became an activist and led protests for action, setting a precedent for ordinary but indignant people everywhere to get involved. Environmental protectionism was no longer a matter of hard-to-read regulations and lengthy, boring legal battles. All of a sudden, it was front page material. The sort of story that sold newspapers and kept people glued to their television sets during the evening news. It was angry, frustrated people demanding that a paralyzed government take some action. It was the image of innocent, unaware children playing in toxic puddles and getting dizzy in toxic basements. Environmentalism had become a public force, no longer a low priority, nor merely an interest in wildlife conservation by hunters and fishermen.

What happened at Love Canal? From 1942 to 1953, Hooker Chemical and Plastics Company placed about twenty-two thousand tons of chemical wastes, from its manufacturing facilities in Niagara Falls, into the Love Canal landfill. Chemical wastes such as trichlorophenol, dioxin, lindane, and chlorobenzenes were placed there. The City of Niagara Falls also used the landfill for disposal of municipal wastes for many years. Some older, long-time residents along the canal allege that the U.S. Army placed chemical warfare agents and debris from the Manhattan Project in the landfill, a fact which is vehemently denied by the Army to this day.

A scary point, frequently overlooked, is that this was a state-of-the art landfill from 1940 to 1955. In fact, it was beyond the state-of-the art, it was the cutting edge of landfill technology. The sides and bottom of the canal provided containment that rival many municipal landfill designs, even today. When it closed the site, Hooker placed a cover over the landfill that was technologically years ahead of its time.

What happened after closure boggles the imagination, however. In 1952, the landfill was sold to the Niagara Falls School District for $1, with a stipulation in the deed that Hooker be absolved of liability, if the industrial wastes contained in the landfill were released as a result of violating the integrity of the landfill cover. Violate the cover is exactly what city, school board, land developers, and residents alike did. They laid sewer lines, roads, utilities, and water lines. They dug out holes for swimming pools. They built homes with basements. They dug holes for sand boxes where their children could play. They removed cubic yard after cubic yard of the protective cover. In building the 99th and the 93rd Street Schools, about seven thousand cubic yards of soil were removed from the cover!

The Love Canal incident precipitated the passage of Superfund in 1980. This law is designed to take care of toxic emergencies *now*, so that fixing blame and liability can wait until *later*. This law changed American property law drastically. No longer can one do anything on his own property, and the rest of the world be damned. If what is on your property affects the environment, then you may be responsible for the resolution of any pollution problem. No longer may you simply pass on your problems to someone else by selling your contaminated property. The liability for environmental damage stays with the source of the contamination. Everyone else who touches the problem along the way becomes tainted and may also share some liability. Gone are the days of *caveat emptor* (let the buyer beware). These days, let the seller beware, too. (More on CERCLA in Chapter 11.)

The Bhopal Chemical Leak

If the Love Canal disaster had been the end of it, CERCLA might have been the last big environmental compliance headache (not counting amendments to other laws). Unfortunately, in India, on December 2, 1984, a Union Carbide Sevin pesticide plant spewed lethal methyl isocyanate (MIC) over nearby Bhopal, killing more than two thousand people, and causing about 100,000 injuries. Eventually, around 300,000 people claimed to suffer some health effect from the accident. Genetic damage among survivors is anticipated as time passes. Arthur Diamond, in *The Bhopal Chemical Leak*, reports that in December 1981, right after pesticide production at Bhopal started, a maintenance man was killed when MIC from a pipe drenched him. Three other workers were also injured in that accident. Forty-six tons of MIC was stored at the facility, and a process safety audit in 1982 indicated that the manual backup safety system was inadequate and should be replaced by an automated system. By 1984, before the big accident, forty-seven employees had been injured or killed by MIC at Union Carbide Bhopal! The world turned its attention to the big accident, its sympathy to the people of Bhopal, its anger to Union Carbide in particular, and its fear onto the chemical industry in general. Chemophobia was spreading.

In 1985, a year after Bhopal, Union Carbide had an MIC incident in Institute, West Virginia. Fortunately, no one died, but Americans sat up and took notice. Chemophobia became an epidemic, due to the accidents of Bhopal and Institute. As if to underscore the already growing fear of toxic chemicals, 40,000 people had to be evacuated from Miamisburg, Ohio, after a train wreck and fire spewed tons of chemicals into the air. The attention of the nation was once again fervently focused on chemicals. Despite having had a sterling safety record, the chemical process industry was about to receive a one-two knockout punch.

Global Concerns over Hazardous Waste

Realistically, environmental managers cannot discount chemical hysteria, nor refute it with any credibility, if not in 100 percent conformance with regulatory requirements. Indeed, some compliance managers wonder if the doomsayers are not right, after all. Industry's continuing inattention to the waste end of business and occasional, but notable, lapses of process safety vigilance, lead to the Stringfellow Acid Pits and the ICMESAs of the world. The drive to make profits, while totally ignoring the effects of process and product on the environment, accumulates a debt to nature and society which eventually must come due.

In 1990, the population of the world was over five billion; by 2000, the population is expected to be more than six billion persons. Developing nations will account for over ninety percent of the population at the turn of the century, and the ecology of earth will be balanced between new and old industrial nations.

Twenty-first century environmental issues will be more global, less local in nature. Already, we see concerted, cooperative efforts by nations to stop depletion of stratospheric ozone. Many nations are now discussing transboundary issues, such as acid rain. One thing we can look for, in the next century, is a proliferation of multinational environmental regulations on issues diverse in character, but interrelated. Figures 1.3 and 1.4 summarize issues on which the nations of the world are already debating and cooperating. The International Earth Summit, in Brazil in 1992, brought hope that issues can be worked out sometime in the next century by international cooperation.

Figure 1.3		
Summary of International Issues		
Issue	**International Response**	**U.S. National Response**
Acid Deposition		CAAA
Air Pollution	BAPMoN	CAAA
	HEAL	
Biodiversity	CBD	
	CITES	
	GBS	
	IBPGR	
	MIRCEN	
	WCMC	
	WCS	
Deforestation	TFAP	
Desertification	ISRIC	
	PACD	
	SADCC	
	WSP	
Global Warming	GEMS	CAAA
	IPCC	
	UN FCCC	
	WGMS	
	WMO WCP	

Figure 1.3 *(cont'd)*

Issue	International Response	U.S. National Response
Hazard Communication	ICCDUP LGEICIT	29 CFR 1910.1200
Hazardous Waste	BCCTMHWD IRPTC	RCRA
Incineration		RCRA/CAAA
Oceans and Coasts	GPACMUMM UNEP RSP	
Ozone Depletion	Ozone Action Program Montreal Protocol	CAAA/TSCA
Sustainable Development	APELL Habitat ICC BCSD UNEP CPP UNEP ECC	
Toxic Cleanup	EHC ICC WICEM IPCS PEEM UNEP IE/PAC	CERCLA RCRA SARA III
Water Supplies	UNEP EMINWA	CWA/SDWA
Wetlands		NEPA

Abbreviation/Acronyms:
APELL = Awareness and Preparedness for Emergencies at Local Level
BAPMoN = Background Air Pollution Monitoring Network
BCCTMHWD = Basel Convention on the Control of Transboundary Movements of Hazardous Wastes and their Disposal
BCSD = Business Convention on Sustainable Development
CAAA = Clean Air Act Amendments of 1990
CBD = Convention on Biological Diversity
CERCLA = Comprehensive Environmental Response, Compensation and Liability Act (Superfund)

Figure 1.3 *(cont'd)*

CITES = Convention on International Trade in Endangered Species of Wild Flora and Fauna
CPP = Cleaner Production Program
CWA = Clean Water Act
ECC = Energy Collaborating Center
EHC = Environmental Health Criteria
EMINWA = Environmentally-sound Management of Inland Waters
FCCC = Framework Convention on Climate Change
Habitat = UN Center for Human Settlements
HEAL = Human Exposure Assessment Location
GBD = Global Biodiversity Strategy
GEMS = Global Environmental Monitoring System
GPACMUMM = Global Plan of Action for the Conservation, Mgmt and Utilization of Marine Mammals
IBPGR = International Board for Plant Genetic Resources
ICC = International Chamber of Commerce
ICCDUP = International Code of Conduct on the Distribution and Use of Pesticides
IE/PAC = Industry and Environment Program Activity Center
IPCC = Intergovernmental Panel on Climate Change
IPCS = International Program on Chemical Safety
IRPTC = International Registry of Potentially Toxic Chemicals
ISRIC = International Soil Reference and Information Center
LGEICIT = London Guidelines for the Exchange of Information on Chemicals in International Trade
MIRCEN = Microbial Genebank and Training Center
NEPA = National Environmental Policy Act
PACD = Plan of Action to Combat Desertification
PEEM = Panel of Experts on Environmental Mgmt for Vector Control
RCRA = Resource Conservation and Recovery Act
RSP = Regional Seas Program
SADCC = Southern African Development Coordination Conference
SARA III = Superfund Amendments and Reauthorization Act Title III
SDWA = Safe Drinking Water Act
TFAP = Tropical Forest Action Plan
TSCA = Toxic Substances Control Act
UN = United Nations
UNEP = United Nations Environment Program
WCP = World Climate Program
WCS = World Conservation Strategy
WCMC = World Conservation Monitoring Center
WGMS = World Glacier Monitoring System
WICEM = World Industry Conference on Environmental Management
WMO = World Meteorological Organization
WSP = World Soils Policy

Figure 1.4

UNEP: United Nations Environmental Programme

Conventions Administered (have the force of treaties)

1973 Washington Convention on International Trade in Endangered Species of Wild Flora and Fauna (CITES)

1979 Bonn Convention on the Conservation of Migratory Species of Wild Animals (CMS)

1985 Vienna Convention for the Protection of the Ozone Layer

1987 Montreal Protocol on Substances that Deplete the Ozone Layer

1989 Basel Convention on the Control of Transboundary Movements of Hazardous Wastes and their Disposal

1990 Amendments of the Montreal Protocol

1992 UN Framework Convention on Climate Change

1992 Convention on Biological Diversity

Guidelines and Non-Binding Agreements

1982 World Charter for Nature

1982 Montevideo Program for the Development and Periodic Review of Environmental Law

1987 London Guidelines on Trade in Harmful Chemicals

1987 Cairo Guidelines and Principles on Hazardous Waste Management

1989 Amendments to London Guidelines

The bugbear of the American environmentalist—hazardous waste—is also taking on an international scope in the 1990s. Several industrialized nations, including the U.S., have adopted strict laws and regulations to control domestic disposal of hazardous waste. Exporting hazardous waste to countries that have less stringent rules for disposal has thus become economically attractive. In the 1980s, exporting waste was a growing business. This has slowed recently because the 1984 RCRA amendments imposed restrictions on exported waste. Now, potential exporters must give each waste's composition and quantity to the receiving government in advance. About one percent of domestic hazardous waste is exported, according to an EPA estimate. However, a lot more unregulated nonhazardous waste is also exported. This latter material includes incinerator ash and municipal solid waste.

Domestic Concerns over Hazardous Waste

Environmentalist organizations are putting the squeeze on traditional industrialized states, like New Jersey and California. Tough laws, much more restrictive than national laws, are enacted in these states. Consequently, companies are opting for less stringently regulated, greener areas. As more polluted states try to clean up, states that are "green" want to stay that way, while attracting industry and jobs, too. What seems like a catch-22 now may turn out to be a mere leveling of the playing field for industrial siting.

On the other hand, the siting of treatment, storage, and disposal facilities (TSDFs) for hazardous waste management is a stress-filled, community-dividing process. The whole topic of incineration, for example, is controversial beyond anything anticipated thirty years ago. As one author writes, "waste incineration has become a lightning rod for environmental activism." Yet, the incinerator was once hailed as the catholicon of waste management, the desired replacement for landfill technology. Right now, a moratorium has been placed on new hazardous waste incinerators. Critics of incineration have questions worthy of consideration, though: What about incomplete combustion? What reactions take place at sub-combustion temperatures? What chemical reactions take place post-combustion? Are dioxins and furans released as a result of combustion? How does ash affect groundwater? Since hazardous waste incineration is currently under a moratorium, attention is being focused on the combustibility of dewatered municipal sewage sludge. Recent developments promise to make incineration of sludge both economically and technically feasible.

Many groups are hard at work drafting legislation to reauthorize Superfund (Comprehensive Emergency Response, Compensation and Liability Act of 1980). One issue under study is the *de minimis* policy of EPA, which currently allows regional administrators to resolve liability of potentially responsible parties (PRPs) which contribute only small (de minimis) amounts of hazardous waste to a Superfund site. In July 1993,

EPA issued a *de micromis* policy, applicable to generators and transporters of hazardous waste. This new policy allows Regional Administrators to estimate a PRP's contribution before a volumetric ranking is available, thus streamlining the settlement process by allowing small contribution PRPs to settle and get out of any more liability from third party lawsuits.

De minimis settlements were originally designed to protect small companies from larger companies, which obviously want to spread the costs of cleanup to as many pocketbooks as possible. To be eligible for a *de minimis* settlement, the total volume of waste shipped to the site by the settling company has to be less than one percent of the total volume. *De micromis* settlements are for PRPs that contribute an extremely small volume of waste—0.001% or less. As in *de minimis* settlements, *de micromis* PRPs are also protected from third party lawsuits. Another innovation is alternative dispute resolution, which considers the circumstances of small volume PRPs, and provides greater flexibility and judgment to the Regional Administrator for reaching settlements. The remedial process is also being streamlined. Standard cleanup remedies are being promoted to expedite matters. Nevertheless, EPA is still studying the biggest question in everyone's mind, "how clean is clean?"

Meanwhile, Congress holds endless hearings to fashion its own innovations. Impediments to innovative cleanup technologies are being studied closely. For example:

A high temperature reactor was proposed for use in cleaning up a contaminated site in Colorado. The reactor operates at nearly 5,000°F and vitrifies (makes glass of) most solid wastes. However, residence time in the reactor is only about 0.1 second (100 milliseconds), much less than the 2 second (2,000 millisecond) residence time EPA typically requires in rotary kilns and incinerators which operate around 1,700°F. So the state-of-the art reactor is not allowed to process waste.

How do you try state-of-the art equipment if you cannot get a permit to do so?

Another problem area is getting permits for innovative mobile technologies. Permits are issued for specific sites, instead of for specific processes. Somehow, Congress must allow EPA to issue permits for mobile treatment processes, with potential for operating at any of several sites. Of course, certain restrictions on temporary siting will need to apply. Perhaps an itinerary similar to a pilot's flight plan can be made part of the permit.

Another Superfund issue in the next century is closed municipal landfills that may soon begin leaking. Who cleans them up? Who pays? If the mood of taxpayers in the 1990s carries into the 21st Century, you can bet EPA will be looking for major industrial and commercial contributors (deep pockets) regardless of blame.

SUSTAINABLE DEVELOPMENT

Whether global or local, more and more government officials and corporate executives are using the phrase "sustainable development," introduced by the World Commission on Environment and Development in 1987. In order to grasp this issue, we must ask: How do we continue mass production of consumer goods when the wastes and by-products of production imperil the planet? How do we continue to produce more energy for factories and homes when the waste materials of production can potentially be devastating?

The International Chamber of Commerce proposes sixteen guiding principles for attaining sustainable development which are listed in Figure 1.5.

Figure 1.5
International Chamber of Commerce
Guiding Principles for Sustainable Development

1. Make environmental management one of the highest corporate functions.
2. Integrate environmental policy throughout organization.
3. Continuously improve corporate environmental policies and processes per achievable global standards.
4. Educate employees to be environmentally responsible.
5. Assess environmental impacts before starting any new activity.
6. Provide products/services that are safe in their intended use.
7. Advise/instruct customers in the safe use of products/services.

Figure 1.5 *(cont'd)*

8. Design/operate facilities to maximize resources/minimize unavoidable wastes.

9. Support research that helps to understand and minimize environmental hazards.

10. Modify activities that demonstrate irreversible negative impacts on the environment.

11. Make effective/comprehensive emergency response plans.

12. Transfer environmentally sound technology.

13. Contribute to environmental awareness in government, industry, and the public

14. Foster openness to concerns and dialogue with employees and the public.

15 Audit environmental compliance performance/periodically report on progress to shareholders/public.

16. Promote these principles with contractors/suppliers.

For the remainder of the 20th century, the International Chamber of Commerce calls on industry to focus on four agenda items: 1) education and open dialogue; 2) pollution prevention and waste minimization; 3) product stewardship; and 4) innovative product design and marketing. Industry must be aggressive in taking initiatives such as these in order to reduce hazards to the environment. Commitment to reduce waste and emissions is required by single-minded executives. Companies must start thinking about the entire life cycle of their products, instead of product design, manufacturing, and marketing only. Formalized consideration of the impact of production is called *life-cycle analysis* and many companies have begun to use this planning tool.

If you think the International Chamber of Commerce has foregone pragmatism for altruism, retired environmental consultant Roy F. Weston says, "it should be obvious that sustainable development is an economic model with limited resources." Sustainable development mandates specific actions of business and government: 1) protect life and natural systems; 2) conserve nonrenewable resources; and 3) assure that the economic system supports the first two actions, as well as fosters efficient use of all resources.

Weston identifies twelve truisms about environmental systems which are outlined in Figure 1.6. Figure 1.7 lists activities which Weston believes we should be concerned with and cautious about. Do not read gloom and doom into this frank treatment of issues. As Weston states, "There is ample evidence that a high standard of living and an acceptable environmental quality are highly compatible."

Figure 1.6
Roy F. Weston
Truisms about Environmental Systems

1. Natural systems are interdependent.
2. Interrelationships among natural/human systems can be highly complex, apparently chaotic, and imprecisely predictable.
3. Energy is essential to life, environmental systems, and human productivity and is a limited resource.
4. The more energy reflected into/out of the atmosphere, the more extreme and violent the weather.
5. Micro decisions/actions, while insignificant themselves, can collectively create a major impact.
6. Micro change in one part of a natural system can prompt macro change in the system as a whole. Likewise, micro change in one system can alter balance among systems.
7. The interval between time of initial contact and time of effect in natural systems can be years.
8. All life forms are vulnerable to natural diseases.
9. Limited resources + unbalanced life systems self-destruct.
10. Individual life forms, including siblings, are not created equal in resistance to disease, sensitivity to environmental factors, adaptability, social behavior, and other significant factors.
11. Environmental degradation is initiated at the local level; local problems collectively create regional and global ones.
12. Those societies with the highest standards of living tend to have the lowest population growth rates.

Figure 1.7
Roy F. Weston
Activities of Concern

1. Destructive use of nonrenewable resources.
2. Dispersive dislocation of nonrenewable resources.
3. Excessive use of renewable resources.
4. Irrecoverable loss of currently available renewable resources due to mismanagement.
5. Development and use of materials foreign to nature.
6. Use and disposal of materials that will bioconcentrate.
7. Overload of natural systems.
8. Lack of technologies and systems for amelioration of the activities listed above.

The President's Council on Sustainable Development—twenty-five representatives from the Cabinet, industry, environmental organizations, and minority affairs organizations—selected global warming as a priority. Subcommittees are developing strategies for sustainable agriculture, environmental justice, and environmental education. One product of the Council is a strategy for how the U.S. might achieve goals outlined in Agenda 21, the UNEP program for sustainable development (UNEP programs are listed in Figure 1.4). The Council will identify specific actions for a national sustainable development strategy.

From Love Canal to the Ukraine, from Seveso to Bhopal, human endeavor to change life for the better has been known to backfire. Occasionally, pollution has been due to acts of maliciousness driven by greed, but more often it has been due to acts of stupidity, driven either by ignorance or by poor judgment, or sometimes by both.

The human race cannot afford for nations to get into finger pointing contests over the issue of wise *versus* stupid stewardship of toxic chemicals. The same chemicals that poison our planet are also beneficial to us in many ways. Collectively, we must decide whether each chemical's liability outweighs its benefits. Too many people in underdeveloped countries sorely need progress in order to have even a small share of the necessities of life taken for granted in the U.S. Too many die every minute from starvation or disease for us to ignore technological possibilities. Eight billion people cannot live in an agrarian society. In the long term, hard questions have to be asked and unpopular decisions may need to be made.

CONCLUSION

Protecting and managing a pristine environment for generations to come has the potential to pull the people of this planet together like nothing has before. New priorities must be set to point the way to international cooperation and understanding. Many millions of people cannot focus on environmental problems today simply because they are too busy surviving from day-to-day. That's why today's environmental problems are mine and yours; we must be able to focus on them in the present.

REFERENCES

"The Bush Administration and The Environment." Washington, D.C.: U.S. Executive Office of The President, 1992.

Carson, Rachel Louise. *Silent Spring*. Boston: Houghton Mifflin, 1962.

Chowdhury, Jayadev. "Plant Siting." *Chemical Engineering*. February, 1992.

Commoner, Barry. *Science and Survival*. New York: Viking Press, 1966.

"Consequences of Wetland Loss and Degradation." *Wetlands Fact Sheet #3*. EPA843-F-93-001c, March 1993.

Diamond, Arthur. *The Bhopal Chemical Leak*. San Diego, California: Lucent Books, 1990.

Esposito, John and Larry J. Silverman. *Vanishing Air: The Ralph Nader Study Group Report on Air Pollution*. New York: Grossman Publishers, 1970.

"Facts about Wetlands." *Wetlands Fact Sheet #5*. EPA843-F-93- 001e.

Faith, W.L. *Air Pollution Control*. 1959.

Finlayson-Pitts, Barbara J. and James N. Pitts, Jr. *Atmospheric Chemistry: Fundamentals and Experimental Techniques*. New York: John Wiley & Sons, 1986.

Fuller, John Grant. *The Poison That Fell from The Sky*. New York: Random House, 1977.

Gibbs, Lois Marie as told to Murray Levine. *Love Canal: My Story*. Albany, New York: State University of New York Press, 1982.

Gore, Al. *Earth in The Balance: Ecology and The Human Spirit*. Boston: Houghton Mifflin, 1992.

Hammer, Mark J. *Water and Wastewater Technology*. 2nd ed. New York: John Wiley & Sons, 1986.

"Holes Poked in Ozone Efforts." *Pollution Engineering*. March 1, 1992.

"In Our Hands: Earth Summit 92." Rio de Janeiro, Brazil: United Nations Conference on Environment and Development, 1991.

Kemmer, Frank N., ed. *The NALCO Water Handbook*. 2nd ed. New York: McGraw-Hill Book Company, 1988.

Lambert, Richard J. "Rethinking Productivity: The Perspective of The Earth as The Primary Corporation." *Population and The Environment*. Spring 1992.

Law Companies Group, Inc. *Washington Update*. September 1993.

Lipfert, Frederick W. *Air Pollution and Community Health: A Critical Review and Data Sourcebook*. New York: Van Nostrand Reinhold, 1994.

Magill, P.L., F.R. Holden and C. Ackley. *Air Pollution Handbook*. 1956.

"Major Milestones in Federal Surface Water Quality Legislation." *Environmental Protection*. July/August 1992.

Nemecek, Sasha. "Holes in Ozone Science: Researchers Look at Loss of The Protective Layer above Our Heads." *Scientific American*. January 1995.

Nemerow, Nelson L. *Industrial Water Pollution: Origins, Characteristics and Treatment*. Reading, MA: Addison-Wesley Publishing Company, 1978.

Novotny, Vladimir and Harvey Olem. *Water Quality: Prevention, Identification, and Management of Diffuse Pollution.* New York: Van Nostrand Reinhold, 1994.

O'Reilly, James T. *Emergency Response to Chemical Accidents: Planning and Coordinating Solutions.* New York: McGraw-Hill Book Company, 1987.

"The President's Message on Environmental Quality." *Environmental Quality: 22nd Annual Report.* Washington, D.C.: Council on Environmental Quality, 1992.

Rasmussen, Dana A. "Enforcement in The U.S. Environmental Protection Agency: Balancing The Carrots and The Sticks." *Environmental Law.* Winter 1992.

Schneider, David. "Global Warming Is Still A Hot Topic: Arrival of Seasons May Show Greenhouse Effect." *Scientific American.* February 1995.

Silverman, Gerald B. "Love Canal: A Retrospective." *Environment Reporter Current Developments.* September 15, 1989.

Simpson, Theodore B. "Limiting Emissions of The Greenhouse Gas, CO_2." *Environmental Progress.* November, 1991.

"The State of The World Environment 1991." Nairobi, Kenya: United Nations Environmental Program, May 1991.

Stern, A.C., ed. *Air Pollution: A Comprehensive Treatise.* 1962.

Stern, Alissa J. "Control of Toxic Substances." *Environmental Law.* Vol. 22, No. 2.

Stix, Gary. "Clean Definitions: The Nation Contemplates What to Do with Superfund." *Scientific American.* December 1993.

Terry, Edith. "Japan's Plan: Deep-Sea Carbon Dioxide Disposal." *Tomorrow: The Global Environmental Magazine.* Vol. 2, No. 2.

UNEP. *20 Years: Two Decades of Achievement and Challenge.* London: A.Banson Production commissioned by UNEP, 1992.

"Values and Functions of Wetlands." *Wetlands Fact Sheet #2.* EPA843-F-93-001b, March 1993.

Vansant, Carl and Michael E. Hilts. "The Status of Waste-to-Energy: What Role in Integrated Waste Management?" *Solid Waste and Power Magazine.* June 1992.

Vincoli, Jeffrey W. *Basic Guide to Environmental Compliance.* New York: Van Nostrand Reinhold, 1993.

Wagner, Travis. In Our Backyard: *A Guide to Understanding Pollution and Its Effects.* New York: Van Nostrand Reinhold,1994.

Wells, Harry W. "Modern Agriculture: Polluter or Protector." *Pollution Engineering.* January 1, 1992.

Weston, Roy F. "Sustainable Development: Make It a *Given,* Not a Goal." *Chemical Engineering Progress.* February 1992.

"Wetlands Protection—Overview." *Wetlands Fact Sheet #1.* EPA843-F-93-001a, March 1993.

Winter, Georg. *Business and The Environment.* Hamburg: McGraw-Hill Book Company GmbH, 1988.

Woolard, E.S., Jr. "An Industry Approach to Sustainable Development." *Issues in Science and Technology.* Spring 1992.

Zwick, David. *Water Wasteland: Ralph Nader's Study Group Report on Water Pollution.* New York: Grossman Publishers, 1971.

2

COPING DAILY WITH COMPLIANCE

As would anyone, the industrial environmental compliance manager wants to do a quality job for his or her company. The newly assigned environmental compliance manager quickly learns, however, that a dichotomy often exists between environmental compliance and what is good for the company.

On the one hand, the usual expectations of performance faced by an employee are to perform well and be a positive contributor to the bottom line in some visible way. On the other hand, compliance with environmental regulations is seen as diametrically opposed to the company's stated mission to exceed "x" millions of dollars in sales and to return "y%" on the investment of the company's stockholders. If the environmental compliance manager fails to do well, the company may be penalized. Money may be paid as a direct fine or equipment may have to be purchased and installed under compliance pressure or any of several compliance sanctions may be imposed including sentencing someone to a jail term. Also, the public may not pay much attention to the plant right now, but if an environmental incident occurs, that company's operations and management will be scrutinized microscopically and its decisions will be tediously dissected by the press. Journalists are not compliance experts but they are tough Monday morning quarterbacks!

So, the typical compliance manager is, at one and the same time, expected to keep the company out of trouble and out of the headlines while not spending or costing a dime that impacts the bottom line. Hence, environmental compliance is still rarely assigned to a trained professional in the environmental engineering discipline with compliance affairs experience. Typically these duties are assigned to a person who is competent in some other field (for example, human resource management, purchasing management, or plant engineering) but untrained in the complexities of laws and regulations of pollution control and prevention engineering. These persons are the nonexpert generalists who keep the vast majority of American businesses more or less in compliance.

The assignment seems to be an impossible, thankless task to the newcomer. Given that regulations are complicated and that the manufacturing plant environmental compliance manager is typically a collateral duty assignment, what must an inexperienced person having these responsibilities do? The task seems overwhelming and the pressure of the dichotomy mentioned above can be tremendous, engendering fear and stress.

The questions worth asking as a novice environmental professional are, How do I best enhance the compliance posture of my plant? What is the most effective way to manage compliance? What is the fastest and least expensive way to make solid gains in compliance status?

Before discussing the basics of environmental management, the person assigned these duties must be clear on one matter: no real dichotomy exists between the environment and the company's interests. The perception that a dichotomy does exist is an illusion born of near-sighted, short term thinking. What is good for the environment *is* good for the company. It may not be immediately obvious, but in the long term the company's best interests *are* best served by operating in an environmentally sound manner. Existing or proposed regulations may not always be the best answer to an environmental problem. We tend to resist when told we have to do something. Regulations do not necessarily represent the best economic path for your company. However, note that whatever path your company takes, it must be consistent with the regulations, so you must know them well.

The effective environmental manager is one who keeps line management informed of issues, successfully encourages them to minimize polluting activities, and keeps them interested in a goal of zero pollution. The aggressive environmental manager knows that any air or water pollution or any hazardous waste generated is not in the company's best interest. That compliance manager takes steps to go beyond the regulations and does not worry moment-to-moment about every detail of the regulations precisely because he has gone beyond them in an effort to protect the environment.

ENHANCING COMPLIANCE MANAGEMENT

The first thing a new compliance manager typically does is jump into a major compliance problem with both feet. This cannot be helped sometimes, but unfortunately such a compliance manager may never again see the light of day. We have all been in that situation at one time or another. Perhaps that is your predicament now. You keep thinking, "as soon as I take care of this one problem I'll be able to catch up and everything will be all right." It is extremely difficult to catch up once we get on such a path. Another environmental compliance headache is only a few weeks down the road. Therefore, the prudent manager of environmental compliance sets priorities and avoids fighting brushfires as much as possible.

Priorities vs. Brushfires

Sound project management practices can help prevent much job-related stress. Treat each issue that arises as a separate project. Assign a project number and/or title to each in order to track progress and make project status reporting easier. Planning for and administering projects consists of several distinct management steps: problem definition, scope of work, budget and schedule, status reports, and completion report.

The first step is to define the problem—not as obvious as it first sounds. Many projects take too long or fall apart completely because the problem to be solved is not clearly understood or because the project aimed at solving the wrong problem. For instance, you get a notice that your company is in violation of its wastewater discharge permit (you knew that already because you reported it on Discharge Monitoring Reports—see Chapter 8). The problem in this case is not that your company is out of compliance. Rather, the problem is that the wastewater treatment plant is not effectively removing contaminants from the effluent (assuming no analytical snafu). The purpose of your project then is to troubleshoot the wastewater plant, isolate the cause or causes of recent noncompliant discharges, and engineer a permanent solution to the problem. If you make the purpose of the project to get into compliance with the state discharge permit you may chase after compliance forever! It is not the purpose of this book to teach project management methods, only to point out the importance and necessity of good project management in a compliance program. If you are weak on project management, many books and project management training seminars are available.

As soon as the problem is defined, determine who your customers are. In order to do a good job of correcting the problem, you must meet your customers' requirements, so you must know your customers. Your management is almost always a customer. Next you need to know whether the state environmental agency or federal EPA or both are customers. In the case of our example, the wastewater plant operators are also your customers. Identifying all customers is very important, as one company found out when it attempted to get an air permit to burn a flammable cleaning fluid in a boiler providing steam for process heat. The cleaning fluid was used to pick up unused motor oil from the plant floor. The strategy for permitting, the information gathered to support the application, and the efforts to get the information were all predicated on air pollution regulations. When the application was submitted to the state air pollution control authority, the authority spent eighteen months reviewing the information and then returned the application with the announcement that the desired activity fell into the realm of hazardous waste management which, at the time, was a matter for the regional EPA office. If the right customer had been identified, a permit would probably have been issued in considerably less time than the twenty-eight months it ended up taking. Do not be afraid to talk to or meet with regulators, permitting authorities, or enforcers in order to determine your customers.

Once customers are known, determine their requirements. You can easily sit down and discuss requirements with your senior management staff. Get their input directly for each problem. As for the state or EPA, you can always get their requirements by finding the appropriate regulations for the problem at hand. However, sometimes you need direct, face-to-face contact with regulators and enforcers. Do not be hesitant to ask for a meeting in order to ensure that you know and understand their requirements thoroughly.

One company spent months preparing air permit applications at considerable expense for ten non-identical production facilities. The company eventually received a letter from the state saying that its policy was not to require permits for facilities such as three of the company's ten. A permit exemption list was available for the asking. A conversation with them in the first place might have uncovered the exemption and saved time and money.

Checking with the customer about requirements is basic and avoids wasted work, expense, and time. Good project management and customer relations allow you to address priorities instead of always fighting brushfires.

Long-Range Planning

Another aspect of good project management is the making of long-range plans. To do this effectively, the environmental compliance manager must keep up with trends in regulations. Even the nonexpert generalist cannot afford to lose track of regulations in the development phase. The best way to keep up is Subscribe, Read, and Attend.

Subscribe to a service that tracks regulations. The *Federal Register* is the most direct and basic subscription service, though many find it hard to read and filled with extraneous information. The *Federal Register* is a daily weekday publication by the federal government that provides a uniform system for publishing all presidential documents, all proposed and final regulations, notices of meetings, and other official documents issued by federal departments and agencies such as the EPA. Some environmental managers prefer to subscribe to one or another of the numerous news services that scan the *Federal Register* and screen information for client subscribers. These subscription services are useful because they have journalists who keep up with the really important information and screen out that which is not relevant. Corporate newsletters are a fine way to keep up with regulations too; however, when it comes down to complying with any particular regulation, make sure you have an up-to-date copy of the actual regulation.

Twice each year, in April and October, the *Federal Register* prints the *Regulatory Plan* and *Unified Agenda of Federal Regulations*. Each executive branch agency's Regulatory Plan contains two sections: 1) a narrative statement of its regulatory priorities, and 2) a description of the most significant regulatory actions that it reasonably expects to propose or issue during the upcoming year. The *Unified Agenda* reports on regulatory activities under development for the next twelve months. Information is included in the *Unified Agenda* which identifies rules that may have a significant economic impact on substantial numbers of small businesses and those that will have an effect on various levels of government.

When Congress passes a law (Act of Congress) it generally authorizes a single federal agency to implement by regulation the specific policy objectives that were set forth in the new law. Sometimes an act requires several agencies to issue regulations to accomplish its objectives, in which case the agencies work with a central coordinator to jointly publish common rules. A public law (PL) is either signed by the President or enacted over his veto and has general applicability. A private law applies only to those persons or entities specifically designated in the bill. Public laws are numbered sequentially throughout the two-year life of each Congress. For instance, PL 80-845, the Water Pollution Control Act (WPCA) of 1948, was the 845th law passed by the 80th Congress and PL 92-500, the WPCA Amendments of 1972 (commonly called the Clean Water Act (CWA)), was the 500th law enacted by the 92nd Congress.

Both the *Regulatory Plan* and *Unified Agenda* list rules by rulemaking stage. *Rule* and *regulation* are interchangeable terms. *Law, act,* and *statute* are also interchangeable terms. However, rules and regulations are not laws; do not confuse the two sets of terms. Rules are administrative details that implement a law's stated policies. Laws are the authority for rules.

In the Prerule Stage, agencies determine whether or how to initiate rulemaking. Such actions occur prior to a Notice of Proposed Rulemaking (NPRMs) and may include Advance Notices of Proposed Rulemaking (ANPRMs) and reviews of existing regulations. An ANPRM is a preliminary notice that an agency is considering a regulatory action and it is issued before a detailed proposed rule is developed. The ANPRM describes the general area that may be subject to regulation and usually asks for public comment on issues and options. ANPRMs are used only when the agency believes it needs more information before proceeding to an NPRM.

The Proposed Rule Stage starts with an NPRM and a comment period. Regulations are not laws, so NPRMs must be placed before the public for review and comment before being finalized. The NPRM includes the time, place, and nature of the public hearing, cites legal authority for the proposed rule, and gives either the terms or substance of the proposed rule or describes issues and subjects involved.

After public commentary is considered, the issuing agency may publish a final rule or an interim final rule or take another final action, such as drop the proposed regulation. Either way, this step is called the Final Rule Stage. Actions or reviews completed by the agency since publishing its last agenda are Completed Actions. *Unified Agenda* data elements are given in Figure 2.1.

Figure 2.1
Unified Agenda **Elements**

Title of Regulation
Legal Authority citations
CFR Citation
Legal Deadline
Abstract
Timetable
Small Entities Affected economically in substantial numbers. Are they businesses, government, or organizations?
Government Levels Affected—federal, state, local, tribal.
Agency Contact—name, title, address, telephone number.
Procurement-related actions (not typically noteworthy in environmental management).

For each pending rule, the Regulatory Agenda contains all the information about the rule that the Unified Agenda does, plus the ones listed in Figure 2.2.

The listing agency may include other information as it wishes. Keeping a copy of the latest Regulatory Plan and Unified Agenda handy allows you to keep up with pending rules that may affect your plant.

Figure 2.2
Additional Elements of Regulatory Agenda

Statement of Need for the regulation.
Summary of the Legal Basis—statute or court order?
Alternatives considered.
Anticipated Costs and Benefits—preliminary estimates.
Risks—magnitude of the risk; amount by which risk will
    be reduced by the rule and relationship of risks and risk reduction
    efforts by the agency.

Laws are not rules, and regulations are not acts. Laws, if general and permanent, are consolidated and codified (systematically arranged) in the *United States Code (USC)*. The *USC* is divided into 50 titles, each covering a broad area of federal law. Figure 2.3 shows *USC* titles pertinent to the environment and Figure 2.4 lists environmental laws with acronyms.

Once a federal agency finalizes a rule it is printed in the *Federal Register*, then codified annually in the *Code of Federal Regulations (CFR)* which is divided into 50 titles and kept up-to-date by the office which prints the *Federal Register*. *CFR* titles do not correspond to *USC* titles. It is easy to confuse the two because the method of citing each is similar. For example, *40 USC* has no relationship to *40 CFR*; the public law codified at *42 USC 6901-81* is implemented by regulations found at *40 CFR 190-299*. Each *CFR* title covers a broad area subject to federal regulation. Figure 2.5 lists *CFR* titles of interest to an environmental manager while Figure 2.6 gives the titles of various federal agencies which regulate the environment in some way. The lead federal agency for environmental matters is EPA (Environmental Protection Agency). Major offices within the EPA are listed in Figure 2.7. The titles of close assistants to the EPA Administrator are given in Figure 2.8. In Figures 2.9 and 2.10, respectively, are lists of EPA Research Laboratories and Regional EPA Offices.

Figure 2.3
Pertinent Titles of USC

<u>U.S. Code</u>

<u>Title</u>	<u>Sections</u>	<u>Subject</u>
5	551 - 559	Administrative Procedures Act
5	701 - 706	Administrative Procedures Act
7	136	Federal Insecticide, Fungicide and Rodenticide Act
15	2601 - 2692	Toxic Substances Control Act
16	661 - 666c	Fish & Wildlife Coordination Act
16	1271 - 1287	Wild and Scenic Rivers Act
16	1361 - 1404	Marine Mammal Protection Act
16	1451 - 1464	Coastal Zone Management Act of 1972
16	1531 - 1544	Endangered Species Act
16	2001 - 2009	Soil and Water Resources Conservation Act of 1977
16	2901 - 2912	Fish & Wildlife Conservation Act of 1980
20	5501 - 5510	National Environmental Education Act of 1984
21	349	Bottled Drinking Water (part of Safe Drinking Water Act)
26	4611 - 4672	Hazardous Substance Response Revenue Act of 1980 (Title II of CERCLA)
33	401 - 413	Rivers and Harbors Act of 1899
33	1251 - 2761	Federal Water Pollution Control Act as amended by Clean Water Act of 1977
33	1401 - 1447f	Marine Protection, Research and Sanctuaries Act of 1972
33	1501 - 1524	Deepwater Port Act of 1974
33	2601 - 2621	Shore Protection Act of 1988
33	4202 - 4204	Shore Protection Act of 1988
42	300f- 300j	Safe Drinking Water Act
42	4321	Pollution Prosecution Act of 1990
42	4321 - 4375	National Environmental Protection Act
42	4368	Environmental Programs Assistance Act of 1984
42	6215	excerpt from National Energy Conservation Policy Act relating to Clean Air Act
42	6901 - 6981	Resource Conservation and Recovery Act of 1976
42	7401 note	Radon Gas and Indoor Air Quality Research Act of 1986

Figure 2.3 *(cont'd)*

<u>U.S. Code</u>

<u>Title</u>	<u>Sections</u>	<u>Subject</u>
42	7401 - 7671p	Clean Air Act
42	9601 - 9675	Comprehensive Emergency Response, Compensation and Liability Act of 1980
42	11000-11050	Emergency Planning and Community Right-to-Know Act of 1986
42	13101-13109	Pollution Prevention Act of 1990
43	1331 - 1351	Outer Continental Shelf Lands Act

Figure 2.4
Environmental Law Titles and Acronyms

<u>Law</u>	<u>Acronym</u>
Aircraft Noise Abatement Act	ANAA
Asbestos Hazard Emergency Response Act	AHERA
Atomic Energy Act	AEA
Aviation Safety and Noise Abatement Act of 1979	ASNAA
Clean Air Act	CAA
Clean Air Act Amendments of 1990	CAAA
Coastal Zone Management Act of 1972	CZMA
Comprehensive Emergency Response, Compensation, and Liability Act of 1980	CERCLA
Deepwater Port Act of 1974	DPA
Emergency Planning and Community Right-to-Know Act of 1986	EPCRA
Endangered Species Act of 1973	ESA
Energy Reorganization Act of 1974	ERA
Energy Supply and Environmental Coordination Act of 1974	ESECA
Environmental Programs Assistance Act of 1984	EPAA
Environmental Quality Improvement Act of 1970	EQIA
Federal Food, Drug and Cosmetics Act	FFDCA

Figure 2.4 *(cont'd)*

Law	Acronym
Federal Insecticide, Fungicide and Rodenticide Act	FIFRA
Federal Water Pollution Control Act	FWPCA
Fish & Wildlife Conservation Act of 1980	FWConA
Fish & Wildlife Coordination Act	FWCA
Hazardous and Solid Waste Amendments	HSWA
Hazardous Material Transportation Act	HMTA
Marine Protection, Research and Sanctuaries Act	MPRSA
Maritime Mammal Protection Act	MMPA
National Environmental Policy Act	NEPA
National Ocean Pollution Planning Act of 1978	NOPPA
Noise Control Act of 1972	NCA
Oil Pollution Act of 1990	OPA
Outer Continental Shelf Lands Act	OCSLA
Pollution Prevention Act of 1990	PPA
Pollution Prosecution Act of 1990	PPrA
Port and Waterways Safety Act	PWSA
Radon Gas and Indoor Air Quality Research Act of 1986	RGIAQRA
Resource Conservation and Recovery Act	RCRA
Rivers and Harbors Act of 1899	RHA
Safe Drinking Water Act	SDWA
Shore Protection Act of 1988	SPA
Solid & Water Resources Conservation Act of 1977	SWRCA
Superfund Amendments and Reauthorization Act	SARA
Surface Mining Control and Reclamation Act	SMCRA
Toxic Substances Control Act	TSCA
Water Quality Act of 1987	WQA
Water Resources Planning Act	WRPA
Water Resources Research Act	WRRA
Wild & Scenic Rivers Act	WSRA

Figure 2.5
Pertinent Titles of CFR

Title	Chapters	Subject
		Energy
10	0- 199	Nuclear Regulatory Commission
10	200- End	Energy Department
18		**Conservation of Power & Water Resources**
21		**Food and Drugs**
		Mineral Resources
30	1- 199	Mine Safety & Health Administration (MSHA)
30	200- 699	Mineral Management Service Bureau
30	700- End	Surface Mining Reclamation and Enforcement
		Navigation and Navigable Waters
33	1- 199	Coast Guard
33	200- End	Corps of Engineers
		Environmental
40	1- 49	Administrative, General, Grants, Assistance
40	50- 99	Air Programs
40	100- 149	Water Programs
40	150- 189	FIFRA—Pesticide Programs
40	190- 299	RCRA, Radiation, Ocean Dumping, Solid Waste, Hazardous Waste
40	300- 399	CERCLA, SARA Title III
40	400- 699	Water Effluent Guidelines and Standards
40	700- End	TSCA, PCB, Asbestos, Lead, Radon
		Public Lands: Interior
43	1- 999	Department of Interior, Reclamation Bureau
43	1000- End	Land Management Bureau
49		**Department of Transportation**
50		**Wildlife and Fisheries**

Figure 2.6
Meet the Regulators

Administrative Office/Suboffice	Acronym
Council on Environmental Quality	CEQ
Department of Agriculture	USDA
Agricultural Research Service	ARS
Agricultural Stabilization & Conservation Service	ASCS
Cooperative State Research Program	CSRP
Farmers' Home Administration	FHA
Soil Conservation Service	SCS
Department of Commerce	DOC
National Bureau of Standards	NBS
National Oceanographic & Atmospheric Administration	NOAA
Department of Defense	DOD
U.S. Army Corps of Engineers	COE
Department of Energy	DOE
Department of Health and Human Services	DHHS
Food and Drug Administration	FDA
National Institute of Environmental Health Sciences	NIEHS
Department of Housing and Urban Development	HUD
Department of the Interior	DOI
Bureau of Indian Affairs	BIA
Bureau of Land Management	BLM
Bureau of Mines	BuMines
Fish and Wildlife Service	FWS
National Park Service	NPS
Office of Surface Mining Reclamation and Enforcement	OSMRE
U.S. Geological Survey	USGS
Department of Justice	DOJ
Department of Labor	DOL
Occupational Safety & Health Administration	OSHA
Department of Transportation	DOT
Federal Aviation Administration	FAA
U.S. Coast Guard	USCG

Figure 2.6 *(cont'd)*

Administrative Office/Suboffice	Acronym
Environmental Protection Agency	EPA
International Joint Commission	IJC
National Aeronautics and Space Administration	NASA
Nuclear Regulatory Commission	NRC

Figure 2.7
Offices of EPA

Administration and Resources Management
Air and Radiation
Enforcement and Compliance Monitoring
External Affairs
General Counsel
Inspector General
Pesticides and Toxic Substances
Policy, Planning and Evaluation
Research and Development
Solid Waste and Emergency Response
Water

Figure 2.8
Close Assistants to the EPA Administrator

Assistant Administrator for International Activities
Associate Administrator for Communications and Public Affairs
Associate Administrator for Congressional and Legislative Affairs
Chief Administrative Law Judge
Deputy Administrator (second in charge)
Director, Civil Rights
Director, Science Advisory
Board Director, Small and Disadvantaged Business Utilization

Refocusing on the need for long-range planning, you should also read all the trade journals you can get your hands on. Many have regular columns which summarize regulation changes, trends, and developments. Make use of this free information. Compliance management is about reading, reading, reading! You cannot afford not to read. A person who hates to read or does not read well is in the wrong job. Summaries and review articles are another good way to keep up with current regulations, plus they usually give clues about issues to look for when reading actual regulations.

Finally, attend every environmental regulation update seminar held in your town. With no travel expenses your supervisor should not object. If you have to travel, convince him or her that you need to attend two such seminars per year. Environmental compliance management depends heavily on continually developing information—which is perishable—so expose yourself to many discussions about pending regulations because this allows you to start proposing and discussing long- range plans for your company.

Making the Quickest Gains

You have taken over a compliance program that is nonexistent or in shambles. How do you make the quickest gains? Put another way, how do you get the biggest bang for your buck when stepping into a bad situation? When taking over a compliance program, the priorities are 1) orders; 2) permits; 3) training; 4) routine operations; and 5) recordkeeping. Perhaps you are surprised that recordkeeping is not first on the list. If you are interested in appearances then perhaps recordkeeping is the highest priority, since enforcement inspections tend to look at recordkeeping first and base the rest of the inspection on the impression the records make. However, if you are interested in the quickest way to achieve a first-class compliance program, this is the order of priorities.

Orders are brushfires but they get management attention and you may as well take advantage of the situation. When your company has violated a regulatory requirement, the enforcement agency issues a compliance order, which is an administrative device to get quick action without a court battle. An order may also assess a civil penalty, but it will always give you tasks to complete or you will pay. Orders give you a compliance schedule (likely as not proposed by your company) with the list of things to do. Do them on time.

Generally, the environmental compliance manager gets a blank check when the company is under a compliance order—an opportune time to get things done! Take advantage of the "fix it now at any cost" attitude your upper management will have and correct the problem, first class. Do not waste this precious opportunity on a bandage or quick-fix; instead isolate and correct the underlying problem.

If any orders are still pending when you take over, keep in mind that exact legal and technical requirements to remedy a noncompliance situation are frequently negotiated within the confines of regulations and permit conditions. Before initial discussions with enforcement authorities, determine their priorities as well as those of the regulatory office (if different from the enforcement office). Know your customer's requirements! Are you going to set a precedent by proposing an innovative corrective action? How extensive is the risk to public health and the environment if the problem is not corrected? Knowing the answers to these questions and the priorities of the authority you deal with allows your management to decide what basic negotiating strategy to take. How soon you must comply and the technical requirements are usually negotiable. Before the negotiations, send two persons down to review state and/or EPA files on your company. These files are public records and you may review them. You may have to make an appointment and some restrictions may apply to seeing draft documents and to making copies.

With facts collected, management should appoint a negotiating team. The members should familiarize themselves with all facts before the initial negotiation session and plan a negotiating strategy which addresses the time it will take to be back in compliance, the choice of corrective technology, how and when the decision will be made that you are back in compliance, and the penalties for noncompliance. Resolve the compliance issue as quickly and cheaply but as effectively as economically feasible because the issue, being a hot one, is probably consuming all your time and you must get on to other projects before they too become critical. Other than that, go for the most complete solution your company can feasibly manage so the same problem will not be revisited.

Figure 2.9
EPA Research Laboratories

Laboratory	Location
Air & Energy Engineering Research Lab	Research Triangle Park, NC
Atmospheric Science Research Lab	Research Triangle Park, NC
Center for Environmental Research Information	Cincinnati, OH
Environmental Criteria & Assessment Office	Cincinnati, OH
Environmental Criteria & Assessment Office	Research Triangle Park, NC
Environmental Monitoring & Support Lab	Cincinnati, OH
Environmental Monitoring Systems Lab	Las Vegas, NV
Environmental Monitoring Systems Lab	Research Triangle Park, NC
Environmental Research Lab	Athens, GA
Environmental Research Lab	Corvallis, OR
Environmental Research Lab	Duluth, MN
Environmental Research Lab	Gulf Breeze, FL
Environmental Research Lab	Narragansett, RI
Health Research Lab	Research Triangle Park, NC
Risk Reduction Engineering Lab	Cincinnati, OH
Rob't S. Kerr Environmental Research Lab	Ada, OK
Walter Engineering Lab	Cincinnati, OH

Figure 2.10
Regional EPA Offices

Region	Location	Covers
I	Boston, MA	Connecticut, Maine, Massachusetts, New Hampshire, Rhode Island, Vermont

Figure 2.10 *(cont'd)*		
Region	**Location**	**Covers**
II	New York, NY	New Jersey, New York, Puerto Rico, Virgin Islands
III	Philadelphia, PA	Delaware, District of Columbia, Maryland, Pennsylvania, Virginia, West Virginia
IV	Atlanta, GA	Alabama, Florida, Georgia, Kentucky, Mississippi, North Carolina, South Carolina, Tennessee
V	Chicago, IL	Illinois, Indiana, Michigan, Minnesota, Ohio, Wisconsin
VI	Dallas, TX	Arkansas, Louisiana, New Mexico, Oklahoma, Texas
VII	Kansas City, MO	Iowa, Kansas, Missouri, Nebraska
VIII	Denver, CO	Colorado, Montana, North Dakota, South Dakota, Utah, Wyoming
IX	San Francisco, CA	Arizona, California, Guam, Hawaii, Nevada
X	Seattle, WA	Alaska, Idaho, Oregon, Washington

Permits are the next priority for establishing a compliance program. Many companies receive a permit, hang a copy of the first page in the lobby and put the permit itself in a file where they promptly forget about it. However, during a compliance inspection, enforcement officials verify whether the conditions of a permit are being followed. Therefore, a permit is a working document, not a file document. It is correct to file the original, but a working copy needs to be kept at the compliance manager's fingertips for frequent reference. (Chapter 5 is about permits.)

Importance of Training

Training is often the weakest area of good environmental programs. So, the third priority is to concentrate on training. The importance of training is recognized by most managers but often training is the first element of business readiness and effectiveness to be shortchanged. Sometimes the worst enemies of the compliance manager are his or her own fellow employees. Untrained employees hurt the compliance effort in two ways. First, untrained employees say inappropriate things when interviewed by compliance inspectors.

One compliance manager was aghast when an employee told a compliance inspector, "I dump hazardous waste down the sewer all the time." The statement was not false, but not entirely true, and it led the inspector on a fact-finding hunt. Some aqueous wastes, having RCRA hazardous characteristics for leachable heavy metals, were allowed, by permit, to be batch dumped into the wastewater treatment plant which neutralizes the wastewater. No penalty. The activity was legal, but the company spent several high-level man-hours in conferences with the enforcement office until all facts were collected and considered and understood.

Second, untrained employees may do inappropriate and noncompliant things.

A RCRA compliance officer was finishing her inspection of hazardous waste storage and commenting on how well run the operation was when an employee walked by with an open pail and tossed its contents out an open back door, about twenty feet from where she was standing. She walked over to the doorway and noticed the grass was dead. "What did you throw out?" she asked the employee, who was taking a smoke break with one foot resting on the up-side-down pail. "Just diesel fuel, Miss. Don't worry, we do it all the time." Use your own favorite EPA nightmare for an ending. Enforcement agencies realize the importance of training too and have begun to focus on verifying training effectiveness during inspections.

Training must be effective or you will revisit the same nagging compliance problems often. Nothing deflates your confidence faster than having a key production line supervisor or senior manager make a statement that indicates that he does not understand the compliance issue under scrutiny.

The secret to ongoing effective compliance management is: *COMPLIANCE BEGINS AND ENDS ON THE LINE.* Train line supervisors and their employees in the details of compliance and make managers aware of regulatory issues and internal compliance efforts.

Training does not just happen. Training is about channeling specific information to persons who need it to perform their jobs properly. Training is about changing behavior and attitudes and improving performance. The economic advantage of training is that if performance is optimized, theoretically, profits will increase or at least be optimized. It can surely be said that if performance is ineffective—or, worse, countereffective—profits will suffer proportionately.

What makes training happen? Buying a video or reading a company procedure is generally not very effective. Four reiterating stages constitute effective training development. These are 1) conducting a needs assessment; 2) setting training goals and objectives; 3) developing learning measurement devices; and 4) developing a lesson plan.

A training policy for your plant should be outlined in a written document that spells out who will be trained and what goals the training will achieve. For instance, how many people from each department are to be trained? Are they identified by name or job task? What areas of training are to be covered? What spaces will be used for training? Having a written policy signed by senior plant management makes it easier to get resources committed to training.

Improving awareness takes time in order to reach the point where employees stop making mistakes that put the company in jeopardy. According to several experts, a major business thrust for the rest of this decade and the early twenty-first century is to become more competitive through effective environmental management. Everyone in the plant is accountable for environmental management. That is the cost return for awareness training. The most difficult goal of training is to keep people continually aware of new regulations and trends while getting them to think, to generate pollution prevention ideas, and to move the plant ahead of the regulations.

Before buying videos or booklets that may or may not cover what she needs, the prudent environmental manager asks, "What end result am I looking for?" Typically, you want hazardous waste handlers, for example, to handle and transfer hazardous waste containers in a manner consistent with RCRA regulations each and every time without error. Then ask, "What specific behaviors does RCRA require of these hazardous waste handlers?" You need to have assurance that each waste handler will behave as required each time he handles waste material. Another question is, "If employees do not behave in the desired manner, how will we make compliance happen?"

Figure 2.11 lists potential questions Kingsley Hendrick gives in *Systematic Safety Training* to determine needs. If you have serious training problems you should consult training experts. The point here is to demonstrate the necessity of effective training for a good compliance program and to show some basic things you can do in-house instead of merely buying training materials which may not complete the training process.

Figure 2.11
Determination of Needs

1. What is the problem?
2. Is it a people or thing problem?
3. What are people doing wrong?
4. What should they be doing?
5. How will we know when the problem is corrected?
6. Is it a problem of ability or willingness?
7. Are solutions available other than training?
8. Would people perform correctly if they knew what was expected of them, how to do it, and why?

After needs assessment, the next training step is to devise training goals and objectives. A training goal is a broad statement of what is expected to be achieved by the training. To continue the example from the previous section, the goal for training might be:

> *Upon completion of this training, affected employees will handle hazardous waste materials and containers in a manner consistent with RCRA regulations.*

This is fine, but so far we have nothing to sink our teeth into.

Objectives give teeth to the goal. Exactly what is it we want the employees to know, to know how to do, and to be willing to do? Objectives are about changing the knowledge, skills, and willingness of adults. Therefore, adult training objectives are principally behavioral in nature. Three types of behavioral objectives are: knowledge, skills, and attitudes (or willingness). Each type of objective has different levels of performance. For an in-depth discussion of training effectiveness and the elements of training, refer to Hendrick's book. The point is that training provides an opportunity to develop or correct attitudes and behaviors. Thus, a sound training program is paramount to a sound compliance program. Is it any wonder that compliance inspectors want to see training records?

Tests and demonstrations of acquired skills are the primary means of measuring learning. A demonstration of skill might involve properly filling out an EPA- approved hazardous waste label or a Uniform Hazardous Waste Manifest. A manual demonstration might be the inspection, under observation of an instructor, of several hazardous waste containers for spills, leaks, and container integrity, orally describing the findings. A more complicated demonstration would be walking through an emergency response, and more difficult still would be a complete emergency drill measured against the clock and an evolving scenario.

Do not use long essay-type tests unless the number of trainees is small and you know for a fact that their level of education, especially their reading and writing skills, is sufficient for such tests. Even then, the purpose of a test is not to create scholars but to reinforce training while measuring the achievement of behavioral objectives. Tests are best if objective (true-false, multiple choice, match two columns of terms) and short. Remember, not everyone reads on the same level so keep it as short and simple as your objectives allow.

Pre-tests and post-tests are recommended but not always necessary. The pre-test tells the instructor where to concentrate his presentation and the post-test measures the achievement of objectives. However, pre-tests backfire in some instances.

A pre-test given to illuminate some myths about certain hazards, which had been circulating among employees, consisted of true-false questions in which each of ten myths were picked apart. A true answer indicated the employee believed the myth, and all correct answers were false. The employees were so angry after the pre-test that they did not listen to the presentation and even refused to cooperate for the post-test. They were humiliated and agitated from having their false ideas challenged.

A pre-test should not be used unless the instructor is well versed enough to modify the remainder of his lesson plan in order to address any weak areas identified and experienced enough to turn emotional reactions into a training opportunity.

Approaches to adult learning must be based on sound principles. Fact: adults are able to learn, but adults must be motivated to learn. Simply telling them that the knowledge, behavior, or skill to be taught is necessary for their performance to be considered satisfactory is generally adequate for their motivation. However, adults are not passive receivers of information but must be involved somehow in the learning experience. Since each adult comes to the training with a unique set of experiences, it is a good idea to have them share their experience in some way. One way is to have small groups discuss a situation and share how they, as individuals, would respond to it. Each group presents its findings to the reassembled class and the instructor concludes the process by summing up and giving feedback on the ideas presented. The entire class can be drawn into such a discussion; however, do not allow the discussion to become negative.

Adults prefer variety, so use several types of training aids and instructional activities. Videos that use talking heads and news anchor presenters quickly bore an adult audience; however, you may have to use such a training aid if you do not have the requisite knowledge yourself. Give a brief introduction for the video in which you mention the training objectives it will satisfy and summarize the major points to look for. After the video, address questions and have a short list of discussion questions prepared in advance, in case the trainees do not have questions. Small group discussions of personal experience relative to the video may also be used effectively.

Keep training sessions around thirty minutes if possible, forty-five minutes if not but an hour maximum. If more time is required to adequately cover a subject (such as HAZWOPER training), schedule additional training 30-60 minutes at a time over a certain time period. Nothing says you cannot do HAZWOPER training, for instance, over the period of a year as long as you repeat the required minimum time each year.

At the beginning of each training session inform the participants why the training is necessary. Adults need to see the purpose of learning or they will tune it out. They need time to become comfortable with what they are learning, so several short sessions are better than one long session for new, complicated material. Reinforce correct behavior in some way to solidify the training process. Positive reinforcement must be immediate.

Three groups of employees used a cleaning process that underwent a change of materials to satisfy Clean Air Act Stratospheric Ozone requirements. All were given a training session on the hazards of the new chemical, but the change for one group was not actually made for four months. After changing the process chemical in the third line, exposure complaints surfaced immediately, whereas employees in the other two work areas, which had made the switch months earlier, had no complaints. The third group slowed down cleaning and would not cooperate with efforts to eliminate emissions except under threat of disciplinary action.

Who must be trained? Who says this training is necessary? These questions are often asked by senior managers who are reluctant to let personnel take time away from production for training. Time amounts to dollars. The best situation is to have a generous training budget that you have control over. But that is rarely the case, so do the best you can with whatever you have. In discussing explicit requirements, do not forget to go through permits to see if any training requirements are spelled out therein.

HAZWOPER

The most extensive training requirements and also the ones most misunderstood and oversold are found in the OSHA (Occupational Safety and Health Administration) Safety Standard 29 CFR 1910.120 "Hazardous Waste Operations and Emergency Response" (HAZWOPER for short). Well-meaning but misinformed persons will insist on telling you that you must give your hazardous waste handlers *forty-hour training*. Companies fearful of noncompliance but ignorant of requirements ask for *forty-hour training for all our employees*. Many of these companies require no additional training at all.

What does your plant require? While HAZWOPER applies to almost everyone, many industrial plants satisfy the requirements by completing training for other regulations. Very few industrial employers need to give forty-hour training to employees. If you have to fight to get training funds, as compliance managers typically do, you certainly do not need to fight for unnecessary funds. Save your energy and your company's money for the real battles.

HAZWOPER applies to hazardous waste sites where employees are exposed to hazardous substances (RCRA corrective action and CERCLA), and to RCRA TSDFs, fire department and other outside emergency responders and to hazardous waste generators only if they provide their own emergency response. Figure 2.12 gives the training requirements in summary.

After initiating effective responses to existing orders and improving permit compliance and training, your fourth priority is to focus attention on routine operations and maintenance of pollution control equipment. Some pollution controls may already have been addressed as a response to an order or while improving permit compliance. Anticipate that day-to-day operations will improve by themselves once training is more effective and regular, but to the extent that routine operations have not been completely addressed already, focus your efforts in the direction of operations and maintenance now. Much of the rest of this book is about routine pollution control operations.

Figure 2.12
HAZWOPER Training Requirements

Type of Hazardous Waste Site	Situation or Employees Covered	Training Required
RCRA TSDF	hazardous waste handlers and supervisors RCRA corrective action	24 hr class + hazard recognition
Outside	first responder, awareness	as necessary
	first responder, operations	8 hrs
	HazMat technician	24 hrs + operators
	HazMat specialist	24 hrs + technician
	on-scene incident commander	8 hrs + control policies
	emergency response refresher	as necessary
RCRA Generator	emergency responders* assigned cleanup duties	Hazard Communication or emerg. response
Superfund	hazardous substance handlers	40 hr classroom 3 days field
	supervisors	40 hr classroom 3 days field 8 hr class 1 day field

---

* = Internal emergency responders require only hazard communication training as long as one such person can perform the cleanup; otherwise, they require first responder operations training.

When routine operations are improved, improve the flow and storage of paperwork, your fifth priority. How is your recordkeeping? As in the case of routine operations, recordkeeping may have been partially addressed in the process of complying with an order or during the improvement of permit compliance or as the result of enhanced training and operations. To the extent that it has not improved, however, now is the time to address recordkeeping.

The easiest part of environmental compliance is the part dreaded by so many: reporting and recordkeeping. These requirements are simple, cut-and-dried—they are spelled out in no uncertain terms, in most cases. Compliance is hard because we see paperwork as telling on ourselves. Recordkeeping does do that, but the sword cuts in both directions, because it also tells how well you have been doing at compliance. Well-prepared, timely reports and well-kept records are the well-intentioned compliance manager's best friends. If you earnestly strive for compliance, you make good faith efforts, and your mistakes are honest and do not harm anyone or the environment, your paper infractions are generally treated as mistakes and penalized only mildly, if at all. When remiss or ineffective, even if well-intentioned and honest, you may be penalized somewhat more severely for your mistakes, especially if any person or the environment is harmed. If you intentionally break rules and attempt to cover your tracks, then whether or not any person or the environment is harmed—but especially so if they are—you can expect maximum sanctions to be levied against you. Never tamper with or falsify reports or records. To do so is a criminal activity. If paperwork has been your downfall, learn to use it to your advantage. Learn to control paperwork so that it works for you, as it should. Each major compliance law and very permit have reporting requirements. Figure 2.13 lists some of them. Three kinds of environmental reports are: dated reports, event reports, and confirmation reports.

Figure 2.13
Reporting Requirements of Major Laws

CAA (CAAA):
    Carbon Tetrachloride Transformer Quarterly Report
    Class I ODS Quarterly Report
    Class II ODS Annual Report
    Emissions Monitoring Report
    Radionuclide Emissions Report
    Vinyl Chloride Emission Source Activities Report

CWA:
    Baseline Monitoring Report
    Discharge Monitoring Report
    Pretreatment Compliance Report
    Stormwater Discharge Monitoring Report

EPCRA (SARA Title III):
    Emergency Release
    Form R, Toxic Chemical Release Inventory
    Supplier Notification
    Tier I/II, Chemical Inventory

RCRA:
    Hazardous Waste Exporter Report
    Hazardous Waste Generator Report
    TSDF Groundwater Report
    TSDF Report
    Used Oil Recycling Activities Report

SDWA:
    Hazardous Waste UIC Biennial Report
    Public Notice of MCL Violations

TSCA:
    Chlorofluoroalkanes Propellant Manufacturing Report
    PCB Activities Annual Report
    TSCA Chemical Inventory Partial Update Report

Dated reports are routinely submitted each year on a certain date. Figure 2.14 lists reports filed annually or more often.

Figure 2.14
List of Ongoing Annual Reports

CAA (CAAA):
  Carbon Tetrachloride Transformer Quarterly Report
  Class I ODS Quarterly Report
  Class II ODS Annual Report
  Emissions Monitoring Report
  Radionuclide Emissions Report
  Vinyl Chloride Emission Source Activities Report

CWA:
  Discharge Monitoring Report
  Pretreatment Compliance Report
  Stormwater Discharge Monitoring Report

EPCRA (SARA Title III):
  Form R, Toxic Chemical Release Inventory
  Supplier Notification
  Tier I/II, Chemical Inventory

RCRA:
  Hazardous Waste Exporter Report
  Hazardous Waste Generator Report (some states biennial)
  TSDF Groundwater Report
  TSDF Report
  Used Oil Recycling Activities Report

SDWA:
  Hazardous Waste UIC Biennial Report (every other year)

TSCA:
  PCB Activities Annual Report

Reports that record events are typically emergency reports. The major report in this category is the EPCRA (SARA Title III) Emergency Release Report. Emergency reporting is also required by your permits.

Confirmation reports either inform the regulatory agency that something has been accomplished as required or report baseline data. The Air Emissions Monitoring Report, Radionuclide Emissions Report and Vinyl Chloride Emission Source Activities Report are in this category. A Baseline Monitoring Report is required of industries that discharge wastewater into a public sewer. RCRA requires confirmation of *clean* on corrective action projects, as does CERCLA at closure of Superfund sites. Under TSCA, the Chlorofluoroalkanes Propellant Manufacturing Report and TSCA Chemical Inventory Partial Update Report are required.

Maintain a file folder for each category in Figure 2.15.

Figure 2.15
File Folder Categories

CAA (CAAA) file drawer:
    Permit application and supporting material
    Permit
    Permit correspondence
    Emissions monitoring data
    Compliance reports submitted
    Inspection reports received and your responses
    Orders/Notices of Violations
        Background
        Order/NOV documents
        Responses

CWA file drawer:
    Permit application and supporting material
    Permit
    Permit correspondence
    Analytical reports/QA/QC documentation
    Baseline Monitoring Report
    Discharge Monitoring Reports
    Inspection reports received and your Responses
    Orders/Notices of Violations
        Background

Figure 2.15 *(cont'd)*

CWA file drawer: *(cont'd)*
    Order/NOV documents
    Responses

EPCRA (SARA Title III) file drawer:
    Release reports and follow-up reports
    Notifications of Facility Emergency Coordinator names
    Notification of hazardous chemical presence
    Tier I/II reports and documentation
    Form R reports and documentation

RCRA file drawer:
    Notification of Regulated Waste Activity/updates
    Manifests open and requests for extension of storage
    Exception reports
    Manifests (closed) for current year
    Manifests (closed) for one year ago
    Manifests (closed) for two years ago
    Manifests (closed) for three years ago
    Land ban notification, stapled to appropriate manifest
    Analytical results from which hazard determination is made (see next section under waste stream files)
    Exemption documentation (one file per exemption claimed)
    Treatability study files (one per study)
    Procedure for removing waste from drip pad and associated collection system at least once every 90 days
    Underground tank file documenting compliance with design, construction, installation and notification
    Underground tank file documenting corrosion protection
    Underground tank repair records

SDWA file drawer:
    Analytical reports/QA/QC documentation

TSCA file drawer:
    Significant adverse reaction file

Periodically review files and weed out handwritten notes and memos that no longer have meaning. Keep internal memos and reports, particularly those discussing policy options and decisions, or evaluating alternative courses of action, in separate file folders from those listed above. The reason for separate file folders is that when an inspector asks to review a file, give her specifically what she asks for and nothing more. This is not being uncooperative, it is just requiring the inspector to do her investigative work instead of you. Besides internal memos and reports, maintain the separate folders listed in Figure 2.16 (this list is not sacred—use your imagination and your own plant's needs to come up with others or delete what you do not need).

Figure 2.16
Internal Correspondence Folders

CAA file drawer:
   Internal memos and reports on air emissions control
   Control equipment maintenance records*
   Operating logs

CWA file drawer:
   Internal memos and reports on wastewater discharges
   Wastewater Treatment System maintenance records
   Operating logs

EPCRA (SARA Title III) file drawer:
   Supplier notifications
   Chemical inventories

RCRA file drawer:
   Internal memos and reports on hazardous waste management
   Inspection logs
   Log of waste removal from drip pad and sumps
   Contractor files (one per contractor with purchase order, contract and audit report)

Figure 2.16 *(cont'd)*

RCRA file drawer *(cont'd)*:
Waste stream files (one/each with MSDS, TCLP and other analytical reports, profiles, sample land ban notification form)
Manifest tracking log
Waste shipment log

SDWA file drawer:
Internal memos and reports on drinking water management

TSCA file drawer:
Internal memos and reports on TSCA management unless maintained elsewhere, *e.g.*, Maintenance Office.

Record retention is such a personal thing that it almost always comes down to the preference of your management, after being properly advised by corporate legal counsel. Most environmental programs require records to be kept for a minimum of three years. Exceptions exist; most noteworthy are the land ban notifications which must be made to the TSDF and filed for five years. If records are an issue in a Notice of Violation, they must be kept until the violation is resolved and then three years more. If records are potentially an issue in litigation, then they should be maintained indefinitely or until it is clear that they are no longer needed.

Some plants retain environmental records indefinitely, presumably so that they will always be able to demonstrate compliance or otherwise protect themselves in litigation or enforcement action. Permanent, unscreened records can go either way in litigation, and if it is known that records were screened, that knowledge may go against you. If your company policy is to maintain records permanently and this policy has not been reviewed in some time, ask the corporate counsel to give an opinion on the matter. Depending on what he or she says, your management may want to revise the company's records retention policy.

Establishing Compliance Assurance

The quickest way to achieve compliance assurance is to effectively address the five issues just discussed (orders, permits, training, routine operations, and recordkeeping) while getting senior management to show genuine interest in compliance on a daily basis. How do you do the latter?

Keep environmental issues before the senior management team and never far from discussions of the bottom line. Get a regular spot on the agenda of senior staff meetings and discuss current environmental issues briefly (five minutes is great; ten minutes at most) to keep them aware but not to draw them away from other matters long enough that their attention wanders. Or set up your own monthly or quarterly environmental awareness briefing to present your material to them. Sometimes this is better because the meeting is shorter and your topic is the sole item on the agenda. You can take more time this way, say 15-30 minutes . Do not present the background of an issue without explaining how it impacts your plant. How much will it cost? How many employee hours will it take to implement? How can implementation be thwarted, possibly leading to enforcement? What dollar amounts can the fines be? What other civil and criminal sanctions can be levied? How can you avoid new regulations?

Do not be all negative all the time. Acknowledge your company for its accomplishments. Mention it if an enforcement inspection is passed with flying colors. Mention how many months your facility has operated without a permit violation. Senior managers will gradually become more interested in environmental compliance and start providing regular guidance to the plant staff about environmental compliance. When senior managers are routinely involved and interested in environmental affairs, you can be assured that everyone else will be pulling in the same direction.

Staffing and Equipment

Proper staffing and equipment also enhance compliance assurance. During the regular management briefing, mention staffing problems. If yours is a small plant and you are responsible for compliance management as a collateral duty then chances of getting others assigned to assist you may be slim but you may be able to get someone assigned to take some of the duties, or you may be able to assign specific tasks to committees or task teams. Seek additional manpower any way you can. For instance, the environmental compliance manager typically relies on others to operate control equipment whether or not these persons report to him directly. Routine inspections may also be assigned to others.

Equipment is another matter. Pollution control equipment is usually considered part of the manufacturing process and is budgeted and operated as such. Sometimes the maintenance department may be responsible for these systems. Occasionally, a plant makes this equipment part of the environmental compliance manager's budget. Keep an eye on expenses and keep management updated on future needs, regardless.

Other needed equipment may include sampling and monitoring devices. While continuous monitoring devices may be considered part of the pollution control equipment or process, manually controlled samplers and monitoring devices probably belong to the compliance manager's office. Alternatively, they may belong to maintenance or some other department and be controlled by the compliance manager. Regardless, keep track of this equipment and keep a list of equipment you would like to have. Slip the highest priority or two into the budget anytime you can. Hopefully you have your own budget and do not have to get other managers to buy equipment on your behalf, but experience says this is not typical.

A recent trend is to consolidate overall responsibility for managing environmental affairs, safety, health, industrial hygiene, ergonomics, fire protection, emergency planning and response into one site-based department. Traditionally, environmental departments concerned themselves only with EPA and state requirements. The new, integrated departments follow DOT, OSHA, MSHA, Workers' Compensation, NRC and other regulations as well as track voluntary standards issued by ANSI, ACGIH, NFPA, and others.

Corporate offices maintain some staffing, primarily to ensure compliance issues are effectively communicated at the plant level, but site-based management is much more effective than corporate headquarters-based management for routine compliance management.

The new breed of expert generalist (as opposed to the part-time, nonexpert generalist) in the profession is just as likely to be a certified industrial hygienist as a professional sanitation engineer. If you are new and inexperienced, do not be impatient with established professionals. If you are a seasoned professional, do not feel threatened by the new breed; environmental compliance work is plentiful enough to keep us all busy for many decades, despite any anti-regulatory moods in our nation's capitol.

FATAL COMPLIANCE MISTAKES

Most compliance-related mistakes, especially significant deeds of noncompliance, are the result of one thing—fear. Sadly, fear drives more compliance programs than reason and wisdom and, unfortunately, fear as being a negative sentiment tends to produce negative results: false recordkeeping, false reporting, and lies are the crimes committed out of fear. Some consultants use fear of penalties and other liabilities to bring in business. Look in any trade journal and you will find at least a dozen advertisements claiming that the EPA is nearing finalization of a certain regulation or increasing enforcement activities, or has just levied a record-breaking fine against some company, while at the same time advising you to use the services of or buy the product of the advertiser in order to keep out of trouble. Professional environmental compliance managers, whether part- or full-time, generalist or specialist, corporate- or site-based, and also consultants, must insist on integrity, honesty, and forthrightness in the day-to-day application of regulations. Professionals must insist on open and frequent communication with compliance authorities, who must also drop the us against them viewpoint. Sooner or later we must realize that we are all in this together, protecting the same atmosphere, surface, and groundwater.

Fortress Syndrome

The fortress syndrome is an "us against them" attitude. The EPA was established in 1971 because the existing pollution control bureaucracies were largely ineffective. The EPA was established by Richard Nixon's conservative administration with the approval of Congress to protect the public from industrial polluters who were not policing themselves. Back then no incentives existed for self-policing, but instead a general belief prevailed that the earth could assimilate any insult and sustain any damage, and this led to poor management of pollution. On the micro-level, in 1971, it was simply no longer true.

A handful of rivers hosted the majority of American heavy industry, and these rivers were polluted to the point of being unusable. The Ohio from Pittsburgh to Cincinnati, the Cuyahoga, the Mississippi from Baton Rouge to New Orleans, and the Chicago Rivers among others were notorious. The Cuyahoga was so polluted it even caught fire! Drinking water contamination in New Orleans was approaching toxic levels.

Heavy concentrations of factories, homes, and vehicles led to terrible air pollution episodes when combined with certain weather patterns in areas such as the Los Angeles basin; from New York to Boston; the Washington, D.C.-Baltimore-Philadelphia corridor; Pittsburgh; Cleveland; the Detroit-Toledo metroplex; and greater Chicago.

Several landfills, such as Love Canal and the Stringfellow Acid Pits, contributed to local pollution problems for the public.

Some industrial plants just did not know any better. Dumping waste into the creek was the way business was conducted. It was neither intentional nor willful in the sense we use today because that was just how things were done. No one thought twice about destroying the quality of the rain ditch behind the plant. What was it good for anyway? Will it pollute the river? Of course not! The ground will soak it up long before it reaches the river! Not to excuse bad practices of the past, but bad practices of today were the standard practice back then.

All that changed in 1971 when Nixon established the Environmental Protection Agency and Congress ratified its mission. EPA exists for the industrialist as well as for the environmental activist.

Compliance officers are not the enemy. They exist to keep us honest. Housewives and other concerned citizens are not our enemy. They are our spouses, neighbors, and friends with legitimate environmental concerns. Environmentalists are not our enemies. None of these people should be viewed as the enemy of an environmental manager.

Little Fish in a Big Pond Syndrome

Another syndrome that leads to noncompliance is the attitude that "they'll never pay attention to us! We're just a little fish in a big pond." These were the famous last words of more than one industrial manager.

The Hopewell kepone case was a tiny business providing specialty chemical products to Allied-Signal. When little businesses make huge contamination, someone eventually sits up and takes notice. Do *not* refuse or counterfeit compliance just because you think you'll be lost in the crowd. The state and federal regulators will drop some pretty high priority projects long enough to track down a poluter no matter how small the business is.

Integrity vs. Expediency

One of the saddest reasons for noncompliance is the excuse of "I was so swamped, I just thought I'd take a shortcut." Tough environmental regulations are here to stay. They will not go away under even the most conservative of Congresses or White Houses because, as the planet approaches having eight billion persons on board, the margin for error decreases. If you truly do not have time, it is time to insist on having a full-time person to handle the environmental compliance duties. If you are already full-time then it's time to push for an assistant.

Legal Trees in a Management Forest

Sometimes the compliance manager is so busy looking at the management forest that he or she cannot see the legal trees. It's not so much that the manager did not have time, but that he or she did not recognize the problem until it was too late. This often happens to well-meaning companies who attempt to minimally meet regulatory requirements and no more. If your goal is simply to comply with regulations, you will be like a puppy chasing its tail—you will have a great time but you won't get anywhere. Zero pollution is the only worthwhile goal.

Ostrich Syndrome

"If we keep a low profile the problem will go away." "If we do not tell anyone that we spilled a tank full of chemicals on the back forty acres no one will ever know." Maybe not, but it is your reputation and your bottom line that will suffer if caught. Problems go away when we work on them logically and intelligently and, preferably, when we have worked out the details with the approval of the enforcement agency.

Lost in the Paperwork Blizzard

Are you snowed under an avalanche of paperwork? Many of us can sympathize with you. We have been or are in the same situation. Somehow, though, whatever it takes, we have to maintain the big picture while coping with the paperwork the best way we can. That mound of paper will not cut any ice if compliance violations are found during an inspection. It will provide no protection if a criminal negligence charge is made against you. Keep your paperwork under control, even if you are behind schedule. Do not let it control you.

ENVIRONMENTAL ETHICS

The Machiavellian management style, while not exactly an anachronism, is definitely losing acceptability in the business world today. Nor is the attitude widely accepted anymore that humans are lords and masters of the Earth and therefore can do with it as we please. Humans are stewards of something much bigger than humankind. Humans are keepers of the puzzle, yet just pieces of it ourselves. This is illustrated poignantly in a letter written by the Salish Indian Chief Seathl—for whom Seattle, Washington is named—to the President of the U.S., asking him to spare the destruction of the beautiful Northwest:

> Every part of this earth is sacred, every shining pine needle, every sandy shore, every mist in the dark woods, every clearing and humming insect is holy. The rocky crest, the juices of the meadow, the beasts and all people, all belong to the same family.
> Teach your children that the earth is our mother.
> Whatever befalls the earth befalls the children of the earth. The water's murmur is the voice of our father's father. We are part of the earth, and the earth is part of us. The rivers are our brothers; they quench our thirst.
> The perfumed flowers are our sisters. The air is precious. For all of us share the same breath. The wind that gave our grandparents breath also receives their last sigh. The wind gave our

children the breath of life. This we know, the earth does not belong to us; we belong to the earth. This we know, all things are connected, like the blood which unites one family. All things are connected. Our God is the same God whose compassion is equal for all. For we did not weave the web of life; we are merely a strand in it. Whatever we do to the web, we do to ourselves. [As quoted by Wm. Fitzgerald in *Seasons of The Earth and Heart*.]

Industrial productivity in the middle of the twentieth century seemed to be at right angles to Chief Seathl. Richard J. Lambert proposes a series of guiding principles (see Figure 2.17) intended to get us to rethink industrial productivity as the 21st century approaches.

Figure 2.17
Lambert's Guiding Principles

1. Learn to see all things swayed by sacred meanings. Even our cities should be transformed into sacred settings for the indwelling of the human spirit.
2. Delight in all creatures as subjects who radiate an interior richness.
3. Be sensitized to the infinitely differentiated splendor of the Earth—and its wealth of resources—which should make our being blink in wonderment.
4. Take time to listen to the voices of a divine presence—like the song of a bird, the wonder of moonlight, and the   wind in the trees.
5. A human imperative is to generate the insights of the mind and the in sounds of the heart to live in compassionate harmony with the Earth.
6. In our race to save our planet, be compassionately engaged with life as an experience of celebration and with human happiness rescaled to embrace Earth's needs.
7. Be educated by the genius of the Earth in its evolutionary splendor, in its emergent life systems, and in the human as its most original mode of expressiveness.
8. With the full substance of our humanity, let us relate in mutually enhancing ways to the entire Earth community.
9. Inspired by the dream of the Earth, let us find enterprises worthy of human energy and sustained development.
10. In the unfolding of this new story, may we put on a new imagination, re-vision the human, and be shaped by an ecological consciousness as a way into the future.

German industrialist Georg Winter, concerned about the quality of his country's environment, took matters into his own hands and turned the negative environmental impact of his company around. Then he went after other industries, pointing out that "there are sound economic reasons why damage on this scale can simply no longer be tolerated." This is the point. Pouring waste out the back door, into the air, and into the sewers and streams eventually has to have a tremendous negative potential. Already it has had some; we can measure that impact to some extent. Georg Winter points out that although environmental damage in Germany shows up as a mere three percent of the domestic national product, certain impacts are not yet measured and included. He lists these unmeasured impacts as follows:

1. loss of habitats,
2. loss of species,
3. loss of environmental quality, and
4. long-term effects that have yet to come to light.

Mr. Winter developed the Integrated System of Environmental Business Management known as the Winter Model: a portrait of the successful company of the twenty-first century.

Addressing other top managers, as well as himself, Georg Winter asks these hard questions of his company:

1. Do I have enough respect and understanding for my colleagues, and do I treat them with at least the sense of responsibility I apply to my natural environment (flora and fauna)?
2. Am I really concerned about the environment or is what I am doing intended to give myself a better image or boost my ego?
3. Am I already acting in exemplary environmental fashion or do my deeds detract from the credibility of what I say?

The "heck" you say! Remember, this man is head of one of the most successful industries in all of Europe, much more so in Germany. He even hired consultants and sent them to his employees' homes to give them ideas about detoxifying their houses and making them greener!

The renowned environmental consultant Roy F. Weston, writing from retirement, calls all environmental professionals to personal accountability by 1) being intellectually honest; 2) caring; 3) being fair; 4) contributing proportionately to ability; 5) expecting reward only appropriate to contribution; 6) behaving ethically; and 7) acting prudently.

One of the largest companies in the business of handling waste streams, with sixty thousand employees, Waste Management, Inc., put its principles in writing, emphasizing the highest standard of environmental conduct. A high-level group of executives responsible for devising written policy statements called their company to responsible stewardship of the environment and committed the company to train employees to enhance awareness and understanding of the environmental policies of the company.

Alcoa, a large generator of wastes, also embarked on a path of clarifying ethics and company policy. Alcoa emphasizes six core values: integrity, safety and health, quality of work, treatment of people, accountability, and profitability.

One of the professional organizations concerned with the environment is the American Society of Safety Engineers (ASSE), which established fundamental canons for its membership, including these:

1. Hold paramount the protection of people, property, and the environment.
2. Advise employers, clients, employees, or appropriate authorities when your professional judgment indicates that the protection of people or the environment is unacceptably at risk.

As employees or consultants, we have a duty to protect the interests of our employers and clients, within the law, of course, and also within the scope of professional obligation and ethics. We have a duty to correct any conditions in our professional relationships which may lead to conflicts with professional ethics.

Ethically acting and morally responsible technical professionals should lead the way to a greener planet in the twenty-first century and can make a difference now. It is imperative that we make a difference. "In the end," writes former Senator, now Vice President Al Gore, "we must restore a balance within ourselves between who we are and what we are doing."

CONCLUSION

In the long run, company interests are best served by operating in an environmentally sound manner. Familiarity with the maze of regulations and their requirements, combined with careful planning and record-keeping, and a properly trained workforce, can greatly simplify day-to-day environmental compliance activities.

REFERENCES

Aquino, John T. "Ethics in The Waste Industry." *Waste Age*. February 1992.

Arbuckle, J. Gordon, *et al. Environmental Law Handbook*. 12th. Ed. Rockville, Maryland: Government Institutes, Inc., 1993.

Baker, Nancy Croft. "Environmental Training Completes Quality Loop." *Waste Tech News*. September/October 1993.

Clean Air Act. Section 114 [42 U.S.C. 7414] revised by PL 95-95, PL 95-190 and PL 101-549. "Recordkeeping, Inspections, Monitoring and Entry."

Daugherty, Jack E. "Riding The Wild Bull: Or, How to Get Started as A New Environmental Manager." *Environment Today*. September, 1992.

Eckhardt, Robert. "Coordinating Regulatory Compliance Programs." *Professional Safety*. November, 1993.

Fitzgerald, William J. *Seasons of The Earth and Heart: Becoming Aware of Nature, Self, and Spirit*. Notre Dame, Indiana: Ave Maria Press, 1991.

Gore, Al. *Earth in The Balance: Ecology and The Human Spirit*. Boston: Houghten Mifflin, 1992.

Grinnell, Thomas E., PhD. "Would You Want to Fly with a Pilot Who only Had Three Days Training?" *Occupational Health & Safety*. April, 1989.

Hendrick, Kingsley. *Systematic Safety Training*. New York: Marcel Dekker, Inc., 1990.

Inglima, Julianne E., Esq. *et al*, eds. *Environmental Compliance Tool Kit.* Washington, D.C.: Thompson Publishing Group, 1994.

Kulick, Steven W. "How Real Would Be The World without Research at Universities." *Waste Management Research Report.* Vol 4., No. 1

Lambert, Richard J. "Rethinking Productivity: The Perspective of The Earth as The Primary Corporation." *Population and The Environment.* Spring 1992.

Miskowski, Diane and Sam N. Popowcer. "The First Steps in Determining Your Plant's Liability." *Pollution Engineering.* November 1986.

Wilson, S.E., CIH. "Training Workers for Hazardous Waste Sites." *Pollution Engineering.* November, 1991.

3

COPING WITH COMPLIANCE AUDITS AND INSPECTIONS

One of the more stressful events in the lives of many compliance managers is to be summoned to the lobby to meet a group of ladies and gentlemen, of whom one says, "Hi! We're here to help you!" Discounting any skeletons that may be hiding in your closet, accept audits and inspections as an opportunity to show off what you have accomplished. You have organized your paperwork, you manage control of emissions and discharges on a daily basis, appropriate personnel have been trained, now is the time to be measured. This is performance measurement under duress, to be sure, but the amount of stress depends on your readiness and willingness to discuss real problems when they arise. In this chapter we examine the audit and inspection processes, hopefully to remove the mystery and, thus, to dissolve the fear. There is a spiritual saying which is apropos here:

Fear knocked at the door.
Faith answered.
No one was there.

When an inspector knocks at the door, you have no reason to get worked up out of fear. Chances are most of your fears are unfounded.

COMPLIANCE AUDITS

Many organizations are working toward standardization of environmental management systems by developing standard audits and registered auditors. The following discussion is not intended to make you an expert auditor. Several fine books are available that can do that including *Environmental Audits*[1]. This discussion is aimed at helping you decide whether your facility needs an audit and giving you a better feel for the process.

To Audit or Not?

What is a true audit process? What purposes can it serve? Should you be audited?

Total compliance is an elusive thing, yet we are required by law to achieve it. Unfortunately, no middle ground exists—we are either in compliance or not in compliance (probably the latter on any given day). The *regulated community* is expected to implement various regulatory programs on their own and monitor their own progress. No one comes in to help set up a compliance management program—you have to do that yourself. The principal purpose of an audit then is to improve the compliance stance of the plant. Another purpose of an environmental audit is that it helps protect your plant from potential liabilities. You would like to know if your plant is exposed to a potential enforcement action or lawsuit in time to correct the situation at a fraction of the cost. Finally, although environmental compliance auditing is still relatively new, tax and accounting audits have been part of good business management for a long time. About ten years ago, advocates of the environmental audit began touting their philosophy, but even in 1996 relatively few plants regularly receive quality audits.

Should you conduct a self-audit? The environmental audit, as an internal management tool, reviews and evaluates facility administration, operations, processes, and procedures. The purpose of this tool is to assess, verify, correct, and improve any instance of noncompliance with environmental regulations and corporate policies. An audit is recommended for three situations. When there has been a change of responsibility such as a new environmental manager, an audit can define his or her scope of work. An audit is a good way to establish a scope of work when new, significant regulations are pending. Finally, you probably should audit every three to five years as a general practice. Self-audits give you a way to keep up with how you are doing, protect

---

[1] Cahill; Government Institutes, Inc.

corporate legal interests, identify cost-effective changes in planning, enhance the corporate image, and indirectly improve relationships with regulatory agencies.

The problem with self-audits as opposed to audits by outsiders is objectiveness and depth of experience. Self-auditors can conduct a perfectly good audit, if they can divorce themselves from office politics, forget about their usual job and job relationships, and bring experience with production processes, environmental compliance management, and/or pollution control equipment to the audit team. That is not to say the team cannot include a rookie or two for training purposes. Often, however, these factors are far less than ideal, so self-audits have been known to fall short of expectations. That is why many companies pay to have outside experts audit them.

Regardless of who does the audit, management's fears prevent companies from effectively using audits to improve compliance. Some companies fear that some wrongful practice or gross omission will be uncovered, forcing them to report themselves. This fear is almost always unfounded inasmuch as all but a very few of these fearful managers have anything of significance to hide anyway. Other managers fear that the audit report cannot be maintained in confidence and that the company's good name may somehow be ruined. This fear is also largely unfounded. If a company is in fact making progress toward correcting noncompliance, the public generally maintains a favorable perception of that company. The last fear is the least understandable, but it exists. Some managers believe that what they do not know will not hurt them! So, reasons not to audit based on fear are usually unfounded if one analyzes the matter rationally. If a true reason to be fearful exists, it is time for your company to retain an attorney.

Should you audit hazardous waste TSDF (Treatment, Storage, or Disposal Facility) contractors? *Yes*, but even if you do, you will not have iron-clad evidence that the TSDF will not violate hazardous waste rules or will not leave you holding the bag at a Superfund site in the future. You can determine how this TSDF stacks up with others if you are willing to invest the time and money. Prudence demands that you be diligent up front, so go for the plant tour, review the Part B permit, find out how waste is tracked from delivery vehicle to ultimate disposal, etc. A TSDF audit is definitely recommended, but always remember it may still have to be cleaned up someday. Keep in mind your audit objective, no matter who owns and operates the TSDF.

Can the average environmental manager assure company executives that the TSDF being considered for a contract does not represent a future blank check for a cleanup? No. In the absolute sense you cannot give such an assurance, but acceptable ways of determining relative risk are available.

One method of choosing a TSDF is called risk-ranking. This requires knowledge of several TSDFs, so it is usually not feasible for a plant-level environmental manager working alone, especially a nonexpert generalist with very little, if any, risk-ranking training and experience. Consultants who specialize in the risk-ranking technique can be called in, yet *no* guarantees can be given.

A recent innovation is to form audit consortiums with other hazardous waste generators. The consortium shares the cost of an in-depth audit of many TSDFs by an experienced audit team equipped to examine operations, recordkeeping, reporting, and financial health. The team puts together a report on each facility audited and may also do a risk-ranking evaluation. The consortium members are allowed to buy any report available. Sound good? It is. Is this the answer to the TSDF audit dilemma? Not entirely. It is certainly a gigantic leap forward, but it still has limitations. The main limitation of the consortium audit report is that, as thorough as it is, you have only a snapshot, static in time, of the TSDF's health. Tomorrow or next year may be an entirely different story.

Think of audits, then, as perishable information. Any audit older than six months is of dubious value. An audit older than one year is essentially worthless. No matter how much you paid for it, the TSDF's regulatory, technical, and financial health tomorrow may be totally different than it is today. That is not to say that an audit is totally worthless—in fact it is highly recommended—it just says that you must go back for an update audit on a regular basis. Bottom line: you could still be responsible for a cleanup. *No* guarantees can be given, *none* whatsoever.

Financial health is the chief factor of interest at the TSDF, not operational compliance; though if the TSDF is grossly out of technical compliance, that should set off warning bells in your mind. At any given time, though, an excellent TSDF may be out of compliance with one regulation or another. Emergency incidents are not the chief deciding factor either, although numerous fires, explosions, spills, or other release incidents tell you something significant. The finest TSDFs may have occasional spills, leaks, or fires. After all, hazards are the nature of the business and unfortunate incidents occur from time to time. Operational compliance and emergency incidents are secondary indicators but financial health is the only true indicator that a company will be around to take care of its waste or residue tomorrow. The typical audit does not address financial health; hence the limitation of TSDF audits.

If having an in-depth financial audit of your TSDF every quarter or semi-annually were feasible, you could at least know when to bail out. But what if you did know? Your bailing out would actually exacerbate the situation and the TSDF would sink into financial nonexistence that much quicker, yet your waste or its residue would still be around to be cleaned up. If you have been in business with the TSDF for only a short time, minimize your losses. But what does minimizing losses mean when you have been in business with a TSDF for thirty years? Bailing out early when they're in trouble may not represent much of a savings, so if your continued business would help them survive some red ink, you may want to consider staying in, but you need an attorney and an accountant, not an engineer, to help you make that judgment.

Nevertheless, audit TSDFs to satisfy yourself and your management that the selected TSDF is technically viable and that it is safe to haul your waste streams there. However meager your action may seem in the future, it should be the best you can do today. Besides monitoring a TSDF, the only other thing you can do is to make sure your business relationship is well defined; that is, your attorney should be involved in helping to construct a sound business arrangement up front in order to minimize losses down the road.

Contract terms and conditions are very important, then, so you, your purchasing office, and your corporate attorney need to develop a boiler-plate contract for your TSDF contractors. The contract must be consistent with federal and state laws and their implementing regulations as a standing public law takes precedence over a contrary contract clause. The TSDF management will probably want to use its own standard contract (after all, its customers' omissions, errors, and other acts of negligence affect its own liability) so you may have to negotiate certain terms and clauses. Be sure to document why you relented on any given boiler-plate clause. Many good reasons to modify clauses will probably come to light, as doing any kind of business is about making trade-offs. Just be sure to document the reasons so you can remember why the contract reads as it does three years from now.

The best approach for selecting a TSDF is to 1) develop a boiler plate contract for the disposal of your waste; 2) request quotes on your waste streams from three to five pre-qualified TSDFs; 3) send complete profiling information and the proposed contract along with the bid package; 4) evaluate the TSDFs on bid economics first; then 5) visit the low bidder for an audit, and 6) complete the purchasing/contracting process if the TSDF is found to be operating in an acceptable manner. Should the audit of the TSDF present any red flags, repeat step five with the next low bidder before completing step six.

If you plan to audit the TSDF yourself, first visit the regulatory agency which oversees TSDF compliance and read the TSDF's files for yourself. Never rely on a telephone discussion—it is futile. Read every page of every folder. Then, armed with information gathered from the compliance files, audit the candidate TSDF. Pay regular return visits to TSDFs to which you actively ship waste. A good rule of thumb is to inspect TSDF's at least as often as Figure 3.1 indicates.

Figure 3.1
Contract TSDF Audit Frequency

Your Waste Generation	TSDF Audit Frequency
2,200 lbs/week or more	quarterly
2,200 lbs/month or more	semiannually
1,100 lbs/month or more	annually
220 lbs/month or more	biennially
less than 220 lbs/month	once per TSDF

Note: This is a recommendation. Typical practice is to audit far less frequently than this figure suggests.

TSDF Auditing Case History

The near futility of auditing TSDFs can be seen in this actual case. The new, but experienced compliance manager for Widget Manufacturing Company (WMC) audited Recycled Stuff, Inc. (RSI), a small solvent recycling facility his company had been using for about 20 years. Before the visit, he had a telephone conversation with the compliance officer at the state hazardous waste division about the RSI site.

"Nothing to report," said the compliance officer, "RSI is in compliance."During the RSI audit, the WMC compliance manager noticed some construction activity where two out-of-service distillation units were lying on the ground. He was told that the construction was due to the upgrading of the RSI tank farm with a concrete dike in order to come into full compliance with Clean Water Act spill control requirements and to expand business. That seemed reasonable as a creek ran across one end of the property and the maximum inventory allowed by the interim permit was currently on-site. The stills on the ground were said to be out-of-service and awaiting overhaul. That too was reasonable.

WMC continued to use RSI for another year until another TSDF won the recycling contract. Four years later, WMC was named as one of several parties responsible for cleaning up RSI, being one of the top ten companies, by volume, which had sent waste there. RSI had gone out of business. It seems company cash flow was approaching dire straits so the owner locked the gate one evening, took his cash and other liquid assets and retired to the Caribbean for health reasons. It turned out that the RSI facility had experienced repeated spills, fires, and explosions over its thirty-year life. One explosion completely destroyed a still just three months before the WMC compliance manager's audit. The average longevity of salaried employees was less than one year and hourly employees only stayed about two years. The new tank farm with its fine containment system was situated over the largest of several spills, about twenty thousand gallons of industrial solvents. Residential neighbors complained numerous times to the hazardous waste compliance office and recently had reported that their well water tasted funny. The property and casualty insurance provider terminated the facility's policy about four days before the owner left suddenly.

All kinds of indicators are visible in hindsight, but a single visit to the TSDF did not show any problems. In fact, the WMC compliance manager, an experienced auditor, wrote that the facility was exceptionally well run and that he was impressed with the design of the new containment system (which hid a large spill). A telephone conversation with the state compliance agent did not reveal anything, even though a serious explosion had occurred just months prior to the conversation.

The lesson to be learned from this audit is that only regular monitoring of TSDFs and their compliance files truly demonstrates due diligence.

Selecting a TSDF—never an easy task for either novice or master—may be called TSDF Roulette. Auditing TSDFs is an iffy business. Worse, no matter what you do, you may still end up holding a cleanup invoice someday. However, being a responsible party at a Superfund site is far less likely than death and taxes, and far more regulatory controls exist now than in the not-too-distant past. The most significant indicator of whether a company is heading toward being a significant uncontrolled release site is its financial health, the least accessible audit factor. Pick a TSDF selection logic that suits your company and stick to it unless you have good reason to change, such as it does not work for you. Perform the best audit your resources are capable of doing. That is the best you can do.

Who Should Be on the Audit Team?

Auditor training deserves special consideration. Ideally, auditors have experience with the regulations, the processes and the manufacturing, maintenance, and compliance procedures. However, one or more of these ideals is almost always sacrificed when considering any one person as a prospective auditor. Typically, the best way to get a team of experienced auditors prepared to audit a particular facility is to have the facility complete an initial survey (pre-audit questionnaire) and return it to the team leader to be distributed to other team members for review. A preliminary survey allows auditors to learn what the plant does and how it does it before arriving at the gate. The survey also allows them to start digging into regulations covering their respective areas of compliance to come up with checklist items and questions to resolve. If the team is well prepared, the environmental audit can go well beyond the compliance assessment received during a regulatory inspection. That is no reflection on compliance inspectors because they do not have preparatory questionnaires, and typically they spend far fewer hours in-plant than an audit team does.

Attorney Involvement

Should attorneys be involved in the audit? The role of the lawyer in protecting the audit report centers around ameliorating the fear that confidentiality cannot be preserved. Even with attorney involvement, confidentiality cannot be guaranteed in every case.

From a layman's perspective, two means of protecting confidentiality may be available: the attorney-client privilege and the work-product doctrine. The attorney-client privilege protects confidential communication between you and the lawyer, but does not protect facts—such as in analytical results showing soil contamination in the backyard. Several restrictions also apply as to the appropriateness of protectable communications, so work closely with your attorney on this. The critical factor in the work-product doctrine is the degree to which litigation is imminent. Many companies have their corporate attorney set up and manage the audit team, which then makes its report to the attorney. Presumably if any potentially litigious matters are uncovered during the audit, confidentiality might be preserved.

Do you have to tell on yourself? In many cases, no. However, if an audit leads to your learning of a problem that must be disclosed under some reporting provisions of a law, regulation, or permit, your obligation to report is not negated. You have the obligation to report these situations even if litigation is pending and an attorney is involved.

For instance, if an audit uncovers the fact that a leaking underground pipe has pumped over 100 pounds of trichloroethylene into the ground, you must report the fact to appropriate authorities under the provisions of SARA Title III even though your attorney is leading the audit team and your neighbor, who has a drinking water well, has threatened to sue you for contaminating his well. The report is required not because of the audit—the audit has little to do with it beyond the fact that the discovery was made during the audit—but because anytime you find out that you have released 100 pounds or more of trichloroethylene you *must* make a report to authorities.

Also, EPA has broad authority to compel a regulated facility to produce environmental compliance information. Normally EPA is not interested in your audits, but let's say for argument's sake that your neighbor calls EPA and says something like, "My well is contaminated and I think it's that ABC Company next door to me." Enforcement agents will arrive and expect to be shown any analytical data whether or not it was obtained by means of an audit. Your attorney will have to inform you of what protection is available in this case or if a lawsuit is pending because confidentiality only goes so far. The other side in compliance enforcement and litigation has a right to specific factual information. You can withhold minutes of discussions in which your staff discussed policy and options about what to do about the situation, for instance, but you cannot withhold analytical reports that show the groundwater beneath your plant is contaminated with trichloroethylene. The confidentiality matter, as you can see, is extremely complicated, so you need to consult an attorney immediately anytime it may become an issue.

Preliminary Work

Before the audit itself starts, the team has some preliminary work to do, as stated above. Pre-audit activities include identifying the scope, selecting the team, allocating resources, developing the audit plan, and accumulating background information. The facility absolutely must cooperate with the audit team during this preliminary phase of the audit.

A preliminary scope essentially identifies what is to be audited. Will the audit look at the whole facility or one operation or one unit process within an operation? Will it cover all regulatory areas (air, water, hazardous waste, etc.) or only some of them or just one? Corporate audit teams may have these details so organized that the preliminary work is minimal, but outside teams need to take time to define the scope and objectives of the audit with their customer.

To maximize potential benefits, the team leader should be given a free hand, within an established budget, to select team members and allocate resources. Outside regulatory expertise may be needed to round out internal process expertise. (See the self-auditing discussion above.)

Development of the audit plan requires accumulation and evaluation of background information (a process called Preliminary Assessment; see pre-audit questionnaire discussion above). This preliminary exercise is extremely tedious but not the least luxurious because it familiarizes the audit team with all materials, locations and practices that could affect compliance.

Among preliminary information the team needs is a topographical map extending at least a mile in all directions. If the facility is located in a corner of a topographical map, be sure to obtain all the quadrants. A street map might supplement the topographical map(s). Other requirements include a construction site drawing showing the physical layout of buildings and plant property, a general description of the plant and its operations, a chemical inventory, and a list of products manufactured. Include a description of any planned modifications or expansions to the plant, with a current schedule for implementation of these planned changes. The team also needs an organization chart depicting not only those with environmental responsibilities but also those with operations, maintenance, human resources, engineering, and research responsibilities.

To round out preliminary requirements, two very important items are needed, if applicable: previous audit reports and any outstanding administrative orders or notices of violations. Sometimes management is reluctant to share these documents but the audit team is crippled without them. The team will verify that previous audit items as well as issues delineated in administrative orders have been corrected or otherwise appropriately addressed.

The legal department and management team should have an opportunity to submit concerns. This can be handled at the in-briefing for small facilities, but for large plants it is better to invite the legal department and management team to an audit team meeting to express their concerns.

Compiling Checklists

Preliminary information must be studied closely and understood in order to develop protocols and checklists for the facility. Preprinted checklists are useful if customized for the audit, but auditing from an unmodified checklist drawn up by a third party gives occasion for lack of depth in the audit. This is especially true if the audit team lacks depth in either processing or regulatory experience.

A checklist is a simple solution to one auditing problem. What do you ask and look for? It suggests interview questions and gives the auditor a road map to better ensure no stone is left unturned. A checklist is not an end in itself but merely a tool, a means to the end. If an inexperienced auditor uses the best checklist without digging deeper, checking further, expanding his inquiry into operations and management from the environmental viewpoint, then that portion of the audit will turn up very little of consequence. A well-prepared checklist is tailored to the facility and the experience of the auditor using it.

A well-prepared checklist is also regulatory-based. Comprehensive assessment of environmental compliance requires extensive analysis of facility performance against numerous environmental statutes and implementing regulations including those listed in Figure 3.2. Inclusion of appropriate amendments to these statutes is implied.

Audit Schedule

An audit should begin with an opening conference. Audit team members, plant management team, and appropriate operating and environmental compliance personnel should attend the briefing, which makes appropriate introductions, covers the auditors' schedule, and assigns contacts, tour guides, and workspace for the audit team. The purpose is to establish reasonable expectations and start friendly in order to head off a fortress mentality where it is "us against them." Misguided expectations can nullify an otherwise excellent audit and even internal auditors are sometimes made to feel like bad guys.

Following the opening conference, an initial walk-around is typically taken, during which the team gets a feel for operations, notes methods and processes that need in-depth examination, and, especially, gains a sense of the flow of materials through the plant in addition to the fate of excess materials.

Figure 3.2
Auditable Environmental Laws

- Clean Air Act
- Clean Water Act
- Comprehensive Environmental Response, Compensation and
  Liability Act
- Emergency Planning and Community Right-to-Know Act
- Federal Insecticide, Fungicide and Rodenticide Act
- Hazardous Materials Transportation Act
- Marine Protection, Research and Sanctuaries Act
- Medical Waste Tracking Act
- Resource Conservation and Recovery Act
- Safe Drinking Water Act
- Toxic Substance Control Act
- Uranium Mill Tailings Radiation Control Act

Sampling is not usually an issue during operational audits; however, on property transaction audits some samples may need to be taken and additional sampling may be recommended in the audit report. Whoever sets up the sampling scheme needs to be familiar with statistical sampling procedures which are beyond the scope of this discussion.

An effective audit evaluates the extent to which protection of the environment is a management priority. An organization where senior management is committed to going beyond the strict requirements of environmental regulations places environmental protection as a high priority. Committed managers establish organizational policies that ensure that regulatory requirements are implemented and that they provide guidance for environmental hazards not specifically addressed in regulations. In a well run facility, appropriate personnel are trained and motivated to work in an environmentally acceptable manner. These personnel understand and comply with government regulations and the company's environmental policies. Relevant environmental developments are communicated expeditiously to facility personnel, where management gives such matters high priority. Committed management teams communicate effectively and promptly with government agencies and the general public when a serious environmental incident has occurred: no hand-wringing, finger-pointing, or hiding of pertinent facts occurs.

Committed managers require outside contractors and service people working on the premises to comply with company policies concerning the protection of the environment. Personnel who carry out environmental duties, especially emergency procedures, are proficient. Concern for protection of the environment is written into other procedures, such as how to operate a particular process. Committed managers apply best management practices, use safe operating procedures, and enforce good housekeeping. Well-run plants have preventive and corrective maintenance systems which minimize environmental harm. These plants use effective sampling and monitoring techniques, test methods, recordkeeping systems and reporting protocols. Committed plants promptly evaluate the causes behind environmental incidents and establish procedures and implement engineering changes to avoid recurrence. When economically feasible, such plants utilize source reduction, recycling, and reuse of materials. These plants have substituted materials or processes that use less hazardous substances wherever they can.

Audit Reports

The audit team holds a closing conference on the last day of the audit. For lengthy audits, a status conference is held at the end of each day and a closing conference on the last day. Oral reports only are given and minutes are not kept except by the audit team secretary. Facility personnel may take limited notes about items for which they are personally responsible. A written audit report is compiled afterwards and given to the team attorney who issues a copy of the report, with legal advice about correcting findings of noncompliance, to the plant manager. Perhaps one or two other persons may have a copy, but each is accounted for at all times in order to protect confidentiality.

SURVIVING COMPLIANCE INSPECTIONS

The heart of even the most seasoned environmental compliance veteran sinks when the receptionist announces, "There are Compliance Officers in the lobby to see you!" A regulatory inspection is the second principal method of determining compliance status (the first being auditing). You can do some things to prepare for such inspections, thereby easing your anxiety.

Once you have experienced an inspection, you will realize that a protocol is followed, that the scope is usually—but not always—limited, and that your company not only has a duty to comply but also has certain rights as the inspected entity. Typically, corporate auditors dig deeper than compliance inspectors, but compliance inspectors have been known to scrutinize closely in certain situations. Auditors, by the way, never issue citations and penalties.

An inspection may sometimes be announced, though the reaction time will be severely limited. The regulatory compliance office may call on Friday for a Monday inspection, but more often they call first thing in the morning for an inspection later the same day. Unannounced inspections are also common, especially in situations where the purpose of the inspection is to gather evidence for civil or criminal proceedings. The best preparation you can make for compliance inspections, then, is to know the regulations and maintain compliance.

What if an inspector shows up on your second day of a new job and you feel totally green? This scenario is not farfetched. One compliance manager who had an inspection on the very first day of his new job fortunately was a veteran. The fact that the compliance inspector had been in the plant longer than the compliance manager (the inspector showed up about fifteen minutes before the new compliance manager arrived that first morning—a Monday, no less) did not phase either the inspector or the compliance manager. The inspection proceeded.

When an inspection happens, you need to know your rights as an individual and as a company, how the inspection should proceed, the responsibilities of the inspector, how to limit potential liability, and how to make follow-up responses to the inspection. For compliance managers who maintain a state of preparation for inspections, know the regulations, are in compliance with the regulations, conduct regular compliance checks, know the gaps in their compliance program, and have a written plan with schedule and budget information for closing the gaps, an inspection is usually only a minor nuisance.

Until 1979, EPA used its inspection authority under various environmental laws to inspect plants in spite of their objections. Congress gives EPA the mandate to inspect the regulated community for each major environmental law. For instance, Section 308 (33 U.S.C. 1318) of the Federal Water Pollution Control Act, titled "Inspections, Monitoring, and Entry," gives EPA the right to enter a plant for the purposes of collecting data in order to develop effluent standards, determine whether the plant is in violation of its permit or the Act, and for other reasons as needed. Presentation of proper credentials is all that is required. Under the Clean Air Act, Section 114 (42 U.S.C. 7414), titled "Recordkeeping, Inspections, Monitoring, and Entry," EPA has the right to enter after presenting proper credentials to inspect records and make copies of them as necessary in order to develop air standards or verify compliance. The Comprehensive Environmental Response, Compensation, and Liability Act (CERCLA or Superfund) gives EPA the right to enter your plant and take samples of any suspected hazardous substance.

Until 1979, EPA occasionally strong-armed its way into plants that were reluctant to cooperate with them. In 1978, the Supreme Court ruled in *Marshall v. Barlow's, Inc.* that an OSHA inspector was not entitled to enter the non-public portions of a work site without either the owner's consent or a search warrant. This decision protects plant owners from penalty or other punishment for insisting upon a warrant. However, environmental laws generally have warrantless search provisions built in, and if entry is refused, the EPA or state can make direct application for an injunction—that is, they can shut your operation down while they inspect and assess your compliance status! Since the warrant process is far more expeditious than the injunctive process, EPA and the state usually prefer to get a warrant, just as their OSHA counterparts are required to do. From the enforcement viewpoint, then, inspections have three potential stages: preparatory, normal entry, and entry with warrant.

Preparation for an inspection includes considering whether a warrant should be obtained before attempting and being refused entry. When surprise is particularly crucial to the inspection, EPA will apply for the warrant beforehand. Another situation where the warrant is obtained first is when a company's prior conduct or prior refusal of inspection entry make it likely that entry will be denied.

Your rights during an inspection include demanding proper credentials of the inspector(s). This is recommended because sales representatives of companies with official-sounding names have been known to use the compliance inspection ruse to tour the plant and recommend their company's product to fix the violations. This practice is not as common as it was once but it does happen. Ask for credentials before you even shake his or her hand.

You have the right to demand a warrant. This is usually not advisable but you should consult with your corporate legal counsel *before* an inspection. Although you cannot be punished for demanding a warrant, the inspector usually returns with the warrant and his or her colleagues. Unless you have something to hide that can be fixed in a very short period of time—an hour or two—do not ask for a warrant, as a rule. In addition, your hurried attempts to correct a compliance problem will most likely be transparent. Inspectors with warrants typically expand the scope of the inspection and, if there have been previous violations or complaints, the warrant may authorize a criminal search as opposed to a civil search. Even if a civil search warrant is obtained, evidence gathered is admissible in criminal court proceedings. So you take a risk when you demand a warrant, even though your right is protected by law.

Inspector's Guidelines for Facility Entry

Generally, the scope of most federal and state compliance inspections is limited to one compliance program such as wastewater pollution control, air pollution control, hazardous waste management, an so on. Sometimes, however, EPA shows up with several inspectors for a multimedia inspection. Most inspections are consensual, meaning plant personnel grant entry and cooperate with the inspector(s). In permitted compliance programs (air, water), your company has given consent to inspections from accepting the permit, so the EPA or state does not need your consent at the door, although they frequently ask for it anyway.

Arriving at the facility, the inspector(s) will present credentials and issue a notice of inspection. If the inspectors are unknown to you, ask for credentials. Entry is considered voluntary and consensual even if plant personnel complain or express displeasure. If the inspector gains entry in a coercive manner, then such an entry is not consensual. Only if the inspector is told to leave the premises is entry considered denied. Consent is not needed to inspect the non-public portion of the plant. For instance, if the inspector sees a violation while standing in the lobby, his observations are admissible evidence in enforcement proceedings whether or not the owner consented and whether or not a search warrant was obtained.

If the owner withdraws consent after the inspection starts, all information gathered up until that time is admissible in enforcement proceedings. The inspector leaves and obtains a warrant to inspect the facility. If the inspector announces that he or she intends to leave and obtain the warrant in order to compel the inspection, this is not considered to be coercion.

The inspector brings a copy of three draft documents to a meeting with the U.S. Attorney: the application for a warrant, an accompanying affidavit, and the warrant itself. The application identifies the statutes and regulations under which EPA seeks the warrant and clearly identifies the site to be inspected including the owner/operator of the site. The affidavit states factual background for seeking the warrant. If the warrant is sought without probable cause, the affidavit recites a neutral administrative scheme, such as a schedule for inspection of plants or a permit, which allows the inspection.

The warrant itself directs an inspector, a U.S. Marshal, or other federal officer to enter a specific location and to perform specifically described inspection functions. Broad warrants are desired by enforcement agents since they are permissible in civil proceedings, but vague or overly broad statements may prevent the magistrate from signing the warrant or prove susceptible to constitutional challenge.

With warrant in hand and a U.S. Marshal, the inspector returns to the plant where entry was denied. The Marshal is principally charged with executing the warrant. If the plant refuses or even threatens to refuse entry, the Marshal has the discretion to leave, seek forcible entry, or do otherwise.

Once entry is made, the inspector conducts the inspection exactly as stated in the warrant. If you are unfortunate enough to be the subject of a warranted search, read the warrant carefully and understand it when entry is requested. If sampling is authorized, the inspector must follow exact protocol, including the presentation of receipts for all samples taken. If records or other property is authorized to be taken, the inspector must receipt the property and maintain an inventory.

After a warrant inspection, the inspector returns the warrant to the magistrate along with the inventory of property and records and samples removed from the property. Without a warrant, a compliance inspection is typically a friendly but serious examination of records and operations. Going through the process of getting a warrant makes inspectors less than amicable and definitely sensitive to any perceived uncooperativeness on your part. Warrants focus the eyes and sharpen the minds of inspectors. With a warrant the inspector is severely limited in the scope of his inspection but not in its depth, and you can count on receiving a notice of violations unless the facility is extremely well managed. But then, why did you demand a warrant in that case? The inspector is responsible for briefing the facility management on the scope of the inspection, examining records and operations, sometimes taking samples, interviewing personnel, and presenting a few brief closing comments to management about how the inspection went. Focus on what the inspector says he found, not on comments about what will happen to you. The inspector does not determine penalties in the field; normally, that is done at the office with input from his superiors. So, at the closing conference, zero in on what he says was not in compliance so you can get to work on it, and don't concern yourself with penalties until you receive a draft compliance order.

Confidential Business Information

Certain processes, equipment, or records about processes or equipment under examination may be confidential for business purposes. In this event the inspector is obligated to attempt to provide protection for the information gathered (only the confidential portions specifically identified by the inspected plant). In fact, sanctions are specified against compliance administrators who negligently allow confidential information to be disseminated. Of course, after the fact, sanctions do not restore the confidentiality of the loose information. In order to claim and protect confidentiality, ask the inspector to provide a written request for the specific confidential information. A handwritten note will do; do not make him leave unless you do not mind if he returns with a search warrant. Ask him to sign a confidentiality agreement. He may not. Your corporate attorney should devise a step-by-step procedure, outlining when and how to declare confidentiality, what sort of confidential information requested by the inspector is acceptable, and what to do if he refuses to make a written request. The procedure should include a standard confidentiality agreement and what to do if an inspector refuses to sign it.

Photographs

Inspectors like photographs because when they return to the office and start writing the inspection report it is easier to remember what they saw when a photograph is available. Photographs also aid in explaining what they saw to their superiors and can be used as evidence in hearings. Many plants, for security reasons, have a no photograph policy. During the opening conference, be sure the issue of photographs is discussed. The inspector may ask about photographs or arrive with a camera hanging from his or her neck. It is perfectly acceptable to insist on no unreviewed photographs. You can request no photographs at all, but be careful about insisting. Generally, plants offer to develop the inspector's film so that photographs can be reviewed from a confidentiality standpoint. Another compromise is to take photographs for the inspector at his direction. Again, the inspected facility reviews the developed film for confidential information before turning it over to the inspector. Upon delivery of photographs, cover them with a letter summarizing trade secret information. You may not withhold a photograph, for obvious reasons. In any case, have double prints made and keep one set for your own files. Even if confidentiality is not a factor at your plant, request copies of photographs anyway.

Collecting Samples

The inspector may wish to take samples or may be required by permit, regulation, or law to take samples. The best approach is to be cooperative but be certain to let the inspector know where the best—most representative—sample point is located. Do not, under any circumstances, try to mislead the inspector about sample collecting. While you do not have to volunteer information, keep in mind that you have reporting obligations if a release has been made to the environment. Protest but do not interfere if the inspector insists on taking a sample at what you consider is an inappropriate location. Mostly, inspectors cooperate reciprocally so if you show them the best sample point, they will normally use it. If evidence is being gathered specifically for enforcement action, or if you suspect a sample may be damaging, ask for a split sample. Your legal counsel may advise that split samples always be taken—ask him now, before an inspection. If you request split samples, the inspector is obligated to divide the sample with you so that your portion can be sent to a laboratory of your choosing. Be sure to determine the parameters for which the sample is to be analyzed. Four sampling rules should be strictly followed in case the situation becomes a legal matter: 1) track each person or entity who handles the sample (chain-of-custody); 2) prevent contamination; 3) use calibrated sampling and analytical equipment; and 4) use scientifically acceptable (standard) methods of analysis.

Chain-of-custody is maintained by having the original sample collector initiate a document describing the sample and signing that he or she has relinquished it to the next person, who signs that he or she has received the sample. That person signs to relinquish it to a third person who signs to receive it and so on, until it ends up in the possession of an analyst who will generate a report that can be used as evidence along with the chain-of-custody document.

Prevent contamination by always using clean containers—not just containers rinsed out with water, even distilled water, but new, unused, clean containers. A properly trained analyst can clean containers sufficiently, but why introduce a potential source of error or misreading? Figure 3.3 lists container and field preparation requirements for samples.

The third and fourth sampling rules require you to enlist a suitably qualified laboratory which has implemented quality control techniques and whose supervisors practice quality assurance. Insist on a tour of the laboratory before contracting with them and discuss requirements during the tour. If you do not get the impression that these people are eager and competent and take pains to track samples and QA/QC, reconsider that contract.

Figure 3.3
Sample Containers, Preservation and Holding Times

Measured on site, no preservative, held in plastic or glass:
Chlorine Residual
pH

Measured on site, EDTA, plastic/glass:
Sulfite

No preservative, held in plastic/glass (days specified):
Cation Exchange Capacity (indefinite)
Chloride (28)
Fluoride (28)

No preservative, held in glass (days specified):
Flash Point (indefinite)
Paint Filter (indefinite)
Phenols (28)

Held at 4°C, no preservative, plastic/glass (days specified):

Acidity/Alkalinity (14)	Residue, Settleable (SS) (2)
BOD (2)	Residue, Total (TS) (7)
Bromide (28)	Residue, Volatile (TVS) (7)
Color (2)	Semi-Volatile Organics (glass)
(7-water) (14-soils)	
Nitrogen, Nitrate (2)	Silica, Dissolved (28)
Nitrogen, Nitrite (2)	Specific Conductance (28)
Pesticides (glass)	Sulfide (indefinite)
(7-water) (14-soils)	
Phosphorus, Ortho (2)	Sulfate (28)
Residue, Filterable (TDS) (7)	Surfactants (MBA) (2)
Residue, Non-Filterable (TSS) (7)	Turbidity (2)

Table 3.3 *(cont'd)*

Nitric Acid (< 2pH), plastic/glass (days specified):
    Hardness (6 months)
    Metal Ions (6 months) except:
        Hexavalent Chromium (24 hours)
        Mercury (28)

Nitric Acid (< 2pH), glass (days specified):
    Total Organic Halides (TOX) (28)

Sodium Hydroxide (pH > 12), plastic/glass (days specified):
    Cyanide (14)

Sodium Thiosulfate (0.008%), sterile plastic/glass:
    Coliform, Fecal (6 hours)   Total (24-30 hours)
    Heterotrophic Plate Count (24 hours)
    Streptococci, Fecal (6 hours)

Sulfuric Acid (< 2pH), plastic/glass (days specified):
    COD (28)
    Nitrogen, Ammonia (28)   Kjeldahl (28)   Nitrate/Nitrite (28)
    Oil & Grease (28)
    Phosphorus, Total (28)

Sulfuric Acid (< 2pH), glass, (days specified):
    Total Organic Carbon (TOC) (28)   Halides (TOX) (28)
    Total Recoverable Petroleum Hydrocarbons (TPH) (28)

Zinc Acetate & Sodium Hydroxide (pH > 9), plastic/glass (days):
    Sulfide (7)

2 Glass Vials, Pres. 1* or 2* for 14 days maximum:
    Halogenated Solvents and other volatile organics

    Preservative method 1: Sodium thiosulfate 0.008%
    Preservative method 2: Hydrochloric acid < 2pH

Reviewing Records

Often the compliance inspection moves directly from the in-briefing to the review of records. At any rate, records will typically be reviewed early in the inspection as the inspector will gauge the level of inspection based on the condition of your recordkeeping. Therefore, recordkeeping is very important!

For that reason it is recommended that files be divided into compliance programs. A logical method for organizing files was discussed in Chapter 2. Each compliance program should have its own filing drawer at a minimum unless your company is a small operation. In that case, divide a single file drawer (or perhaps two) into these programs by using different colors of hanging folders or some other scheme of division. When a RCRA inspector is reviewing hazardous waste management records, she does not need to be sorting through documents belonging to other compliance programs such as wastewater. This is not merely for the inspector's convenience. If inspectors recognize a violation of the law under another compliance program, they are required to file a report with the appropriate compliance office about what they observed.

Logs and records on permits should be maintained separately from other information. Do not voluntarily release other information during the inspection unless it is specifically asked for by the inspector. Be friendly and cooperative but show her only what she asks to see.

Interviews

Typically, inspectors will talk to one or two employees about compliance activities in order to determine levels of awareness and training effectiveness or to uncover mismanagement practices. The best approach for all employees to take during an inspection is to be friendly and courteous and to answer the inspector's questions promptly and straightforward to the best of their ability.

It is far better to say "I don't know" than to try to bluff a compliance inspector with what one thinks he wants to hear. If an employee is asked about recordkeeping and is not directly involved, the best answer is: "You'll have to ask my supervisor, she keeps track of that."

If asked why a certain procedure is done or how it is done, an acceptable answer is: "My supervisor told me to do it this way." Or, "My supervisor will tell me how to do it." Or, "My supervisor tells me when and how to do it."

Instruct employees to be perfectly honest but not to volunteer information. If the inspector does not ask the question, do not give the answer.

In one real situation an inspector had already looked at the plant's hazardous waste manifest file and had satisfied himself after looking through only a few manifests that everything was in order.

While touring the hazardous waste storage area, he asked an employee, "Who fills out manifests?" "My supervisor does," the employee replied, then added, "but I used to until I botched up so many of them that the supervisor took it over last August."

It should come as no surprise that the inspector revisited the manifest file and issued seventeen citations for manifest errors!

In another situation an inspection was almost complete when the inspector saw an employee pushing a drum marked HAZARDOUS WASTE on a hand truck.

He asked the employee, "Where are you going with that hazardous waste?"

"I don't handle hazardous waste," the employee said, "I was told not to mess with the stuff."

Inquiries into where the drum came from and what was in it revealed that it was indeed hazardous waste and that particular employee routinely moved it from its accumulation point to the hazardous waste storage area. After a brief investigation, twenty-three citations were issued for training, container management, accumulation management, and other violations. These violations may have been uncovered anyway and this plant certainly needed to learn this hard lesson, but there are cheaper ways of learning proper hazardous waste management than what those twenty-three citations cost. If the employee had answered the question directly, the plant would have had cheaper options to explore, but since he volunteered information—well, that's the cost of noncompliance.

In another case a state inspector was reviewing an industrial wastewater plant when he encountered one of the operators.

Seizing the opportunity, the inspector said to him, "Tell me how this system works," in spite of the fact that the supervisor was in the very process of giving the inspector a guided tour of the wastewater treatment process.

The operator began to tell the inspector how the wastewater treatment system worked. Then, to the consternation of his supervisor, the man broke down and starting spilling his guts and begging for leniency for everything he had ever done wrong. Apparently he had harbored these guilt feelings for years and his conscience was bothering him. The funny thing is that none of the things he confessed were violations, they were little operating and maintenance errors he had made—snafus which did not affect effluent quality—but the man considered them major sins.

The inspector started to wonder about the operation and maintenance of the plant and the capability of the operating staff to run the system, so he spent much more time reviewing records and reports than he had originally intended. Eleven recordkeeping citations were issued with a minimal penalty, but the point is, the citations might have been avoided.

None of these cases required the interviewer to find the administrative violations. If the inspectors had been more thorough in the first place, they would have uncovered the violations anyway. The point is, that what employees say in interviews can turn an inspection around—and these were not employees with an ax to grind with management. You cannot plan for what employees may say during an inspection; however, some preparatory actions are advisable.

Effective training is the principal preventive measure for disastrous interviews. If employee relations are strained, then double training efforts. Ill feelings between employees and management often impact compliance inspections. Role play an inspection interview with employees involved in compliance management. Have them explain the knowledge or demonstrate the skills they receive in training. Give written examinations, not to prove anything to inspectors, but to reinforce learning.

Teamwork building also helps ensure that employee quips have minimal impact on compliance inspections. Mostly, preventive measures are standard business management practices.

A final word about not volunteering information: use your judgment. If carried to the extreme, this tactic is uncooperative. Do not make the inspector's job unnecessarily difficult. If the question asked is begging a trivial or meaningless answer, be courteous and restate the question, "Don't you mean to ask -----?" Just don't start talking about the lack of placards or confusion concerning the DOT Hazardous Materials Table if the inspector asks to see your manifests.

Briefings

Inspectors have two briefings with plant management. At the opening conference, explained above, the inspector will want to be introduced to key management personnel, especially those involved directly in the compliance area (air emissions, wastewater, hazardous waste) to be inspected. The plant manager or senior management person responsible for the plant and its operations should be present. If that person is out of the plant or not available, the next senior person should be present. At the closing conference, the inspector gives his or her impression of the inspection. Do not bank on the inspector's favorable remarks at the closing conference.

Time after time I have heard phrases such as "outstanding operation," "well-run plant," "a superb compliance program," "I think you are doing an excellent job here," from the inspector only to receive a Notice of Violations letter six to eight weeks later.

Be friendly, courteous, and cooperative no matter what the inspector says. If violations are pointed out, ask when you may expect to receive a Notice of Violations letter. If you have a concern or issue, simply state what bothers you. Keep the proceedings on a business-like basis.

Immediately after the inspector leaves, sit down and compose a letter report regarding the inspection to corporate counsel in order to establish attorney-client privilege.

Inspection Report

Six to eight weeks after the inspection, depending on case-load backlog, turnaround time for sample analysis, and other factors at the compliance office, you will receive a letter report of the inspection. If violations were found, the covering letter will be titled "Notice of Violations." If major violations are involved, you may also receive a draft compliance order such as an administrative order or agreed order.

Administrative orders authorized under the Clean Water Act are used to require compliance of persons in violation of their permit or requirements under the Act. This type of order outlines a compliance schedule that must be followed in order to avoid further trouble. It may allow up to thirty days for a specific operation and maintenance requirement to be implemented. Failure to comply on schedule may lead to criminal prosecution for *knowing violations* (a legal term defined under the CWA) unless a good faith effort to comply is demonstrated. Similar compliance orders are issued under the authority of other environmental laws as well. Agreed orders are negotiated in good faith between an out-of-compliance facility and the compliance authority. The agreed order may include a penalty, but often the payment of some or all of it is contingent on performance during a probationary period. As long as all issues are addressed effectively and on time as agreed, no penalty or liability to your plant will occur.

Follow up with corrective action as soon as possible and track your responses to the Notice of Violation in letters to the compliance office until all matters have been recognized by the agency as closed. If a particular requirement in the NOV or order is impractical to comply with, the plant manager should promptly inquire about right of appeal or right to obtain a variance. Prepare well for meetings and maintain a cooperative relationship with the agency, as this engenders willingness to negotiate and usually—although no guarantees can be made—means lower penalties will be assessed. Factors such as significant harm to public health or the environment, promptness of abatement activity, probability of continued compliance, and cooperativeness are considered in the assessment of penalties.

CONCLUSION

In summary, audits are excellent tools for maintaining compliance. TSDF audits have severe limitations but are the best we can do for the present. The best way to be prepared for compliance audits is to be in compliance. No one will fault a beginner with not knowing the ropes, but on each subsequent visit, there ought to be some measurable progress.

REFERENCES

Arbuckle, J. Gordon, *et al. Environmental Law Handbook*. 12th. Ed. Rockville, MD: Government Institutes, Inc., 1993.

Bergeson, Lynn L., Esq. "When Audits uncover Violations." *Pollution Engineering*. August, 1991.

Bleiweiss, Shell J. "Legal Considerations in Environmental Audit Decisions." *Chemical Engineering Progress*. January 1987.

Cahill, Lawrence B. *Environmental Audits,* 7th Edition. Rockville, MD: Government Institutes, Inc., 1996.

Clean Air Act. Section 114 [42 U.S.C. 7414] revised by PL 95-95, PL 95-190 and PL 101-549. "Recordkeeping, Inspections, Monitoring and Entry."

Comprehensive Environmental Response, Compensation and Liability Act. Section 104(e) revised by PL 99-499. "Information Gathering and Access."

Daugherty, Jack E. "Riding The Wild Bull: Or, How to Get Started as A New Environmental Manager." *Environment Today*. September, 1992.

Eckhardt, Robert. "Coordinating Regulatory Compliance Programs." *Professional Safety*. November, 1993.

EPA 600/4-79-020. *Methods for Analysis of Water and Wastes*. March 1983.

EPA 600/4-82-057. *Test Methods for Organic Chemical Analysis of Municipal and Industrial Wastewater*. July 1982.

EPA SW-846. 3d Ed. *Test Methods for Evaluating Solid Waste, Physical/Chemical Methods*. November 1990.

Federal Water Pollution Control Act. Section 308 [33 U.S.C. 1318] revised by PL 100-4. "Inspections, Monitoring and Entry."

Friedman, Gary E. "Environmental Insurance, Permits & Audits." Presentation at 1986 Regulatory Update Conference by Mississippi Manufacturers' Association.

Hawkins, August E. "Back to Basics: Successful Environmental Compliance Inspections." *Pollution Engineering*. January 1989.

Inglima, Julianne E., Esq. *et al*, eds. *Environmental Compliance Tool Kit*. Washington, D.C.: Thompson Publishing Group, 1994.

Miskowski, Diane and Sam N. Popowcer. "The First Steps in Determining Your Plant's Liability." *Pollution Engineering*. November 1986.

Nemeth, John C., PhD, CEP. "Environmental Auditing Helps Assess Risks, Improve Profits." *Environmental Management News*. July/August 1986.

---. "Positive Benefits Derived from Careful Environmental Audit." *Environmental Management News*. September/October 1986.

Rasmussen, Dana A. "Enforcement in The U.S. Environmental Protection Agency: Balancing The Carrots and The Sticks." *Environmental Law*. Winter 1992.

Shields, Jacqueline, ed. *Air Emissions, Baselines, and Environmental Auditing*. New York: Van Nostrand Reinhold, 1993.

Swiss, Samantha. "No Pain, No Gain: Are Standards A Hindrance or A Sign of Progress for Environmental Auditing Worldwide?" *Environment Risk*. March, 1992.

Thomas, Lee. "EPA Policy on Environmental Auditing." Published at *50 FR 46504*, November 8, 1985.

U.S. EPA, Assistant Administrator for Enforcement. "Conduct of Inspections After The Barlow's Decision." Memorandum issued April 11, 1979.

4

POLLUTION PREVENTION

The least interesting question to an aggressive environmental manager is "what's new in the way of regulations?" Why? Because he or she is always ahead of regulations. That feat does not involve mental telepathy or psychic powers, nor does such a manager consult 1-900 telephone numbers for help. The reason his or her company stays in compliance is because it is always finding ways to reduce its environmental impact. It is always reducing the quantity and toxicity of waste generated. It is always minimizing air emissions. It is always reducing water usage. Waste minimization or pollution prevention is second nature to such a manager and his or her company.

The reduction or elimination of the generation of hazardous waste as expeditiously as possible and wherever feasible is the policy of the United States as declared by Congress in 1984. This policy, stated in the amended Resource Conservation and Recovery Act, states that any waste generated in spite of well intentioned efforts is to be treated, stored, or disposed of so as to minimize present and future threats to human health and the environment. Once waste is generated it is subject to end-of-pipe treatment, storage, or disposal and subject to various regulations which can be onerous to comply with from day-to-day. End-of-pipe waste is subject to permit conditions under the Clean Air Act (if emitted to the atmosphere) or the Clean Water Act (if discharged to the waters of the U.S.) or to solid waste regulations (if otherwise managed). On the other hand, reduction of waste at the source has the potential to significantly decrease the quantity of pollutants entering our air, water, and soil.

The Pollution Prevention Act of 1990 clarifies that it is national policy to reduce waste at the source whenever feasible. The same law directs the EPA to collect information for a multi-media technology transfer to enable more companies to reduce waste, and provides financial assistance to the States to implement this policy and promote source reduction. Basically, source reduction, or pollution prevention or waste minimization, is the reduction or elimination of the *creation* of pollution.

COMPLIANCE STRATEGY

If keeping up with regulations is not the best strategy then what is? Regulations mostly address effective pollution control. This means, for example, that you have generated a waste stream which is contaminated with some toxic chemical or hazardous physical characteristic of a chemical and now you are going to control it somehow before it does harm to persons or the environment. When the effectiveness of controls are less than ideal you typically pay a penalty for violating the conditions of a permit or the requirements of some regulation.

Pollution Prevention vs. Pollution Control

Pollution prevention is a much better strategy than pollution control because it means you do not create the waste in the first place. It can be achieved by using energy, water, and other resources more efficiently before creating a waste stream and then having to recycle or dispose of it. Waste minimization is the reduction of generated waste—particularly hazardous waste—to the extent technically and economically feasible. Any source reduction or recycling activity is waste minimization if it 1) reduces total volume or quantity of waste (especially hazardous waste); or 2) reduces the toxicity of hazardous waste; or 3) both reduces total volume or quantity and toxicity of hazardous waste. Overall, the reduction must be consistent with the goal of minimizing present and future threats to human health and the environment.

A material is recycled if it is used, reused, or reclaimed. Used or reused means it is used as an ingredient of a product. A material may also be used or reused if it is an effective substitute for a commercial product. However, when distinct components are recovered as separate end products, the material is neither used not reused. If spent sodium hydroxide were used as an ingredient to make soda ash it would be a reused material. If heavy metals are recovered from the sodium hydroxide at the same time, then the material does not meet the regulatory definition of used or reused.

A reclaimed material is processed to recover a useful product or if it is regenerated. Recovery of lead from spent batteries is reclamation as is the regeneration of spent solvents.

Pollution Prevention vs. Waste Minimization

While the terms pollution prevention and waste minimization are often used interchangeably, they are not exactly the same. Waste minimization is a more generic term that includes source reduction and recycling. Pollution prevention, or source reduction, is an activity that reduces or eliminates the generation of pollution at the source. Recycling regains or recovers waste material but does not reduce or eliminate pollution at the source. Reclamation is the recovery of valuable materials from contaminated materials but also does not reduce or eliminate pollution at its source. While neither recycling or reclamation are pollution prevention, recycling is waste minimization in that it avoids waste disposal by diverting the waste material to a process which can return it to usefulness. Reclamation is not waste minimization because it still leaves waste material, usually almost all of it, to be dealt with somehow.

DRIVING FORCES

Why would your facility want to get on this national bandwagon of pollution prevention? What is in it for you and your company? Other than being our national policy it turns out that there are several reasons why the prevention of pollution and minimization of waste should be a high priority with your company.

Economics

The chief reason to make pollution prevention a priority is the bottom line on your company's annual report. Pollution prevention is economically attractive. Waste represents inefficiency, ineffectiveness, and reduced quality. Some amount of residual material will always exist, but we want to optimize our profits by minimizing that material, if it is waste.

Think of this: when your waste streams have not been minimized you are paying for it four-fold! First, it is product lost and, therefore, income that will never be collected. Secondly, it is typically labor intensive so you have to pay again to have it moved around and managed on your property. Third, you have to dispose of it in a legitimate fashion so you must have control equipment or a TSDF contract for transportation and disposal. Fourth, now your ongoing liability potential has increased by an unknown amount of money which you may never pay but, then again, you may. Wouldn't you rather avoid all this cost?

The potential liability of a hazardous waste is the ongoing risk the material represents if you treat, store, or dispose of it. You could put a dollar amount on land disposal cost increases, however the final cost will not be known until you and I are history. The potential savings to be realized from waste minimization efforts is based on three real and measurable costs, as opposed to a potential liability which is typically not measurable and hardly predictable. First, the cost of disposal is real and measurable. Congress has banned landfilling of untreated wastes and—as landfills approach their capacity—the cost increase has been dramatic in recent memory. The cost of activities associated with landfill disposal has also gone up. Transportation and analysis of waste, for instance, are much more expensive than just a few years ago. Secondly, you can also measure the cost of alternative treatment technologies. Incineration, neutralization, oxidation, and all treatment or destruction technologies have gotten very expensive. Finally, you can certainly measure savings in your raw material and manufacturing costs that are due to your waste minimization efforts.

Pollution Prevention Act of 1990

Another incentive for practicing waste minimization is the 1990 Pollution Prevention Act. The 1984 Hazardous and Solid Waste Amendments (HSWA) required generators to certify, under threat of penalty and prison, on hazardous waste manifests that a waste minimization program is in place and is being used for source reduction. The law requires EPA to verify the effectiveness of these programs so a new section was added to Form R, Toxic Chemical Release Inventory Report, which many companies are required to file each July 1. This is how EPA verifies that you are making some progress minimizing waste and preventing pollution.

EPA Regulations

EPA collects source reduction information in order to evaluate the effectiveness of programs that have been implemented. As currently written, the information is voluntary and relatively few companies provide it.

EPA Guidance

EPA has been generating, if slowly, guidance documents for different industries relative to waste minimization. EPA report 625/7-88/003, *Waste Minimization Opportunity Manual* is an essential guidance tool for companies earnestly attempting to minimize waste. By virtue of their mandate from Congress, EPA transfers reports and other documents to states, which are to make them available to interested parties.

Barriers

Lack of awareness and information is most frequently cited as the reason more companies are not aggressively engaged in pollution prevention. Managers are so focused on production at any cost that they fail to see the opportunity to save money by preventing the generation of waste streams. As the popular total quality management programs take hold, more managers are asking, "How else can we save money and make a quality product?" This is the cue for the environmental compliance manager to plug for pollution prevention. After all, waste equals dollars off the bottom line. Therefore, minimized waste represents an improved bottom line.

State Programs

Many states have source reduction programs. Most work along the following lines. A local college or university is chosen to manage the information clearinghouse for the technology transfer from EPA. Often this same organization provides waste minimization audits typically at no cost—although the report remains in the public domain—and source reduction advice. Some states have an office in the department that is responsible for environmental regulation and regulatory compliance. This office monitors source reduction activities within the state and, where required, examines source reduction plans on site. Sometimes grant money is available for waste reduction research and implementation and, in a few cases, tax incentives are involved.

Voluntary Programs

Many companies got the message early on and have implemented waste minimization programs that are already realizing bottom line savings. Member companies of the Chemical Manufacturers Association (CMA) developed the Responsible Care program for instance. CMA also has issued a pollution prevention workcode, which is available to member companies. The American Institute of Chemical Engineers established the Center for Waste Reduction Technologies (CWRT). The Three M Company is renown for its 3Ps or Pollution Prevention Pays program. As of early 1993, over 700 companies were participating in EPA's 33/50 program.

Here are some resource telephone numbers you can try for more information.

American Institute of Chemical Engineers
    New York, N.Y.   212/705-7407

Chemical Manufacturers Association
    Washington, D.C.   202/887-1100

EPA Pollution Prevention Information Clearinghouse
    Arlington, VA   703/821-4800

Synthetic Organic Chemical Manufacturers Association
    Washington, D.C.   202/659-0060

Check with your industry's trade association and with your state for other resource numbers.

ORGANIZING FOR POLLUTION PREVENTION

Do you want to be a hero? Sell your management on waste minimization. When they are sold on the positive benefits of a concentrated and effective waste minimization effort the management team will take the ball and run with it. After all, improving the bottom line is part of all job descriptions. You will have their commitment and backing as never before but get them to spread their commitment and enthusiasm by frequently discussing and mentioning waste minimization to employees in various and many ways.

Selecting a Team

In order to get started on minimizing waste you need a team to review operations and evaluate opportunities for waste minimization. No magic number of team members is required. In fact, the size of your plant staff will necessarily limit you somewhat. The personnel chosen should represent departments or organizations which contribute in some manner to waste generation or management. The facility engineering or buildings and grounds maintenance departments should be represented. The environmental management, process engineering, safety and health, quality assurance, procurement, legal, and finance departments should also be involved. It is a good idea to have at least one line supervisor from production on the team. Outsiders might include representatives from sister facilities who have already undergone this assessment or who have needed skills. A consultant may also be desirable. A process engineering consultant is typically more helpful than a compliance management consultant for waste minimization audits.

A key skill necessary for waste minimization audits is process knowledge. Related skills include knowledge of cost of processing, knowledge of material availability and procurement options, and skills necessary for the design and operation of a process.

The audit team needs a champion who holds them accountable for work output and provides the authority necessary to break through barriers to success. For instance, the champion's help may be needed to get beyond paradigm paralysis: "We've always done it this way; no other way will work." The champion insures that support and commitment of other managers are sustained. Sometimes the champion may be needed to gain access to a busy senior manager who may have key information. Who is selected as the champion is not as important as the authority she has. Finally, the champion must be a leader. Leaders have five natural and five learned qualities that both make them recognizable as leaders and give them the talent to lead.

The five natural qualities are: 1) initiative; 2) willingness to take risks; 3) a sense of responsibility; 4) personal authenticity; and 4) generosity. Initiative is the ability to perceive an opportunity and reach a decision to grasp it. A person with initiative has the courage to act on his or her decisions and, at the same time, to cooperate with others in deciding and acting. By being willing to take risks, leaders are not afraid to act just because they may be wrong. Fear of taking action is probably the number one reason many plants are not in full compliance at any given time. Effective waste minimization requires risk-taking and leaders who can observe the situation, make a judgment about what seems right, and then act. It is not all risk, however. Most companies find real savings on their bottom line when they minimize waste. Sometimes the leader must take a stand, alone, and tread on thin ice. Sometimes a leader must stick his or her neck out. The leader is the one who feels a sense of personal responsibility for the mission and goals of the company and can see that waste minimization is more compatible with those goals than pollution control. A leader is authentic. That means the leader is truthful with himself or herself. Like a saying from the 1960s, "What you see is what you get." In business, we don't often put a value on generosity, but it is important that a leader has this quality. Leaders give what they have, what they are, and what they can be. They give themselves totally. If your waste minimization leader does not have these natural qualities, tell him or her to get back in the line and find someone who does exhibit them consistently.

The military is fond of claiming that leadership is learned not born, and that they can take almost anyone and infuse into them the qualities of leadership by training and drill. In business, we do not have the luxury of leadership training schools and endless drills. Our leaders have to be more or less natural ones. Yet, certain leadership qualities must be learned. First, good leaders tend to be well-rounded individuals. More important than from which college they obtained their diploma or its discipline field, the leader's interests and aptitudes make him or her stand out among colleagues. Second, leaders are better-than-average communicators. Third, they also tend to be more mentally and emotionally mature, on the average, than those they lead. Fourth, they have a powerful inner drive to achieve the mission and goals of their assignment. This personal motivation is connected with a sense of responsibility, but the deep inner motivation is learned. Many earnest employees feel a sense of responsibility and ownership for their work, but, until that sense is translated into drive, they are not leaders. Fifth, technical ability is less important to a leader than learned managerial and supervisory ability.

Setting Goals

As in any other project, success is assured when clearly defined goals and objectives are consistent with policy set by senior management. Devise qualitative goals and quantitative objectives. One company president said that the only worthwhile goal is zero discharge. Another commendable goal is a significant reduction of pollutants into the environment. These may be referred to as overall goals for the waste minimization/pollution prevention program.

Intermediate to an ultimate or overall program goal, your waste minimization program should identify long-range but intermediate goals. Converting a particular process to an inherently safer one may be such a goal. Short term goals can be set for each year or other reporting period. *In 1996 we will eliminate all vapor degreasers*, for instance.

Not every goal will turn out to be economically or technically feasible so identify reasonable alternatives. Not every waste stream can be reduced but many can be. The Office of Technology Assessment determined in 1986 that an opportunity existed to reduce waste generation by ten percent per year over the next five years. Although this did not happen, the potential, presumably, still exists. EPA, in a similar assessment, reported to Congress in 1986 that thirty-three percent of the then-current waste generation could be eliminated. That eventually led to the 33/50 program in which EPA challenged leading companies to reduce the release of seventeen target chemicals by thirty-three percent by 1992 and by fifty percent by 1995. These chemicals were:

Benzene	Methyl isobutyl ketone
Cadmium & its compounds	Methylene chloride
Carbon tetrachloride	Nickel & its compounds
Chloroform	Tetrachloroethylene
Chromium & its compounds	Toluene
Cyanide compounds/HCN	1,1,1-Trichloroethane
Lead & its compounds	Trichloroethylene
Mercury & its compounds	Xylenes
Methyl ethyl ketone	

The report that generated the 33/50 program found that of the seventeen target chemicals, benzene had the greatest production at nearly twelve billion pounds, toluene accounted for the greatest air emissions at 274 million pounds, one million pounds of chloroform was the greatest amount discharged to water, 7.5 million pounds of cyanide compounds were the most injected into deep-wells, chromium and lead compounds accounted for the most released to land at fifty-five million pounds, nearly eight million pounds of toluene and xylenes were transferred to POTWs and over one hundred million pounds of toluene and xylenes were transferred to other facilities. Toluene, xylenes, and 1,1,1-trichloroethane are released by over three thousand facilities each.

POLLUTION PREVENTION/WASTE MINIMIZATION ASSESSMENTS

The assessment or audit is the next phase of the waste minimization program. The information collected and evaluated during this time will be used to define alternatives to waste generation.

Material Balance

In order to determine which waste streams are generated and their quantities, a material balance of the plant is performed. A material balance includes qualitative and quantitative information. In principle, the material balance is based on the Law of the Conservation of Matter devised by Newton centuries ago. This law simply states that given a defined *system* we can account for the material flows and changes in inventory of material within that system. This law does not hold for systems where nuclear transformations are occurring but few industries deal with radioactive process materials.

Let us define our plant as the system. A block flow diagram showing all inputs to the plant, products, wastes, air emissions, and water discharges provides a qualitative assessment of the plant that identifies inflows (*influents* if the material is in the liquid state) and outflows (*effluents* if liquid, emissions if gaseous). When stream volumes and/or mass quantities are added to the diagram a quantitative tool is available. The actual mass balance is the sum of product weights or volumes minus the sum of all inflow materials' volumes or weights. The difference less unused inflow material accumulated as inventory is waste. The simplest expression of the mass balance is:

$$Accumulation = Input - Output \qquad [4.1]$$

In physical processes inputs, outputs, and accumulations can be measured in weight (pounds, kilograms, tons) or volume (cubic feet, cubic meters, gallons) but where chemical changes are occurring the streams must be tracked in lb-moles and converted to weight or volume. In this case, the material (or mass) balance must be defined as:

$$Accumulation = Input - Output + Generation - Consumption \qquad [4.2]$$

Partial material balances may sometimes be used to determine auxiliary streams. For instance, in machining plants, a partial material balance of cleaning processes would be calculated because the amount of raw material becoming product is not really germane to the cleaning solvent material balance as the amount of soiled metal parts going into the cleaning process equals the clean metal parts coming out. The soils have some finite weight and volume but these are infinitesimal when compared to the product material and the solvent weights and volumes. Here the material balance for the cleaning solvent is as Eq. 4.3.

Material balance information is obtained from process flow diagrams for chemical processes. For manufacturing processes one typically has to search purchase records, take an actual inventory of unused materials, gather product records and waste stream records.

$$WASTE = Out_{air} + Out_{water} + Out_{hazardwaste} = In\text{-}Stored \qquad [4.3]$$

For RCRA hazardous wastes, waste stream data will be available from manifests. If the company has had a policy of requiring manifests or equivalent documents for nonhazardous waste streams information from those documents can be used for the material balance.

If you have recycled streams, do not let them confuse the issue. The thing to remember about recycle situations, where no chemical reaction is taking place, is that, once the process is running, it is in steady state; no accumulation or consumption of material takes place in the process or in the recycle stream without chemical reaction. Beyond these few simple cases you should engage qualified chemical engineers to calculate a mass balance or learn to use a mass balance algorithm.

Energy Balance

Just as mass is conserved within a defined system so is energy. Actually, both mass and energy are in conservation with each other but for our purposes we can consider them as two separate conservation principles. Therefore, for a given system:

$$Accumulation = Input - Output + Generation - Consumption \qquad [4.4]$$

For a closed system, where no mass is transferred in or out and no chemical reaction is taking place:

$$\Delta E = E_{in} - E_{out} = Q - W \qquad [4.5]$$

where:

Q = heat absorbed from surroundings

W = mechanical work done by the system on the surroundings.
Beyond this simplest of cases the energy balance quickly becomes too complicated to explain here. Any chemical or mechanical engineer should be able to calculate an energy balance for you.

Collecting Data

The purpose of gathering data is to answer the questions in Figure 4.1 as follows.

Figure 4.1
Waste Minimization Questions

1. What waste streams are generated?
2. Quantify each waste stream.
3. Identify the processes or operations from which these streams come.
4. What makes them hazardous, if anything?
5. What input materials generate the waste?
6. What quantity of the input material enters the waste?
7. How much are fugitive losses?
8. How efficient is the process?
9. Are any unnecessary wastes generated by mixing otherwise recyclable hazardous wastes with other process wastes?
10. Do housekeeping practices limit the quantity of wastes generated?
11. List these housekeeping practices.
12. What types of process controls are in use to improve or maintain process efficiency?

LIFE CYCLE ASSESSMENTS

Recently EPA has been pushing a concept which originated in the European Community: the Life Cycle Assessment. This assessment does not define the plant as the system around which the mass balance is calculated. Rather it looks at the product you make from cradle to grave. That is, it not only considers the impact of your plant on the environment but also the impact of your purchase of raw materials, finished materials from other industries, the environmental impact of your product in the hands of its user, the fate of your product, and its subsequent impact on the environment. Naturally, EPA—which has been tasked by Congress to regulate industrial wastes from cradle to grave—is interested in such an assessment of your product before it is ever manufactured. In the 21st century, the Life Cycle Analysis promises to be a major plant design requirement for construction permits.

Problem Definition

After waste streams are identified, each potential waste minimization opportunity is a separate project to be scheduled according to priorities and availability of funding. Initially the option must be studied for feasibility so it is important to issue a document which spells out precisely the problem to be solved, which is to eliminate or minimize or detoxify stream X if feasible to do so.

Besides giving background material and stating the problem in terms of a goal to eliminate a waste stream, the Problem Definition document assigns persons to complete the study, recommends a study budget for analytical and bench scale feasibility experiments, sets a timetable, and names milestones for the project.

Prioritizing Problems

The EPA has established a hierarchy of priorities for waste minimization studies. Source reduction opportunities should be explored first, followed by recycling opportunities, then reclamation opportunities. Waste treatment on-site is a lesser priority. The least desirable option is disposal of residuals. Right now the great majority of waste is shipped off-site for treatment and disposal.

TECHNICAL ASSESSMENT OF ALTERNATIVES

The technical assessment looks at each of various waste minimization options, in order of priority, and determines whether it will work under the circumstances of the process. When management approves the Problem Definition it becomes the feasibility study plan. The study will address technical feasibility, economic feasibility, and technical options for implementation.

Technical Feasibility

Will the option under consideration work? Often it has to be tried out in the laboratory (bench testing), in a pilot plant (pilot testing), or in operational process equipment (operational testing). Sometimes it is necessary to rent equipment to conduct tests. Careful records of experiment and test design should be kept in order not to duplicate unnecessarily and to remember later what worked or failed and why. Not every option works. Some work well in the laboratory and for inexplicable reasons do not do well on larger scales.

When the ban on CFCs was announced in 1987, even before the timetable was accelerated, an aerospace parts manufacturer foresaw the need to convert metal parts cleaning from vapor degreasing with CFCs—which clean superbly to aerospace standards—to some alternative. A team was formed to study the options and make an appropriate recommendation to management. After five years of testing HAP solvent vapor degreasing, alkaline degreasing, flammable degreasing, degreasers derived from citrus chemicals, and perfluorinated chemicals, among others, this company found that about forty percent of its simpler, nonferrous parts could be cleaned in alkaline aqueous baths but that the remainder required vapor degreasing due to flash rusting and complexity of geometry. Some successful bench scale tests did not fare well when repeated in operational size equipment.

Economic Feasibility

The strength and major incentive for waste minimization is the economic payback it offers. Therefore, after passing the technical hurdle an option must offer some improvement to the bottom line after paying for itself. Standard engineering economic analyses, which look at incremental costs and cost savings, can be used for this evaluation.

TECHNICAL ALTERNATIVES

Source reduction techniques are good operating practices, inventory and material control, substitution of material, process modifications, new technology, and volume reduction. Recycling techniques are examined as the next priority.

Good Operating Practices

Procedural and administrative measures which a company can use to minimize waste are called good operating practices. These apply to the human interface with the manufacturing process. Procedures and management practices that improve operational efficiency are easy to implement and cost little to nothing.

Personnel management practices such as training, incentives, bonuses, and participatory programs encourage employees to reduce wasteful practices and give them rewards for suggesting other efficiency improvement ideas. Loss prevention practices reduce losses due to spills and leaks. Waste segregation practices minimize the volume of hazardous waste by preventing nonhazardous wastes from being mixed with hazardous ones. Cost accounting practices that allocate the cost of waste treatment and disposal to the generating departments give these work centers incentive to improve their profitability by minimizing waste.

Inventory and Material Control

Material handling practices reduce loss of materials due to mishandling. Inventory practices reduce loss of materials due to expired shelf life and improper storage conditions. Installation of containment areas and isolation of hazardous materials reduce losses during storage. Production scheduling can be adjusted to reduce the frequency of equipment cleaning and minimize shutdowns and startups which typically generate "off-spec" materials.

Substitution

Hazardous materials that enter the production process can sometimes be reduced or eliminated by making changes of raw material. In some cases, purer materials are available. Sometimes impurities in raw materials carry over to waste streams as residuals which make those streams hazardous. Changing to raw materials with lower levels of contaminants can eliminate this problem. In other cases, a completely different material may be substituted in order to eliminate the contaminants in the waste stream. These possibilities require thorough economic analysis, needless to say.

Process Modification

A good example of a process modification is the change from cyanide chemistry to noncyanide chemistry in the metal finishing business. Process modification can require extension change and modification so engineers need to study the possibility thoroughly and present an economic analysis which they have confidence in to convince the top management to authorize expenditures for such drastic operational changes.

New Technology

Technology changes are process and equipment modifications which reduce waste. Minor changes can often be accomplished with little fanfare and cost. Other technological improvements require a large capital outlay. These may include changes in the production process, equipment, layout, or piping. Such improvements may involve the implementation of automation. Process operating changes may be implemented, such as temperatures, pressures, flow rates, and residence times.

Volume Reduction

Reducing the volume of the waste stream is another alternative. This can be achieved by filtration, evaporation, and other concentrating processes.

New or Altered Product

As a manufacturer you may decide to alter your product so that less waste results from its use. The EPA gives an example of the paint manufacturing industry where increased applications are being found for water-based paints which emit less VOC air pollution and do not contain the toxic solvents found in many solvent-based paints.

Recycling/Reuse

When a waste material is returned to the process for further use as a replacement for input material it is said to be recycled. It may also be recycled by being sent to another process as raw material. Energy recovery is a good reuse of waste. See Figure 4.2 for the energy value of common waste materials.

Figure 4.2
Energy Value of Common Waste Streams

Waste Stream	BTU/lb
Grounds, coffee	10,000
Paper	
Boxes, corrugated	7,040
Cartons, coated, mild	11,330
Magazines	5,250
Newspapers	7,975
Organic Chemicals	
Naphthalene	17,298
Paraffin	18,000
Starch	8,530
Sugar, dextrose	6,730
Sugar, glucose	6,730
Sugar, sucrose	7,100
Vegetable oils	16,900

Figure 4.2 *(cont'd)*

Waste Stream	BTU/lb
Resins	
Latex	10,000
Melamine formaldehyde	8,650
Phenol formaldehyde	15,100
Polyethylene	21,407
Polypropylene	21,092
Polystyrene	18,400
Polyurethane	8,025
Polyurethane (foamed)	13,000
Polyvinyl acetate	9,800
Polyvinyl chloride	8,600
Urea formaldehyde	7,600
Synthetic Materials	
Nylon	11,600
Saran	5,000
Tar, asphalt	17,100
Pitch	15,100
Woods	
Beech	7,550
Birch	7,600
Oak	7,200
Pine	8,000
Sawdust, pressed	7,300

After "Technical Talk: Waste-to-Energy Values," *Environmental Protection News*, October 8, 1991.

DATA INTERPRETATION

Most process engineers have the skills necessary to examine technical options and evaluate their technical and economic feasibility. Academic disciplines such as mechanical and chemical engineering in particular receive this type of training as part of their undergraduate preparation. Consultants who are process wise can also assist your company in making these evaluations. Regulatory compliance is a marginal issue so verify the process experience of environmental consultants who claim to be ready to help you with waste minimization.

CONCLUSION

To date there has not been a general movement by industry to implement waste minimization measures. This is unfortunate as it is wasteful of potential cost savings. Get your management excited about waste minimization now and prove yourself worthy of their confidence in you by claiming those cost savings.

REFERENCES

Azar, Jack. "Asset Recycling at Xerox." *EPA Journal.* July-September 1993.

Basta, Nicholas with Kent Gilges. "Recycling Loop Closes for Solvents." *Chemical Engineering.* June 1991.

Berglund, R.L. and C.T. Lawson. "Preventing Pollution in The CPI." *Chemical Engineering.* February 1992.

Browner, Carol M. "Pollution Prevention Takes Center Stage." *EPA Journal.* July-September 1993.

Cebon, Peter. "Corporate Obstacles to Pollution Prevention." *EPA Journal.* July-September 1993.

Chadha, Nick and Charles S. Parmele. "Minimize Emissions of Air Toxics via Process Changes." *Chemical Engineering Progress.* January 1993.

Cheremisinoff, Paul N., PE. "Hazard Analysis for Waste Reduction. *The National Environmental Journal.* March/April 1992.

Clearwater, Scott W. and Joanne Scanlon. "Legal Incentives for Minimizing Waste." *Environmental Progress*. August 1991.

DeVries, Douglas. "Yankee Thrift as Pollution Prevention at Hyde Manufacturing." *EPA Journal*. July-September 1993.

Doerr, William W. "Plan for The Future with Pollution Prevention." *Chemical Engineering Progress*. January 1993.

Duke L. Donald. "Hazardous Waste Minimization Policy and Implementation: An Industry Case Study." A paper given at Hazardous Materials Management Conference and Exhibition. Anaheim, California, April 17-19, 1990.

EPA/625/7-88/003. *Waste Minimization Opportunity Assessment Manual*. July 1988.

Ferrante, Louise M. "Preparing to Meet Waste Minimization Mandates." *The National Environmental Journal*. November/December 1993.

---. "Waste Minimization Is A Serious Business." *The National Environmental Journal*. March/April 1992.

Freeman, Harry, *et al*. "Industrial Pollution Prevention: A Critical Review." *Journal of The Air & Waste Management Association*. May 1992.

Gammill, Laura M. "Proactive Approach to Pollution Prevention." *Pollution Engineering*. February 15, 1993.

Haimann, Theo and Raymond L. Hilgert. *Supervision: Concepts and Practices of Management*. 2d. Ed. Cincinnati: South-Western Publishing Company, 1977.

Hill, Darryl C. "Establishing A Waste Minimization Program." *Professional Safety*. August 1992.

Himmelblau, David M. *Basic Principles and Calculations in Chemical Engineering*. 5th. Ed. Engelwood Cliffs, NJ: Prentice Hall, 1989.

Jacobs, Richard A. "Design Your Process for Waste Minimization." *Chemical Engineering Progress*. June 1991.

Katin, Robert A. "Minimizing Waste at Operating Plants." *Chemical Engineering Progress*. July 1991.

Kling, David and Eric Schaeffer. "EPA's Flagship Programs." *EPA Journal*. July-September 1993.

Kraft, Robert L. "Incorporate Environmental Reviews into Facility Design." *Chemical Engineering Progress*. August 1992.

McIlvaine, Robert, Sally Halderman and Joseph Schwartz. "Can Air Toxics and VOC Reduction Goals Be Met?" *Pollution Engineering*. February 15, 1992.

Mooney, Gregory A., PE. "Shrinking The Waste Stream." *Pollution Engineering*. March 1, 1992.

Pickett, Lael. "Using Sorbents for Waste Minimization." *Engineer's Digest*. October 1993.

Price, Roger L. "Pollution Prevention Audits." *Industrial Safety & Hygiene News*. September 1992.

Rittmeyer, Robert W., PE. "Prepare An Effective Pollution-Prevention Program." *Chemical Engineering Progress*. May 1991.

Rossiter, Alan P., H. Dennis Spriggs and Howard Klee, Jr. "Apply Process Integration to Waste Minimization." *Chemical Engineering Progress*. January 1993.

Shapiro, Ellen. "Three Case Studies: An Introduction." *EPA Journal*. July-September 1993.

Smith, R. Blake. "Reducing Waste." *Occupational Health & Safety*. June 1992.

Spearot, Rebecca M., PhD, PE. "Pollution Prevention Makes Good Sense." *Environmental Protection*. June 1993.

Steward, F.A. and W.J. McLay. "Waste Minimization Alternate Recovery Technologies." *Metal Finishing Guidebook & Directory*. 1989.

Tejera, Frank. "Cutting Waste at Borden." *EPA Journal*. July-September 1993.

Underwood, Joanne D. "Going Green for Profit." *EPA Journal*. July-September 1993.

White, Allen L. "Accounting for Pollution Prevention." *EPA Journal*. July-September 1993.

Yates, William. "Leveraging Recovery." *Products Finishing*. February 1988.

5

PERMITTING

PERMITTING AS A LAST RESORT

The general public wants assurances that the air it breathes will be healthy and not harm property, crops, livestock or wildlife; that the water it drinks, cooks with, swims in, boats on, and fishes in will be safe for these uses; and, because of a strong fear of chemicals, it also wants assurance that hazardous waste will be properly handled somewhere else. To be sure, the public's wish to be totally safe from chemicals is behind the national policy of waste minimization. It is also behind other environmental laws implemented by so many complicated EPA regulations requiring end-of-pipe controls on polluted waste streams. If waste minimization is the first line of defense against mismanagement of hazardous chemicals in the environment and controls are the second line of defense, then permits are the last resort, the last ditch effort to protect the public from the presence of unwanted hazardous materials in the environment.

Despite the best of efforts to prevent pollution in the first place and to control it on-site in the second, some amount of pollution reaches facility boundaries. When production or maintenance has significant impact on the environment despite all efforts, the plant needs a permit. Of course the question is: "What is significant?" What industry commonly considers significant is typically far greater than what environmental activists consider significant so EPA generally interprets significant as somewhere between these extremes. Essentially a permit is an individualized law applied to your plant allowing either air or water discharges up to a certain concentration of specific contaminants.

If you put any water-based waste into a storm ditch, creek, river or lake or into a public sewer or emit any air emissions or generate and treat, store, or dispose into the ground a bulk liquid waste, containerized waste or any solid waste, then you need to apply for a permit. You need to apply for a permit while planning to do these things, not after a new facility is built and production and waste generation are in full swing. Some states have streamlined permitting processes and various compliance offices coordinate their activities to expedite acting on all necessary permits for a facility. Other states have hopelessly complicated processes with little or no coordination between compliance offices, much less communication.

As soon as your company selects a site for a new plant, if you have not already done so, establish contact with the city, county, and state to determine the requirements for permits. Ideally the site selection team has already obtained this information as part of its decision making process. From the city and county you need zoning plans and general community planning information. Some municipalities require a use permit and most require building permits for construction. Contact the local sanitation district to determine requirements for connecting process wastewater discharges to the sewer. Also contact the state about anticipated industrial wastewater discharges and air emissions. If outside city limits, contact the state or the regional EPA office (as appropriate) about wastewater and air permitting. If the new site is near the coast, additional permitting may be required before construction starts. If you are told a permit is not necessary by the locality, go to the state. If the state says no permit required, go to the regional EPA office. Do not stop until all authorities indicate that a permit is not required or you receive an application. You cannot count on a locality telling you that, although it does not require a permit, the state or federal agency does.

If the site is going to be on or impact federal property, such as that managed by the Bureau of Land Management or the Forest Service, an Environmental Impact Statement (EIS) may be required. Congress, by virtue of the National Environmental Policy Act of 1970 (NEPA), makes federal agencies responsible for land areas under their control. Some companies, such as mining and logging companies, among others, use federal lands. Companies that plan to construct alongside a navigable river or on coastal wetland property may require an EIS. Some states require an EIS of all permit applicants.

In any of these cases, your company must submit a Notice of Intent (NOI) or a Plan of Operations to the federal (or state) lead agency. The

NOI to a federal agency is published in the *Federal Register*. Federal agencies requiring an EIS are given in Figure 5.1.

| **Figure 5.1** |
| **Federal Agencies Requiring EIS** |

Corps of Engineers	if navigable waters are involved
Department of Energy	if an energy project is involved
Department of Interior	if federal lands or mining involved
Environmental Protection Agency	if historical site, archaeological site, wetlands, floodplain, agricultural land, coastal zone, wild and scenic river, fish and wildlife protection, endangered species, displaced human population, alter the character of a residential area, park lands, preserves or state implementation plan for air quality involved

Criteria published by the Council on Environmental Quality is used by the lead agency to determine whether an EIS is required or not. Figure 5.2 gives the required format.

If an emergency situation makes it necessary to take action that will have a significant environmental impact but is the lesser of two evils, the lead agency must contact the EPA Office of External Affairs before taking action. A private company involved in the matter should ensure the lead agency has made this notification.

In nonemergency situations a joint meeting is held between the lead agency and the company in order to agree on hiring a third party to prepare the EIS. The lead agency may prepare the EIS with its own staff but this can take up to 30 months. Consultants recommended by both parties are considered and one is chosen jointly. The company pays the consultant fee, although the consultant is responsible to and directed by the lead agency.

Figure 5.2
EIS Format

Title (Cover) Sheet
(Executive) Summary
Table of Contents
Purpose/Need
Proposed Action and Alternatives
Affected Environment
Environmental Consequences
Preparers
Distribution
Index
Appendices

Figure 5.3
Baseline Studies for EIS

Air quality	Land use
Archaeological	Meteorology
Biology, terrestrial and aquatic	Noise
Climatology	Seismology
Demography	Socioeconomics
Geology	Soils
Historical	Topography
Hydrology	Water Quality

The consultant prepares a scoping document, conducts baseline studies (*see* Figure 5.3), participates in all meetings as expert witness and prepares the EIS. When complete (it may take 18 months for the consultant or 30 months for an agency) the EIS is distributed for public review.

With or without an EIS, a permit must meet applicable standards so a planning meeting with the permit issuing authority is helpful in order to understand what regulations apply and what issues must be addressed before operational start up. A meeting minimizes, if not eliminates, costly delays. Communication with authorities during the plant design phase allows time to work out problems in case the company's plans do not meet environmental standards.

Typically the permitting agency works with you to improve the environmental impact of your project. Do not be afraid to frankly discuss plans or to negotiate differences between your position and the authority's. That is not to say you will be able to do anything you want to do but do not hesitate to ask.

The permitting process has four phases: application preparation, application review, public participation, and issuance. Preparation by the applicant involves measurements and calculations and review by the permit authority verifies this information. The rest is procedural.

MEASUREMENTS AND ASSESSMENTS FOR APPLICATIONS

Whether you are considering a new facility or auditing an existing facility, these questions are paramount:

1. What permits are required for the industrial processes?
2. Whom do you contact for information about permitting in your state or EPA region?
3. Do state permits satisfy federal requirements as well?
4. What operation requirements will a permit impose?
5. How long will it take you to get the permit once you submit an application?

Concerning how long it takes, you have probably heard many horror stories. Four basic reasons why permitting may take longer than expected are:

1. If the original application was incomplete, the permit will be delayed while missing information is requested and obtained.

2. Some applications generate more than one kind of permit or require coordination between different agencies or offices within agencies.
3. Some state permits must be approved at the federal level.
4. Applications for controversial or environmentally sensitive projects require public hearings with substantial lead times required for public notice to be given.

In order to improve your chances of getting the permit you need in a timely fashion, here are some hints.

Before preparing the application, schedule a meeting with the permit authority in order to find out what they really need to know in order to write the permit. Simply and directly tell them what your plans are and listen to their comments. If you do not like some comments, you can test them on the rigidity of their position but do not do or say anything to make them think you are trying to compromise their integrity. Remember, the process is impersonal; they are just trying to do their jobs as best they can.

Do not question their honesty or sincerity. Do ask them to quote applicable regulations, but if you have not completed your own homework do not be upset if they have not done theirs, either. If you have done your homework, the initial meeting (ideally before your company commits capital) is the right time and place to get interpretations of regulations. Do not hesitate to ask for their help interpreting confusing or complex regulatory requirements or to challenge their interpretations within the limits of business civility.

Avoid an adversarial relationship at all costs. Therefore, avoid the temptation to bring a lawyer to the initial meeting. No matter how pleasant and friendly she is, the presence of an attorney puts matters on a different footing as if by convention. Do not bring anyone who is quick-tempered or has a rash or impetuous personality. Each person representing your company at the fact finding meeting should personify the ideal ambassador for your company. That is not to say you cannot send tough negotiators, just make sure they are cool-headed, tough but civil negotiators.

Try to make contact with as many levels of the regulatory staff as you can at the initial meeting. (Be sure to get names and telephone numbers or collect business cards.)

Work within the system and go over people's heads only as a last resort. Even then, be extremely careful about how you talk about those persons who have worked on your file. Do not gossip about or slander anyone at the agency. That should go without saying but I have seen it happen. As public servants they must serve your company's needs but there are many justifiable reasons for denying a permit and they have another side to serve too—the public. Do not give them an incentive to deny your permit on some technicality.

If you feel you have been treated badly, consider whether the matter can wait until after the permit is issued. If you must register a bona fide complaint, do so in a professional manner. You will not be punished, as they are professionals too, though the staff may seem a little cool afterwards. If the situation is unbearable, consult with your corporate counsel. Remember this sword cuts in both directions and at times the agency will want to bring in their counsel due to behavior by representatives of your company.

Maintaining a good relationship with the agency does not mean that your agreements rest on individual relationships. What would happen if the agency contact moves on to another job? What if you get a new plant manager whom the agency permit writers dislike instantly? What you want to achieve is a sound, friendly, professional relationship between your company in the private sector and the regulatory agency in the public sector, yet proceed as two companies negotiating a mutually beneficial agreement. Nothing more.

For a new source permit, get as many branches of the regulatory staff (air, water, hazardous waste) into the initial meeting as you can.
Frankly discuss your plans and desires. It is one thing for them to tell you at a friendly meeting that you simply cannot do such and such, but quite another for them to come into your plant, find you doing it and then tell you. Do not be afraid to propose new and unusual ways to comply with regulations, especially if those solutions are more efficient than normal solutions. Avoid disputes over technical information. Disputes are one-sided and therefore options are lost when the agency becomes insistent and stops negotiating. Remember, however, they may not allow you to do anything 1) against the law, 2) in conflict with established regulations, or 3) which may harm people or the environment.

Inventories

An inventory is important for any type permit: emission inventory for air quality, water balance for water quality, and waste stream profile for solid waste management. Air permit applications require an inventory of processes or equipment that emits gases or vapors, the identity of pollutants, volumetric flow rates, and other pertinent information. Wastewater permit applications require a water balance of the plant with a list of anticipated pollutants in each wastewater stream as well as their concentration in the stream. A permit to manage hazardous waste (a RCRA "Part B") requires an inventory of anticipated solid waste streams to be managed, their hazardous constituents and characteristics, etc.

Inventories are nothing more than a mass balance as discussed in the previous chapter. A mass or inventory equates the input of material to the consumption, accumulation, and loss of that material. To complete an inventory you must account for all streams of material flowing into the process and all streams flowing outward. Any accumulation or depletion of each material within the process must also be considered. A complicating factor is the impact of control devices and chemical reactions on the inventory. Therefore, you may need chemical engineering assistance to complete an accurate inventory. If it cannot be calculated from process information then the inventory must be completed using some other method.

One alternative method is to search the literature for information about similar waste streams (from sources such as the emission factors found in the EPA publication AP-42, for instance). An emission factor is a ratio of pollutant released to a process-related measurement such as tons of production per day, tons of raw material consumed, number of gadgets produced, etc.

Process engineering calculations are also an acceptable source of information for an inventory. Reaction kinetics, equations of state, vapor-liquid equilibrium, mass transfer and other physical, chemical, and chemical engineering techniques are often required. Process design information, unit operation data, equipment design specifications, and emission data from similar processes are sources of information for performing engineering calculations to obtain an emission inventory.

The final alternative is to conduct stack or discharge testing. This method is available only for existing plants, of course. Testing must strictly use EPA Reference Methods and adhere to the exact number of traverses (sampling positions inside the stack), determine velocity profile, volumetric flow and moisture content as required in the Reference Methods. Variations can lead to the test report being rejected as inaccurate. Experienced stack sampling engineers can propose modified methods which will be acceptable to EPA if your process or stack does not allow for the use of an approved method. Modified methods should be proposed to and approved by EPA or the state in advance of the test.

Preparing inventories for plants in the design phase is not always easy. Emissions from planned facilities are required in order to determine if a New Source Review is applicable and what limitations will be imposed on the new plant. Coordination between the plant design team and the environmental manager is crucial. King and McGrath discuss an iterative process for designers, environmental managers, and permit application reviewers (shown in Figure 5.4). Remind the design team to practice waste minimization when reviewing preliminary plant designs. Figure 5.5 gives often over-looked air sources.

Figure 5.4
Steps in Designing and Permitting A New Plant

1. Process concepts.
2. Project constraints.
3. Project schedule.
4. Protocols for regulatory agencies.
5. Preliminary design.
6. Design options.
7. Environmental impact.
8. Permit application(s).
9. Comments from regulators and public.
10. Regulatory approval of design.
11. Detailed design.
12. Construction.
13. Start up.
14. Operation.

Figure 5.4 *(cont'd)*

15. Compliance verification.
16. Monitor operations.

Figure 5.5
Frequently Over-looked Air Sources

Analyzer (online) returns
Bleed valves
Compressors
Cooling towers (via heat exchanger leaks)
Degassing (line, pump, vessel)
Filters
Fluid, seal or lubricating
Fugitives (valves, flanges, seals, packings)
Loading operations
Maintenance releases
Metal emissions (compounds from catalyst)
Packed beds (regeneration or backwash)
Pressure relief seal pots
Purges, inert or non-condensable
Samples
Solid wastes
Stormwater runoff
Tanks
Transfer operations
Traps, steam
Vents, process
Waste oil
Wastewater collection and treatment

Adapted from Knepper.

For each storage tank containing volatile organic chemicals collect the following information: type of tank (fixed roof, floating roof, horizontal, etc.), type of seals for floating roof tanks (primary, secondary, liquid, vapor, mechanical), throughput (amount of material added during the year), and liquid composition. Identity of components and percentage of each are required so that chemical and physical properties can be extracted from handbooks and other data bases. When solutions consist of components quite similar in nature, straight-chain hydrocarbons for instance, Raoult's law is used to calculate vapor composition.

$$p_i = p^* x_i \qquad [5.1]$$

where p_i is the partial pressure of component i in the gas phase and x_i is the liquid-phase mole fraction. Where $x_i = 1$, $p_i = p^*$. The term, p^*, is the vapor pressure of the component. If y_i is the gas-phase mole fraction, then we can define an equilibrium constant K_i by assuming Dalton's law applies to the gas phase:

$$K_i = \frac{y_i}{x_i} = \frac{p^*}{p_i} \qquad [5.2]$$

What does this mean? We can use this relationship to calculate the vapor losses from a storage tank. If chemical engineering is not your strong suit, the calculation procedure may be found in AP-42. Breathing loss is estimated by this formula:

$$L_B = 2.26 \times 10^{-2} M_V \left(\frac{P}{P_A - P}\right)^{0.68} D^{1.73} H^{0.51} \Delta T^{0.50} F_p C K_c \qquad [5.3]$$

where:
  L_B = breathing loss, lb/yr
  M_V = molecular weight of vapor, lb/lb-mole
  P = true vapor pressure, psia
  P_A = average atmospheric pressure, psia
  D = tank diameter, ft
  H = average vapor space height, ft

T = average ambient diurnal temperature (delta represents
daily change), °F
F_P = paint factor, dimensionless
C = adjustment factor for small tanks, dimensionless
K_C = product factor, dimensionless

AP-42 gives information about the various factors and also product information for common petroleum chemicals. EPA-450/4-88-004 is also useful as a data resource. Material speciation is found in EPA-450/2-90-001a.

The working loss of a tank is the amount of vapor lost when loading and unloading. This can be estimated by the following equation:

$$L_W = 2.40 \times 10^{-5} M_V PVNK_N K_C \qquad [5.4]$$

where:
L_W = working loss, lb/yr
V = tank capacity, gallons
N = number of capacity turnovers during the year, dimensionless
K_N = turnover factor from AP-42

To estimate total losses you also need to know the control efficiency of any vapor recovery unit installed. Storage tank emissions are significant in very large refineries with massive tanks, but tanks of the 6,000 to 8,000 gallon variety usually lose only a few pounds of VOC per year.

Fugitive emissions from tanks occur where valves, pumps, flanges, relief valves, and relief flanges are leaking. When making an inventory, determine the type of service for these potentially leaky components: gas, light, or heavy liquid. Count the number of each. Estimate fugitive emissions by multiplying the number of each type of component by an emissions factor from AP 42 to determine overall losses. Speciation profiles are found in EPA-450/2-90-001a.

Transfer operations are the loading and unloading of trucks, rail cars, barges, and ships. For your inventory, determine the components and whether the fill pipe is submerged or not. If not, it is called splash loading. Submerged loading is where the fill pipe enters from overhead and is submerged. If the fill pipe enters from the bottom of the tank, it is called bottom loading. A procedure for calculating the losses may be found in AP-42. Calculated emissions also depend on whether a vapor control system is installed and, if so, its efficiency.

What do wastewater treatment facilities have to do with air inventories? VOCs contained in wastewater evaporate and are emitted. Sources of emissions in wastewater plants include process drains, sumps, collection systems, oil/water separators, air flotation systems, secondary treatment equipment, and in-plant sludge treatment. If VOC's contaminate your plant's wastewater, collect a number of representative samples over a period of time (three samples in two weeks) in order to define the emissions. Data needed are flow rate, discharge temperature, and HAP/VOC concentrations representative of normal operations.

Speciation profiles, mentioned above, are lists of chemical compositions of various organic compounds, or metal compounds by specific processes or equipment. These profiles were developed from actual source tests, stream compositions, and engineering calculations. Generally, they are accepted by EPA as a good ball park estimate.

The 1990 Clean Air Act Amendments put more emphasis on emission inventories than the law previously did. Emission inventories under the CAAA are more complicated due to emphasis on speciation. Hazardous air pollutants, SARA releases, and other air toxics must now be identified and quantified by species.

Fugitive emissions from equipment leaks and unvented processes are often ignored. Fugitives may also result from a lack of exhaust ducting, as many small manufacturing plants emit processes vapors into the general shop atmosphere, which is controlled by dilution ventilation. Several options exist for quantifying process fugitives. Emission factors from AP-42 may be multiplied by a total process component count, where the component is one type of leaking equipment. Emissions may also be calculated from solubility or thermodynamic equilibrium data. Air monitoring techniques also provide an estimate of fugitives. The air emissions inventory must also account for the combustion of fuels, including waste fuel. Figure 5.6 gives information required about combustion sources.

Figure 5.6
Combustion Source Information

Capacity of burner (MMBTU/hr)
Utilization factor (hr/yr)
Fuel Type (natural gas, refinery gas, coal, fuel oil, coke)
Lower heating value (BTU/ft^3, BTU/gal, BTU/lb, etc.)

Air emission inventories are required in order to determine applicable regulations on a facility-specific basis. They are also the basis for enforcement and permit fees. Inventories are also used to update regional air quality plans, demonstrate emission reductions, and support Ambient Air Quality Analyses.

Source and Ambient Sampling and Monitoring

Source monitoring is the process of collecting and testing samples from an air emissions stream, wastewater discharge, or hazardous waste stream, although the term is usually applied to air emissions. Ambient sampling in air pollution compliance pertains to the collection and testing of air samples for background levels of pollutants of interest. In wastewater and land releases (RCRA and CERCLA matters), this is called background monitoring.

Should you conduct monitoring when applying for a permit? Unless you have an acceptable way to estimate emissions from an existing facility, you must. In the case of a facility in the design phase, you cannot; just make your best estimate for the application. The permit authority will require a demonstration of compliance in the form of monitoring as soon as the plant is built and operating.

Although you will be concerned about cost, concentrate on the qualifications of your potential monitoring contractors. This is critical business. The future operating comfort of your plant depends on it. Bear in mind that you usually get what you pay for, so be hard-nosed with your procurement department and select the best qualified firm you can practically afford, preferably one with which you are familiar and with which you have had good experience in the past.

Particle Size Determination

Determining particle size is very important in the regulation and control of particulate matter. Permit conditions for the site may be expressed in terms of total particulate matter (PM) on the state operating permit but federal standards are expressed in terms of PM-10, particulate matter smaller than 10 microns in diameter. Current emphasis is on PM that can be inhaled into the lungs which typically is smaller than 10 microns in diameter. Nose hair, cilia (fine hair-like structures in the nasal and laryngeal passages), and natural settling tend to remove larger particle sizes before they reach the bronchial passage. EPA defines inhalable dust (PM) as any which enters the body but is trapped in the nose, throat, or upper respiratory tract. MSHA (Mine Safety and Health Administration) defines respirable dust as that fraction of airborne dust that passes a size-selecting device with particle size characteristics shown in Figure 5.7:

Figure 5.7
Respirable Dust Characteristics

Aerodynamic Diameter, microns	Percent of dust passing selector (% coarser than)
2.0	90
2.5	75
3.5	50
5.0	25
10.0	0

Total dust is all airborne PM regardless of size or composition. Environmental scientists generally consider anything greater than 2.5 microns as coarse particles and anything smaller as fine particles. Larger fine particles, 0.08 to 2 micron diameters, are known as the *accumulation range* while ultrafine *transient range* particles, less than 0.08 micron diameter, are also called the *Aitken nuclei range*.

PM-10 causes respiratory irritation and can lead to or complicate respiratory diseases. Children who were chronically exposed to PM-10 over threshold amounts have shown reduced lung capacity. Total PM is implicated in reduced visibility and unpleasant odors in communities.

The design of air pollution control equipment for PM is based on particle size. Operation and maintenance of such equipment as baghouses, cyclones, electrostatic precipitators, and other particulate scrubbers are based on the efficiency of removal of certain particle sizes.

Calculations. Although the diameter of PM is discussed as if it were spherical, typically PM comes in assorted, irregular shapes resulting in no true diameter. Therefore an equivalent diameter is used in design and regulatory control. Engineering practice defines the size of irregular shapes in terms of effective diameters (aerodynamic, Martin's, and Feret's among others). The aerodynamic diameter (D_a) is particularly useful as instruments are available to measure it directly.

$$D_a = D_g k \sqrt{\frac{\varrho_p}{\varrho_o}} \qquad [5.5]$$

D_g is the geometric diameter, ρ is the density of the particle, if the buoyant forces of air are neglected, and ρ_g is the reference density, 1 g/cm^3. The shape factor, k, is 1.0 for a sphere. Martin's and Feret's diameters are now considered nearly obsolete among atmospheric chemists, but are used for determining statistical averages by other scientists. Particle sizes are reported either in graph form, or as a set of numbers, such as 97-10 microns. This example means that 97% of the particles were finer (smaller diameter) than 10 microns. Conversely, 3% of the particles in this particular batch were coarser (larger diameter) than 10 microns. Sometimes you may see a report such as 90+5 microns. This means that 90% were coarser than 5 microns, while 10% were finer. In reading particle size graphs, study the information carefully until you understand whether it is reporting percentage finer than or coarser than because more than a few environmental managers have come to grief over such a simple misunderstanding.

Plume Mass and Opacity

A direct relationship exists between the amount of particulate matter in air emissions and visibility through the plume. This relationship is distorted by the amount of water vapor droplets in the plume, which tend to show up as white smoke, but is not smoke. Nevertheless, this crude method is successfully used by smoke readers for inspecting stacks. The color or opacity of the smoke, in the inspector's judgment, issuing from the stack is compared to a standard Ringelmann chart numbered from zero to five. Zero is assigned to a plume with no opacity or an invisible plume. Five is assigned to a solid black plume with zero visibility. Besides moisture, smoke reading of plumes is complicated by the inspector's experience, the position of the sun in relationship to the plume, and the diameter of the stack.

PSD Analysis and Atmospheric Diffusion Modeling

Congress, fearing that air quality might be sacrificed in attainment areas, which could potentially get more new facilities because tighter emission controls are required in nonattainment areas, established the Prevention of Significant Deterioration (PSD) program for any major source seeking a new source permit, or wanting to make a major modification to an existing source in an attainment area. A major source is one which would emit over 250 tons per year (TPY) of a regulated pollutant, or over 100 TPY of a regulated pollutant, if the industry falls within any one of twenty-eight listed source categories (fugitives must be counted). Figure 5.8 gives these categories.

If any of these process plants is located in an attainment area and seeks a permit for a major modification, it must demonstrate that the facility's emissions will not cause the ambient air quality to degrade below a preset significant level. The facility will be required to utilize the best available technology (BACT) for controlling each pollutant that will be emitted in significant amounts. A major modification is any physical change in the method of operation resulting in a significant net emissions increase of any regulated pollutant. Significant increases are defined in terms of each pollutant in Figure 5.9. Net emission increases that are significant for VOC are regulated for ozone attainment.

Figure 5.8
Source Categories Subject to PSD

> 250 MMBTU/hr Steam Generation
Coal Cleaning
Kraft Pulp Mill
Portland Cement
Primary Zinc Smelter
Iron and Steel Mill
Primary Aluminum Reduction
Primary Copper Smelter

Municipal Incinerator > 250TPD
Hydrofluoric Acid
Sulfuric Acid
Nitric Acid
Petroleum Refinery
Lime Plant
Phosphate Rock Beneficiation
Coke Oven Batteries
Sulfur Recovery
Carbon Black Furnace Process
Primary Lead Smelter
Fuel Conversion
Sintering Plant
Secondary Metal Production
Chemical Process Plants

Fossil Fuel Boilers > 250 MMBTU/hr cumulative

Petroleum Storage & Transfer > 300,000 bbl
Taconite Ore Processing
Charcoal Production
Glass Fiber Processing

Figure 5.9
Significant Increases

Pollutant	TPY
Carbon Monoxide	100
Nitrogen Oxides	40
Sulfur Dioxide	40
Particulate Matter	25
PM_{10}	15
Ozone, VOC increase	40
Lead	0.6
Asbestos	0.007
Beryllium	0.0004
Mercury	0.1
Vinyl Chloride	1
Fluorides	3
Sulfuric Acid Mist	7
Hydrogen Sulfide	10
Total Reduced Sulfur (TRS)	10
Organics, MWC (1)	3×10^{-6}
Metals, MWC	15
Acid Gases, MWC	40

Note: MWC = Municipal Waste Combustor
(1) = dioxins/furans

BACT is the maximum emission reduction achievable (considering economics, energy consumption, and environmental protection) and must be at least as effective as any NSPS applicable to the source. No list is available from which you may choose BACT equipment. The company and state negotiate BACT for the specific facility.

The process works like this: The applicant completes an engineering study to determine which equipment can accomplish the required reductions in emissions from the process to be permitted, how much reduction can be expected and at what cost to install. A preliminary technical and economic decision made by the permit seeker is presented to the state along with the equipment information and decision logic. If the state agrees with the selection, then the applicant goes with it. If the state does not agree, the two sides negotiate the acceptable alternatives to the unacceptable features of the proposed equipment. In some cases, a company may have to deal with a regional EPA office or with an Air Quality Management District instead of the state air pollution control office. Needless to say, the EPA has strict control of the whole process (cf "4.2.1 The PSD Program" Arbuckle, *et al*).

Although large companies—especially chemical and mineral processing plants—routinely do engineering studies before making budget decisions, smaller companies tend to do "catalog" engineering, that is, selecting the cheapest of several dissimilar sales presentations without benefit of an objective feasibility analysis. The PSD process forces technical and economic feasibility studies as preliminary to the decision-making process. If you do not spend the money for a feasibility study up front, you will spend it on engineers who have to troubleshoot and design modifications on the tail end of your project. If you have someone come in to troubleshoot, that means your company may also be paying penalties until the problem is resolved. Pay now to do it right the first time or pay double when you are under the gun. The point is to do the engineering up front in your compliance project, where it belongs.

Once BACT is selected and approved, the plant which wanted to modify operations may, permit-to-construct in hand, begin. The PSD process assures that the major modification will not have significant impact on the air quality in the region.

DISPERSION MODELING

Dispersion models are used to make air emission inventories for air quality management districts. Dispersion is a phenomenon in which one gaseous specie gradually mixes with other gaseous species. Aerosols (solid particles dispersed in air) or colloids (solids dispersed in water) or liquids will disperse much as if they were gaseous. If you have ever seen sun tea being made, you have seen a dispersion. A dispersion requires a driving force. The usual driving force in air pollution is concentration difference (called gradient). The pollutant species, given time and ideal conditions, will seek to disperse, or diffuse, until it is in equal concentration everywhere as shown by this simple equation provided by Sadar.

$$C = \frac{Q S}{U} \qquad\qquad [5.6]$$

C is the concentration of pollutant downstream at some receptor, Q is the emission rate, S is a function of atmospheric stability and U is wind speed with consistent units.

The Gaussian plume model is a better mathematical representation of what is going on and yields a bell-shaped curve of concentration along the path of dispersion with the highest concentrations being at the centerline and tapering off to undetectable at the edges of the plume. Most computer models acceptable to EPA are based on the Gaussian equation, which calculates the concentration of the pollutant at ground level in grams per cubic meter (1-hour average assumed) and is expressed as:

$$X = \frac{Q}{\pi \sigma_y \sigma_z u} \qquad\qquad [5.7]$$

where σ_y is the crosswind dispersion factor, in meters, σ_z is the vertical dispersion factor, in meters, and u is the wind speed in meters per second.

However, conditions are not ideal everywhere so in real life this equalization may never happen. Temperature and pressure differences in the atmosphere, wind, the presence of chemically reactive species, precipitation, mountains, and buildings all affect the dispersion process. Nor do these factors operate independently of each other in all cases. So, you see, dispersions are quite complicated in real life though they can be described mathematically, or modeled, in ideal situations. Dispersion occurs most readily when the atmosphere is unstable. Atmospheric stability is defined in Figure 5.10.

Figure 5.10
Atmospheric Stability

Weather	Atmospheric Stability	Classification
Sunny, >60° over horizon; light wind	Strong Instability	A
Sunny, 35-60° over horizon; light wind	Moderate Instability	B
Partly sunny, 15-35° over horizon; light to moderate wind	Slight Instability	C
Cloudy skies day or night, winds at any speed or clear and moderate to strong wind	Neutral	D
Night: mostly cloudy, light wind	Slight Stability	E
Night: partly cloudy or clear; light wind	Moderate Stability	F

Nevertheless, environmental engineers rely on air dispersion modeling to predict pollutant concentrations in various locations as the pollutant plume disperses from the stack. Industries estimate emissions and submit this information on state operating permit application forms. Data from industry is merged with meteorological data in a computer model based on dispersion of low concentrations of gases and aerosols in the atmosphere. The model estimates ambient concentrations at the fence line of an industrial source or in a school yard or nearby residence. In short, a map of concentration gradients can be drawn by the computer using the modeling output data. Figure 5.11, derived from Sadar, lists some models acceptable to EPA. As a nonexpert compliance manager, assure yourself that whoever is chosen to conduct modeling for you has both modeling and chemical process experience.

Figure 5.11
EPA Accepted Plume Models

Model	Use
COMPLEX I	rural
ISCST2	rural; urban
ISCLT2	rural; urban
LONGZ	urban
MPTER	rural
SCREEN	rural; urban
SHORTZ	urban

Most areas in the U.S. are classified as rural for dispersion modeling. The urban designation requires that heavy industry account for more than 50% of total area within a 3 km radius of the source. Selection of a model also depends on the type of averaging period (hourly, daily, monthly seasonal, seasonal, annual), type of source (point, area, volume) and terrain (simple or complex). Point sources are stacks. A large liquid spill is an area source while a large storage pile is a volume source. Simple terrain means the ground is no higher than the source height. If ground level exceeds the source height the terrain is complex.

Permits are granted or denied by virtue of model runs. Dispersion models are inaccurate inasmuch as they do not fit real life. So, some permit applicants are not going to be happy about the results of dispersion modeling. Three alternatives exist to having the state issue or deny a permit based on one or two dispersion model runs. Those who like to do things themselves are referred to specialized discussions of dispersion modeling such as that by Brophy who covers four main categories of dispersion models commercially available: screening models, refined models, transportation models, and accidental release models.

One alternative to dispersion modeling is receptor modeling whereby data from monitoring sites located remotely from a facility are analyzed and compared with previously collected data on sources of emissions in the area. Most industries do not have ready access to such information nor could they easily and anywhere establish monitoring stations without trespassing. For the most part, receptor modeling is not a practical alternative.

A second alternative is to have a consulting firm develop a model which more closely resembles real conditions at the plant. This is about the best you can do. A variation of the same theme is to run many different trials of a standard model, playing "what if" with variables. It takes some field work to verify that a favorable run is realistic. The state may want to know about all your runs, not just a favorable one, so be prepared to explain the reality of each. Multiple runs may be required if the state's modeling resources are back-logged and the overworked staff judges that your company has the wherewithal to conduct such studies under their scrutiny.

RISK ASSESSMENT

The fourth alternative to having the state conduct a dispersion model run is to undertake a risk assessment which estimates the magnitude of health effects that may occur as the result of exposure resulting from the pollutants emitted. Toxicity, exposure, and opportunity for dosing of a population are considered when calculating health risk. The nature and source of data affects the acceptability of risk. The less solid the data is, the more the burden of proof is on the polluting facility. The question is, "Given the magnitude of uncertainty about this particular study, what will happen to an exposed population?" Risk assessment is becoming a major influence in the decision-making process. The risk assessment proper is only one phase of a three phase process involving multiple disciplines: chemistry, biology, geology, toxicology, epidemiology, medicine, statistics, economics, public policy, and so on.

The first phase is data collection and research. The purpose of this phase is to accumulate information about exposure and its effects, examine scientific data for gaps, examine public policy and regulatory issues, and review site specific factors. The level of detail and the need to generate experiments to fill data gaps is also determined in this phase.

Qualitatively, the next phase enumerates hazards to human health and the environment. What chemical, physical, or biological agents are potentially harmful? With this information sorted out, two subordinate studies are conducted in parallel: the Toxicity Assessment and the Exposure Assessment.

Toxicity Assessment

The Toxicity Assessment is important because no two chemicals (or physical or biological stressors) have the same effect on either human health or the environment. All chemicals affect human health to some extent but not all are hazardous enough to cause serious health concerns. Paracelsus (1493-1541) wrote: "All substances are poisons: there is none which is not a poison. The right dose differentiates a poison and a remedy." The purpose of the Toxicity Assessment is to identify and quantify human health and ecological effects caused by the stressor(s) [or the pollutant(s) as the case may be].

The response of the body to chemical dose is plotted in the *dose-response relationship*. As dose increases so does the response, that is, the observable effects of dose. Do not confuse dose, exposure, and effect. When a liquid solvent evaporates into the air, an exposure to a certain concentration of that solvent occurs. Exposure is a potential. When you are exposed to X ppm of solvent A, you do not necessarily receive X ppm into your body. The solvent must diffuse in the atmosphere, wind currents carry it here and there, moisture may absorb some or all of it, and some of it may condense onto a cold metal surface. You may be partially protected by the clothing you are wearing. Many things may prevent all the solvent that is available (the exposure) from reaching your body. The amount of solvent that you actually receive is called a dose. Strictly speaking, many so-called dose-response curves are actually exposure-response curves when the facts of the study methodology are revealed.

Each chemical has one or more target organs on which it acts adversely. Not all the material received as dose may make it to the target organs. The human body has a natural detoxifying system which protects us until it is overwhelmed. Therefore, a response to a dose is actually a response to some lesser amount that is delivered to target organs, not the entire dose. Normally, we do not know how much material arrives at the target organ(s), so we watch for a response and relate observed effects on health to either dose or exposure. Obviously, a dose-response curve is better than an exposure-response curve due to attenuation of the species in the atmosphere. The question is, "How is intake, or dose, related to adverse effects?"

Most pollutants have a *threshold response*. That is to say that a dose smaller than the threshold amount will have no observed response as the body's various systems are capable of coping with the intrusion and detoxifying themselves, while a dose greater than the threshold amount overwhelms these systems, so that a response is observed. This means that if we can control the exposure, that is, reduce the emission at the source, we can prevent someone from having a health effect due to the pollutant. PM and the acidic pollutants SO_2 and NO_x are like this. Other pollutants, especially carcinogens (cancer-causing agents), have no dose threshold and exhibit health effects at any exposure. Some risk exists, in other words, no matter how small the dose of a carcinogen.

The response of carcinogens is tracked by the cancer slope factor (CSF) or potency factor (pf). Although the fear of chemicals, chemophobia, leads otherwise rational persons to presume that all chemicals are carcinogens, fewer than one hundred known carcinogens are known among over 600,000 chemicals currently manufactured and millions of chemicals known to modern humanity, according to the Chemical Manufacturers' Association.

Exposure Assessment

The Exposure Assessment looks at the potential for coming into contact with chemicals that cause unwanted health effects (or effects on the environment). The magnitude, frequency, duration, and routes of exposure of humans and the environment are determined during the study. Standard assumptions must be made in order to quantify some of these factors. Figure 5.12 gives exposure assessment assumptions generally acceptable to EPA. When presenting risk assessment reports to EPA or state compliance agencies, it is better to agree on assumptions in advance. The purpose of the exposure assessment is to measure or predict the spatial and temporal distribution of a stressor (chemical, physical, or biological) and the effect of its contact with ecological systems including humans.

Figure 5.12
Standard Exposure Factors

Factor	Adult	Child
Body Weight (kg)	70	10-16
Body Surface Area (m²)	1.9	1.4
Water Ingested (l/day)	2	1
Air Inhaled (m³/day)	20	5
Soil Ingested (mg/day)	100 (70 years)	200 (5 years)
Fish Consumed (g/day)	6.5	---
Life Exposure (years)	70	---

After Kolluru.

The *risk assessment* goes a step beyond the exposure and toxicity assessments to evaluate the likelihood of adverse effects in populations and ecological systems caused by exposure to the stressor. Scientific uncertainties must be addressed in detail. One definition of risk is that it is *the uncertainty of safety*. At the statistical level, we can quantify risk fairly well. For instance, insurance companies can tell you the likelihood that a certain number of people who are your age will die this year with great accuracy, but they cannot tell with any accuracy whether you, or I, or any particular individual will die.

If your company is conducting a risk assessment, avoid prejudging the nature and magnitude of the risk. The tendency, because we work around chemicals, is to downplay risk. This is a game we play to avoid dealing with the risk on a daily basis, which would stress us out. That is not to say that we are inherently in danger.

Plan for risk assessment from the very beginning of your permitting project, when you can do it in a positive, controlled fashion. If you go back and do it later in response to public concerns, you will be on the defensive and the manner in which the assessment is conducted will likely be out of your hands. Once risk has been analyzed, your job has just begun. How people view that risk is more likely to affect the outcome of your permit application than the actual risk value will.

Alternatives to Comparative Risk Assessment

Current alternatives to comparative risk assessment are not very attractive to industry. One controversial alternative is the *environmental justice* paradigm. Proponents of environmental justice maintain that uncorrected environmental damage has been disproportionate in poor and minority areas. For instance, environmental justice advocates claim that either no attention or delayed attention is paid to problems in poor and minority neighborhoods where hazardous waste facilities are typically sited.

Another alternative paradigm is that of *pollution prevention*, which requires massive cultural and economic changes, not only in industry, but in society at large. One reason that pollution exists is convenience. Modern society thrives on convenience. If pollution prevention is going to work, we have to change the *culture of convenience*, the way we think and do things. We have to find new ways of looking at production and waste and devise new ways of accounting for the material flowing into and out of industrial processes. Society must eventually give up the internal combustion automobile, learn to use less energy, etc. Only so many pollution prevention innovations can be implemented in industry without making drastic cultural changes. It will take a veritable revolution of thought before pollution prevention pays huge dividends.

The *technological innovation* paradigm is a variation of the pollution prevention theme. This paradigm assumes that certain aging industries are ripe for new technologies, which will produce less pollution. A fine dream, but too few industries are ready for such a change; they just are not ripe enough.

What, in the final analysis, is risk? And how can we convince the public, assuming the evidence is on our side, that the chemicals we use to make the things they enjoy are safe? A myth among industrial environmental managers is that people in general are fanatics for safety and that they are fundamentally against anything hazardous. *NIMBY* (Not In My Back Yard) is an expression frequently heard in environmental war stories. Experts have found, however, that, given the opportunity to participate in the planning process, the public can be quite sensible about risks. Unfortunately, managers and technicians tend to get scientific and discuss risk in terms of the number of deaths and injuries expected. An unemotional, scientific discussion about the statistical body count is sure to turn concerned citizens into irrational crusaders. Morgan points out that working for a few hours in a coal mine, eating peanut butter sandwiches every day for a month, or living next to a nuclear power plant for five years are all activities which increase the risk of death by about one in a million. If you use this information at a public hearing for a permit for your company, you will be run out of the room because the general public does not view risk that way.

Nontechnical people (In this sense any industrial manager is a technician.) look at risk completely differently, but just as logically, as technical persons do. They just use a different logic. Do not berate them for using a different logic, though, and never suggest that your point of view is the only acceptable one.

Risk Communication

Generally, people want to understand the process that introduces risk and to know how equitably the danger is distributed. They also want to know how well individuals can control their exposure and whether the risk is assumed voluntarily. When you throw in the example of eating peanut butter sandwiches, for instance, you ask them to compare voluntary risks to the risk of having your new polluting process right next door to them. Voluntary risk they accept, but an equal involuntary risk they do not accept. Involuntary risk is perceived as being more dreadful than voluntary risk. A sky diver or bungee jumper, for instance, may sincerely refuse to live next door to a nuclear power plant. Involuntary risk is generally perceived as being less understood than voluntary risk. Yet, who in the general public—you and I included—fully understand why we are at risk for eating peanut butter sandwiches or Japanese puffer fish which kill one person in every two hundred who eat them? Industrial risk imposed involuntarily is generally perceived as exposing more people than acceptable voluntary risks do. Do not quote risk statistics for natural disasters at this point, unless you want a free trip out of town on a rail with a new suit of tar and feathers.

Covello and Allen give seven cardinal rules for risk communication, which are listed in Figure 5.13, but we also need to consider the research of Morgan when we talk about risk communication.

Figure 5.13
Rules of Risk Communication

1. Involve the public as a legitimate planning partner.
2. Plan carefully and evaluate efforts.
3. Listen to specific concerns of the public.
4. Be honest, frank, and open.
5. Coordinate and collaborate with other credible sources.
6. Meet media needs.
7. Speak clearly and be compassionate.

According to Morgan, experimental psychologists have found that people unconsciously use a number of heuristics when making judgments about the uncertainty of risk. A *heuristic* is an aid or guide used in learning. Heuristics work up to a point then typically they fail and let us down. Therefore heuristics lead to bias and introduce errors in all but a limited number of cases. Risk perception heuristics are no different according to the researchers mentioned above. People tend to underestimate the frequency of common causes of death such as stroke, cancer, and car accidents by a factor of ten and overestimate the frequency of uncommon causes of death (such as botulism) by a factor of one hundred or one thousand. Researchers believe this happens because people judge the likelihood of events in terms of how easily they can recall examples. The grieving process tends to help us forget about heart attacks and strokes but media hype insures that we remember botulism deaths. Since an entire generation has Bhopal forever burned into its memory, what do you think the chances are of siting a methyl isocyanate plant in your community? Or a landfill? Or even a recycling plant?

So never stand up in a public hearing and tell the audience they are safer with your plant next door than they are smoking a cigarette, even if it is true. Or that 1 part per billion is like one inch between here and the moon or some such. They will not buy it, in fact they will detest it and you will be perceived as the enemy. In order to effectively communicate risk, Morgan suggests we first learn what people already know. Then, he says, develop messages to fill the information gaps. Test and refine these messages until surveys of the public verify that the revised messages convey the intended information. The objective of risk communication, he says, is to provide people with a basis for an informed decision; therefore, an effective message must contain information that helps them in that task. The essence of good risk communication, Morgan continues, is very simple: learn what people already believe, tailor subsequent communication to this knowledge and to the decisions people face and then subject the message to careful evaluation. He believes that, given sufficient time to reflect on balanced information, people generally do a remarkable job of deciding what problems are important and systematically address the facts. You stand a better chance of having the public in your corner if you enhance public understanding of your project in language that 1) does not confuse them and 2) does not offend them.

Before leaving the subject of risk assessment let us briefly examine how requirements are mandated for risk management. Statutory (Congressional) risk management mandates are broadly classified as three kinds of standards: pure-risk, technology-based, and reasonable-risk. Pure-risk standards are expressed or implied in only a few statutory provisions. The *Delaney Clause* of the Federal Food, Drug, and Cosmetic Act prohibits the approval of any food additive that has been found to induce cancer. The Clean Air Act has the National Ambient Air Quality Standards which protect the public health with an adequate margin of safety without regard to technology or cost factors. The more common technology-based standards focus on the effectiveness and cost of alternative control technologies. The pretreatment standards for industrial wastewater discharges are technology-based. The new MACT standards under the Clean Air Act Amendments of 1990 are also technology based. Reasonable risk standards attempt to balance risks against potential benefits. The Federal Insecticide, Fungicide and Rodenticide Act requires the registration of pesticides which EPA finds will not cause "unreasonable adverse effects on the environment." The Toxic Substance Control Act forces EPA to act if it finds that a chemical substance "presents or will present an unreasonable risk of injury to health or the environment." Risk management standards affect plant operations in many ways but most often through permit limitations.

DATA INTERPRETATION

Once information has been gathered for the permit application, material balances made, models runs, risk assessment, etc., it is important to sift through it for the purposes of a quality assurance review. Does it all make sense? If not, what is needed? What does the data mean?

The best way to present emissions data is to tie it to production. Graphic representation quickly shows how many pounds of pollutant are expected per ton of product. This works best in plants where production is nearly continuous and product is uniform, such as a chemical processing plant. Larger manufacturing plants have pretty good success tracking emissions against production, too.

Many small manufacturing plants do not measure production in tons. For instance, automotive electrical wiring harness production is measured in terms of units. The raw materials consumed in these plants are measured in terms of a few pounds per day. This is an extreme example since these plants' emissions are difficult if not impossible to measure. A good emissions measure in this case might be pounds of pollutant per 1,000 harness units. Many manufacturing plants operate in terms of widgets per day, though, and unless every widget is geometrically alike and weigh closely the same, production measurement gets fuzzy unless each individual unit gets weighed. Unless the widgets are made in lots, then lot weight can be determined. That still leaves many plants which manufacture custom-made gadgets. Determining an average weight per gadget is one way to simplify the problem.

For instance, what does pounds of pollutant per 1,000 gadgets mean when 200 gadget models of varying weights and sizes are possible? What does pounds of emissions per ton of product mean when five gadgets may be shipped to customer A on one day, forty to customer B seven days later, etc. Sporadic shipping confuses the product measurement. Also, the production shop may have a certain amount of unassembled metal parts undergoing emitting processes which have no relationship at all to daily shipments. In fact, from one manufacturing process to the next there may be no connection whatsoever between each process' production. Alternatively, the same equipment may be used to manufacture parts for vastly different products. Manufacturing plants composed of machine shops can present data in terms of pounds per ton of product, pounds per unit of each model produced, or, if all else fails, in terms of pounds per hour. The latter measure does not allow variation from the norm, so if production on any given day is atypical the plant could be operating in violation of its permit depending on how much at variance the production is.

WASTE CHARACTERIZATION

Besides knowing the air emissions and wastewater discharges, the compliance manager must also know the other waste streams well. Nearly everything that is not an air emission or wastewater discharge is solid waste. Therefore an inventory of waste streams is in order. Once the inventory of streams is complete the next step is to characterize each one as explained below.

Solid Waste

Solid waste is not a scientific term but a regulatory one. In fact, solid waste may not be in the solid state at all. For instance, a liquid waste in a 55-gallon drum is a solid waste. So is a bulk liquid waste stored in a tank. A gaseous waste which is stored in a compressed gas cylinder is a solid waste. The definition of solid waste found in the Resource Conservation and Recovery Act (RCRA) [42 USC Sections 6901-81] is broad, as shown in Figure 5.14.

As a generator of solid waste, you have a responsibility to characterize (describe the hazards of) your waste streams. The first thing you need to do has already been stated above. Make an inventory of *all* waste streams no matter where they end up in the environment: air, water, soil. What processes do they come from? What raw materials or other chemicals go into them? What chemical reactions, if any, have taken place? How many pounds or tons or gallons per hour are generated? *Etc.* This is part of the plant material balance discussed above.

Figure 5.14
RCRA Solid Waste

This is solid waste	if from these sources
garbage, refuse, sludge	waste treatment plants, water supply treatment plants, air pollution control facilities.
other discarded material, including solid, liquid, semisolid or contained activities gaseous materials	industrial, commercial, mining, agricultural, and community activities

This is not solid waste	if from these sources
solid or dissolved material	domestic sewage
solid or dissolved material	irrigation return flows
industrial discharges	point sources subject to permits under Section 402 CWA
source, special nuclear or by-product material	defined by Atomic Energy Act of 1954

Waste streams that are covered by an air or water permit can be subtracted from your overall list if the emitted stream comes straight from the generating process. If, for instance, a waste aqueous machine-coolant is transported from the Machining Department to a sump in the wastewater plant it is solid waste, not wastewater. Treating and discharging it as wastewater is fine if the baseline report or a permit modification application lists machines as a source of wastewater and coolant is reported as a batch wastewater discharge and the wastewater treatment system effectively removes any contaminants within the limits stated on the permit. However, the coolant is still a solid waste and until proved otherwise, presumed to be hazardous waste. Returning to your inventory, you should end up with a list of all waste streams not dealt with as air emissions or wastewater discharge and some, such as the machine coolant, that are.

Next study 40 CFR 261 the EPA regulation which defines solid and hazardous waste.

Hazardous Waste

The set of all solid wastes completely contains the set of all hazardous wastes, a subset. No material is a hazardous waste unless it is a solid waste. Not all solid wastes, however, are hazardous wastes. Any material on your waste stream inventory that does not fit the definition of solid waste may be removed from the list. Be careful and think this through as the definition of solid waste is very broad. Few waste streams from industrial plants fail to fit the definition of solid waste. To the extent that such waste streams do exist you can be assured they are not hazardous waste. Even so, some industrial facilities prefer to treat such streams as hazardous waste anyway in order to reduce potential future liabilities.

With the remaining solid waste streams on your list it is time to determine if any are hazardous waste. The regulation on waste identification (40 CFR 261) can confuse newcomers to the profession but it is really very simple. A solid waste is also a hazardous waste in one of two ways: it is either defined as such by a list or it has a hazardous characteristic determined by testing. Before we determine whether these apply to our solid waste inventory we first must consider solid wastes that EPA has explicitly exempted from being hazardous (nonhazardous by definition, in other words). Figure 5.15 lists these exemptions.

If a material becomes a solid waste while still contained in a process vessel, a product or raw material storage tank, pipeline or transport vehicle it is exempt from hazardous waste regulations until it is removed for disposal. This important exemption means very few manufacturing plants that generate hazardous waste require hazardous waste management (RCRA Part B) permits. Another important exemption is provided for samples (quantity limits apply) collected for analysis, characterization, or treatability study. This means that a sample of waste material shipped to a distant laboratory is not labeled Hazardous Waste although it may yet be a DOT hazardous material and will have to be labeled appropriately.

Figure 5.15
Exempt Solid Waste

household waste
agricultural waste used as fertilizer
mining overburden returned to the mine site
utility waste from coal combustion
drilling waste from oil and natural gas exploration
    wastes from the extraction, beneficiation, and processing of ores and
minerals including coal
waste dusts from cement kilns
wastes generated by the end users of arsenical-treated wood
wastes bearing chromium from certain sources

Lists of Hazardous Wastes

After going through the waste stream inventory from the viewpoint of whether each stream is a solid waste and after having considered any exemptions, we go to the lists in 40 CFR 261 where you will find four lists but two of them are actually sublists of a larger list so the three lists typically referred to in print are: hazardous wastes from nonspecific sources (F-list); hazardous wastes from specific sources (K-list); and commercial chemical products (P- and U-lists). The four-place alphanumeric designation given in these lists is called the hazardous waste number or just the waste number.

If your business, no matter what it is, engages in any of the waste producing activities listed in 40 CFR 261.31 (the F-list) the wastes from those activities are hazardous wastes by definition. For instance, if you have a vapor degreaser which uses a chlorinated solvent to clean metal parts, the waste solvent is an F001 hazardous waste. The aqueous cleaning solution you use to clean the degreaser sumps are also considered F001 by the mixture rule. The rags used to dry the degreaser sumps after you cleaned them are even considered F001 by the mixture rule. Any discarded protective equipment used to allow an employee to clean the sumps and which were presumably contaminated with solvent are also F001 wastes by the mixture rule.

The most important point about the F-list is that, regardless of your industry, if your plant engages in any of the listed activities, the waste streams described in the list are hazardous waste. A discussion of delisting and variances is given below. Delisting and variances notwithstanding, such waste streams are hazardous just because they are listed. Be sure to read the description of each waste number carefully.

Case-in-point: A routine cleanup of an agricultural waste was proceeding in a hot, arid western state. The previous owner of the farm had been paid to receive off-spec pesticides but had not used them. Approximately three tons of materials were stored in thirty-gallon fiber drums in a storage shed on the property. The farm was repossessed during a bankruptcy proceeding. The new owner and mortgage company naturally wanted the material removed with no residual liability. Initial examination of the drum labels and shipping papers led to the conclusion that a relatively innocuous agricultural pesticide was contained in the drums in dilute concentration (hence, off-spec). Statistical sampling of the material verified this conclusion. The project seemed simple enough: repack spilled material and damaged drums and ship the entire quantity to an incinerator.

The project was executed in mid-summer when it was 110° in the shade but with no shade trees within one hundred miles. The encapsulated remediation workers could work about fifteen minutes before having to take a break to drink a pint of electrolyte solution. During one work session, a worker was transferring material from a damaged drum. A wadded up plastic liner was in the bottom of the damaged drum. He picked it up, stretched it out, and nearly fainted. The label on the liner read "**WARNING: Contains Dioxin!**" Immediately we stopped work, opened several undamaged drums and transferred their contents. Five of five drums contained wadded up plastic liners with the same label warning! Each of these drums showed evidence that the liners had once been part of the drum itself. That is, pieces of the liner remained in the top ring of the drum where it had been cut away!

The original work plan was put on hold while we collected samples from the bottoms of the drums. The original samples had been collected from the top of each drum based on the assumption that the material was homogeneous. Five new samples were hand carried to the laboratory fifteen hundred miles away where they were immediately tested for dioxin species and precursors. Five of five samples were *hot*—having high concentrations of dioxin precursor species! We had found an illicit disposal facility for dioxin, the deadliest chemical currently known to humankind. This changed our waste from being hazardous by characteristic (due to a minor, diluted constituent) to F026, a listed waste and one which, at the time, could not be disposed of anywhere in the country except by incineration (hence the "midnight" disposal). After conferring with two states and the EPA, the waste was sent to an approved, permitted incinerator where it was slowly blended with combustible materials. Nearly two years later the last of the material was destroyed.

The point of this diversion is that once we fully understood the meaning of the F026 listing description we realized that it gave clues which should have led us into a deeper investigation in the first place. It is easy to browse through a listing description and conclude that this waste has nothing to do with my situation when it fact it may.

More often than missing a listing is the situation where a listing is applied erroneously. Such was the case of a machining plant with an inventory of thirty-three hazardous waste streams. A closer examination revealed eight hazardous and twenty nonhazardous waste streams. Five of the streams merely duplicated other streams but with different brand names. For instance, eight F001 streams were on the original inventory when only three different solvents were in use. All could have been combined into one F001 waste stream, but in order to practice strict segregation of waste for recycling, it was decided that three different F001's were better: one F001 waste stream for each of the solvents in use. The other five were just different brand names for the same chemicals. This plant had also classified two waste streams as F007 yet had no electroplating operations. The two waste streams were properly characterized as D003 for cyanide content. The same situation applied to three waste streams classified F006 when none of the listed processes were used in the plant. These streams were D007 for chromium.

The next list is found at 40 CFR 261.32, Hazardous Wastes from Specific Sources. Whereas the F-list is process specific, the K-list is specific to industries. If your wastewater treatment facility generates a sludge, it is not a K-waste unless your plant is involved in the production of one of the inorganic pigments listed (K002-7) or uses the mercury cell process in chlorine production (K106) or is from the production of chlordane (K032), creosote (K035), disulfoton (K037), phorate or toxaphene (K040-1), from the manufacturing and processing of explosives (K044 or 46) or from the production of veterinary pharmaceuticals using arsenic or organoarsenic compounds.

When commercial chemical products, intermediates, or residues are declared waste material they are hazardous wastes if listed at 40 CFR 261.33, where you will find two sublists. The P-list represents acute hazardous wastes that are regulated in volumes of one quart or more. Other toxic materials that are not as acutely hazardous as the P-wastes are listed in the U-list.

Let's say that your plant uses zinc cyanide in a plating bath. If you use all the material, the waste is F007. A certain amount of the material is kept in inventory to make fresh bath solution from time to time. This material is not hazardous waste. Why? Because it is not a waste. For argument's sake, let's say that your pollution prevention program has somehow been able to eliminate the need for this particular plating bath and zinc cyanide is not needed elsewhere. All the material in inventory now has no usefulness to you. By RCRA definition, it is a waste material and a solid waste at that. So, by virtue of the P-list it is now a hazardous waste (P121)!

Now, let's revise this example. The plating need was eliminated but in its place is a metal finishing process which utilizes potassium cyanide. Is the waste from this process F007? No, but it may be D003 (characteristic for reactivity due to cyanide). Later this process too is eliminated. Unused potassium cyanide shipped as a waste is hazardous waste and is numbered P098.

Consider F001 solvent again: the waste from degreasing operations. The assigned material handler who routinely fills and drains degreasers is on the way to refill a degreaser with a drum of trichloroethylene resting on the tines of a forklift. Keeping his load close to the ground for safety causes the bottom rim of the drum to scrape across the concrete floor as he starts up an incline and this shaves metal off the rim. Liquid starts leaking out rapidly. He stops but before help arrives about two gallons have leaked out. Someone throws absorbent clay on the spill and it is swept up with a broom and put into a five gallon bucket. The rest of the material in the original drum is added to the degreaser but now we have two hazardous waste streams. The spent degreasing solvent is F001, as always. The residue from the spill is U228. The residue from cleaning the degreaser is F001, though.

Before leaving the lists, a few items must be cleaned up. You may have noticed that the list gives a code letter enclosed in parentheses (). These codes, summarized in Figure 5.16, tell you why EPA has listed this particular waste material as hazardous.

Figure 5.16
EPA Hazard Codes

Ignitible Waste	(I)
Corrosive Waste	(C)
Reactive Waste	(R)
Acute Hazardous Waste	(H)
Toxic Waste	(T)

This logic becomes important when applying for delisting, as discussed below.

The relationship between the F- and K-lists (wastes from nonspecific and specific processes) and the P- and U-lists (commercial chemicals) is the difference between used as intended and unused or used in some manner not intended. Spent trichloroethylene used in degreasing metal parts is F001 but a drum of unused trichloroethylene shipped as a waste for any reason is U228. Toluene used as a thinner for paint is part of the waste paint (D001, F003, F005). Waste paint contains several solvents in the F003 and F005 listing and all are ignitable. A drum of unused toluene declared and shipped as waste is U220.

You may hear people discuss the Appendix VIII list which is for reference only. Do not designate a solid waste as hazardous just because it has a constituent listed in Appendix VIII. Use Appendix VIII only when evaluating Material Safety Data Sheets (MSDSs) and other vendor information to determine whether your waste might be hazardous. Never use it to declare your waste hazardous.

Always remember, your material cannot be a hazardous waste if it is not a waste in the first place. A material coming out of a process to be recycled is not a hazardous waste even if it is stored for a brief period. An unused material is not necessarily a waste. However, this is no loophole to skirt around RCRA hazardous waste regulations. If, for instance, you take a waste stream from a process to lengthy storage as speculation for future recovery of material, your scheme requires a RCRA permit. If a recycled material is applied to the land and the local RCRA compliance authority decides this is use constituting disposal, a RCRA Part B is needed. If a recycling scheme involves burning of material for energy recovery, a permit is required. Reclamation of certain constituents from the hazardous waste (as opposed to recycling the entire stream) requires a permit. Consequently, these kinds of management strategies should be implemented only after negotiations with the regulators.

In one case, a machining plant bought a distillation unit to recycle degreasing solvent. The capacity of the unit was greater than their needs so they invited sister plants within the company to ship solvents to be recycled. This sounds like a good idea, doesn't it? It is. Unfortunately, the sister plants shipped more solvent to be reclaimed than could be used as reclaimed material due to customer quality requirements for cleaning processes. The receiving plant, not wanting to process the material it could not use, stored the excess used material in a side yard. A RCRA inspector alleged that this constituted storage of a hazardous waste without a permit. The receiving plants and the shipping plants were fined. The receiving plant 1) received hazardous waste from off-site without a waste analysis plan or accounting for material, 2) received it from a transporter who did not have an EPA ID number, 3) stored hazardous waste for longer than ninety days without a permit to do so, and 4) treated hazardous waste without a permit. The shipping plants 1) sent hazardous waste to an unpermitted TSDF, 2) used transportation without an EPA ID number, and 3) did not use Uniform Hazardous Waste Manifests. Recycling is good and permissible but think it through. A true recycling scheme is exempt from most RCRA requirements but a sham operation, even an accidentally sham operation, is not. Allow a state or local RCRA compliance authority to review your plans. Do not allow regulations to kill your vision but make sure your vision is clear, logical, and reality-based.

Hazardous Characteristics

After a thorough review of exemptions and the hazardous waste lists, any solid wastes remaining on the inventory have another hurtle to pass. You still have the burden of proving that your solid waste is not hazardous. The hazardous characteristics of concern are ignitability, corrosivity, reactivity, and toxicity.

Ignitability. The hazardous characteristic of ignitability is a rough measure of how easily a waste material will catch on fire, at least the vapors over the material. Fire is the first and prime hazard because it kills or maims right now whereas other hazards give us some amount of time to react in order to protect ourselves and others. If a waste liquid has a flash point less than 140°F it is hazardous waste. This definition does not apply to aqueous solutions which contain less than 10% alcohol by volume (such as beer, ale, and some wines).

The flash point is the temperature at which the vapor over a liquid pool ignites and is measured in one of two instruments per EPA methods: a Pensky-Martens Closed Cup Tester or a Setaflash Closed Cup Tester. Open cup testers have their own protocols. If a nonliquid waste is capable of causing a fire due to friction, absorption of moisture, or spontaneous chemical changes at STP (77°F, 1 atmosphere), it is a hazardous waste if it burns vigorously and persistently after ignition. A waste compressed gas that will catch on fire when released into air at STP is a hazardous waste. Finally, waste oxidizers are considered ignitable hazardous wastes by definition. Ignitable wastes are designated by the D001 code.

Corrosivity. After fire the next most critical hazard is skin contact with corrosive materials that can cause chemical burns. In fact, any waste material which quickly burns or destroys flesh is a hazardous waste. It is also a corrosive waste if it corrodes, weakens, or damages metals after only a short time. Aqueous wastes having a pH less than or equal to 2 (acidic) or greater than or equal to 12.5 (alkaline) are hazardous wastes. Alternatively, an aqueous waste liquid that corrodes SAE 1020 steel at a rate greater than 6.35 mpy (mm/year) or 0.250 ipy (inch/year) at 130°F is a corrosive hazardous waste.

Nonaqueous waste liquids are hazardous waste if they produce a solution ≤ 2 pH or ≥ 12.5 pH when mixed with an equivalent weight of water. Nonliquid waste materials are hazardous wastes if they corrode SAE 1020 steel at rates greater than 6.36 mpy (0.250 ipy) when mixed with an equivalent weight of water and maintained at 130°F. All these wastes exhibit the characteristic of corrosivity and are designated by the D002 code.

You may be thinking, "But what about cyanide? Isn't cyanide more dangerous than fire or acid?" No. Hazard is not exactly equivalent to danger. Hazard is equal to danger times the probability of the disaster. Hazard and danger are exactly equivalent only when the probability is 1.0 that the disastrous event will occur. Other factors also mitigate danger. In the case of waste reactives, they are the third priority because they require at least a two step event to be hazardous and that lowers the probability, though not the danger, of the material itself. That is why reactives are third priority in concern.

Reactivity. If a waste material is normally unstable and readily undergoes violent change without detonating, it is also a reactive waste. A waste material that reacts violently with water is a hazardous waste. Waste materials which form potentially explosive mixtures with water are reactive hazardous waste. Waste sodium metal is a good example of this kind of reactive. If toxic gas, vapor, or fume is emitted from a waste material when mixed with water, and the quantity emitted is sufficient to endanger human health or the environment, that material is a reactive hazardous waste. If a cyanide or sulfide bearing aqueous waste releases toxic gases at pH conditions between 2.0 and 12.5, and in sufficient quantity to endanger human health or the environment, it is a hazardous waste. A waste which is capable of detonation or explosive decomposition when subjected to standard temperature and pressure is a reactive waste. A material is also a hazardous waste if it will detonate or explosively react when subjected to a strong initiating source or if heated under confinement. Oil-soaked ammonium nitrate is one such reactive. DOT Forbidden Explosives are also hazardous wastes under this category. All these hazardous waste materials are reactives designated by the D003 code.

Toxicity. Toxic hazardous wastes are capable of inducing illness, disease, or genetic damage in humans or animals. If the toxic constituent affects people or animals after only a short period of exposure, it is acutely toxic. Chronic toxicity damages bodies after a long period of exposure at near background levels of concentration. The toxicity of a chemical is also affected by the potential routes of exposure: ingestion, inhalation, or dermal absorption.

Mercury from dry cell batteries, or discarded thermostats, or fluorescent light bulbs evaporates slowly and inhalation of low doses over a period of time can affect the central nervous system of exposed individuals. Remember the Mad Hatter in *Alice in Wonderland*? His madness was common among felt hatters and was due to mercury exposure. Mercury can also present acute effects after a single high dose.

Lead can also give acute effects after a single high dose. Ingested lead in low concentrations affects the central nervous system. Congress recently added a new title to the Toxic Substances Control Act to deal with lead exposure to children in public housing projects. Many older housing projects were built when lead-based paint was in vogue and now that the paint is peeling children are being affected by eating the chips. Why not just train them not to eat paint chips? Lead-based paint has a sweet, candy-like taste. How do you teach a hungry three year old not to eat candy?

Chemicals that change cellular or genetic structures in bodies are either carcinogens, mutagens, or teratogens. Carcinogens induce or catalyze uncontrolled growth of cells (cancer). Some known carcinogens are benzene, asbestos, and hexavalent chromium. Teratogens damage otherwise viable embryos or fetuses. Sometimes this damage ends in the aborted delivery of the fetus and other times it affects the normal development of the fetus. The drug phthalidamide, which made news in the 1950s, is a widely known teratogen. The movie *Teenaged Mutant Ninja Turtles* popularized the notion that mutagens evolve exposed individuals into totally new creatures. Mutagens do alter the genetic structure of the exposed individual but two things are erroneous about the Hollywood notion of mutagens. One, the exposed individual will notice no changes whatsoever, rather his as-yet-unconceived offspring will. Whereas a teratogen damages an embryo or fetus already conceived and developing in an exposed female, a mutagen damages the chromosomes of an exposed male or female who passes these damaged chromosomes on to offspring conceived after the damage occurs. Two, chromosome damage does not create new beings, rather it alters the developmental possibilities of the human or animal body as it currently exists. Evolution is the work of natural selection over many generations, not the result of passing on chromosome damage from one particular generation to the next. So, the toxic goo at the bottom of Love Canal or Stringfellow Acid Pits is not creating any upright walking, surfer lingo talking, pizza eating reptiles who perform oriental marshal arts. It's an entertaining idea, maybe, but not science.

Toxic hazardous wastes are designated according to Figure 5.17. These regulatory levels refer to the concentration of the toxic constituent in an acidic extract of the waste material after grinding.

| | **Figure 5.17** | |
| | **Toxic Waste Codes** | |
Code	Toxic Constituent	Regulatory Level, mg/l
D004	Arsenic	5.0
D005	Barium	100.0
D006	Cadmium	1.0
D007	Chromium	5.0
D008	Lead	5.0
D009	Mercury	0.2
D010	Selenium	1.0
D011	Silver	5.0
D012	Endrin	0.02
D013	Lindane	0.4
D014	Methoxychlor	10.0
D015	Toxaphene	0.5
D016	2,4-D	10.0
D017	2,4,5-TP (Silvex)	1.0
D018	Benzene	0.5
D019	Carbon Tetrachloride	1.0
D020	Chlordane	0.03
D021	Chlorobenzene	100.0
D022	Chloroform	6.0

Table 5.17 *(cont'd)*

Code	Toxic Constituent	Regulatory Level, mg/l
D023	o-Cresol	200.0[1]
D024	m-Cresol	200.0[1]
D025	p-Cresol	200.0[1]
D026	Cresol	200.0[1]
D027	1,4-Dichlorobenzene	7.5
D028	1,2-Dichloroethane	0.5
D029	1,1-Dichloroethylene	0.7
D030	2,4-Dinitrotoluene	0.13
D031	Heptachlor (and its epoxide)	0.008
D032	Hexachlorobenzene	0.13
D033	Hexachlorobutadiene	0.5
D034	Hexachloroethane	3.0
D035	Methyl Ethyl Ketone	200.0
D036	Nitrobenzene	2.0
D037	Pentachlorophenol	100.0
D038	Pyridine	5.0[2]
D039	Tetrachloroethylene	0.7
D040	Trichloroethylene	0.5
D041	2,4,5-Trichlorophenol	400.0
D042	2,4,6-Trichlorophenol	2.0
D043	Vinyl Chloride	0.2[1]

[1] If ortho-, meta- and para-Cresol concentrations cannot be differentiated, the total Cresol (D026) concentration is used. Total isomers of Cresol cannot exceed 200.0 mg/l. [2] If the quantitation limit (limit of detection) is greater than the calculated regulatory limit, then the quantitation limit becomes the regulatory level.

If the concentration is lower than the limits given, the waste does not have the characteristic of toxicity for the constituent. Concentrations greater than or equal to the regulatory level in the extract means the waste material is a hazardous waste. You are obligated to have a sample of unlisted waste subjected to the Toxic Characteristic Leachate Procedure (TCLP or TEE-Clip) for these potential constituents unless you have a reasonable argument to declare any constituent not present by virtue of your knowledge of the waste material and the process(es) that generated it. Only one TCLP is required on a representative sample unless the generating process(es) change or materials are substituted. Even if all you do is buy raw material from a new supplier, run a new TCLP. You never know.

Some TSDF contractors may require that you provide them with a TCLP less than one year old in order to do business. That is negotiable with them. It is not necessarily a regulatory requirement for you; it is for them.

Now you have split your original solid waste inventory into two categories: hazardous and nonhazardous waste streams. The definition of hazardous waste by listing is not perfect. Certainly the lists do not include all hazardous wastes and just as certainly they include some wastes that are not hazardous. Therefore, EPA has provided a procedure for delisting waste streams on an individual, case-by-case basis. The burden of proof is on the delisting petitioner and not many waste streams have been delisted over the past twenty years.

The delisting petitioner must rigorously prove that the waste stream is not hazardous due to facility-specific variations in 1) raw materials, 2) processes, and/or 3) other specific factors. The procedure requires representative sampling of the waste for characterization, especially for the characteristic(s) for which the waste stream was listed in the first place. Remember those hazard codes out to the side in the lists? Of course, sampling and testing must be conducted in accordance with EPA approved protocols. You must also demonstrate that the waste stream has no hazardous characteristics which would otherwise make it a hazardous waste by scanning for constituents listed in Appendix VIII of 40 CFR 262. If EPA is convinced, it will delist that one waste stream for your facility. Sorry, you cannot ride someone else's coat-tails on delisting but must prove your own case. EPA has two years from the day they receive a *complete* delisting petition to review and act on it.

Land disposal restrictions are an apparent point of confusion for nonexpert generalists in hazardous waste management but are not really that difficult to grasp. In 1984, Congress made it our national policy to discourage disposal of hazardous wastes in landfills, recognizing that, ultimately, some residual will end up in the ground anyway. In the early 1980s, industry had little incentive to treat hazardous waste to the point it became a nonhazardous residual or to recycle or reclaim materials, with a few notable exceptions. The land ban restrictions were intended by Congress to be the driving force for new technologies for treating waste, for waste minimization, and for recycling and reclamation. After all, the prime law controlling hazardous waste is the Resource Conservation and Recovery Act (RCRA) and until 1984 there was very little resource conservation going on, much less resource recovery. Instead it was all ending up in landfills, which are potential Stringfellow Acid Pits and Love Canals because no one can guarantee, despite financial assurance, that even the biggest and best landfills will not go bankrupt, leaving the taxpaying citizen with the invoice for the corrective action. Hence, the origin of land ban restrictions. Essentially, certain wastes (nearly all) are prohibited from storage in landfills, application on the land as nutrients, deepwell injection, and so forth, unless they have been treated to remove or reduce the hazardous characteristics or constituents. The effect of the land bans on generators of hazardous waste is a discussion reserved for another chapter.

Hazardous vs. Solid Waste

At the beginning of this section we discussed the relationship of solid and hazardous waste. Since the set of all solid waste contains both hazardous and nonhazardous waste, all hazardous wastes are solid wastes. In fact, if the waste stream is somehow not a solid waste it is impossible for it to be a hazardous waste. No non-waste material is hazardous waste. It may be a hazardous material but the key word in this discussion is waste. A lot of confusion exists about this very basic definition. As long as a material has an intended use, it is not a waste stream. On the other hand, as soon as a material has no intended use, it is a waste, no matter where in the process it happens to be. As long as it remains in process it is not regulated as a solid waste but it is a solid waste (unless exempted). Understanding this definition and its implications is absolutely vital to managing hazardous waste in compliance with regulations.

Understanding mixtures is also crucial in managing hazardous wastes. A good rule of thumb is: do not mix wastes, keep each waste stream segregated from others. If you think you have a reason to violate this heuristic, make sure you understand the implications before you do. For instance, if your plant uses three different degreasing solvents (F001) and you cannot recycle them separately, you can mix them together. However, if they are recyclable streams you may complicate the recycling process by mixing them. Ask the recycling contractor about it. A similar example is the mixing of the aqueous cleaning solution used to clean a vapor degreaser with spent F001 solvent removed from the degreaser. Water in a solvent requires more energy, hence cost, when distilling. Although you can mix the two streams, the additional cost of recycling will be passed on to you.

Another mixing situation is the use of chlorinated solvent spray guns at metalworking machines. The F001 solvent mixes with the machine coolant (typically a nonhazardous waste stream) rendering it a hazardous waste when removed from the machine. The moral of this example is: segregate not only waste streams but move upstream into the process and segregate hazardous materials from nonhazardous as best you can (waste minimization). If a shipment of waste oil from your plant that usually costs $1,000 is ever invoiced for $15,000 due to high chloride content, you will appreciate this advice. Also, be very careful about intentional mixing of hazardous wastes with nonhazardous materials. This can be construed as treatment of hazardous waste and requires a RCRA Part B permit. Do you have one for the mixing activity?

Any waste or by-product generated due to treatment, storage, or disposal of hazardous waste is hazardous waste by definition. In other words, any residue or material derived from a hazardous waste is also hazardous waste.

Recycled materials are solid waste under certain conditions as discussed earlier. Discuss planned recycling activities with the RCRA compliance authority if a residue is applied to land, or the accumulation and storage of the material before or after recycling is long-term, or the material or residue is to be burned for energy or some constituents will be reclaimed. These activities may require a RCRA permit.

Regulated recycling has some notable restrictions. Sludges and process by-products that are hazardous by characteristic(s) only and not listed by EPA as hazardous waste are not solid waste when reclaimed. Also, you can reclaim or accumulate speculatively commercial products (which have not been used). These are not solid waste unless you declare them such and ship them to a TSDF. Waste material that is directly and totally reused in the generating process or totally used in another process as feedstock is not solid waste. Total use or reuse means none of it is being reclaimed and all of the material is involved as a raw material, though it may border on being off-spec. A waste material that can be used as a substitute for a commercial product is not a solid waste as long as it has an intended use.

Empty containers can be solid waste and therefore are potential hazardous waste. If a container has no intended use and once contained a hazardous material that would be a hazardous waste by listing or characteristic, then the container itself is hazardous waste unless certain conditions apply. Some plants crush all their drums and ship them off-site as hazardous waste. To avoid having to handle containers as hazardous waste merely requires some common sense management.

As long as 1) no constituent of a mixture held in a container as a commercial product was listed as an acutely hazardous waste and 2a) the residue amounts to less than three inches, or 2b) the residue amounts to less than 1% of the volume if the container has a volume greater than 110 gallons, it is empty per regulations and may be handled as solid waste. If the residual volume exceeds this amount or the material or a constituent is listed as an acutely hazardous waste, the container itself must be handled as a hazardous waste. If a container that held a material listed as an acutely hazardous waste is triple rinsed with steam or clean water and afterwards holds less than one inch of residue, the container is empty and exempt from hazardous waste regulations.

CONTROL OPTIONS

The need to obtain a permit implies that a plant has something greater than zero discharge. Some waste stream is being added to the atmosphere (Air Operating Permit) or surface water (either NPDES or Pretreatment Permit) or a hazardous waste is being treated, stored, or disposed (RCRA Part B Permit). Air or water permits put a limit on the pollutants that may be discharged from the plant by means of permit limitations while the land ban restrictions limit the TSDF discharges. Operating within limits requires one or more of three tactics: source control, fugitive control, emission reduction.

Source Control

This tactic starts back in the process. Can raw materials be changed? The process? Anything to reduce the pollutant load in the discharge stream. A healthy pollution prevention effort is your best tool to control pollution at the source. Get everyone excited about it. Become a pollution prevention cheerleader.

Fugitive Control

The next tactic is to reduce or eliminate fugitive emissions from leaky valves, pumps, and fittings. Reduce the VOC content of coatings. Eliminate vapor degreasers.

Emission Reduction

The final tactic, emission reduction, is the subject of subsequent chapters. When all else fails, you must put some sort of emission controls on the end of your stack or wastewater discharge pipe. Emission reduction amounts to end-of-pipe controls.

DATA TRACKING AND REPORTING

Your permit will require the collection of waste stream samples, analysis, and evaluation of pollutant loading.

Organizing and Maintaining Data

Maintain files of 1) sampling records, manifests, and chain-of-custody forms, 2) analytical reports, 3) calculations performed to evaluate permitted waste streams and 4) reports to authorities by media. Organization of files was discussed earlier.

Computerizing Data

Many companies are tracking analysis of waste streams in computerized databases. This allows easy statistical analysis, graphic presentation of data, report generation, and other advantages.

Reporting to Enforcement Agencies

Permits require some form of regular reporting to the enforcement authority to inform it how you are doing relative to your discharge limitations. The reporting is not on the honor system. You must maintain data files as discussed above in order to demonstrate to a compliance inspector how you arrive at the numbers in your reports.

In wastewater compliance, your NPDES permit will require the submission of a Discharge Monitoring Report (DMR) on a regular basis. Pretreatment permits require a regular compliance report, too, and many jurisdictions require that you use the NPDES DMR forms. However frequently you must submit, the DMR is a formatted report on carbonless paper generated by the enforcement agency's computer specifically for your facility. You calculate pollutant loadings in your discharge and fill in the blanks. Excursions must be reported orally by telephone, usually long before you send the DMR.

Working with wastewater parameters is easy. To convert from ppm (parts per million) to mass units (pounds per day) all you need to know is the concentration in ppm or milligrams per liter (mg/l) and the flow rate of your wastewater stream. For a solution of chemicals in water, mg/l = ppm. This does not hold true for the concentration of chemicals in oils or other chemicals (where ppm = mg/l X specific gravity), but for water the two units are essentially identical (specific gravity is nearly equal to 1.0 for water).

To convert from concentration units in water to mass units in water, use a simple formula:

$$lb/day = MGD \times 8.34 \times ppm \qquad\qquad [5.8]$$

where:

MGD = million gallons per day (GPD/1,000,000)
8.34 = density of water, lb/gallon

In air emission monitoring, maintain records of analyses and report only when you have an *exceedance*. Calculations in air monitoring are complicated and far beyond the scope of our discussion here. For air emissions you need to 1) take continuing education courses on how to do the calculations, 2) hire a specialized staff member, or 3) contract a consulting firm or stack tester to do it for you.

PERMITS BY MEDIA

The discussion below takes a brief look at permits according to media: water, air, hazardous waste.

Wastewater Permits

Water pollution control laws and regulations are broad and encompass many, but not all, industrial operations. Water pollution control programs operate by permit issuance, review of engineering, and other technical documents which describe the wastewater treatment system, field inspections, overview of self-monitoring reports, and enforcement. Wastewater permits are required for all discharges of wastes to waters of the U.S. (or state waters), any industrial wastewater to publicly owned treatment works (POTW or sewer district) and, in some cases, for operation of other wastewater disposal systems, whether or not they have a discharge, such as storage basins, land farming, and recycling systems, among other activities.

Application for wastewater discharge permits must be made on forms provided by EPA or the state authority. If the form does not fit the situation, fill it out as completely as possible and provide additional information by means of tables, drawings, and appendices to the form.

An application for a wastewater permit must be submitted at least 180 days (six months) before the regulated activity begins. When the office writing the permit receives the application, it will make a preliminary determination of completeness. You will be required to supply missing information before the permitting process continues. When complete, the application will be reviewed to make a preliminary determination of applicability.

A draft permit is forwarded to the applicant for review and comment. The applicant has thirty days to request a meeting to discuss changes. Minor changes may be discussed over the telephone but typically a face-to-face is required for more substantial changes. A letter covering a marked up draft permit may also be appropriate in some cases.

Once the applicant and the permit writing office agree on the draft (silence is consent to go ahead after the comment period expires) public comment is invited. The permit writing office files a public notice of the proposed permit (usually in the local newspaper) and the public has thirty days to file a petition for a public hearing. If the permitting authority decides that public interest is significant, a hearing will be scheduled, giving the public at least thirty days notice. After public input, the permit writing office recommends approval or denial of the permit to the permit authority. Final decisions of the permit authority are appealed in court.

Types of Permits. For industry, one or both of two basic wastewater permits is required: NPDES and indirect discharge permits.

An NPDES permit must be obtained before discharging wastewater into the waters of the U.S. Any material added to water or any physical characteristic imparted to water (heat, pH, color) is a pollutant. A plant must obtain an NPDES permit if it is a point source, that is, a discreet discharge point. A rain ditch, pipe, or container is a point source. A lawn, parking lot, hillside, or field is an area source. Process wastewater and stormwater runoff must be permitted. Many times an NPDES permit will be required for noncontact cooling water discharged to the waters of the U.S.

Application for an NPDES permit must be filed before construction begins. If your plant is already operating and has no permit, contact your permitting authority immediately unless you have correspondence in your files that explicitly exempts your operations. Applications for renewal of a permit must be received by the authority at least 180 days prior to expiration of the old one. If your application for renewal is received on time, the old permit continues in force while the permitting agency writes and approves the new one. If you file late, you are technically operating without a permit after midnight the day it expires. Timely submission of the renewal application makes the difference between operating in compliance after that or not.

In addition to the limitations placed on your discharge stream (flow, concentrations of specific pollutants, mass limits, pH, temperature, *etc.*), the CWA permits have special, boiler-plate provisions. These clauses are

1) bypass, 2) upset, 3) halt or abate, 4) duty to mitigate, 5) notification, and 6) operation and maintenance.

By virtue of the permit, no waste stream may be diverted from any part of a treatment facility. When this happens it is called *bypass* and it is prohibited where it causes the discharge limits to be exceeded. Bypass is allowed in emergency conditions in order to avoid severe property damage, personal injury, or loss of life, but the burden of proof is on the permittee. If a large quantity of flammable solvent were accidentally spilled into your floor sumps, you may bypass the treatment system in order to prevent an explosion. However, now you face soil and surface water cleanup if it were an NPDES discharge. If it were a pretreatment discharge, fines and litigation are possible should the bypassed discharge get into the city sewers and explode. If faced with an emergency bypass, choose the lesser of the evils unless you can divert to some containment area. Bypass is allowed if it does not cause discharge limits to be exceeded but only for essential maintenance to insure efficient operation. You may not routinely bypass for no particular reason.

Upset is the unintentional, temporary violation of discharge limitations due to factors beyond your control. An upset is your defense against noncompliant discharges if you have a technology-based permit and if you file a notice within 24-hours of the upset event. Permit violations caused by operational error, improper design, inadequate facilities, lack of preventive maintenance, carelessness, or improper operation are not upsets. Therefore, when claiming an upset you can expect a visit from an enforcement official who will want you to demonstrate to her the specific cause of the upset: that you were operating the system properly at the time, that the system is being maintained properly, *etc.* Since it is usually difficult, if not impossible, to determine the exact cause of an upset, circumstantial evidence will usually suffice. Be able to convince the inspector you did a thorough job of investigating the matter even if you did not determine the exact cause. You should also demonstrate to her that a positive corrective action has been or is being implemented. If you have a water quality model based permit, sorry, no upsets.

As a permittee you are required to control your discharge within limits at all times. That is the implication of the discharge limits in your permit. So, what is required if you cannot control the discharge? Whatever is necessary to get back into compliance and stay in compliance. If it takes shutting down the production operation to do that, then that's what it takes. Often you can curtail production to get back into compliance without a complete shutdown. Some small facilities store wastewater for awhile. One very small facility contains wastewater in drums until they get the wastewater system under control. (Be careful of RCRA rules here.) Another facility rented five 10,000 gallon over-the-road tankers for the duration of their indefensible upset. The *halt or reduce activity* clause requires you to do whatever is necessary (without violating some other rule) to maintain compliance. The expected solution, besides finding the problem and fixing it, is to control the discharge by reducing or halting production. If you choose to accumulate wastewater during a frustrating plant upset, be sure to segregate those aqueous streams treated as wastewater that are otherwise hazardous waste. If the storage exceeds 90-days you will violate RCRA generator status. If you have a RCRA Permit for storage, does it include storage of aqueous wastes normally treated in the wastewater system?

If preventive measures have been taken and your discharge is still noncompliant for whatever reason, and before you can halt it, the environment is damaged in some way, then you have a *duty to mitigate*. This clause in your permit requires all reasonable steps to be taken to minimize or prevent environmental damage and prompt mitigation once it does occur.

If you perform any physical alterations or add equipment, you must provide the permit authority with *notification*. Permit authorities have interpreted this clause to mean alterations or additions which could significantly change the nature of the discharge or which would increase the quantity of pollutants.

You are required to provide *proper operation and maintenance* for your treatment system. Generally, an inspector likes to see an operator's daily log sheet and maintenance checklists or other administrative evidence that maintenance is being routinely performed. Of course, the wastewater treatment systems should give the appearance that maintenance is being performed, as physical evidence. That is why housekeeping is so important.

An indirect discharge (or pretreatment) permit is required of any industry discharging wastewater into the public sewer. The local sewage treatment plant (POTW) receives a State Operating Permit from your state and an NPDES Permit to discharge effluent into a nearby stream. The POTW typically cannot deal with certain industrial wastewaters, therefore the industry must treat the wastewater before discharging it into the sewer (hence, pretreatment). Not every industrial facility has to pretreat wastewater but most do. A pretreatment permit is required for the reasons listed in Figure 5.18.

The local POTW is supposed to develop and implement a pretreatment permit program. In many localities this is not how the pretreatment program works. While some POTWs have developed and received approval for administering permit programs, most have not. The state compliance authorities, and in a few cases the regional EPA office, administer the pretreatment permit program in most states.

Regardless who administers the pretreatment program, if your plant discharges any industrial wastes to a public sewer system, a permit is required if you meet the conditions outlined in Figure 5.18. If you do not have one, go in search of the permitting authority. Start with the regional EPA office if none are found among the state, county, or municipal government listings of your telephone directory.

Figure 5.18
Who Needs A Pretreatment Permit?

A plant needs to obtain a pretreatment permit if it discharges into a public sewer and the wastewater:

1. Is subject to federal pretreatment standards,
2. Would cause interference with the proper operation of the POTW,
3. Would pass through the POTW causing it to violate state water quality standards,
4. Would contaminate the POTW's sludges so that they could not be properly disposed as nonhazardous solid waste,
5. Amounts to 25,000 gallons per day or more, even if none of the above apply, or
6. Amounts to 5% or more of the POTW's intake, even if none of the above apply.

How to Get a Wastewater Permit. The procedure to get a wastewater permit has some similarities to getting an air permit. First, establish effluent limits. This will require a thorough search through the CWA regulations. Categorical dischargers have technology-based limits spelled out in the regulations. Next, establish a proposed compliance schedule for your plant. A date when it will be in full compliance and major milestones on the way to achieving full compliance. When NPDES and pretreatment regulations were first implemented back in the early 1980s, deadlines for compliance were established. If you do not have a permit but are required to have one, the bad news is this: you have long passed all deadlines. As new regulations and treatment standards are promulgated (issued) there will be additional guidelines for certain facilities but the original deadlines have come and gone. Applications for new facilities or newly regulated facilities are required to be in the authority's hands 180 days prior to startup or by the deadline stated in the new standard. Applications from existing facilities should be submitted as soon as possible after discovering a permit is required. It is a good idea, in many instances, to have the corporate attorney write a letter to the authority explaining that the requirement has been discovered and suggesting a date for delivery of the permit application.

Operating Requirements. Wastewater treatment (or pretreatment) facilities must be operated at maximum expected efficiency at all times. Monitoring, recordkeeping, and other requirements stated in the permit have the full force of law, and all terms and conditions in the permit must be complied with exactly. Other requirements in regulations, even though not explicitly mentioned in the permit, are also implicit. Any process modification, which may result in an increased volume of wastewater or an increased pollutant load, must be reported to the permit authority in advance for approval.

Notices, Hearings, and Appeals. The permit writing office will post notice of the pending permit once the draft is written, while the permit is in review. Interested parties have thirty days to submit written comments or to file a petition for a public hearing. The permitting authority decides whether sufficient public interest for a hearing exists and, if so, schedules one giving a minimum of thirty days notice. After the hearing, all comments from the hearing, and written comments received, are considered with regard to the permit request and the authority makes a decision to approve or deny the permit. Final decisions are appealed to chancery court or court of equity or equivalent.

Air Permits

Besides state and local air regulations, emissions into the air are regulated by the National Ambient Air Quality Standards (NAAQS), regulations for the Prevention of Significant Deterioration (PSD), New Source Performance Standards (NSPS), and National Emission Standards for Hazardous Air Pollutants (NESHAP). These regulations collectively define the maximum permissible ambient concentrations of air contaminants and establish technology-based air emission standards. The air permit program works through the issuance of permits with public participation (in some cases), review of engineering and technical documents which define the emitting processes and their controls, and field inspections which verify data submissions.

NAAQS define ambient concentration levels that are acceptable in the U.S. These levels apply across your fence line and in the atmosphere over your plant. Stated in terms of maximum concentrations, NAAQS are not emission limits for industry, rather they are the goal that defines what clean is with regard to air quality. Air Quality Management Districts (AQMD) are charged with the responsibility of achieving and maintaining the NAAQS within the district. When the AQMD achieves NAAQS level for a pollutant, it has become an attainment area for that pollutant. That is, the AQMD has attained the national goal with respect to the pollutant. A nonattainment area then is an AQMD where a pollutant concentration goal has not been achieved. NAAQS are defined for criteria pollutants and are indirectly enforced on industrial plants by modeling during the permit process. The goal of Title I of CAAA is to get nonattainment areas into compliance with NAAQS. Typically, it is easier to get a new source permit or to get approval to significantly increase an existing source in an attainment area than in a nonattainment area. Primary NAAQS are listed in Figure 5.19.

Figure 5.19
Primary NAAQS

Criteria Pollutant	Primary NAAQS
Ozone (O_3)	0.120 ppm (1-hr average)
Carbon Monoxide (CO)	9 ppm (8-hr average)
	35 ppm (1-hr average)
Particulate Matter (PM-10)	150 $\mu g/m^3$ (24-hr average)
	50 $\mu g/m^3$ (annual average)
Sulfur Dioxide (SO_2)	0.140 ppm (24-hr average)
	0.03 ppm (annual average)
Nitrogen Oxides (NO_x as NO_2)	0.053 ppm (annual average)
Lead (Pb)	1.5 $\mu g/m^3$ (quarterly avg)

Only thirteen states have no nonattainment areas for ozone and three of these have borders with nonattainment areas. Ozone is the one NAAQS that affects U.S. industry more than any of the others. Power plants contribute heavily to sulfur dioxide and nitrogen dioxide but many industries emit volatile organic chemicals (VOCs) which react with sunlight to produce ozone in the troposphere where it has environmental consequences on humans, animals, and plants. Ozone is the major contributor to urban smog as known in the U.S. The south coast of California (San Francisco, Santa Barbara, Los Angeles, San Diego) and the northeast corridor (from Delaware, Maryland, and Pennsylvania northeastward including those states; called the Northeast Transport Region) are major nonattainment areas. Elevated ozone levels are worse in the summer months because of the warm temperatures and extended hours of sunlight during a day. Temperature, sunlight, and VOCs inevitably lead to smog. Therefore states and AQMDs restrict VOC emissions of industry.

Whether or not your plant is considered a major source and the extent to which it is regulated for VOCs depends on the ozone attainment in your AQMD. Figure 5.20 shows the thresholds which define major source for some nonattainment situations. Figure 5.21 shows how the classification of an ozone nonattainment area redefines major source. A major source may also be categorical, that is, one of a list of twenty-eight categories established by Congress.

In order to achieve NAAQS, the state or AQMD adopts regulations that require sources to obtain operating permits and install reasonably available control technology (RACT) for VOC and NO_x emissions. This control equipment is defined as technology generally recognized to be technically and economically achievable for a majority of existing sources. Permitting authorities will use facility air emission inventories to determine whether RACT is applicable. Unlike ozone, carbon monoxide attainment does not affect industry that much. If a source has the potential to emit more than 50 TPY, it must be required to install control equipment. Mostly, however, CO is a matter of motor vehicle and transportation control measures rather than industrial control.

Figure 5.20
Major Source Threshold

Source Situation	Potential to Emit, TPY
VOC emitter in ozone non-attainment area	10 - 100
VOC emitter in Northeast Transport Region	50
NO_x emitter in ozone non-attainment area	10 - 100
NO_x emitter in Northeast Transport Region	100
CO in a serious nonattainment area	50
PM in a serious PM-10 nonattainment area	70

TPY = tons per year

Figure 5.21			
Ozone Nonattainment Area Specifications			
Ozone Classification	Level, ppm	Major VOC Source	Compliance Date
Extreme	>0.280	10 TPY	11/2010
Severe	0.180-0.280	25 TPY	11/2005-07
Serious	0.160-0.180	50 TPY	11/1999
Moderate	0.138-0.160	100 TPY	11/1996
Marginal	0.121-0.138	100 TPY	11/1993

All areas that are nonattainment for particulate matter must implement reasonably available control measures (RACM). After December 31, 1994, these areas must require best available control measures (BACM) with an attainment deadline of December 31, 2001.

EPA was mandated by the Clean Air Act Amendments of 1990 to develop technology-based regulation of sources of hazardous air pollutants (HAPs) and to limit their emissions over the next ten years (to 2000). Limits are to be placed on 174 categories of industrial sources emitting substantial quantities of HAPs by placing emission allowances on each source. EPA does not have to be paralyzed while trying to conduct risk assessments of these pollutants because they have been declared HAPs by law. However, EPA must still establish an allowance or limit which reflects the maximum achievable control technology (MACT) for that category. MACT are the controls used by the cleanest 12% of a source category. Affected sources are given three years after the effective date of a MACT standard to comply. The accuracy of the emission inventory, by the way, will be an important factor in determining the applicability of MACT, especially for borderline facilities. After MACT has been implemented, EPA is to conduct residual risk determinations to further control categories of sources whose emissions still present major health risks. Again, an accurate emissions inventory will influence residual risk outcome for those facilities with marginally high risk. Figure 5.22 gives the EPA implementation schedule for Title III CAAA dealing with HAPs.

Figure 5.22
Title III Hazardous Air Pollutants

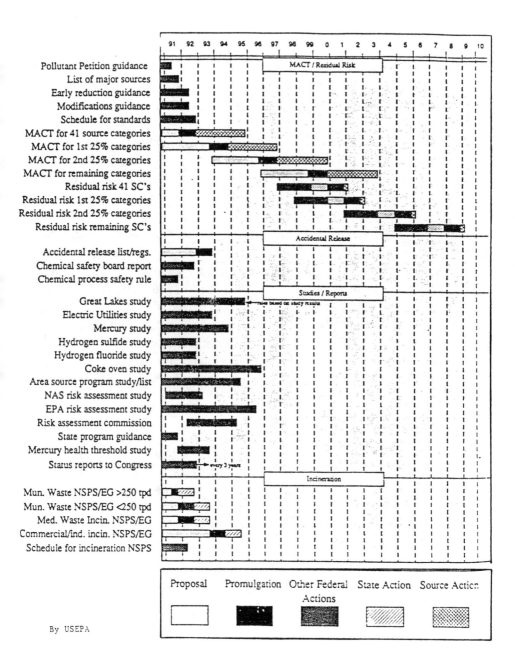

By USEPA

Types of Permits. A permit is required for the construction and operation of sources emitting air contaminants. Applications are generally submitted on forms supplied by the state or regional EPA office. However, if the form does not fit your situation, submit pertinent information in your own format (which must be easily understandable, of course). Engineering data accompanies the permit application in order to define emission rates, types of emitting processes, and stack parameters. Additional information may be required after the agency reviews the initial submittal.

If your company proposes to construct a new facility ("source" in air permitting language) or just plans on modifying an existing source, an application for a permit to construct an air emission source is required 180 days (six months) *before* construction or installation commences. Do you make decisions more quickly than that? Sorry, you may attempt to negotiate a quicker groundbreaking date but 180 days is the requirement if your attempt is unsuccessful. Do not expect to get an agreement if you have already started construction. Will you have to pay a penalty if you have already begun construction, or completed it, and then, for whatever reason, begin the permitting process? It depends. You certainly can be made to pay a penalty. However, it depends on whether you impacted the environment significantly, applied late before, and so on.

State operating permits are required of plants that have begun normal production operations and emit air contaminants. Very few industrial plants do not emit air contaminants.

Title V Operating Permits. Nearly all sources of air emissions are required to apply for and obtain an operating permit under the mandate of the Clean Air Act Amendments of 1990. This is called the Title V operating permit or the federal operating permit. Existing major sources, new sources and even sources whose operations were grandfathered (that is, exempt from permit requirements because it pre-existed regulations) must have the new operating permit in order to operate. Permitted facilities may not operate in violation of their permit. A facility that must have a permit under the law may not operate without one. Permitted facilities must comply with the permit conditions which will contain all the requirements for compliance with air quality regulations. These requirements have been referred to as a compliance shield for the permittee. The shield is a two-edged sword, cutting in both directions, though. Permitted facilities must submit an annual (sometimes more often)certification that reasonable inquiry has been made into the accuracy of compliance information, both in the permit application and subsequent information. The certification must also describe any periods of noncompliance, state how the situation was corrected and list steps taken to prevent recurrence of the problem. The potential consequences for the corporate officer who signs the certification are "unprecedented in their severity," per Kuryla and Jones.

Who needs to have a Title V Permit? Major Title V sources are HAP emitters of 10 TPY or more of one HAP species or 25 TPY or more of all HAP species or 100 TPY or more of all other pollutants. A source which may emit more than a threshold quantity of certain air toxics must have a permit. Any source subject to a HAP Standard or a new source subject to a New Source Performance Standard require a federal operating permit. Electric generating units subject to Title IV (acid rain) must have a permit. Figure 5.23 gives a decision tree to determine whether you need a Title V Permit. If in doubt, ask the state or regional EPA office.

Figure 5.23
Title V: Operating Permits

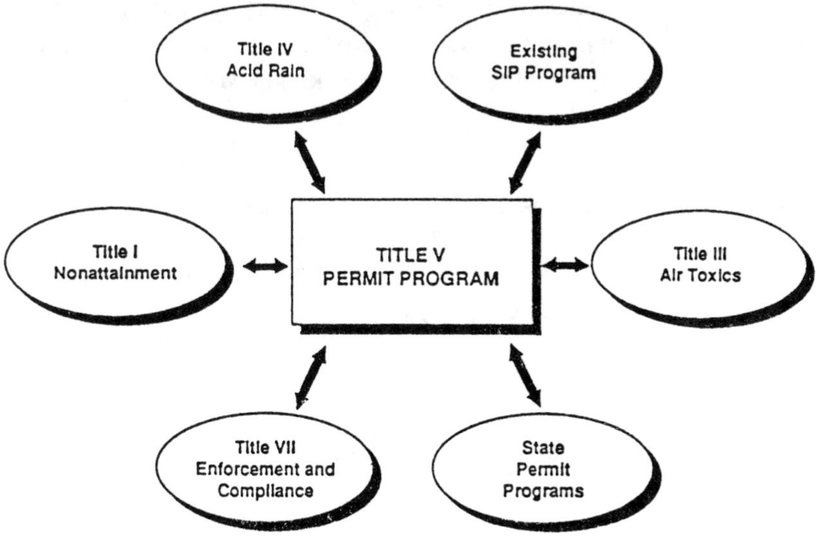

Prevention of Significant Deterioration. What if you operate a process that has air emissions in an attainment area? A PSD (Prevention of Significant Deterioration) Permit is required if you build or modify a major source in an attainment area. How does EPA define a major source and major modification in an attainment area? The PSD program applies to major sources emitting over 250 TPY or to any of twenty-eight categories of industries which emit over 100 TPY.

How to Get an Air Permit. After receiving your completed application the permit writing office will review it for completeness. If not satisfactory, you will receive a letter itemizing informational requirements. Once all data is received, the writing office will review the information in detail and come to its own conclusions about the impact of your plant on the atmosphere. That is why your information is so critical. The more it is technically complete and logically presented the quicker it can be verified as accurate. Usually, within six months this office will recommend approval, denial, or conditional approval to the permitting authority. Typically, you may make an appeal to the permitting authority within a specified time frame (usually twenty days) if you are not happy with the decision.

Plan the steps necessary to obtain a permit and do them. This includes identifying sources, making an emissions inventory, preparing documents to support the application (such as drawings and plans), researching applicable regulations, and, if required, making a MACT determination. Permits are the critical documents for compliance. Figure 5.24 shows how the Title V Permit controls compliance with the other pieces of CAAA.

Figure 5.24
Do You Need A Federal Permit?

1. Determine sources.

2. Inventory emissions.

3. 10 TPY any HAP or 25 TPY combination?

4. 100 TPY of any pollutant or combination?

Figure 5.24 *(cont'd)*

5. Major Stationary Source for VOC, NOx, PM-10 in nonattainment area?
If yes to any 3-5, Major Source --> PERMIT
If no to all 3-5, go to 6

6. Is source an industry category subject to new source performance standards (NSPS)?
If yes, go to 7
If no, go to 8

7. Built or modified after NSPS rulemaking?
If no, go to 8
If yes, go to 10

8. Any amount of toxic pollutants emitted?
9. Is source a fossil-fuel-fired device subject to acid rain regulations?
If yes, go to 10
If no, go to 11

10. Is category exempt from permitting?
If yes, go to 12
If no, go to 13

11. Does source require specific air permits from EPA regardless?
If no, go to 12
If yes, go to 13

12. No federal permit required. State operating permit may be required.

13. Federal permit required but state may defer.

After Kuryla and Jones.

The process typically includes application submittal, review, public hearing, and approval or denial by the authority. Certain permits require public hearing by their nature, as defined by regulation, but others may come to a public hearing if the public expresses any significant interest in it. Two or three inquiries may be all that is required to be considered significant interest in some quarters.

A permit usually specifies operating requirements such as emission limits, methods of operation of processes and control equipment, operation and maintenance requirements of control equipment, emissions testing, self-monitoring requirements, and reporting requirements. These conditions are tailored to the individual plant which must strictly comply with them.

RCRA Permits

Generators of hazardous waste are allowed ninety days to store the hazardous waste in containers or tanks before shipping it to a permitted TSDF (treatment, storage, disposal facility). This period is given to allow for the accumulation of a truckload of containers or a full-tank for bulk shipments. At the end of ninety days the generator must ship regardless of the amount accumulated or get into a permitting situation.

Notification of Hazardous Waste Activity. If you are a generator, you must submit a notification to EPA, usually via a state RCRA authority, that you are engaged in such activities and report the EPA Waste Numbers of the different waste streams you handle. This is accomplished by filling out EPA Form 8700-12, Notification of Regulated Waste Activities, which is also used to report used oil activities. This notification only has to be submitted once unless changes occur in waste streams, which change the EPA Waste Numbers reported, or new waste streams with different numbers. It is a good idea to review waste streams periodically and file a revised copy of the 8700-12 to insure you have reported all the different Waste Numbers your plant generates. By regulation, you have thirty days after generating a new stream to report it on 8700-12 (unless it is the same waste number as another stream).

What is a Generator? If you generate 2,200 pounds or more of hazardous waste in any single month or if you accumulate 2,200 pounds in any time period, you are a generator. If you generate less than 2,200 pounds but more than 220 pounds in any given month and accumulate less than 2,200 pounds before shipping the waste off-site, you are a small quantity generator. A very small quantity generator is one who generates 220 pounds or less in any given month and ships it off-site before accumulating 2,200 pounds. Conditional exemptions from most regulations are given to the latter category of facilities. Only 2.2 pounds of acutely hazardous waste makes one a generator.

Do you need a permit? Hazardous waste activities except for generator storage for shipment less than ninety days require a RCRA permit. Nonhazardous waste activities, such as the processing or disposal of any solid waste or sludge, typically require a Solid Waste Permit from state authorities. Exemptions from the latter include disposal on your own property for nonhazardous solid waste. Applications for solid waste permits include site location, hydrological conditions, geological conditions, content and quantity of waste, engineering specifications, facility operating plan, and ultimate disposition of the waste. It goes without saying that this waste can have no impact on the environment and your management should investigate all alternatives thoroughly before deciding to dispose or process solid waste on site unless that is your business.

Permits issued under the authority of the Resource Conservation and Recovery Act (RCRA) are required for the operation and modification of existing facilities or for the construction of new facilities for the treatment, storage, or disposal of hazardous waste. The application for a hazardous waste permit consists of two parts: Part A and Part B. A permit is required in order to construct and operate a new facility, however, land treatment facilities and incinerators may go through a trial period in order to demonstrate their ability to perform properly under operating conditions. This period is called a trial burn for incinerators and a land treatment demonstration for land treatment facilities. These facilities then obtain a temporary permit that is enforced during the trial period. Once the demonstration is completed successfully the facility applies to modify its permit to set final operating conditions based on trial data.

As in other types of permitting situations the process for obtaining a RCRA permit is 1) submittal of an application, 2) administrative review of the application, 3) draft permit, 4) public comment, 5) finalizing permit, and 6) modifying, maintaining, or terminating permit. The RCRA permit process is unique in that the application is submitted in two phases. Another unique feature of the RCRA permitting process is that other laws may affect the permitting process. These laws are the Wild and Scenic Rivers Act, the National Historic Preservation Act of 1966, the Endangered Species Act, the Coastal Zone Management Act, and the Fish and Wildlife Coordination Act. Whenever one of these laws applies in the location desired for the permitted facility its procedures must also be followed. The regulation at 40 CFR 270.3 discusses the impact of these laws on the RCRA permitting process.

Preparing a Part A Application. Part A is brief and includes general information to let the authority know the facility exists and what is intended. A standard form is provided by EPA or the state RCRA authority. Site location information must be included. This part also identifies facility status: existing, modification, planned. Techniques of treatment, storage, or disposal used at the facility must be identified. The type and quantity of wastes must be described. A scale drawing of the facility and, if available, photographs are included in the Part A application.

Preparing a Part B Application. The Part B is a much more extensive document. A Part B typically requires several three-ring binders to assemble all the information required. Detailed technical information is required in no specific format, although a checklist will be provided to you. You may have heard horror stories about time and money invested in Part B applications but the process of preparing one is straightforward and most haggling is caused by the failure of the preparer to follow directions. Other reasons many expensive Part B applications are turned down are poor site selection or failure to involve the community in the planning and decision-making processes. Consequently, it is absolutely essential to make contact with the assigned project officer of the permitting authority and to have frequent telephone conversations and meetings with her.

The Part B includes an extensive description of the facility. The results of chemical analysis of waste streams must be included. Also, the results of physical testing are included. One section describes the security procedures at the facility and lists available security equipment as well as fire protection and emergency communication equipment. A copy of the hazardous waste contingency plan is made part of the application. A description of procedures, structures, and equipment used to prevent leaks, spills, accidents, exposures, and contamination is another major requirement. Procedures, structures, and equipment to mitigate impact of equipment failure are also required. Permitted RCRA facilities require demonstrations of financial security and a history of compliance. Also the commercial facility must demonstrate the need for its services in order to receive a permit.

Facilities that existed before November 19, 1980 were granted Interim Status and given deadlines for submitting their Part B applications. The last of these deadlines expired in 1988. New facilities submit their Part A and B simultaneously at least 180 days prior to the date on which physical construction starts. Sometimes, though, a Part A is accepted in advance by the state RCRA authority in order to investigate siting acceptability. After the administrative review, the permit authority either approves the application or issues a Notice of Deficiency. The TSDF owner/operator then must supply additional information in order for the application process to proceed. EPA reviews the application after the state authority and both EPA and the state must find it acceptable. Evaluation is lengthy—up to three years. The RCRA permit incorporates the application as conditions to be met by the permittee. Other permit conditions may also be spelled out as well as a compliance schedule if the facility is not already in compliance. The permit is good for ten years except land disposal permits which expire in five years.

Stormwater Permits

Amendments to the Federal Water Pollution Control Act (now called Clean Water Act) in 1972 required the issuance of an NPDES permit to any point source discharging a pollutant to navigable waters of the U.S. The Water Quality Act of 1987 added Section 402(p) to the Clean Water Act, requiring NPDES permits for stormwater discharges from industrial activities. EPA stormwater regulations promulgated on November 16, 1990 set forth which industrial activities require permits. Stormwater permits are required for many industries, mining operations, permitted

TSDFs, landfills, salvage yards, transportation facilities, large wastewater treatment plants, and construction sites covering more than five acres. Industries identified by certain Standard Industrial Classification (SIC) codes require permits only if material handling equipment or activities, raw materials, intermediate products, products, waste materials, by-products, or industrial machinery are exposed to stormwater.

Types of Permits. There were originally three ways to get a stormwater permit: NOI for general permit, group application, individual application. The group application is no longer available.

Many industrial facilities choose to submit a Notice of Intent (NOI) for General Stormwater Permit Coverage. The NOI gives basic information about the facility and receiving stream. An NOI must be submitted at least ninety days prior to commencing operations. NOIs for construction sites must be submitted at least forty-five days prior to commencing construction activity. Other facilities, when the regulations first came into effect, chose to submit a two part application with a group of facilities with similar stormwater discharges. In Part 1 of the application, each facility submitted nonquantitative information on who and where they were. The group submitted one Part 1 for everyone in the group on or before September 30, 1991. Part 2, containing detailed information on each plant plus sampling data on at least ten percent of the plants in the group of ten members or more, was due on October 1, 1992. According to Perrich, the EPA received over 1,300 group applications instead of an expected 100 and quickly began encouraging groups to disband in favor of individual or general permit application processes. Today the process is not available.

The individual application is submitted by one plant for itself and consists of completing EPA Forms 1 and 2F. This is the normal NPDES approach to permitting. These applications were initially due on October 1, 1992 for existing facilities and now must be submitted at least ninety days prior to commencement of regulated activities for new plants. The individual application is similar to an NPDES permit application. A site map and estimate of impervious areas (areas where stormwater will run off instead of soaking into the ground) is required. Also any materials which may be exposed to stormwater must be identified. Associated outdoors materials management and on-site disposal practices must be discussed in the application. The location and description of existing structural and nonstructural controls to reduce pollutants in stormwater runoff must also be described. Structural controls include catchment basins, containment ponds, diversion dikes, etc. Nonstructural controls amount to management practices and policies on housekeeping, where work is performed, training, etc. All stormwater outfalls must be evaluated for unpermitted, non-stormwater discharges and a certification that this evaluation has been performed must be included with the application. Information about spills or leaks of toxic or hazardous pollutants within the previous three years must also be submitted with the application. Finally, quantitative data must be submitted for samples collected on-site during storm events.

How to Get a Stormwater Permit. The best avenue available is to submit an NOI for a general permit. This permit is considered the easier route you can take. The terms are not onerous so follow the permit requirements exactly so as not to jeopardize your status. Some facilities may find it to their advantage to submit an individual application for an individual permit.

Notices and Hearings. EPA has forty-five days to review and comment on individual stormwater applications. The public is given thirty days to make written comments after the posting of a notice about the draft permit. EPA has ninety days to review a state's draft general permit. Interested persons may request to receive regular lists of pending permits. All information on the permits not classified as confidential is available for public inspection during normal business hours at the permitting authority. During the public comment period any person or agency may file a petition with the authority for a public hearing. Persons aggrieved by the issuance of a stormwater permit may appeal the action within thirty days after issuance of the permit.

CONCLUSION

This discussion is merely the tip of an iceberg. Permitting activities and decisions for any one medium we have examined could, by itself, be the subject of an extensive book. If you are a nonexpert generalist, you should now have a better grasp of what it means to obtain and hold a permit. The process can be frustrating at times, so do your best to cooperate and communicate with the permitting authority early and often. In the next chapter, we will take a closer look at some of the regulations requiring these permits and in the following three chapters how to control and manage these media in order to maintain compliance.

REFERENCES

American Petroleum Institute. *Evaporative Loss from External Floating Roof Tanks*. API Publication 2517. February 1989.

Arbuckle, J. Gordon, *et al*. *Environmental Law Handbook*. 12th. Ed. Rockville, MD: Government Institutes, Inc., 1993.

Ashland Chemical Company. *The 1990 Clean Air Act: An Overview*. Bulletin 1905, 1991.

Ayers, Kenneth W., *et al*. *Environmental Science and Technology Handbook*. Rockville, MD: Government Institutes, Inc., 1994.

Brophy, Robert. "Software Programs Model Air Emissions." *Environmental Protection*. November/December, 1991.

California Air Resources Board. *Technical Guidance Document for The Emission Inventory Criteria and Guidelines Regulation for AB2588 (Air Toxics "Hot Spots" Information and Assessment Act of 1987*. August 1989.

Cox, John W. "The Hazardous Materials Manager and The Clean Air Act Amendments of 1990." Academy of Hazardous Materials Managers. Fourth Annual Meeting, Rockville, MD, October 2-4, 1991.

Dufour, James T., *Environmental Organizer*. Sacramento, CA: California Chamber of Commerce, 1992.

----. *Hazardous Waste Management*. Sacramento, CA: California Chamber of Commerce, 1992.

EPA 340/1-80-008. *Petroleum Refinery Enforcement Manual*. March 1980.

---- 450/2-90-001a. *Air Emissions Species Manual: Volume I (Volatile Organic Compound Species Profiles)*. 2d. Ed. January 1990.

---- 450/2-90-001b. *Air Emissions Species Manual: Volume II (Particulate Matter Species Profiles)*. 2d. Ed. January 1990.

---- 450/2-90-011. *Toxic Air Pollutant Emission Factors—A Compilation for Selected Air Toxic Compounds and Sources*. October 1990.

---- 450/3-85-001b. *VOC Emissions from Petroleum Refinery Wastewater Systems—Background Information Document*. December 1987.

---- 450/3-88-010. *Protocols for Generating Unit-Specific Emission Estimates for Equipment Leaks of VOC (Volatile Organic Compounds) and VHAP (Volatile Hazardous Air Pollutants)*. October 1988.

---- 450/3-90-04. *Industrial Wastewater Volatile Organic Compound Emissions (Background Information for BACT/LAER Determination)*. January 1990.

---- 450/4-88-004. *Estimating Air Toxics Emissions from Organic Liquid Storage Tanks*. October 1988.

----450/4-90-015. *Protocol for The Field Validation of Emission Concentrations from Stationary Sources*. April 1990.

Finkel, Adam M. and Dominic Golding. "Alternative Paradigms: Comparative Risk Is Not The Only Model." *EPA Journal*, January/February/March 1993.

Finlayson-Pitts, Barbara J. and James N. Pitts, Jr. *Atmospheric Chemistry: Fundamentals and Experimental Techniques*. New York: John Wiley & Sons, 1986.

Flatow, Stuart. "The Right Way to Communicate Risk." *Safety & Health*. August 1993.

Frye, Russell S., Esq., *et al. Clean Water Act Permit Guidance Manual*. New York: Executive Enterprises Publications Co., Inc., 1988.

----. *Clean Water Act Update*. New York: Executive Enterprises Co., Inc., 1987.

Heilshorn, Elyse D. and J. Jeffrey MacDougall. "Identify and Track Hazardous Wastes Effectively." *Chemical Engineering Progress*. November 1992.

Himmelblau, David M. *Basic Principles and Calculations in Chemical Engineering*. 3d Ed. Englewood Cliffs, NJ: Prentice- Hall, 1989.

King, Geoffrey P. and Michael J. McGrath. "Plant Designers Face A Circular Dilemma." *Chemical Engineering*. June 1991.

Klaber, Kathryn Z., Kenneth N. Weiss and John W. Gallagher. "Charting A Compliance Course through The Clean Air Act Amendments." *The National Environmental Journal*. November/December 1993.

Knepper, Teresa R. "HAZOP Doubles as Emissions Inventory Tool." *Pollution Engineering*. March 1994.

Kolluru, Rao V. "Understand The Basics of Risk Assessment." *Chemical Engineering Progress*. March 1991.

Kuryla, Matthew and Stephen C. Jones. "Air Pollution Permits: New Regulations Determine Procedures and Cost." *Chemical Engineering*. November 1991.

Lipfert, Frederick W. *Air Pollution and Community Health: A Critical Review and Data Sourcebook*. New York: Van Nostrand Reinhold, 1994.

Mississippi Department of Environmental Quality. *Environmental Permit Directory*. March 1992.

Mody, Vinit and Raj Jakhete. *Dust Control Handbook*. Park Ridge, New Jersey: Noyes Data Corporation, 1988.

Mohin, Timothy J. "CAA Title III Challenges EPA." *Environmental Protection*. June 1992.

Morgan, M. Granger. "Risk Analysis and Management." *Scientific American*. July 1993.

Parkinson, Gerald. "New Models to Control Old Pollution Sources." *Chemical Engineering*, December 1, 1980.

Passow, Nancy R. "Preparing The Environmental Impact Statement." *Chemical Engineering*. December 15, 1980.

Patrick, David R., ed. *Toxic Air Pollution Handbook*. New York: Van Nostrand Reinhold, 1994.

Patton, Dorothy. "The ABC's of Risk Assessment: Some Basic Principles Can Help People Understand Why Controversies Occur." *EPA Journal*. January/February/March 1993.

Perrich, Jerry. "How to Cope with Confusing Storm Water Permits." *Pollution Engineering*. March 1994.

Ross, Douglas M. and McDonald, Robert A. "Environmental Impact Statements: The "Third-Party" Approach." *Engineering & Mining Journal*. April 1981.

Sadar, Anthony J. "Dispersion Modeling." *Environmental Protection*. March 1993.

Scheuplein, Robert J. "Uncertainty and The Flavors of Risk: Let's Give Risk Assessment A Reality Check." *EPA Journal*. January/February/March 1993.

Shields, Jacqueline, ed. *Air Emissions, Baselines & Environmental Auditing*. New York: Van Nostrand Reinhold, 1993.

Strom, Peter F. and Gregory S. Opheim. "Mission-Oriented Risk Assessment." *Professional Safety*. June 1993.

Suthersan, Suthan S. and Gisella M. Spreizer. "Integrated Remediation Approaches: Combining Technology, Risk Assessment and Environmental Statistics." *The National Environmental Journal*. May/June 1993.

Wentz, Charles A. *Hazardous Waste Management*. New York: McGraw-Hill, 1989.

Williams, Chris. "Assessing Risk: Toxicity in Perspective." *Environmental Protection*. August 1993.

----. "Using Ecological Risk Assessment Methods." *Environmental Protection*. January 1994.

6

REGULATING ENVIRONMENTAL HAZARDS

Before discussing end-of-pipe pollution controls, let us examine regulations concerning each medium: air, water, solid waste. This will neither be exhaustive nor scholarly but will briefly examine Congress' attempt to legislate eco-stewardship and EPA's logic in devising various regulations, not with the understanding of an insider but from the viewpoint of what implications these laws and regulations have on our business. For our purposes it suffices to summarize ideas discussed in previous chapters that we may next consider how to manage each major media of pollution considering each law and its regulations as a whole. To the uninitiated, a maze of confusing rules and regulations hangs over the head of the environmental compliance manager, so in this chapter we will learn to navigate our way through these hard-to-read documents.

GENERAL

Recall that rules and regulations are not laws nor vice versa. Congress considers various bills which if approved by both houses become law. While being debated by Congress, the document is a bill and has no force in law. When passed, it becomes law unless vetoed by the President and even then Congress gets another shot at it. Laws are "acts" of Congress, hence, we refer to the Clean Air Act or the Clean Water Act. Acts are laws of the land and take priority over any regulation, state or local law, any consensus standard, or industrial or military specification. However, the matter of understanding and living with the laws of an advanced society is not always simple and so we have attorneys, courts, regulators, and federal agencies. Environmental laws typically develop as a hodgepodge of enactments in which congress addresses, over a period of several years, some pressing issue that affects a broad spectrum of citizens.

When a complex law covers technical issues, such as pollution control, it rarely gives sufficient detail about how the regulated community is to comply with it. Day-to-day application and enforcement of a given law is, therefore, left to an office in the Executive Branch such as EPA, OSHA or DOT, among other agencies. These agencies implement the will of the legislature—which, theoretically, is the will of the people, tempered by the policies and philosophy of the incumbent president—by promulgating rules and regulations. Promulgation implies that the agency officially publishes the regulation or in some way actively issues the regulation, as opposed to the passive issuance of many laws. That does not mean, however, that ignorance becomes an excuse for the regulated community, as many have learned the hard way. All private and corporate citizens and alien residents of this country are bound by these laws and regulations. The law says we have to do something, or perhaps to refrain from doing something, while the regulation tells us how to do it or not do it in compliance with the law. Regulations also give ground rules for deciding whether or not we have completed some action properly or improperly. Finally, regulations usually spell out in detail what is going to happen to us procedurally if we commit a prohibited act or neglect a required act, as well as telling us our administrative rights as citizens while awaiting the news of our fate in the system.

Regulations are neither a luxury nor an option that we can either have or not have if we so choose. Each time a new law is passed by Congress, some federal or state agency *must* issue a new set of regulations or revise an old set of regulations in order to implement that law. This procedure has precious few exceptions and, unless Congress begins enacting minutely detailed laws (may this never happen), few exceptions will be the rule. Regulations are not arbitrary documents that oppressive federal agencies dream up just to harass hapless taxpaying citizens or to abrogate property rights, as some would lead us to believe. They document the means of implementing, administering, and enforcing the will of the people as ratified by Congress. To say that we want no more regulations by federal agencies is civic ignorance. To hear a congressman—a member of the very body that makes law—say that is downright scary and we know immediately that we are listening to a hebetudinous public servant.

Typically only one federal executive agency implements, administers, and enforces a given law. Occasionally, one agency implements and administers while another enforces. At the implementing agency, a person or committee is assigned to write implementing rules. When the draft rule is chopped (approved), the document is published in the *Federal Register* (FR) as an Advanced Notice of Proposed Rulemaking (ANPR). A preamble is placed before the actual draft regulation in order to solicit public comment and explain the history, the philosophy, and, hopefully, the science of the rule, but the preamble is not the rule itself.

When the commentary deadline has passed, the implementing agency considers the merits of any comments received and a revised draft is published in the *FR* as a Notice of Proposed Rulemaking (NPRM). Sometimes the ANPRM stage is skipped and the agency proceeds directly to the NPRM. After ironing out further comments, the agency publishes the final rule, in which the wording is now binding on all affected citizens and alien residents.

Finding your way in the Code of Federal Regulations (CFR) is not as difficult as it first appears. The CFR, similar to the USC, is a codified body of documents to help you find regulations when you need them. While USC codifies laws, CFR codifies regulations. Hence, you would not search USC for regulations nor search CFR for a law. The CFR is divided into chapters which identify implementing agency and parts and sections which identify the specific regulations. EPA regulations are found in Chapter 40 (as spoken but written 40 CFR). Keep in mind that the terms *regulation*, *rule*, and *standard* are interchangeable when referring to federal or state regulations.

To really confuse matters, though, other documents, also referred to as standards and codes, have no direct relationship to federal or state laws. Consensus standards and codes are issued by quasi-governmental bodies such as self-regulating professional societies. For instance, the National Fire Code is a set of standards issued by the National Fire Protection Association. Other such bodies include the American National Standards Institute (ANSI), American Society of Mechanical Engineers (ASME) and the American Institute of Chemical Engineers (AIChE), but other bodies write consensus standards too.

A voluntary or consensus standard must not be confused with regulatory standards such as an EPA regulation. Codes are typically binding among practitioners of a profession but not among the population in general. A voluntary standard contains provisions on when, how, and where something shall or shall not be done. Codes and standards both contain mandatory provisions by using the word *shall* to indicate requirements and *will* or *may* to indicate recommendations or guidance. Explanatory material is typically included in codes and standards as fine print: notes, footnotes, or appendices. Such codes are often adopted into law by reference. Unfortunately, the double use of the terms codes and standards can only be determined by the context in which they appear unless some modifying adjective is used such as voluntary, consensus, federal, state, or local.

A recommended practice (RP) is similar in content and structure to a voluntary code or standard but contains only nonmandatory language. In an RP, the word *should* is frequently used to indicate recommendations in the body of the text. A guide is a document that is advisory or informative in nature and contains only nonmandatory language. RPs and guides, or guidance documents, are strictly for voluntary use and are not necessarily intended by their developers to be adopted into law.

NATIONAL ENVIRONMENTAL POLICY

During the post-World War II years, U.S. industry boomed. Many new consumer products were introduced, making life so much easier and enjoyable. America enjoyed one of the higher standards of living in the world. The hidden cost for this lifestyle has been the by-products of industrial production. During the boom years, some of this material has been recycled. Some has even been marketed to secondary markets and other industries. Most by-products, however, are treated as waste and pumped into air, rivers and streams, sewers, or holes in the ground. The management of waste by disposal in the back yard of the plant was at one time state-of-the art environmental management, even if unsightly.

As people moved from the country to the city, they naturally settled close to their work. In the 1940s, 1950s, and early 1960s, it was common for subdivisions to spring up next to a factory or industrial park. Waste from the factory and company housing placed into the environment eventually claimed its toll. At first, the problem was strictly a local emergency and often was exacerbated only by weather. Slowly the public began to recognize and fear chronic problems associated with air and water pollution and the storage of waste in the ground and Congress was pressed hard to do something about it.

By 1969, environmental scandals were second only to the war in Vietnam in terms of news worthiness. Congress wished to halt the spread of environmental disasters but its legislative powers were dissipated in a federal bureaucracy that was scattered among several agencies with various agendas and priorities. Various degrees of efficiency and effectiveness existed as well. So in 1969, Congress decided that a first step to environmental restoration and protection was the passage of a consistent national policy on the environment.

The National Environmental Policy Act (NEPA) has four purposes:
1.   To encourage productive and enjoyable harmony between humans and the environment;
2.   To promote efforts that prevent or eliminate damage to the environment and biosphere and stimulate the health and welfare of humans;
3.   To enrich the understanding of the ecological systems and natural resources important to the nation; and
4.   To establish a Council on Environmental Quality.

In NEPA, Congress acknowledged that humans have a profound impact on the environment and identified five potentially negative influences on the environment: 1) population growth; 2) high-density urbanization; 3) industrial expansion; 4) resource exploitation, and 5) new and expanding technological advances. The policy of the U.S. is to use all practicable means and measures, including financial and technical assistance, to foster and promote the general welfare, to create and maintain conditions under which humans and nature can exist in productive harmony, and to fulfill the social, economic, and other requirements of present and future generations of Americans.

LAWS AND RULES ABOUT AIR POLLUTION

Air pollution damages human health, the environment, and our property such as concrete, structures and ornaments. Because of significant air pollution episodes attributed to scores of deaths in

Pennsylvania and New York, and the growing problem of air quality in many major U.S. cities, most notably Los Angeles, Congress passed the Clean Air Act (CAA) in 1970 to establish a national goal of achieving pristine quality air everywhere. This was the first national environmental law to be passed by Congress after the formation of EPA. Conversely, it was EPA's first major new law to enforce and regulate. The purpose of the law is to protect and enhance air resources so as to promote public health and welfare and the productive capacity of our population. CAA was passed because most of our nation's population is located in urban corridors crossing state boundaries where air pollution increasingly threatens public health and welfare. Air pollution in some areas causes haze and reduces visibility to the point of interfering with aviation. CAA is probably the least amended environmental law enacted in the U.S. One amendment was passed in 1977 but the only other, and more significant, amendment was the Clean Air Act Amendment of 1990 (CAAA) which corrects some of the problems with CAA.

CAAA has six major titles as shown in Figure 6.1.

Figure 6.1
Titles of the Clean Air Act as Amended in 1990

I: Air Pollution Prevention and Control
II: Emission Standards for Moving Sources
III: General
IV: Acid Deposition Control
V: Permits
VI: Stratospheric Ozone Protection

The original air pollution control law was passed in 1955 and in 1967 Congress added Title II, the Motor Vehicle Air Pollution Control Act. Later, Congress determined that changes were needed and in 1970 a totally restructured federal/state scheme of pollution control was passed as CAA. In 1977, provisions were added for 1) the Prevention of Significant Deterioration, 2) imposing stringent standards on areas failing to attain NAAQS, 3) restricting use of dispersion techniques, and 4) strengthening enforcement. Today we have CAAA, which evolved in hodgepodge fashion over forty years. Figure 6.2 outlines its history.

Figure 6.2
History of the Clean Air Act

Clean Air Act of 1955
The Motor Vehicle Air Pollution Control Act of 1963 (Title II)
Air Quality Act of 1967
Clean Air Amendments of 1970
Technical Amendments to CAA 1973, 1974
CAA Amendments of 1977
Technical Amendments to CAA 1977
1978, 1980, 1981, 1982, 1983
PL 101-549 of 1990 (CAAA)
(Titles IV, V, VI and X)

Title I establishes ambient air standards for criteria pollutants which the states are required to achieve. States put controls on industrial emissions as necessary to achieve the Standards, making it easier to get an air permit in some states than in others. EPA directly establishes rules for controlling emissions of Hazardous Air Pollutants (HAPs) and several categories of new industrial sources.

The four major programs of CAA before 1990 were 1) National Ambient Air Quality Standards (NAAQS), 2) New Source Performance Standards (NSPS), 3) National Emission Standards for Hazardous Air Pollutants (NESHAPs) and 4) monitoring and recordkeeping. CAAA adds programs for Acid Deposition and Stratospheric Ozone Protection and orders a change in the program for controlling HAPs. From 1970 to 1990, EPA only established seven NESHAPs so Congress expressed its impatience in CAAA by expanding the control of hazardous air pollutants through source control standards.

NAAQS

CAA determined that six ubiquitous pollutants (particulate matter, carbon monoxide, sulfur dioxide, nitrogen dioxide, ozone, and lead, which are collectively called criteria pollutants) were major concerns for human health and environmental quality. EPA established air quality criteria for these pollutants in two parts called National Ambient Air Quality Standards (NAAQS—pronounced "nacks"). Primary NAAQS were developed to protect human health with an adequate margin of safety by making the air quality clean enough to protect the most sensitive subpopulation. Secondary NAAQS protect the common welfare from known or anticipated adverse effects from the criteria pollutants. An area that has air quality as good as or better than primary NAAQS is called an attainment area while a nonattainment area has not achieved primary NAAQS. EPA estimated in 1993 that over ninety million Americans still live in nonattainment areas.

Your plant's permit limits may have no directly identifiable relationship with NAAQS and don't even look for ozone on a permit. Ozone contributes to smog and is itself a form of air pollution but in order to control ozone, states limit the emissions of unburned hydrocarbons and volatile organic compounds (VOCs). NAAQS are ceilings of acceptability in the various air quality control regions throughout the country. Being the same standard in all such regions, NAAQS are national ceilings of acceptability. Each state is responsible for developing a plan to achieve NAAQS within each AQMD within the state. This is called a State Implementation Plan or SIP (outlined in Figure 6.3).

Figure 6.3
State Implementation Plans (SIP)

description of air quality
inventory of sources
compliance schedule for attaining NAAQS
description of permitting process
monitoring and reporting requirements for permittees
enforcement procedures

SIP also includes the state's plans for maintaining NAAQS once attained. SIP is a contract between the state and its citizenry for their common good. Remember that when you are negotiating permit limits. Before siting a plant anywhere, whether in a heavily industrialized or primitive area, understand how SIP affects your plans. Existing and new plants both are subject to enforceable emissions limitations stated in the SIP approved by EPA.

New Source Performance Standards are established by EPA in 40 CFR 60. Under Section 111 of the CAA, industrial facilities are subject to NSPS for their particular industrial category if the facility is constructed or modified after the date EPA proposed the NSPS. These standards are technology forcing and based on best demonstrated technology systems. NSPS reflect economically achievable air pollution controls and apply to all states in order to discourage industries from shopping around for sites where less stringent air pollution control technology is required. Each industrial category having an NSPS is given concentration limits for various pollutants, monitoring requirements, and reporting requirements. Required monitoring may be continuous or periodical, although CAAA forces more processes to install continuous monitoring. Reporting includes anticipated startup date, actual startup date, and physical or operational changes which may increase emissions, continuous monitoring results, date for conducting opacity observations, malfunctions, inoperative monitoring devices with estimated date of repair.

Performance testing is required within sixty days after achieving maximum production rate but not later than 180 days after startup. Tests must be conducted in accordance with approved methods.

Under CAAA, cities that do not meet primary NAAQS must attain NAAQS by deadlines set in the law. Most cities had six years (1996 deadline) but Los Angeles (the worst problem) had twenty years (2010). State programs complement EPA efforts on behalf of those cities. Ninety-six cities failed NAAQS for ozone (ranked from marginal to extreme) in 1994. The more severe cases must institute more rigorous controls to achieve attainment. States may have to initiate or upgrade inspection and/or maintenance programs in order to get all cities into compliance. Vapor recovery may have to be installed at gasoline filling stations in order to comply. Hydrocarbon emissions may have to be reduced from even small sources. For instance, one facility located in the Los Angeles area must log the weight of paint containers before and after painting each day and is allowed to emit merely three pounds per day of VOCs.

Nonattainment cities may have to adopt transportation controls to offset growth in vehicle miles traveled daily. One Los Angeles facility must attain a ratio of 1.7 persons per car per day driven to work so this plant adopted a disincentive program for commuters that charges $40 per month to park in the company lot. However, members of car pools each receive $50 per month extra pay. This program discourages driving alone yet this plant still barely meets its employee per car per day ratio. Americans are die-hard automobilists so the reduction of emissions from vehicular travel is an uphill battle.

Major stationary sources of nitrogen oxides have to reduce emissions if located in any of ninety-six cities failing NOx NAAQS. Forty-one cities fail for carbon monoxide (ranked moderate to serious) and states may have to initiate tighter controls for these cities. Seventy-two cities fail to attain NAAQS for PM-10 and are ranked moderate. Their states will have to implement Reasonably Available Control Technology (RACT) and possibly even curtail use of wood stoves and residential fireplaces.

Air Quality Management Districts

EPA established Air Quality Management Districts (AQMD) throughout the country to manage NAAQS. Each AQMD is a geographical area responsible for attaining air quality conditions in its area that exceed the standard. That is to say, the AQMD must achieve for each criteria pollutant an ambient concentration level that is something less than the NAAQS. As explained above, AQMDs that have achieved this for a particular pollutant are designated attainment areas for that pollutant. Within each AQMD industry is granted permit limitations which help the AQMD maintain or reach its attainment status. Any increase of a criteria pollutant in a nonattainment AQMD must be offset by reductions elsewhere so that the net change is toward attainment. Consequently, it is easier to get a permit to burn fossil fuels in an attainment area for sulfur dioxide and NOx than it is to get one in a nonattainment area for those two pollutants. At least the chances of getting higher, more manageable, emission limits is greater in the attainment area. Ozone being a major pollution problem in the Los Angeles Basin (South Coast Air Quality

Management District or SCAQMD), what do you think are your chances of locating a major industrial coatings operations within the SCAQMD compared to, say, an AQMD in the state of Wyoming? Slim, but not impossible. States or AQMDs themselves can impose stricter standards than NAAQS. Consequently, you have to install reasonably available control technology (RACT) in order to get a permit for an existing source in a nonattainment area. New sources require even more restrictive measures in order to get a permit in a nonattainment area.

Ozone transport regions are areas where transport of air pollutants between one or more states contributes significantly to the nonattainment of the ozone NAAQS in one or more of the states involved. The sky literally cooks in these regions as ozone and VOCs react in the troposphere. CAA establishes by law one such region, which includes Connecticut, Delaware, Maine, Maryland, Massachusetts, New Hampshire, New Jersey, New York, Pennsylvania, Rhode Island, Vermont, and the District of Columbia. Within the ozone transport region VOC reduction targets are established. For instance, a stationary source that potentially emits 50 TPY (tons per year) or more of VOCs is classified as a major source and is subject to the requirements of major sources in moderate nonattainment areas. Similarly, nitrogen oxide reduction targets are set for major sources in the transport region. Marginal nonattainment areas require Reasonably Available Control Technologies (RACT) for industries emitting nonattained pollutants.

Prevention of Significant Deterioration

Should we move our plants to where the sky is blue all day and the air is clear? Not necessarily. While it may be difficult to get an air permit in the urban location of choice, that does not mean the process is effortless in pristine areas. If fact, when you want to locate in such an area, if your proposed plant is going to be a major emitter of criteria pollutants or air toxics, the permit process includes a Prevention of Significant Deterioration (PSD) Review. The purpose of the PSD program is to maintain attainment areas in their pristine condition. That means that if your proposed plant would increase ambient air pollution levels more than a designated amount, the permit will be denied unless you agree to install

Best Available Control Technology (BACT) to bring the emissions level down.

Listed national parks, national wilderness areas, and all parks with international borders (with Canada or Mexico) are designated Class I areas for PSD and allowable pollutant limits are very stringent. Somewhat less stringent are the levels of increase allowed for Class II areas and even less stringent levels are demanded in Class III areas.

Hazardous Air Pollutants

Any air pollutant for which no NAAQS is established but which may reasonably be anticipated to result in an increase in mortality rate or a serious incapacitating or irreversible illness is a Hazardous Air Pollutant (HAP). The original CAA required EPA to list HAPs and to establish for each an emissions standard called NESHAP (National Emission Standards for Hazardous Air Pollutants) within 180 days after listing. The process of conducting risk assessments in order to establish a NESHAP is so very tedious that twenty years after CAA, EPA had only developed seven NESHAPS (arsenic, asbestos, beryllium, mercury, radionuclides, vinyl chloride). Consequently, CAAA demands additional regulation of 186 air toxics, or HAPS, by source category similar to NSPS and establishes timetables for EPA to promulgate new regulations. HAPs typically are carcinogens, mutagens, or teratogens, that is, they are cancer producing or reproductive toxins. If EPA does not establish emission standards on time then each facility requesting a new or modified permit must itself conduct engineering studies to determine the Maximum Available Control Technology (MACT) for its source processes.

Source Categories

CAAA requires EPA to issue emission standards for some 166 major source categories and eight different area source categories of air toxics. The list is down from the over four hundred categories debated by Congress for many weeks. Figure 6.4 gives the HAPs source and area categories and their required promulgation dates. *Major sources* are large emitters whereas small sources are designated *area sources*. Do not confuse these terms with similar terms (point and area sources) used in water pollution but which have different meanings.

Figure 6.4

HAP Standard Source Categories

By November 15, 1992
    Commercial Dry Cleaning—Transfer Machines   (Perchloroethylene)
      [major and area]
    Commercial Dry Cleaning—Dry to Dry Machines   (Perchloroethylene)
      [area only]
    Industrial Dry Cleaning—Dry to Dry Machines   (Perchloroethylene)
    Industrial Dry Cleaning—Transfer Machines   (Perchloroethylene)
    Synthetic Organic Chemical Manufacturing

By December 31, 1992
    Coke Ovens
    Acrylonitrile-Butadiene-Styrene Production
    Aerospace Industries
    Asbestos Processing [major and area]
    Butyral Rubber Production
    Chromic Acid Anodizing [major and area]
    Commercial Sterilization [major and area]
    Decorative Chromium Electroplating [major and area]
    Epichlorohydrin Elastomers Production
    Epoxy Resins Production
    Ethylene-Propylene Elastomers
    Gasoline Distribution—Stage 1
    Halogenated Solvent Cleaners [major and area]
    Hard Chromium Electroplating [major and area]
    Hypalon (TM) Production
    Industrial Process Cooling Towers
    Magnetic Tapes
    Methyl Methacrylate-Acrylonitrile-Butadiene-Styrene Production
    Methyl Methacrylate-Butadiene-Styrene Terpolymers
    Neoprene Production
    Nitrile Butadiene Rubber Production
    Nonnylon Polyamide Production
    Petroleum Refineries—Other Sources

Figure 6.4 *(cont'd)*

By December 31, 1992 *(cont'd)*
   Polybutadiene Rubber Production
   Polyethylene Terephthalate Production
   Polystyrene Production
   Polysulfide Rubber Production
   Printing/Publishing
   Secondary Lead Smelting
   Shipbuilding and Ship Repair
   Solid Waste Treatment, Storage and Disposal Facilities
   Styrene-Acrylonitrile Production
   Styrene-Butadiene Rubber and Latex Production
   Wood Furniture

By November 15, 1995
   Publicly Owned Treatment Works (POTW)

By November 15, 1997
   Acetal Resins
   Acrylic Fibers/Monoacrylic Fibers
   Aerosol Can Filling Facilities
   Amino Resins Production
   Autos and Light Duty Trucks
   Benzyltrimethylammonium Chloride Production
   Butadiene Dimers Production
   Carboxymethylcellulose Production
   Cellophane Production
   Chelating Agents Production
   Chlorine Production
   Chloroneb Production
   Chromium Chemicals Manufacturing
   Chromium Refractories Production
   Cyanuric Chloride Production
   Electric Arc Furnace—Non-stainless Steel
   Electric Arc Furnace—Stainless Steel
   Ferroalloys Production
   Flexible Polyurethane Foam Production
   Hydrazine Production
   Hydrochloric Acid Production

Figure 6.4 *(cont'd)*

By November 15, 1997 *(cont'd)*
  Hydrogen Cyanide Production
  Hydrogen Fluoride Production
  Iron and Steel Manufacturing
  Iron Foundries
  Mineral Wool Production
  Municipal Landfills
  Nylon 6 Production
  Oil and Natural Gas Production
  Paper and Other Webs
  Petroleum Refineries—Catalytic Cracking/Catalytic Reformers/Sulfur Plants
  Pharmaceutical Production
  Phenolic Resins Production
  Phosphate Fertilizer Production
  Phosphoric Acid Manufacturing
  Photographic Chemicals Production
  Polycarbonates Production
  Polyesters Resin Production
  Polyether Polyols Production
  Polymethyl Methacrylate Resins Production
  Polyvinyl Acetate Emulsions Production
  Polyvinyl Alcohol Production
  Polyvinyl Butyral Production
  Portland Cement Manufacturing
  Primary Aluminum Production
  Primary Copper Smelting
  Primary Lead Smelting
  Pulp and Paper Production
  Rayon Production
  Reinforced Plastic Composites Production
  Rubber Chemicals Production
  Secondary Aluminum Production
  Semiconductor Manufacturing
  Sewage Sludge Incineration
  Sodium Cyanide Production
  Stationary Internal Combustion Engines
  Stationary Turbines

Figure 6.4 *(cont'd)*

By November 15, 1997 *(cont'd)*
 Steel Foundries
 Steel Pickling—Hydrochloric Acid Process
 Wood Treatment
 Wool Fiberglass Manufacturing

By November 15, 2000
 Alkyd Resins Production
 Alumina Production
 Ammonium Sulfate-Caprolactam By-product Plants
 Antimony Oxides Manufacturing
 Asphalt/Coal Tar Application
 Asphalt Concrete Manufacturing
 Asphalt Processing
 Asphalt Roofing Manufacturing
 Baker's Yeast Manufacture
 Boat Manufacturing
 Butadiene-Furfural Cotrimer
 Captafol Production
 Captan Production
 Carbonyl Sulfide Production
 Cellulose Ethers Production
 Cellulose Food Casing Manufacture
 Chlorinated Paraffins Production
 4-Chloro-2-Methylphenoxyacetic Acid Production
 Chlorothalonil Production
 Clay Products Manufacturing
 Coke By-product Plants
 2,4-D Salts and Esters Production
 Dacthal (TM) Production
 4,6-Dinitro-o-cresol Production
 Dodecanedioic Acid Production
 Dry Cleaning (Petroleum)
 Engine Test Facilities
 Ethylidene Norbornene Production
 Explosives Production
 Flat Wood Paneling
 Fume Silica Production

Figure 6.4 *(cont'd)*

By November 15, 2000 *(cont'd)*
Hazardous Waste Incineration
Industrial Boilers
Institutional/Commercial Boilers
Large Appliances
Lead Acid Battery Manufacturing
Lime Manufacturing
Maleic Anhydride Copolymers Production
Metal Cans
Metal Coils
Metal Furniture
Metal Parts and Products (Miscellaneous)
Methylcellulose Production
OBPA/1,3-Diisocyanate Production
Organic Liquids Distribution (Nongasoline)
Paints, Coatings, Adhesives (Manufacture of)
Paint Stripper Users
Phthalate Plasticizers Production
Plastic Parts and Products
Plywood/Particle Board Manufacturing
Polymerized Vinylidene Chloride
Polyvinyl Chloride and Copolymers
Primary Magnesium Refining
Printing, Coating, Dyeing of Fabrics
Process Heaters
Quaternary Ammonium Compounds Production
Rocket Engine Test Firing
Site Remediation
Sodium Pentachlorophenate Production
Spandex Production
Symmetrical Tetrachloropyridine Production
Taconite Iron Ore Processing
Tire Production
Tordon (TM) Acid Production
Uranium Hexafluoride Production
Vegetable Oil Production

Existing major sources must install MACT (Maximum Achievable Control Technology) based on a categorical survey. MACT may include process changes, product changes, operational or management practices, or pollution control equipment. Any of these or any combination may be used to comply. EPA will conduct an engineering study of each category and determine the controls implemented by the best twelve percent of all sources in the category. Once MACT is established, all major sources in the category must meet the removal efficiencies of the best twelve percent. New major sources must implement emissions control practices or install emissions control equipment which are at least as effective as the best.

Enforcement provisions are found at Section 113 under Title I of CAA. Civil penalties can mount up to $25,000 per day of violation to a maximum of $200,000. Field inspectors can issue immediate citations for up to $5,000 per day of a violation. Certain actions, such as falsifying records, are considered criminal activities and are punishable with individual as well as organizational fines as well as individual imprisonment. A knowing violation is a felony and subject to fines up to $250,000 and imprisonment up to five years. Each violation is a separate punishable offense. A corporation may be fined up to $500,000 for each criminal violation.

A knowing release of an air toxic which puts another person into imminent danger of serious bodily harm may be fined up to $250,000 per day and receive up to 15 years in prison. A corporation or other business entity may be fined up to $1,000,000 per day. EPA is authorized to pay a bounty of up to $10,000 to anyone who provides information of a potential violation leading to a civil penalty or criminal conviction.

Acid Precipitation

Acid rain provisions are also made in the amendments of 1990. A two-phased, market-based system has been devised for control of sulfur dioxide emissions from power plants and is expected to reduce emissions by fifty percent. By the year 2000, total annual emissions are to be capped at 8.9 million tons, a reduction of ten million tons from 1980 levels. Plants will be given allowances based on fixed emission rates set by law, based on previous fossil-fuel use. Utilities will pay penalties if emissions exceed the allowances held by permit. On the other hand, unused allowances may be banked or sold.

In Phase I, large, high-emission utilities located in eastern and Midwestern states must achieve reductions by 1995. Phase II commences on January 1, 2000 and imposes limits on smaller, cleaner utilities as well as tightens limits on Phase I plants.

Oxides of nitrogen emissions must also be reduced by the utilities but instead of allowances the EPA will set performance standards. All acid rain sources must install continuous emission monitoring devices to assure compliance.

Stratospheric Ozone Depletion

Elimination of ozone depleting chemicals (ODCs) is discussed at length in earlier chapters and the phase-out date of the Class I ODCs has passed.

LAWS AND RULES ABOUT WASTEWATER

Although it is commonly known as the Clean Water Act a more appropriate name of the law pertaining to water pollution is the Federal Water Pollution Control Act, PL 92-500, passed on October 18, 1972, less than a year after the EPA was born under President Nixon. The nation's prime water pollution control law was amended, not replaced, by the Clean Water Act (CWA) of 1977 but it has retained the name of those amendments as a popular title ever since. Before the 1972 law, municipalities, counties, and sometimes states, regulated industrial dischargers of water pollution. The trouble with that system was that enforcement was lax and regulations were haphazardly written. Also, pollution of river basins usually affects a number of states.

Consequently, industrial wastewater dischargers were pretty much free until 1972 to put any waste stream into the nearest body of water or land depression, including many wastes now considered hazardous by RCRA, such as plating waste. Most companies did this. It was the way the business of waste management was done in those days. Earlier national attempts to clean up the nation's waterways were the Water Quality Act of 1965, the Clean Water Restoration Act of 1966 and the Water Quality Improvement Act of 1970, none of which were particularly effective. A scandalous discharge into a storm channel in Indianapolis and the Cuyahoga River fire near Cleveland in the 1950s precipitated national outrage and Congress was forced to take action to end such abuses of water resources.

The law in 1972 addressed the discharge of pollutants into navigable waters of the U.S. and the newly established EPA was given the authority to enforce it. For the first time, authority and enforcement power were centralized at the federal level. A goal was set to re-establish water quality sufficient for the protection and propagation of fish, shellfish, and wildlife and for recreation in and on the water by July 1, 1983. A policy was also established prohibiting the discharge of toxic materials in toxic amounts. The federal government would assist financially in the construction of publicly owned treatment works to eliminate raw sewage discharges. Among other policies established in 1972, Congress committed itself to establish programs to control nonpoint sources of pollution (stormwater runoff) in an expeditious manner. Stormwater control took until 1992 to happen and, even then, the lawmakers and EPA have not tackled runoff from agricultural lands, the largest source of nonpoint pollution. Figure 6.5 outlines the CWA.

Essentially CWA was to restore and maintain the chemical, physical, and biological integrity of the nation's waters. In 1995, twenty-three years after the law was passed, the U.S. still has not met any goal set by the 92nd Congress for clean water.

Under CWA, Congress recognizes, preserves, and protects the primary responsibilities and rights of states to prevent, reduce, and eliminate pollution by making the state the primary regulatory authority for wastewater discharges and the federal EPA and local governments secondary regulatory authorities. Some municipalities do issue local regulations, however, which have major impact for plants that discharge into their POTW. Such municipalities may actually enforce wastewater discharge regulations.

In CWA, Congress set up six national programs to achieve water quality goals: NPDES permitting, pretreatment requirements, new source performance standards, stormwater discharges, wetlands dredge and fill program, and enforcement.

Figure 6.5
Organization of the CWA

Title I	Research and related programs
Title II	Grants for construction of treatment works
Title III	Standards and enforcement
301	Effluent limitations
302	Water quality related effluent limitations
303	Water quality standards & implementation plans
304	Information and guidelines
305	Water quality inventory
306	National standards of performance
307	Toxic and pretreatment effluent standards
308	Inspections, monitoring and entry
309	Federal enforcement
311	Oil and hazardous substance liability
316	Thermal discharges
319	Nonpoint source management program
Title IV	Permits and licenses
402	National Pollutant Discharge Elimination System
404	Permits for dredged or fill material
405	Disposal of sewage sludge
Title V	General provisions
Title VI	State water pollution control revolving funds

Significant section numbers are given under major titles.

Permit Program

The NPDES permit system regulations are found at 40 CFR 122. An NPDES permit is required for any discharge from a point source directly into waters of the U.S. The previous chapter discusses how to get such a permit. Water quality standards (WQS) are one way in which Congress intended for the states to regulate industrial and nonpoint source direct dischargers. CWA authorized EPA to assist states in developing WQS based on usage of water bodies and the states to implement the standards. These are similar to the NAAQS of CAA except that they are set state by state rather than for the nation. Of course, EPA must approve each state's

WQS which is protected by the National Pollutant Discharge Elimination System (NPDES) of permits for direct dischargers. Industries discharging wastewater to any body of surface water are required to have an NPDES permit. POTWs also require an NPDES as they are the ultimate discharge point for industries discharging wastewater into the sewer. Each state adopts WQS for each stream or lake in its inventory. These standards are based on the intended use of the water, such as commercial or recreational fishing, or water recreation, such as swimming, or underwater diving.

Technology-based standards are the other way that discharge limits are decided and represent the minimum level of control that is imposed. For industrial dischargers these standards are referred to as BPT, BCT, and BAT. BPT is Best Practicable Control Technology Currently Available and is used to set effluent limitations for pollutants which require a substantial level of control. BCT is Best Conventional Pollutant Control Technology for effluent limitations of conventional pollutants: BOD, TSS, pH, fecal coliform, oil and grease listed at 40 CFR 401.16. BAT is Best Available Technology Economically Achievable for effluent limitations of toxic pollutants. Nonconventional, nontoxic pollutants are ammonia, chlorine, color, iron, and total phenols listed at 40 CFR 122.21(m)(2). The priority pollutants, or water toxics, are listed at 40 CFR 122 Appendix D, Tables II-IV. To achieve effluent limits on toxic pollutants, BAT is determined by selecting the very best treatment systems with economically achievable performance of various ages, sizes, processes, or other shared characteristics. Sources that existed before compliance deadlines passed for BAT were permitted to have BPT.

Pretreatment Program

The second program established by the CWA to achieve national goals is the pretreatment program. While NPDES regulates direct discharges into streams and lakes, the pretreatment program covers indirect discharges going through a public sewer to a POTW and then to a stream or lake. Congress intended for EPA to set up a program to regulate industries which discharge into and potentially interfere with or overwhelm POTWs. Industries are expected to pretreat wastewater before discharging to the sewer in order that the POTW can effectively treat any remaining pollutants in excess of its NPDES limits. Three types of requirements apply to industrial discharges to POTWs: general pretreatment requirements, categorical pretreatment standards, and local pretreatment standards.

General pretreatment standards are found at 40 CFR 403. Significant industrial users and categorical dischargers are subject to the general standards. An industrial user is "significant" if it discharges 25,000 gallons per day or five percent of the average dry weather hydraulic capacity of the POTW or five percent of the average dry weather organic capacity. The hydraulic capacity is the volumetric flow rate through the POTW which is typically expressed in millions of gallons per day (MGD). Thus for a 1 MGD sewage plant, significant users contribute at least 50,000 gpd. Organic capacity refers to the amount of organic throughput as measured by pounds of BOD. However, where a reasonable potential for having an adverse effect on the POTW exists, a smaller discharge may be declared to be significant.

General standards contain both general and specific prohibitions which apply to all industries. Pass through and interference, the general prohibitions, are discussed under Pretreatment Permits in the last chapter. Pretreaters are specifically prohibited from discharging fire or explosion hazards into the sewer. Any liquid with a flash point less than 140°F is a fire or explosion hazard by definition (also a RCRA hazardous waste due to ignitability). Liquids with less than 5 pH are specifically prohibited. Solids or viscous liquids which could interfere with flow are prohibited. Also specifically prohibited are oxygen demanding pollutants, which may interfere with POTW operations, wastewater temperature exceeding 104°F, any kind of oil which may by pass or interfere with the POTW, pollutants which may release toxic gases, vapors or fumes and pollutants trucked or hauled to the POTW.

Categorical standards developed by EPA for various industries include metal molding and casting, metal finishing, rubber processing, electroplating, plastics molding and forming, meat processing, fertilizer manufacturing, battery manufacturing, coil coating, and pulp and paper mills, among others. These standards set limits on end-of-pipe discharges. If categorical standards that apply to a facility are particularly tough to meet, the facility can theoretically seek relief by obtaining a variance from the permitting authority for fundamentally different factors between the facility as it exists and operates and the typical categorical facility used by

EPA to devise the standard. This procedure is discussed at 40 CFR 403.13. Realistically, it is difficult to get approval for a variance and then it is possible only if 1) another categorical standard specifically controls the pollutants for which the applicant seeks alternative controls; 2) the situation of the controlled discharge is fundamentally different from factors considered by EPA when the standard was established; and 3) the request is made exactly per 403.13.

Local pretreatment standards are requirements in addition to the federal standards. A POTW is required to develop its own pretreatment program if it has greater than 5 MGD design flow and receives wastewater from industrial users and industrial pollutants which either interfere with or pass through the treatment system or EPA or the state judges that circumstances warrant local standards or the POTW wants to obtain approval to grant removal credits. The latter are used by some municipalities to attract industry by granting them permits that have easier limitations than the federal standard allows. As you might guess, this can only be done under very strict circumstances where the POTW can remove the difference in the pollutant load of the waste stream. Specific limits set by a POTW on the industries it serves are binding and enforceable by the state and federal authorities as well as local. Permitting for pretreatment, discussed in the last chapter, requires an application but is a relatively simple process compared to NPDES permitting. Congress expected that once EPA determined categorical standards for existing plants any new source which came on stream after that would be able to improve on those standards due to the availability of enhanced treatment systems which had been developed in the interim.

New Source Performance Standards

New Source Performance Standards (NSPS) are the third program Congress set up to achieve its national water quality goals. Therefore, in each of the categorical standards, one section addresses NSPS, which are more restrictive, if only slightly so.

A major source of pollutants, that until recently was not well regulated, is the nonpoint source or area source. The pretreatment permit system covers only point sources and whereas the NPDES program covers both point and area sources not much was done with area sources until stormwater regulations were finalized in the early 1990s. This is the fourth major program established by Congress in CWA.

Stormwater Regulations

Stormwater regulations established three methods of making application for a permit: individual application, group application, and notice of intent to be included under a general permit. These application routes are discussed in Chapter 5, which also covers the two kinds of permits: general and individual. While presumably improving the quality of the nation's waters, the largest category of area dischargers, row crops, is still not regulated or controlled. Congress still has to wrestle with that but by the turn of the century the water quality picture could be bleak, if Congress fails to act decisively.

Under Section 404 of CWA, Congress required a permit for any dredging or filling activity in navigable waters, including wetlands. This is the fifth Congressional program for restoring water quality to our nation. The Army Corps of Engineers administers the permitting program but EPA has veto power. Wetlands are often hotly contested between extreme environmentalists who defend every wetland regardless and extreme conservatives and land developers who want to turn every single acre of "useless" land in America into a shopping mall or apartment complex.

Wetlands

Wetlands are areas inundated or saturated by surface or groundwater at a frequency and duration sufficient to support a prevalence of vegetation adapted for life in saturate soil conditions. Wetlands generally include swamps, bogs, and similar areas. Normal ongoing farming, silviculture, and ranching operations are exempt from wetlands protection. So is maintenance and emergency reconstruction of river dikes. Farm ponds, irrigation ditches, drainage ditches, farm roads, and forest roads are also exempt from wetlands protection. These exemptions only apply if the activities do not change the flow, circulation, or reach of the source waters. A more extensive discussion of the wetland issues may be found in Chapter 1.

Enforcement

Enforcement is the sixth program Congress established for improving water quality. One of the major problems before CWA was that when major water polluters were found out, the laws of the day had no teeth, whether state or federal. CWA fixes that problem by outlining administrative remedies, civil liabilities and criminal liability. The enforcement authority no longer has to drag a defiant facility to court as it did pre-1972. The implication of the law is that for the common good of all citizens the enforcement authority uses its sovereignty to forego the usual legal formalities with an individual polluter, so long as approved procedures are used.

No limits apply to the amount for which citizens can sue a polluter under CWA, though surprisingly few suits have been filed. Civil liabilities imposed by the compliance authority are fixed by law shown in Figure 6.6.

Figure 6.6
CWA Civil Liabilities

Class I Civil Penalty
    $10,000 per violation
    $25,000 maximum per penalty
    Written notice of intent to issue order
    Administrative hearing, if requested within 30 days

Class II Civil Penalty
    $10,000 per violation
    $125,000 maximum per penalty
    Legal procedure @ 5 USC 554

Criminal sanctions are shown in Figure 6.7. Knowing endangerment means knowing at the time of the violation that the culpable action places another person in imminent danger of death or serious bodily injury.

Figure 6.7
CWA Criminal Liabilities

Negligent Violations

First Conviction
Minimum Fine: $ 2,500 per day of violation
Maximum Fine: $25,000 per day of violation
Subsequent Convictions
Fine: up to $50,000 per day of violation
Imprisonment: up to 2 years
Or both fine and imprisonment

Knowing Violations

First Conviction
Minimum Fine: $ 5,000 per day of violation
Maximum Fine: $50,000 per day of violation
Imprisonment: up to 3 years
Or both fine and imprisonment
Subsequent Conviction
Fine: up to $100,000 per day of violation
Imprisonment: up to 6 years
Or both fine and imprisonment

Knowing Endangerment

First Conviction
Individual: up to $250,000 per day of violation
Organization: up to $1,000,000 per day of violation
Imprisonment: up to 15 years
Or both fine and imprisonment
Subsequent Conviction
Individual: up to $500,000 per day of violation
Organization: up to $2,000,000 per day of violation
Imprisonment: up to 30 years
Or both fine and imprisonment

DECIPHERING LAWS AND RULES ABOUT HAZARDOUS WASTE

EPA regulations concerning hazardous waste were issued as a result of the Resource Conservation and Recovery Act (RCRA) of 1976 (PL 94-580) and manage hazardous wastes from cradle-to-grave, that is, from generation to disposal. All industries which generate, store, transport, or dispose of hazardous waste must meet the same strict standards for compliance.

The Solid Waste Disposal Act (SWDA) of 1965 was the nation's first attempt to address land disposal. The Resource Recovery Act of 1970 amended SWDA but the widest known environmental law ever is RCRA of 1976 which again amended SWDA. 1984 amendments called the Hazardous and Solid Waste Amendments (HSWA) were a major expansion of SWDA's scope, even as amended by RCRA.

RCRA

As it stands today, SWDA is commonly referred to as RCRA and of all its provisions four subtitles are most noteworthy of mention. Subtitle C establishes the cradle-to-grave system for managing hazardous waste from generation through disposal. Subtitle D is a system for managing nonhazardous wastes in nonsecure landfills. Subtitle I pertains to underground storage tanks (UST) used to store petroleum products and hazardous substances. Subtitle J sets up a national system for tracking medical waste (Medical Waste Tracking Act of 1988).

CERCLA

The Comprehensive Emergency Response, Compensation and Liability Act or Superfund or CERCLA (pronounced SIRK'-la), was enacted by Congress in 1980 as the result of several highly publicized landfill disasters, most notably Love Canal. The intent of Congress was to address actual or potential uncontrolled releases of hazardous substances to the environment with stiff regulatory requirements. If a release is controlled it is regulated by some other environmental law depending on its nature. Therefore, CERCLA primarily covers inactive sites, though, in some cases, it also covers actively managed sites which are not covered by

RCRA. CERCLA applies to both landbased facilities and to vessels at sea. Unlike RCRA and other basic regulatory programs, CERCLA is self-implementing with regulations issued as guidance documents defining policy rather than rules to be followed.

CERCLA establishes a mechanism of response for the immediate cleanup of hazardous substance contamination from accidental spills or from abandoned or uncontrolled hazardous waste sites that may result in long-term environmental damage. A CERCLA release is any spilling, leaking, pumping, pouring, emitting, emptying, discharging, injecting, escaping, leaching, dumping, or disposing of hazardous substances into the environment. The Superfund Amendments and Reauthorization Act (SARA) of 1986 added the abandonment or discarding of barrels, containers, or other closed containers holding hazardous substances. Exposures regulated by other laws are excluded from coverage.

Many people seem to use the terms hazardous materials, hazardous substances, and hazardous waste interchangeably. These words have entirely different meanings, however. It is important to understand that for the purposes of CERCLA, which regulates the uncontrolled release of hazardous substances into the environment, the term *hazardous substance* means almost every possible hazardous material—whether it is a solid, liquid, or gaseous chemical, a chemical mixture, a mineral, a composite material, or you name it. The universe of hazardous substances certainly includes all *hazardous materials* and all *hazardous wastes* as well as *hazardous discharges* and *toxic pollutants* under CWA, *hazardous air pollutants* under CAAA and *imminently hazardous chemical substances* or *mixtures* defined under the Toxic Substances Control Act (TSCA). Just in case any material slips by all these lists, it may also be covered by CERCLA Section 102. Any other unlisted substance which "will or may reasonably be anticipated to cause" any type of adverse effects in organisms and/or their offspring are also included. Petroleum and natural gas are not included as CERCLA hazardous substances.

In understanding CERCLA it is important to recognize that not all hazardous substances are covered by it, only those which have been released to the *environment*. The environment means waters such as navigable waters, waters of the contiguous zone, any other surface water, groundwater or drinking water, land surface or subsurface, or the ambient air.

A CERCLA release comes from a *facility*. That is any structure, installation, equipment, landfill impoundment, storage vessel, vehicle, or any site or area where hazardous substances have been deposited or otherwise have come to be located. The simple presence of a hazardous substance at a site qualifies that site as a facility under CERCLA. That is very important: it is *the presence of the material not the nature of the site* that qualifies it as a facility under CERCLA.

The language of this law makes certain parties *strictly liable* for response costs incurred as the result of a release or a threatened release of hazardous substances. This liability is both *joint*, shared in ownership or action, and *several*, not shared but distinct and separate. If you are confused that should explain why most companies consult an attorney as soon as the possibility of a CERCLA action is known to exist. All environmental media are covered by this law: air, water, groundwater and soil.

EPA was to develop a comprehensive program for setting priorities for cleaning up the worst existing uncontrolled hazardous substance (not necessarily hazardous waste) sites. For the common good the law intended to make responsible parties pay for those clean-ups whenever possible. It did this by doing something totally alien to English common law (but not alien to law in the orient nor to common justice in many other countries): fix responsibility without regard to blame. In our English common law system we first look for a guilty party when a wrong has been done or a negligence has caused damage and we make them pay. To Americans and Englishmen, that is justice.

The trouble with the English common law is that, in the case of uncontrolled hazardous substance sites such as Love Canal, the drum dump in Kentucky, the Stringfellow Acid Pits, Times Beach, Missouri and many other cases, it is 1) hard to tell the bad guys from good guys, or 2) the not-so-good guys from not-so-bad guys, or else 3) the bad guys have disappeared altogether along with the purse. Under our English system of law this presents a checkmate or else the taxpayer is the grand loser.

In other parts of the world the correction of a legal mess is not so much on the shoulders of a bad guy as a responsible guy who may not be guilty at all. What does this mean? Well, did you help make the mess by sending some stuff to that place to make the mess with in the first place? Yes? Well, you may not be a bad guy but you are definitely a potentially responsible party (PRP) and you will receive a letter of greetings and salutations from the CERCLA office of the EPA region where the mess is located and it will invite you to a meeting of PRPs and EPA to discuss how everybody is going to clean up the mess. Unless you and your PRP friends take charge and form a committee with solid leadership and present a united front, the EPA will tell you how and when and how much and what and who. You pay, period.

This system was designed to get a potentially dangerous mess cleaned up as quickly as possible without taking time to point fingers and haggle over who is to blame and pays or should pay. PRPs are to pool resources and clean up the mess within 120 days under EPA direction.

Whenever possible, EPA requires PRPs to clean up the site directly. Five acceptable defenses are available to exclude oneself from the PRP list: 1) act of God, 2) act of war, 3) third party defense, 4) innocent purchaser (also called innocent landowner), and 5) involuntary acquisition (good only for state or local government seizure). When EPA has to take over the cleanup operation because of foot dragging or because PRPs cannot be located or have no funds or cannot cooperate long enough to do it themselves, it performs the cleanup action then takes the PRPs to court to recover the response costs. All costs associated with the cleanup, removal, emergency response, remedial action, and related enforcement activities are recoverable under CERCLA. EPA is authorized to subpoena, enter and inspect, take remedial actions and acquire property for remedial action if the state involved will accept the property immediately after cleanup is complete. EPA may also prepare toxicological profiles of health-threatening substances and conduct health assessments at National Priority List sites.

What kinds of actions may EPA take to get a site cleaned up? Basically two: removal or remediation. Removal actions are short term actions taken to protect the public from imminent threats. They include activities such as temporary evacuation, installing fences, providing alternative water supplies, and removing waste and contaminated materials. They may also include such ongoing activities as monitoring groundwater. These are mostly activities learned from the Love Canal incident. Remedial actions are longer term or more permanent actions requiring extensive studies such as dredging, excavating, and treating groundwater.

CERCLA limits remedial actions to National Priority List sites but no limits are placed on cost or duration of these activities.

Who can be a PRP? Who would be responsible but not necessarily blameworthy for an uncontrolled hazardous substance in the environment? Congress established that any individual or company is a potentially responsible party (PRP) if they contributed materials to the contamination problems or even only potentially contributed. The current owners or operators of the facility are PRPs for one but they are often missing. The previous owner or operator are PRPs if the current ones are nowhere to be found. Also, all facility owners and operators at the time of any hazardous substance disposal on-site are PRPs. Anyone who arranged for disposal or treatment of a hazardous substance at the facility (such as a generator contracting for disposal of hazardous waste), and, finally, any party that transported hazardous substances to the site or arranged the transportation of the substance are PRPs.

Between EPA and PRP attorneys, others have been included as PRPs from time to time. Some survived court challenges and some did not. Anyone who lent money to the facility for capital expansion or operating cash may be included as a PRP by virtue of participation in ownership. Anyone who is current owner by virtue of being a lender who foreclosed on the property may be a PRP. The key is whether lending PRPs participated in the management of the facility through the loan. The innocent landowner defense may be used, but remember defenses are only relevant during the cost-recovery phase, which is after the clean-up checks have been written. At least that is the way it was supposed to have been. It does not always work that smoothly with court battles starting as soon as PRP letters are opened.

CERCLA makes PRPs strictly liable. Among other things that means ignorance is not a defense. It also means innocence as we lay people normally think of it is not an issue. A PRP is liable for recovery of costs. SARA Section 113(f)(1) allows certain PRPs to resolve their liabilities and, hence, become immune from contribution actions in future court decisions. This means they may make a settlement with the government for the cleanup, pay up front and not worry about the post-cleanup law suits. Those qualified PRPs who choose not to settle remain liable for excess costs. Liability is limited to the cost of response plus $50 million for natural resource damages except where the release was willful or caused by a violation of a regulation. If the release was approved, such as by permit, damage to natural resources has no liability.

Congress did not intend for the nation to deal with minute quantities of hazardous substances so CERCLA authorizes EPA to establish a list of Reportable Quantities (RQ). An RQ is a specific listed amount for each hazardous substance and if it is released in less than 24 hours the National Response Center must be notified. This is how it works. Say, for example, that compound X has an RQ of 10 pounds. If you spill 11 pounds of X, it is a reportable event under CERCLA. If you spill 9 pounds, it is not reportable. Let's say, though, that you come in on Monday morning and find that 29 pounds of X leaked out onto the ground over the weekend since Friday's inspection of the storage area. That is not an RQ. However, if you find 41 pounds leaked out, call NRC.

National Contingency Plan

The National Contingency Plan (NCP) is our nation's plan for responding to oil and hazardous substance spills beyond regional response capabilities. Each EPA region is required to have its own contingency plan with response teams and coordinators designated. All government responses under CERCLA are required to follow NCP procedures. Releases in excess of an RQ must be reported immediately to the National Response Center.

The NCP provides a methodology for dealing with releases of hazardous substances covered by CERCLA and oil, which is not (oil spills are covered by CWA). The three elements of this method may be divided into four phases. The elements of response are 1) site identification, 2) site listing and 3) site cleanup.

Preliminary Assessment/Site Investigation (PA/SI) is the first phase of the NCP response method during which information is gathered off-site (PA) to identify it as a potential problem and on-site (SI) if inadequate off-site information is available. All that can be answered at the end of the first phase is: do we have a problem to investigate or not? The Remedial Investigation/Feasibility Study (RI/FS) is the phase where additional information is gathered to determine 1) how bad the problem really is, 2) whether to list the site on NPL, and 3) technical alternatives for cleanup. This phase is entered if immediate removal of the problem contamination is not feasible. The purpose of RI is to get enough information to characterize site conditions such as 1) source and extent of contamination, 2) potential pathways of exposure, and 3) extent of human exposure. RI is a comprehensive evaluation of contamination in soil, groundwater, or surface water and specific site characteristics such as geology and hydrology. The extent of human exposure is estimated by conducting a risk assessment. FS presents cleanup alternatives based on information gathered during RI and verified sometimes by laboratory experiments. The process of selecting a suitable remediation method is immortalized as the record of decision (ROD), a public record for which public input is invited by EPA.

After the RI/FS process and ROD have been properly completed, the Remedial Design/Remedial Action step is scheduled and implemented. Operations and maintenance of the remedial process may take years or decades to complete. Several rules must be followed for a cleanup. Destruction- or treatment-based technologies are given priority by EPA. Experimental or unproven technologies can be approved where feasibility is demonstrated especially where conventional technology is infeasible. Unless the cleanup is total, EPA will review the site every five years and take additional action as it feels is warranted. It reports to Congress on all such sites. The remedy selected must meet the requirements of other laws such as CWA, CAAA, TSCA, SDWA, and RCRA. State and federal criteria must be met, not just standards, but informal criteria must also be met. SDWA maximum contaminant levels (MCLs) are used where drinking water is involved. Alternative contaminant levels (ACLs) may only be used within the site owner's property boundaries. Where ACLs cannot be met then RCRA groundwater standards must be met by meeting SDWA standards or showing no excess above background.

EPA gives PRPs notice of anticipated remedial action and solicits their active participation and it is usually to their advantage to cooperate. After the notification, a sixty-day moratorium on RI/FS goes into effect to see if PRPs will finance up front. If none agree within sixty days, EPA initiates the RI/FS after thirty more days or ninety total days so far. If the PRPs agree to finance, they must reach an agreement with the ninety-day period. An enforcement action moratorium of sixty days begins upon PRP notification. EPA initiates remedial action after another sixty days, or one hundred twenty days into the project if the PRPs have not agreed to remediate. If they do agree, they have the same one hundred twenty day period to finalize their agreement with each other. Small volume PRPs can make *de minimis* settlements with EPA and the PRP committee in which they agree to pay a fixed amount and get out of further participation and enforcement actions. De minimis settlements over $500,000 need the U.S. Attorney General's approval. Volume of waste is the criteria for distributing cost among PRPs who are also authorized to seek redress from insurance carriers and self-insurance pools.

That is CERCLA in a nutshell. Unless Congress does something creative, the stalemate over who is responsible and who cleans up such as that which occurred at Love Canal will be repeated at many uncontrolled hazardous substance sites over and over again. The placing of responsibility instead of fixing blame, at least during the clean-up phase, is the best we can hope for but Congress must prohibit lawsuits from being heard before completion of cleanup and prohibit injunctions on clean-up activities. Let the fighting begin when the site is clean.

In 1986, CERCLA was reauthorized and amended in a law known as SARA, or Superfund Amendments and Reauthorization Act. Title III of SARA, called Emergency Planning and Community Right-to-Know Act (EPCRA), provides that every March 1 industrial facilities must file an Inventory Report of hazardous substances stored on site per section 312 of the law. This is the Tier I or II report as accepted by local authorities. Every July 1, SARA III Section 313 requires a Toxic Inventory called Form R to be filed by manufacturing facilities for toxic substances used in qualities greater than a threshold amount.

Conclusion

Laws and regulations need not be dreadful. Exposure to them through conferences and seminars improves understanding. Refer to the original wording anytime you have a question, but consult review articles and books to get differing views or interpretations. Continually work on a better understanding—that is how you become and expert.

REFERENCES

Arbuckle, J. Gordon, *et al. Environmental Law Handbook.* 12th ed. Rockville, MD: Government Institutes, Inc., 1993.

Ashland Chemical. *The 1990 Clean Air Act: An Overview.* Bulletin 1905, 1991.

EPA 400-K-93-001. *The Plain English Guide to The Clean Air Act.* April 1993.

Milner, John E. and Charles A. Waggoner. "Overview of Major Federal Environmental Acts and Regulations for The General Practitioner." *Mississippi Law Journal.* December 1990.

7

CONTROLLING AIR POLLUTION

Now comes the fun part of industrial environmental management: selecting and operating the equipment that cleans the streams at the end of the pipe. The waste has been minimized. A permit has been obtained. Now it is time to select the best control equipment and learn how to operate it efficiently and effectively.

HOW DUST AND OTHER PARTICULATE MATTER IS COLLECTED

In the popular vocabulary, dust is powdered earth or any other finely divided material which is easily suspended in the atmosphere. When we were young, watching dust motes in a shaft of sunlight in an otherwise dark room was fascinating. In science and engineering, dust is fine particles of any material, thus particulate matter (PM). Actually, PM can be either solid or liquid. A fairly stable suspension of such particles in any gas, especially air, is called an aerosol. Fog is an aerosol, rain is not, yet both are natural PM and play a role in anthropogenic pollution. The words *aerosol* and *particulate matter* are not interchangeable, however, as the term aerosol includes the gas as well as the PM. From a pollution standpoint, PM includes solid or liquid particles ranging in diameter from 0.002 microns to about 10 microns. Anything smaller gets into molecular chemistry and anything larger drops out so fast it cannot be an air pollutant. It may, however, be an environmental release to the soil, hence a groundwater polluter.

Primary PM is released directly to the atmosphere, such as rock dust from a cement crushing and grinding operation or PM from a rice processing plant. Metal fines, heavy metal laden-mist from metal finishing baths, acid gases, alkaline mists, and others can be primary PM. Smoke is an aerosol of soot (primary PM), hot air, and other gases released in the combustion process. Other PM may be formed by chemical reactions in the atmosphere and this is called secondary PM. Photochemical smog is produced by chemical reactions which produce secondary PM as a by-product. Originally smog was the result of the chemical reaction between smoke, sunlight, and fog or SMoke + fOG, hence the name. What is popularly called smog today is the ground-level ozone haze we see in large cities such as Los Angeles. Control of ground-level ozone will be discussed later.

Soot is worthy of a brief discussion owing to its environmental significance. In essence, soot is a carbonaceous solid produced in combustion from a gas phase hydrocarbon species and thus the formation of soot is fuel dependent. Primary soot spheres range in diameter from 10 to 40 nm, however they tend to agglomerate in larger bodies consisting of spheres numbering into the hundreds. Soot agglomerates are captured by electrostatic precipitators with low efficiency.

Sources of PM other than burning fuel include mineral processing plants, plants where a dusty product is made such as fertilizer prills, unpaved roads, and plowing and clearing of crop fields. These are all *anthropogenic* (human-made) sources. Nature produces PM in wind storms, especially where human activity has caused die-back of vegetation, and volcanic eruptions. Volcanoes, in fact, put out many more tons of PM than humans do into the atmosphere and you will hear this brought up often. However, volcanic PM is merely a peak on the graph of PM versus a time line whereas anthropogenic PM continues to increase in concentration in the atmosphere. Volcanoes vomit PM occasionally, humans dump it out continuously in ever-increasing amounts.

Remember that PM has effects on human health, the environment, and property. Excessive PM in the troposphere leads to nose and throat irritation, lung damage, bronchitis, and pre-mature death as people in London, New York, and Donora, Pennsylvania can attest. PM also causes the haze that reduces the visibility in Los Angeles, New York, Mexico City, and other large metropolitan areas. PM such as ashes, soot, smoke, and dust blacken buildings, structure, and personal property, such as furniture and clothing.

Moderate PM nonattainment areas were to achieve attainment by December 31, 1994 in accordance to the dictates of the CAAA. Figure 7.1 lists these areas.

Figure 7.1
PM Moderate Nonattainment Areas

AQMD	State	AQMD	State
Ada County	Idaho	Lane County	Oregon
Adams County	Colorado	LaSalle County	Illinois
Allegheny County	Pennsylvania	Libbey County	Montana
Anchorage	Alaska	Liberty-Lincoln-	
Archuleta County	Colorado	Portview-Glassport	
Arostook County	Maine	boroughs-Clairton	Pennsylvania
Bannock County	Idaho	Lincoln County	Montana
Bonner County	Idaho	Madera County	California
Boulder County	Colorado	Madison County	Illinois
Brooke County	West Virginia	Maricopa County	Arizona
Butte County	Montana	Mono County	California
Cook County	Illinois	Nogales	Arizona
Cuyahoga County	Ohio	Oglesby County	Illinois
Denver County	Colorado	Olmstead County	Minnesota
Dona Ana County	New Mexico	Paul's Spur	Arizona
El Paso County	Texas	Pierce County	Washington
Flathead County	Montana	Pima County	Arizona
Fremont County	Colorado	Pinal County	Arizona
Gila County	Arizona	Pitkin County	Colorado
Inyo County	California	Power County	Idaho
Jackson County	Oregon	Prowers County	Colorado
Jefferson County	Ohio	Ramsey County	Minnesota
Josephine County	Oregon	Riverside County	
Juneau	Alaska	(eastern)	California
Kern County	California	Rosebud County	Montana
King County	Washington	Salt Lake County	Utah
Klamath Falls Co.	Oregon	San Bernardino Co.	California
Lake County	Indiana	San Miguel County	Colorado
Lake Missoula Co.	Montana	Santa Cruz County	Arizona

Figure 7.1 *(cont'd)*

AQMD	State	AQMD	State
Sheridan County	Wyoming	Walla Walla Co.	Washington
Shoshone County	Idaho	Washoe County	Nevada
Silver Bow County	Montana	Wayne County	Michigan
Spokane County	Washington	Yakima County	Washington
Stanislaus County	California	Yuma	Arizona
Thurston County	Washington		
Union County	Oregon		
Utah County	Utah		

Figure 7.2 lists Serious Nonattainment areas for PM which have until December 31, 2001 to achieve attainment.

Figure 7.2
PM Serious Nonattainment Areas

AQMD	State
Coachella Valley	California
Las Vegas	Nevada
Owens Valley	California
San Joaquin Valley	California
South Coast Air Basin	California

Although we generally discuss PM as spherical bodies, they are rarely so simple geometry in real life. Therefore particle radius and diameter is an approximation of size and has no real meaning if you examine PM under a microscope. However, for years atmospheric scientists, industrial hygienists, and air pollution control engineers have fared well by speaking of a particle's *effective diameter* or *equivalent* diameter. The most commonly used effective diameter is the aerodynamic diameter, D_a, which is the diameter of a sphere of unit density (1.0 g/cm³) having the same terminal velocity as the particle being examined. Aerodynamic diameter is useful for determining residence time of the particle in air. This information is used by industrial hygienists to determine where in the respiratory system the particle will deposit. Mathematically, aerodynamic diameter is

$$D_a = D_g k \sqrt{\frac{\rho_p}{\rho 0}}$$ [7.1]

Coarse PM (from 2 to 100+ microns) is typically generated by mechanical processes, whether natural or of human origin. Processes such as grinding, windstorms, and erosion produce coarse particles. Because they are relatively large, these particles settle out of the atmosphere by sedimentation (fallout) except on windy days when re-entrainment may complicate the process. Washout by precipitation is another way in which coarse particles are removed from the atmosphere. Convective wind currents may carry coarse PM far downwind from their source as evidenced in volcanic ash settling thousands of miles away from the eruption.

Medium sized PM (from 0.08 to 2 microns) is collected when combustion vapors of low volatility and other similar vapors condense. They are also formed by the coagulation of very fine particle size PM. This size PM is called the accumulation range and particles of this size contain far more organics than coarse PM does (not counting windborne biological particles). Also, water soluble inorganics (NH_4^+, NO_3^- and SO_4^{2-} among others) tend to collect on PM in this size range.

The finest particles, called the Aitken nuclei, range from less than 0.002 to about 0.08 microns. These are strictly anthropogenic, as are most of the accumulation range PM, and combustion processes account for most fine PM. Dirty combustion produces significant amounts of accumulation range PM while clean combustion produces particles mostly in the Aitken nuclei range. In pristine areas over the ocean and the North American continent, the concentration of Aitken nuclei PM is from four to ten times less than the average concentration over North America. Also, anthropogenic contribution is negligible in the background concentrations. Urban areas, especially where freeways are dense, have Aitken nuclei PM concentrations greater than 10,000 times background levels. Particles which settle by gravity, or sedimentation, also called fallout, do so in accordance with Stokes' Law:

$$\upsilon = \frac{D^2 \rho g}{18\eta}$$ [7.2]

where
  D = particle diameter
  g = gravitational constant
  η = gas viscosity
  ρ = particle density
  υ = particle velocity relative to the gas

This equation allows us to calculate the settling time for particles of any given size. Typically, we use a statistical average size to determine how bulk PM will behave, but with a computer we can determine how each size increment will behave. The Stokes equation is good for particle sizes greater than or equal to 1.5 microns.

When particles are finer than that we must apply a correction factor (a number greater than 1 since it will take longer for the particles to settle than Stokes predicts).

$$\upsilon = \frac{D^2 \rho g C}{18\eta}$$ [7.3]

C is often called the Cunningham correction factor, and despite the involved history in the name, let us simply say here that C can be approximated quite handily by this equation:

$$C = 1 + \frac{2.514l}{D}$$ [7.4]

This approximation is good for particles in the range of 0.1 to 1.5 microns. The smaller particles have a significant correction factor. Particles with diameters of 10 microns or greater settle out relatively rapidly, faster than 0.1 cm/sec. When the diameter is less than 1 micron, a particle remains suspended for much longer periods of time, allowing them to participate in atmospheric transformations such as smog cooking. Since these finer particles are anthropogenic and not volcanic or from some other natural source, we must look for human sources to control.

These smallest of particles have a random zigzag motion as they settle. Compare mentally a feather and a bowling ball dropped from the roof of your plant. The movement of the feather, and very fine PM, is called Brownian diffusion. The equations given above are hopelessly inadequate when dealing with very fine particles which settle in accordance with Ficke's first law of diffusion which more accurately describes Brownian movement. For spherical particles this equation is

$$U = \sqrt{\frac{4}{3} \frac{gD_p}{f_d} \frac{\rho_p - \rho}{\rho}}$$

[7.5]

The grain is a discreet particle. Grain limitations are placed on pollution sources because particle size by itself does not describe a polluted gas stream or indicate the magnitude of the problem. Figure 7.3 lists some standard grain loads and mean particle sizes for selected processes according to Rich.

Figure 7.3
Grain Load and Mean Particle Size: Selected Processes

	Grains/scf	microns
Asphalt Plant Rotary Dryer	30	20
Boiler		
Chain grate	1	7
Cyclone	1	5
Pulverizer	5	8
Stoker	4	10
Carbon Black Production		
Natural gas cracking	11	0.1
Oil cracking	30	0.1

Figure 7.3 *(cont'd)*

	Grains/scf	microns
Cement Industry		
Dryer	8	15
Kiln, wet process	5	10
Ceramics		
Glaze, vitreous spray	3	8
Grinding	5	7
Raw product handling	1	5
Refractory sizing	8	15
Chemical Handling Production		
Bin venting	1	7
Copperas roasting kiln	150	mist
Crushing/Grinding	4	10
Dry ice plant	25	fog
Furfural flash dryer	1	0.5
Kiln/Cooler	10	15
Material Handling	4	8
Phosphoric acid plant	150	mist
Pneumatic conveying	30	30
Roaster	10	15
Screening	3	8
Sulfuric acid concentrator	100	mist
Sulfuric acid contact plant		
after absorbers	1.5	mist
after roaster	3	mist
$TiCl_4$ plant, TiO dryer	3	fume
Vaporized phosphorus	0.5	10
Weighing	3	8
Coal Handling		
Bunker ventilation	2	6
Dedusting, air cleaning	8	15
Drying	7	4
Material handling	4	8

Figure 7.3 *(cont'd)*

	Grains/<u>scf</u>	<u>microns</u>
Fertilizer Production		
Ammoniator	3	7
Bagging	5	7
Dryer	7	7
Dryer, ammonium chloride	0.3	0.5
Handling	5	7
Screening	5	7
Foundry		
Abrasive cleaning	4	7
Electric arc	1	1
Sand handling	4	7
Shakeout, enclosed	5	5
Shakeout, side hood	3	5
Swing frame grinder	4	15
Tumbling mill	10	15
Grain Elevator		
Bin ventilation	1	8
Coolers	4	8
Feed mill	4	8
Flour handling	4	8
Grain dryers	1	30
Grain handling	1	12
Gypsum Processing		
Dryer (wet-gas basis)	65	15
Kettle (dry-gas basis)	15	2
Rotary calciner (wet)	40	15
Iron & Steel Processing		
Blast furnace (iron)	13	10
Blast furnace (steel)	15	8
Coke screening	5	14
Electric arc	0.4	3
Electric furnace	10	0.5
Ferrous cupola	4	8
Gray iron cupola	2	5

Figure 7.3 *(cont'd)*

	Grains/scf	microns
Iron & Steel Processing *(cont'd)*		
Hot strip mill	1	3
Oxygen steel converter	9	2
Rotary kiln, iron reduct	6	25
Sintering		
Bed exhaust	2	7
End dump screen	5	7
Steel electric furnace	1	5
Steel open hearth	4	7
Steel, open hearth, oxygen lance	3	2
Steel, open hearth, scrap	1	0.5
Taconite ore crushing/screening	15	40
Metal Working		
Abrasive cut-off	1	15
Buffing	1	3
Cast iron machining	4	8
Grinding	1	15
Polishing	1	3
Portable grinders	1	10
Swing frame grinders	1	10
Mineral Processing		
Asphalt stone dryer	10	30
Cement clinker cooler	4	20
Cement grinding	4	4
Cement kiln	15	7
Cement rock dryer	4	7
Crushing/screening	8	8
Dryers, kilns	5	15
Lime kiln	7	25
Material handling	5	7
Mineral Wool Cupola	0.1	75
Miscellaneous Processes		
Acid mist	1	mist
Acid pickling	4	mist

Figure 7.3 *(cont'd)*

	Grains/scf	microns
Miscellaneous Processes *(cont'd)*		
Bakery	4	8
Bronzing	4	8
Leather buffing	4	8
Leather sanding	4	6
Paper cutting	4	8
Paper grinding	5	8
Non-ferrous Metal Processing		
Ajax furnace, aluminum alloy	4	0.4
Aluminum sweat furnace	0.2	4
Converter furnace	5	12
Copper roaster	10	12
Crucible	1	5
Reverberatory brass	4	0.2
Reverberatory furnace	3	8
Reverberatory lead	2	0.4
Secondary lead blast	5	1
Tin smelting (reverberatory)	3	8
Zinc sintering	3	0.5
Zinc sweat furnace	0.2	4
Petroleum Processing		
Catalytic reformer dust	0.1	20
Powered catalyst recovery	10	7
TCC catalyst regenerator	500	fume
Pharmaceutical/Food Products		
Bagging	1	10
Blending	1	10
Pharmaceutical/Food Products		
Grinder	1	10
Mixer	1	10
Sugar granulator	4	7
Weighing	1	10
Pickling Tank (HCl fumes)	25	fume

Figure 7.3 *(cont'd)*

	Grains/scf	microns
Plastic Processing		
Plastic finishing	4	7
Raw material processing	4	10
Rubber Processing		
Batchout rolls	1	4
Grinding/buffing	4	15
Mixer	4	4
Talc dusting	4	7
Sludge Burning Incinerator	4	5
Sodium Disposal Incinerator	2	0.5
Wood Processing		
Hogging	8	15
Sanding	4	5
Sawing	4	15
Waste conveying	8	15

The grain loading of a coal-fired boiler flue gas can be estimated by

$$C = \frac{240,000(\% \, ash/100)}{T[7.6 \times 10^{-6}(HHV)(100 + \alpha) + 1 - (\% \, ash/100)]} \qquad [7.6]$$

where

C = flue gas dust, grains/ft^3

T = flue gas temperature, R (°F + 460)

α = percent excess air

HHV = higher heating value of coal, BTU/lb

In general, to control PM we must slow down its velocity relative to the carrier gas. This is accomplished by either changing direction (cyclone), impaction (bag filter), bubbling the carrier through water (wet scrubber), or attracting negatively charged particles to a positive plate (electrostatic precipitators). Variations on these devices are available but typically they represent our alternatives for add-on control. This discussion presumes that no control has been ruled out as a viable alternative, that waste minimization techniques such as process modification have been practiced and that closing the plant is economically unattractive.

Hoods and Ducts

First, we must ask some questions and find their answers. Is a hood needed to capture emissions? Will a fan or blower be required?

A hood will probably not be required if the carrier is totally contained within process ducting. However, often a process unit will emit into the air irrespective of ducting. In this case we need a hood to capture emissions. Typically, two types of capture hoods are used in air pollution control: canopy type and semi-enclosed hoods.

Canopies are usually located with a definite gap between them and the actual source; therefore, they capture noncontaminated air as well as contaminated. When using a canopy expect some exposure to personnel. They are used to collect contaminated air over process tanks such as plating tanks. They require larger fans due to the larger volumetric flow. When capturing contaminants from cold process tanks, contaminant movement dictates the capture velocity as shown in Figure 7.4.

When capturing contaminants from cold processes, design the canopy hood so that it extends beyond the process by forty percent of the distance between the hood and the source. That is, if the hood is located three feet over a plating tank (the maximum distance for a canopy hood) then the hood should extend 14.4 inches (36 in. X 0.4) beyond the plating tank.

Figure 7.4
Canopy Hoods for Cold Processes

Contaminant Release	Typical Process	Capture Velocity
At virtually no velocity into still air.	Evaporation from a tank.	50 - 100 ft/min
At low velocity into moderately still air.	Intermittent container filling; low speed conveyor transfer.	100 - 200 ft/min

---

Figure 7.4 *(cont'd)*

Contaminant Release	Typical Process	Capture Velocity
By active generation into rapidly moving air.	Barrel filling; conveyor loading.	200 - 500 ft/min
At high velocity into very rapidly moving air.	Grinding; blasting.	500 - 2,000 ft/min

After Vatavuk + Neveril.

Instead of using Figure 7.4, you can use this equation,

$$v = \frac{V}{1.4pz}$$ [7.7]

attributed to the American Conference of Governmental Industrial Hygienists, to design your capture hood where

v = minimum capture velocity, ft/min
V = ventilation rate, ft³/min
p = open perimeter, ft
z = vertical distance between hood and source, ft

For hot processes, the canopy hood should be low and may be circular or rectangular. For a circular hood

$$V = 4.7D^{2.33}\Delta T^{0.42}$$ [7.8]

but for rectangular hoods

$$V = 6.2W^{1.33}L\Delta T^{0.42}$$ [7.9]

where   D = hood diameter, ft

L = hood length, ft
W = hood width, ft
ΔT = difference in temperature between the hot source and
ambient air, °F.

These equations are derived using calculus methods, which means that
they depend on certain assumptions being true.

Semi-enclosed hoods require smaller fans because comparatively little
noncontaminated air is being pulled into the system. These hoods provide
a higher degree of protection meaning less exposure to personnel. Since
these hoods often affect the equipment from which they capture emissions
it is best to have the process equipment designer do the hood design or
recommend a hood designer to you in order to preserve the process
guarantee.

Figure 7.5
Duct Velocities

Dust Density	Type of Dust	Duct Velocity
Light	Gas, smoke, zinc oxide, aluminum oxide, flour, lint, VOC.	2,000 ft/min
Medium-to-light	Grain, sawdust, plastic, rubber.	3,000 ft/min
Medium-to-heavy	Steel furnace, cement, sandblasting, grinding, other industrial heavy dusts.	4,000 ft/min
Heavy	Metal turnings, foundry shakeout.	5,000 ft/min

Ground-rules, which the buyer should know about these enclosures,
are to provide: 1) adequate volume to allow internal circulation of PM-
laden gas, 2) removable sections for ease of maintenance, 3) a hinged
access door for routine inspection and maintenance, and 4) dust curtains
at open ends to reduce fugitive emissions of PM. When selecting the

location of a pickup hood for a conveyor, choose the place which will prevent dust from escaping, not necessarily the place which will collect the most dust. Otherwise you will soon have fallout from fugitive dust all over the place.

The velocity required in a duct handling PM depends on the type of PM as shown in Figure 7.5.

In order to prevent settling of dust in ducts, a minimum velocity must be maintained and that may be determined by this equation for horizontal ducts.

$$V_v = 0.27 V_h d^{0.2} \qquad [7.10]$$

For vertical ducts, this equation is used.

$$V_h = 105[\frac{s}{(s+1)}]d^{0.4} \qquad [7.11]$$

where

V_h = horizontal duct velocity, ft/min
V_v = vertical duct velocity, ft/min
s = specific gravity of the PM
d = PM diameter, microns

From required entrainment velocity, a duct diameter can be selected,

$$D = 13.54(Q/V)^{1/2} \qquad [7.12]$$

where,

D = duct diameter, in.
Q = volumetric flow rate, ft³/min
V = V_h or V_v as appropriate

These equations demonstrate the importance of knowing particle size of PM in gas streams. However, the entrainment velocity should be calculated for the larger particle sizes, not the average, in order to avoid settling in the duct system. Also the duct system designer needs to account for low velocity pockets near fittings such as tees, elbows, and valves.

Gases flow from areas of high pressure to low pressure according to the equation

$$Q = A V \qquad\qquad [7.13]$$

where Q is volumetric airflow, V is velocity, and A is the duct cross-sectional area in consistent units. For combustion processes, the volumetric airflow can be estimated as

$$V_{std} = \frac{\Delta H_{gross}}{100} (1 + \frac{\% \; excess \, air}{100}) \qquad\qquad [7.14]$$

where

V_{std} = volume of flue gas at standard conditions, scf/lb fuel
ΔH_{gross} = heat of combustion, BTU/lb

The actual flow rate is

$$Q = V_{std} (\frac{460 + T}{492}) \qquad\qquad [7.15]$$

where T is the absolute temperature of the flue gas in degrees Rankin.

The driving force in gas flow is pressure but three kinds of pressure must be understood. Static pressure (SP) is the force that compresses or expands a gas and which is measured with ordinary gauges. Numerically, SP is the difference between the gauge reading and atmospheric pressure. When SP is above atmospheric, it has a positive magnitude and when it is less than atmospheric pressure, SP has a negative sign. Velocity pressure (VP) is the pressure required to accelerate gas from rest to any particular velocity. It is calculated by

$$VP = (V/4005)^2 \qquad\qquad [7.16]$$

which is valid only when g = 32.2 ft/sec^2 and air density ρ = 0.075 lb/ft^3, otherwise a correction factor must be used. VP exists only when the gas is in motion and acts in the direction of positive airflow. Hence, it is always positive in sign. Total pressure is the algebraic sum of SP and VP:

$$TP = SP + VP \qquad\qquad [7.17]$$

TP represents the pressure necessary to start and sustain air movement.

Fans

Centrifugal fans are used to create the pressure difference required in a duct system to move gas streams. Either the backward-curved or radial-tip type centrifugal fan is commonly used.

The backward-curved fan is the more efficient of the two common types but its application is restricted to relatively dust-free, low-temperature environments. Therefore, a backward-curved fan must be installed downstream of the primary pollution control device. In Figure 7.6, according to Vatavuk and Neveril, are the four Classes of backward-curved fans.

Figure 7.6
Backward-curved Fans

Class	Stastic Pressure in. water	Velocity ft/min
I	5 2.5	2,300 3,200
II	8.5 4.5	3,000 4,175
III	13.50 6.75	3,780 5,260
IV	above 13.5-6.75	above 5,260

Better suited to dust-laden gas streams, though less efficient, are the radial-tip fans. These tough air movers can be installed upstream of the pollution control devices. These fans are almost exclusively used when the control device is a venturi scrubber. They can withstand abrasive dust, higher temperatures and higher pressures than the backward-curved fans. They create static pressures of 20 to 80 inches of water and can operate at temperatures to 600°F. Flows range from 25,000 to 250,000 cfm. Regardless of the type fan, certain laws apply, as shown in Figure 7.7.

Figure 7.7
Basic Fan Laws

Variable	With Speed Change	With Density Change
Volume	Varies directly with speed $CFM_2 = CFM_1 (RPM_2/RPM_1)$	Does not change with density
Pressure	Varies with square of speed $P_2 = P_1 (RPM_2/RPM_1)^2$	Varies directly with density $P_2 = P_1 (D_2/D_1)$
Horsepower	Varies with cube of speed $HP_2 = HP_1 (RPM_2/RPM_1)^3$	Varies directly with density $HP_2 = HP_1 (D_2/D_1)$

Power consumption of fans is typically specified as an efficiency, either mechanical or static.

$$ME = \frac{(Q \times TP)}{(6,356 BHP)} \times 100\% \qquad [7.18]$$

$$SE = \frac{(Q \times SP)}{(6,356 BHP)} \times 100\% \qquad [7.19]$$

Figure 7.8 gives limits of dust handling equipment discussed below and Figure 7.9 lists applications for dust removal equipment in hot gas service. Not every piece of dust control equipment is suitable for any application. Selection of the wrong—that is, inappropriate—device accounts for much of the air pollution control problems in industry because none of these devices requires very much in the way of maintenance. As you can see, careful attention must be paid to the problem in the engineering design phase, else the compliance office will pay close attention to dust removal *ad infinitum*.

Wet Scrubbers

The use of water to aid dust collection can be used effectively in several devices. For instance, the cyclone and electrostatic precipitator can be operated in the wet mode. In this section, though, we will examine the use of tower or Venturi equipment, or both, with a liquid to remove particles.

Figure 7.8
Limits of Dust Handling Equipment

Maximum Design Values	Cyclone/ Multi- cyclone	Electrostatic Precipitator dry wet	Filter bed bag	Scrubber
Temperature, °F	2912	842 176	932 662	428
Pressure, psia	1450	14.5 43.5	14.5 29.0	435
Minimum Grain, microns	3	<0.1	1 <0.1	<0.1

Figure 7.9
Hot Gas Dust Removal

Application	Dust Control Device
Increase specific separation efficiency.	Dry Electrostatic Precipitator
Pre-clean to relieve subsequent removal or process units.	Cyclone
Recycle hot dust.	Cyclone
Remove dust from gas with high acid condensation point.	Dry Electrostatic Precipitator Fabric Filter
Remove stack gas without cooler.	Packed-bed Filter Dry Electrostatic Precipitator Fabric Filter
Separate high-melting residue in liquid form.	Cyclone
Wet removal of dust using boiling liquid.	Scrubber
Wet removal of dust using pressurized water.	Scrubber

Some of the more widely used scrubbers are the Venturi scrubbers, which are commonly high-energy (large pressure drop) units but can be used in a lower energy consuming arrangement. These scrubbers generally have a vertical downflow duct inlet. A flooded-wall entry section, called a quencher, receives the gas stream and prevents dust from building up at the entry. An adjustable throat (which is not really a Venturi but somewhere along the way the name has stuck) provides the pressure drop or Venturi effect. Below the Venturi throat but ahead of the actual separator device (usually a wet-cyclone or spray tower) a flooded elbow reduces erosion by abrasive particles. The Venturi throat (especially a true Venturi) is sometimes fitted with refractory brick to prevent erosion.

Figure 7.10
Typical Wetted Tower Separator

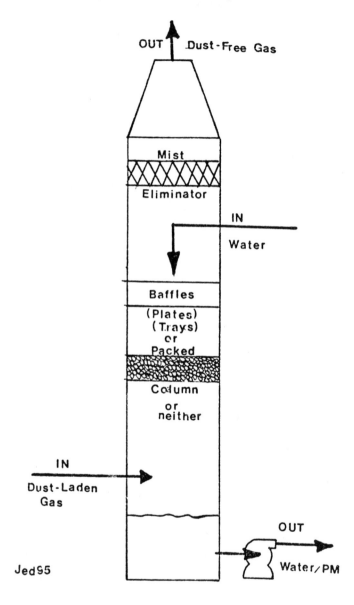

Wet Scrubber

The scrubber itself may be a spray tower, a plate column, a packed-bed, or a wet-cyclone. (Figure 7.10 shows a typical wetted tower separator.) Column or tower can be used interchangeably. Typically, the water is recirculated in these scrubbers and the wet dust is disposed of as a sludge. Figure 7.11 shows the relative energy consumption in terms of pressure drop of various scrubbers.

Figure 7.11
Scrubber Pressure Drop

Low-energy	0.5 to 2.5 in. water gauge
Low-to medium-energy	2.6 to 6 i.w.g.
Medium- to high-energy	6 to 15 i.w.g.
High-energy	>15 i.w.g.

Typical scrubber efficiencies are shown in Figure 7.12.

Figure 7.12
Scrubber Efficiencies

Type Scrubber	Pressure Drop, i.w.g.	Removal Efficiency, % @ grain size
Gravity-spray	1 to 2	70 @ 10 microns
Wet cyclone	2 to 8	90+ @ 5 microns
Packed-bed		90+ @ 1 micron
Venturi		98+ @ 1 micron

Volumetric airflow rate is the most important process variable other than grain size when selecting a scrubber. The actual gas volume at the inlet of the scrubber determines the size of the equipment and, hence, cost.

The pressure drop under operating conditions is the next most important factor. This parameter determines fan size along with volumetric flow. Finally, it is important to know the characteristics of the wet dust and water mixture (sludge) in order to select materials of construction. If the mixture will be corrosive, and this is not accounted for in design, you will spend many dollars replacing downstream duct fittings and the tower itself may fail prematurely. On the other hand, with proper selection of materials, a scrubber can be expected to last for many years.

Venturis and spray towers are most often used for removal of PM but also can be used to remove gaseous emissions, as discussed later. Spray towers are not particularly suitable for very fine PM; however, an innovation on the spray design called a reverse jet scrubber can achieve 90+ percent removal of these particles with around 50 psig water. Packed-beds can be used for PM but because this application requires high maintenance due to plugging, it is typically avoided. Certainly, packed-beds are better suited to removal of gaseous pollutants. Plate towers can be used for PM but the design must consider the fact that a plate has different efficiencies for each particle size. Particles larger than an optimum size can be readily removed but smaller PM is not effectively removed no matter how many additional plates are added to the design.

The chief disadvantage of wet scrubbing is that the pollutant is transferred to another media, either wastewater or solid waste. Therefore, when a scrubber has been selected the plant staff needs to plan for the disposal of the wastewater or sludge in accordance with appropriate regulations. An offsetting advantage of wet scrubbing is that both PM and gaseous pollutants, especially inorganics, can be controlled simultaneously. A spray scrubber is particularly advantageous in hot gas situations. The spray cools the incoming gas until both are at the same temperature as the gas is saturated by the scrubbing liquor (adiabatic cooling). If this is accomplished in a preliminary step, four distinct advantages are gained: 1) the volume of gas entering downstream stages is reduced, 2) evaporation in downstream stages is eliminated, 3) the corrosive effect of the hot gas is mitigated down stream, and 4) the saturation of the gas helps remove certain contaminants downstream.

Where inorganic gas such as sulfur dioxide, nitrogen oxides, chlorine, fluorine, are included in the waste gas stream the wet scrubber must be injected with an alkaline solution such as caustic soda to neutralize the formation of acid in the scrubber but also to remove the inorganic gas pollutant. This use of scrubbers is discussed in more detail later.

Scrubber efficiency is determined by measuring the PM in the scrubber waste liquid and residual PM in the clean air stream leaving the scrubber. Efficiency, % = Solids in effluent/(Solids in effluent + PM Emissions) X 100. Figure 7.13 gives some tips on operating scrubbers to remove PM.

Figure 7.13
Tips on Operating Wet Scrubbers to Remove PM

Keep all areas flooded.
Ensure scrubber installation is precisely vertical.
Maintain liquid seal.
Keep drain clear.
Spray water at fan inlet to prevent buildup on blades.
Clean fan regularly.
Record all pressure drops under clean conditions.
Check recycle and bleed flow daily.

Cyclones

Due to the ease of operation, many plant engineers prefer cyclonic separators for removing PM from gas streams (*see* Figure 7.14) especially as precleaners for baghouses or wet scrubbers. As a precleaner, cyclones generally remove the 20-30 micron range coarse particles. Reverse flow cyclones with tangential or involute inlets are very popular. Heumann's Law of cyclone design is: "use only cyclones whose performance parameters have been determined or verified by actual testing on a cyclone of the same family [geometry]."

As PM falls in a fluid under the force of gravity, it accelerates until the frictional drag in the fluid balances the gravitational forces, whereupon it continues to fall at constant velocity. This is the terminal velocity or free-settling velocity. For spherically shaped particles, such as we assume our PM is:

$$u_t = [\frac{4g_L D_p (\rho_s - \rho)}{3\rho v C}]^{1/2}$$

[7.20]

Figure 7.14
Typical Cyclone Separator

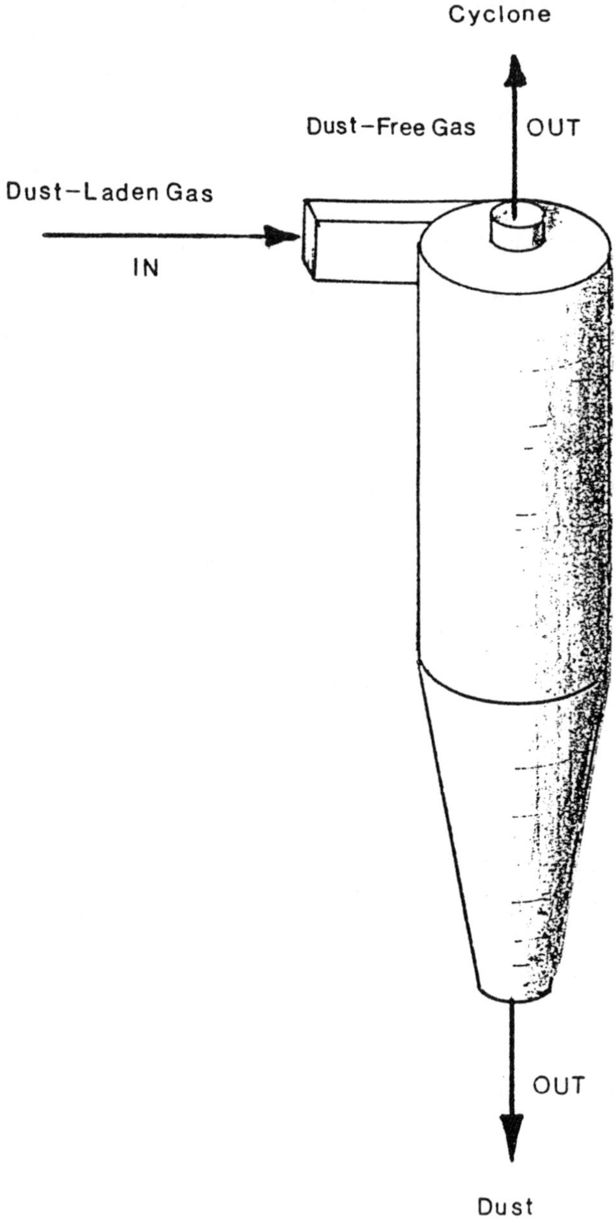

Cyclones use gravity and centrifugal forces to remove PM from a gas stream. As the dust-laden gas enters the cyclone at an angle it throws particles toward the wall of the chamber at forces up to 5 G's (in low-resistance cyclones with large diameters) which halts their motion relative to the gas. In small, high resistance cyclones the G-force on the incoming particles can be as high as 2,500. The PM slides down the wall into a hopper underneath the cyclone. Two vortexes are created as the dust-laden gas enters the cyclone. One, the larger vortex, spirals downward and carries most of the coarser PM with it. An inner vortex is created which spirals upward, carrying finer particles with it.

However, since cyclones remove coarse particles more effectively than fine particles, they can rarely be used alone. Typically, we see a bank of cyclones upstream of either a bank of baghouse filters or a large electrostatic precipitator. Sometimes a series of cyclones are used to remove finer and finer particles. Also multi-tubed cyclones can be very effective dust collectors and have been used as primary control devices quite successfully.

Cyclone efficiency is measured in terms of pressure drop and percent removal. Pressure drop is measured as the difference in static pressure between the gas streams in and out of the cyclone. Constantinescu gives pressure drop as:

$$\Delta P = 0.192 N_H \rho_g u^2 / 2g_c \qquad [7.21]$$

where
ΔP = pressure drop, iwg
N_H = $4ab/(D-2b)^2$, dimensionless
a = inlet height, in
b = inlet width, in
D = cyclone diameter, in
ρ_g = particle density, lb_m/ft^3
u = gas inlet velocity, ft/sec

Cyclone diameter is related to pressure drop by:

$$D = \sqrt{\frac{0.192 \rho_g U^2 (2ab)}{g_c \Delta P} + 2b} \qquad\qquad [7.22]$$

Finally, diameter and height are related to flow rate by:

$$H = 4.32 Q/D \qquad\qquad [7.23]$$

Pressure drop is an indicator of energy consumption as it takes more blower horsepower to move air against a large pressure drop than it does against a lesser difference.

Figure 7.15 shows some advantages and disadvantages of using cyclones to remove PM and Figure 7.16 gives some operational tips.

Percent removal compares the percent of each particle size separated from the incoming gas stream. The larger particle sizes will be removed in the 90-100 percent range, whereas the least particle sizes—5 microns and less—will approach 0 percent removal efficiency.

Figure 7.15
Cyclones

Advantages	Disadvantages
Ease of operation.	Precise installation is critical.
90+% efficiency for coarse.	<90% efficiency for fines.
Can be used at high temperatures.	High temperature design is feasible but expensive.
Can remove a specific size particle.	Cannot process sticky dust.

Figure 7.16
Tips on Operating Cyclones

Install large diameter roughing cyclone upstream.
Line high-efficiency cyclone with refractory.
Keep gas stream above dewpoint.
Clean cyclone routinely.
Install turning vanes in elbow preceding inlet.
Allow exhaust fan to operate a few minutes after shutdown.
Record clean pressure drops.

It is these finer particles that find their way into the lungs of humans. Overall removal efficiency, then, depends on the nature of the PM.

Saltation velocity is defined in Zanker's review article as the minimum fluid velocity that prevents solid particles from settling out before the cyclone. Zanker offers this simplified equation for saltation velocity:

$$U_s = 0.926 \rho_p^{1/3} [(b/D_c)/(1 - b/D_c)]^{1/3} b^{0.067} U_i^{2/} \qquad [7.24]$$

Once a cyclone is installed do not modify it in any way without having the design engineer's approval. Your permit will probably prohibit modifications without advance approval by the permit authority anyway and they will require the designer's approval evidenced by her professional seal on the design documents. Approval notwithstanding, physical modifications can be devastating to the efficiency of the cyclone.

Electrostatic Precipitation

With PM that is easily ionized (given an electric charge) the control device of choice is usually an electrostatic precipitator (EP) (See Figure 7.17) Charged wires or grids attract the ionized PM with an opposite charge. Adhesive properties of the particles and the electric field prevent the particles from being re-entrained in the gas stream. Some mechanical device such as a rapper is used to dislodge the collected particles which fall into hoppers. Cleaning the EP can usually be done without interrupting the gas flow.

EPs are the control device of choice when the gas stream is laden with PM smaller than 10 microns with the size curve skewed towards the submicron range. These devices routinely achieve removal efficiencies exceeding 99 percent and can operate at temperatures up to 1,000°F. Typical operation is at 700° or less. Pressure drop typically runs 1/2 iwg at velocities of 2 to 8 ft/sec. Operating voltages may be as high as 100,000 V.

The Deutsch equation is used to determine plate-area-to-efficiency:

$$E = 1 - e^{-\omega(A/Q)} \qquad [7.25]$$

where E = collection efficiency; ω = drift velocity, ft/sec; A = plate area, ft^2; and Q = flow rate (actual), ft^3/sec. Efficiency is improved by larger collector surface area and decreased gas flow rate. Either of these changes increases the time particles spend in the electrical field this enhancing collection. Decreasing gas velocity, increasing gas temperature or increasing the voltage field will also enhance PM removal efficiency since the particle migration velocity towards the collecting electrodes is increased.

Figure 7.17
Electrostatic Precipitator

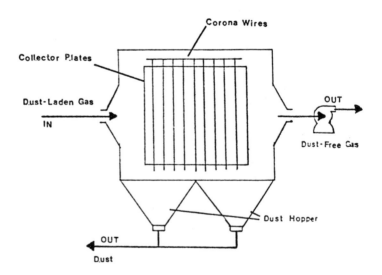

Electrical characteristics of PM have significant effect on collection efficiency and plate area. PM resistivity varies with temperature and moisture content of the flue gas. These characteristics are summarized in Figure 7.18.

Figure 7.18
Effect of Electrostatic Properties on EP's

PM Conductivity	PM Resistivity	EP Problem	Correction
Too high	Too low	bleed charge 1) before, or 2) after elec-trode impact	secondary control
Too low	Too high	not easily charged	very large EP

Moist gas streams at low temperature require insulated equipment in order to prevent dielectric corrosion. Operating tips for EPs are given in Figure 7.19.

Figure 7.19
Tips for Operating Electrostatic Precipitators

Establish removal efficiency with new EP.
Record clean pressure drop.

Filtration

When speaking of cleaning gas streams the filter usually referred is the fabric filter, or the bag house, which can achieve efficiencies of 99 percent. No wonder they are so ubiquitous in industry.

Typically PM-laden gas enters the bag house at the bottom (*see* Figure 7.20) and loses velocity as it expands into the plenum chamber, or the house. Under pressure, the gas passes through the filter, or bag, and exits at the top of the structure into an exit plenum which collects the gas and routes it to a stack through and induced-draft fan. Alternatively, the gas is fed to the filter through its core and the captured PM drops down through the bag. Either way, the impact of PM on the filter medium, diffusion of the gas in the bag house, gravity settling of the PM and the electrostatic attraction of the particles to the medium combine to make the bag house an effective means of removing PM. Figure 7.21 lists the advantages and disadvantages of baghouses. Figure 7.22 gives some operating tips for baghouses.

Figure 7.20
Baghouse

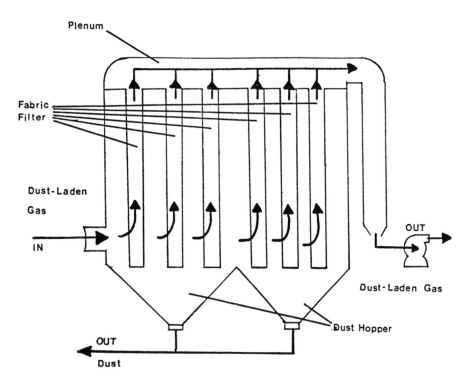

Figure 7.21
Bag Houses

Advantages

Efficiencies exceeding 99%.

Performance independent of
flowrate.

Uniform efficiency over range
of particle sizes.

Efficiency independent of
particle resistivity.

Disadvantages

Bypass due to damaged fabric.

High maintenance.

Cementation of filter cake.

PM adhesion to bag.

Figure 7.22
Tips for Operating Baghouses

Clean rows of bags randomly.
Replace leaking bags immediately.
Check and adjust bag tension often.
Don't clean bags too frequently.
Clean bags for 10 minutes after shutdown.
Check pressure drop often.
Inspect bags thoroughly quarterly.

To prevent excessive pressure drop, the bag filters are periodically shaken by a mechanical means, reverse air stream, or pulsed jet air stream to remove the dust which has built up on it. Older bag houses may have to be manually shaken though these units are antiques now.

The filter fabric may be felt or woven synthetic. The latter are preferred now and are woven with a specific application in mind. The fabric vendor will choose material based on operating temperature, shaking method, and physical and chemical characteristics of the gas stream and particulate. Woven bags typically require air velocities of two feet per minute (fpm) or less, whereas the felt bags can handle velocities of five fpm or higher.

Fabric filter performance is affected by air-to-cloth ratio and pressure drop. The air-to-cloth ratio is a design parameter which is fixed unless modifications are made to the bag house in the field. Figure 7.23 gives some design values. This ratio is calculated by dividing the volumetric flowrate of the gas (ft^3/min) by the surface area of filter medium (ft). Small bag houses with large pressure drops have a high ratio.

Pressure drop across the filter provides an indication of energy consumption and need for cleaning or replacement of bags. Normally, the bag house is operated with a pressure drop from 6-8 inches of water. Excessive pressure drop indicates the accumulated PM on the fabric is too thick and needs to be shaken or pulsed. Pressure drops less than six probably mean that breaches exist in the bags or perhaps even some bags are missing.

Figure 7.23
Typical Air-to-Cloth Ratios

Cleaning Mechanism	Filter Fabric	Typical Air-to-cloth Ratio
Mechanical Shaker	Woven	2 - 3.5
Reverse-air	Woven	2 - 3.5
Pulse-jet	Felt	5 - 12

HOW OFFENSIVE GASES AND VAPORS ARE CONTROLLED

Air streams which contain contaminants other than PM are not effectively removed in cyclones and baghouses though some species can be removed by EP and most can be absorbed in water or some other liquid such as an acid or caustic.

Absorption

The absorber, which is a special wet scrubber, has long been the device of choice for removing gases that are soluble in water. Many heavy industries and power plants will upgrade or retrofit their existing scrubbers to meet CAAA requirements since this will undoubtedly be cheaper than new technology which has not paid its just dues through demonstrated performance anyway. Certainly SO_2 is most effectively removed by wet scrubbing. A certain amount of NO_x is easily absorbed in water but to get down to concentration levels required by law some other control equipment is also needed.

Sulfur compounds are easily soluble in water. Sulfur dioxide (SO_2) and sulfur trioxide (SO_3) are pollutants from the combustion of sulfur-bearing fuels such as coal, sour gas, and certain fuel oils. Other sources are sulfuric acid plants, petroleum refineries, and smelters. Gas streams contaminated with sulfur oxides are absorbed in thick slurries of caustic materials. Often two stages are used to increase removal efficiencies. Some sulfur scrubbing technologies are summarized in Figure 7.24.

Figure 7.24
Sulfur Removal Processes

Lime/Limestone Slurry
Sodium-Alkali
Dual-Alkali
Ammonium Thiosulfate
Illinois Institute of Technology
Dry Scrubbing
Selexol
Kellogg Weir System
Buffered Citrate Absorption
Magnesium Oxide
Wellman-Lord
Resox
Allied Chemical
Chiyoda
Shell/UOP Copper Oxide Adsorption
Integrated Fly Ash Removal
Pircon-Peck
Bergbau-Forschung/Foster Wheeler (BF-FW)

In the Kellogg-Weir Process the absorption of SO_2 is described as:

$$P_o/P_i = e^{-\Phi} \qquad [7.26]$$

where P_o and P_i are the outlet and inlet concentrations of SO_2 in the flue gas. When the overall mass transfer is roughly equal to the gas mass transfer, Φ is:

$$\Phi = 12\sqrt{\frac{Du}{\Pi d}\frac{lNL}{vdG}} \qquad [7.27]$$

D is the diffusivity of SO_2 in the gas phase and u is the relative velocity between the alkaline spray droplets and the contaminated gas. The mean diameter of the droplets is d, the mean distance they travel is l and their actual velocity is v. N is the number of spray stages. Volumetric gas flow is G and liquid flow rate is L.

Diameter of a packed tower and flooding rates are calculated by:

$$G = b\exp[-6.15 + 3.17\sqrt{-1 - 1.2\ln(ab^2)}] \qquad [7.28]$$

$$a = \frac{AV^{0.2}}{g_c e^3(DG)(DL)} \qquad [7.29]$$

$$b = L[(DG)(DL)]^{1/2} \qquad [7.30]$$

where

A = specific surface area, ft^2/ft^3
DG = density of gas, lb/ft^3
DIA = packed-tower diameter, ft
DL = density of liquid, lb/ft^3
e = fraction of void space in packing, no units
G = superficial gas rate, $lb/hr\ ft^2$

L = superficial liquid rate, lb/hr ft^2
L/G = control parameter
V = viscosity of liquid, cP
W = flowrate of gas, lb/hr

After calculating the control parameter, this expression should fall within this range:

$$0.2 < (L/G)[(DG)(DL)]^{1/2} < 7.00 \qquad [7.31]$$

The usual wet scrubbing process involves slurries of lime or limestone or some other alkaline material. Magnesium compounds have been used to scrub sulfur dioxide as well as two stages of alkaline solutions. Determination of the optimum point at which to inject these slurries is critical for maximum SO_2 removal. Sorbent slurry works best at a critical temperature range (typically 1400-2300°F). Reactivity of the slurry, which is related to pore volume and surface area of the solids in the slurry, is also very critical for removal efficiency.

All these systems produce a waste stream which few plants can use. Some have produced ammonium sulfate fertilizer or gypsum or sulfuric acid but this is not economically feasible in all but a few cases. Dry scrubbing or dry absorption utilizes a fine spray of high-solids slurry of alkaline material mixed with the flue gas in a spray dryer. Another scheme moves the flue gas through a bed of powdered absorbent, or in some cases, adsorbent. Some even integrate the fly ash from the combustor to achieve dry scrubbing. These systems are generally less expensive and easier to maintain and operate than wet scrubbing of sulfur dioxide.

The point of this discussion is to give you an appreciation for the science involved. Gas-scrubbing is not a black art and scrubbers cannot be picked out of a catalog. These formula apply to a very specific situation (an SO_2 removal process invented by Alexander Weir in combination with Pullman Kellog's magnesium- promoted lime slurry chemistry) so for your situation a designer should start with fundamental chemistry and physics and develop the appropriate mathematical expressions for removing pollutants from your contaminated gas in certain types of equipment for certain removal processes. Selection of the lowest cost from the catalogs of the next three sales engineers who come through the door has led more than one company down the path to compliance orders and fines. You cannot make a silk purse from a sow's ear.

Figure 7.25
Tips for Scrubbing Acid Gases

Pay strict attention to pH control.
Check liquid/gas ratios often.
Control temperatures above dewpoint.
Atomization of alkaline stream is critical.

Nitrogen compounds are more difficult to remove from an air stream than the sulfur compounds are. Many utilities are opting for low-NO_x burners in order to avoid as much post-combustion control as possible. Typically, NO_x is generated thermally by the following chemical reaction:

$$2N_2 + 3O_2 \rightarrow 2NO + 2NO_2 \qquad [7.32]$$

This type NO_x increases in flue gas exponentially with temperature and at temperatures above 2,000°F is predominant. A source of NO_x which predominates at lower temperatures, called prompt NO_x, is made thusly:

$$CH_4 + 5O_2 + 2N_2 \rightarrow 2NO + 2NO_2 + CO_2 + 2H_2O \qquad [7.33]$$

This is no straightforward burning of methane. Methane, here, represents hydrocarbon radicals that form in flue gas during the combustion process before firebox temperatures reach a sufficient temperature (2,000°) to prevent their formation. Finally, in the burning of coal and fuel oil, the formation of NO_x is:

$$R_3N + O_2 \rightarrow NO + NO_2 + CO_2 + H_2O \qquad [7.34]$$

where R represents any hydrocarbon radical binding nitrogen. Methane and propane have insignificant amounts of organo-nitrogen.

Post-combustion control of NO_x amounts to absorbing it in water to form nitric acid according to the following reactions:

$$H_2O\,(l) + 3NO_2\,(g) \rightleftharpoons 2HNO_3\,(aq) + NO\,(g) \qquad [7.35]$$

The NO is oxidized at 100 psi at 1,688°F:

$$2NO\,(g) + O_2 \rightarrow 2NO_2\,(g) \qquad [7.36]$$

or else it remains a gaseous contaminant. NO_2 removal is enhanced by operating the absorption tower under pressure and cooling with countercurrent strength of nitric acid. That is, at the top of the absorber, where clean gas is exiting, pure water or dilute acid is introduced and at the bottom, where the heavily contaminated gas enters, the concentrated acid is drawn off. Warm air is introduced into a short raschig ring (small cylinder packing) section located between the tower and the acid trap downstream, oxidizing NO and bleaching acid. In pollution control, the quantity of acid production is not sufficient to be commercially viable, so the acid stream is typically neutralized with caustic soda or some alkaline material and disposed as wastewater or neutral sludge.

NO_x is produced in serious quantities in combustion processes, however. For instance, when burning methane in pure oxygen:

$$CH_4 + 2O_2 \rightarrow CO_2 + 2H_2O \qquad [7.37]$$

but when air is used as the source of oxygen:

$$CH_4 + 2O_2 + 7.52N_2 \rightarrow CO_2 + 2H_2O + 7.52N_2 \qquad [7.38]$$

For every volume of natural gas burned, 7.52 volumes of nitrogen are emitted in the flue gas with NO_x formation reactions going on.

Transfer units are numbers that assist chemical engineers to design absorbers by determining the height of packing and column required. This number depends on capture efficiency and where inlet solute concentration is less than three percent by volume:

$$N_u = \frac{\ln\left[(1 - \frac{MG_M}{J_M})(\frac{Y_1 - MX_2}{Y_2 - MX_2}) + \frac{MG_M}{J_M}\right]}{(1 - \frac{MG_M}{J_M})}$$

[7.39]

M is the slope of the solute-solvent equilibrium curve and J_M and G_M are liquid and gas molar flow rates. As you see, the mathematics of absorber design are not easy and the chemical engineering design procedures become specialized and beyond the scope of this management book.

Absorbers are columns of varying design. One of the more common types is the plate column which entrains liquids on plates through the tower while the gas rises through each pool of liquid. This contact allows the opportunity for absorption. Packed towers are also common. The minimum allowable capacity of an absorber is determined by the need for effective dispersion and contacting of the contaminated gas and acid. An efficient absorber has a high liquid (absorbent) to gas (absorbate) ratio, low temperature, high contaminant loading in the inlet gas stream and large surface areas for contact of liquid and gas. Therefore, have an absorber column designed for your specific application, do not try to select it from a catalog.

The most common problems with absorbers are related to process conditions, which must be maintained identical with design parameters. Sometimes towers suffer internal problems such as collapsed trays, plugged beds, and inadequate cooling for various reasons. Rarely is troubleshooting simple, so it is best to call in an absorption tower expert right away.

Adsorption

When molecules of a fluid contact and adhere to the surface of a solid by virtue of van der Waals forces, the process is adsorption and is very useful in pollution control. Many organics adhere exothermally to activated carbon, charcoal or coal though wet gases tend to clog the surface area of activated carbons, plugging the bed. To avoid this place a refrigeration unit upstream of the carbon bed. By using a series of beds, a gas stream can almost be completely stripped of VOCs/HAPs. When the bed is plugged by either moisture or organics then breakthrough occurs and VOCs/HAPs show up in the emissions again.

The contaminant is called the adsorbate and the granulated solid carbon species is the adsorbent. Transfer of adsorbate from dirty gas to the adsorbent is controlled by diffusion, a mass transfer phenomenon. The degree of adsorption available depends on the driving force: difference (gradient) between mass transfer from the gas phase to the solid surface. Adsorbents have large surface area per unit weight.

Figure 7.26
Carbon-Based Adsorbents

Carbon Source	Shapes Available
Bituminous Coal	Granular, Powder
Lignite	Granular, Powder
Peat	Granular, Powder, Cylinders
Petroleum	Granular, Cylinders
Shell	Granular
Wood	Granular

after Perry

Figure 7.26 shows some of the geometries available based on the source of carbon. The properties of some carbon adsorbents are given in Figure 7.27.

Figure 7.27
Properties of Carbon Adsorbents

Property	Activated	Other
Bulk Density	22-34 lb/ft^3	16-44 lb/ft^3
Pore Volume	0.009 - 0.02 ft^3/lb	0.02 - 0.03 ft^3/lb
Pore Diameter, average	15 - 25 Angstroms	18 - 40 Angstroms

The process of adsorption is modeled by the Freundlich relationship:

$$(\frac{x}{m})^n = kc \qquad [7.40]$$

where

> x = weight of adsorbate
> m = weight of adsorbent
> c = concentration in equilibrium with adsorbate
> k & n = constants determined experimentally at fixed temperature

The weight of adsorbate, if VOC, is calculated on the basis of 1,000 scf of gas stream. Determine the parts per million volumes (ppm) of VOC in the gas stream and calculate:

$$x = (ppm)(M)/359,000 = lb\,VOC/1,000\,scf \qquad [7.41]$$

The carbon requirement is equation 7.42.

$$lbcarbon/1,000scf = 100x/((lbVOC/100lbC)$$ [7.42]

The operating capacity (lb VOC/100 lb carbon) is usually supplied by the adsorbent supplier. Patrick provides operating capacities for some VOC as summarized in Figure 7.28.

**Figure 7.28
Carbon Operating Capacities**

VOC Species	Operating Capacity lb/100 lb C
Benzene	6
Butyl Acetate	8
n-Butyl Alcohol	8
Cyclohexane	6
Ethyl Acetate	8
Ethyl Alcohol	8
Heptane	6
Hexane	6
Isopropyl Acetate	8
Methyl Acetate	7
Methyl Alcohol	7
Toluene	7
Trichlorotrifluoroethane	8
Xylene	10

The time it takes to saturate the adsorbent with adsorbate is called the loading time and is expressed as:

$$T = \frac{16.67d\rho}{vC}$$ [7.43]

where

τ = loading time, hr
d = bed depth, ft
ρ = density, lb/ft^3
v = velocity, fpm, and

The typical application of adsorption technology to gas-stream cleaning is fixed-bed adsorbers. A column is designed to carry sufficient adsorbent to last a given period of time given certain gas-stream contaminant loading, temperature, moisture, and flow rate parameters. The event when the adsorbent is used up and the contaminant appears in unacceptable quantities in the flue gas is called break through. When break through occurs, the column must be taken offline for changing adsorbent or restoring it to its original clean condition. This is called reactivation. Two adsorption columns are typically used side-by-side so that one can be reactivated while one is separating contaminant from the off-gas. For absorber design, you are referred to Treybal and other texts on the subject. However, it is not the black-art that some would have you believe. Therefore, if you are operating an adsorber and it is not performing as desired after reactivation, calibrate all instruments (pressure, temperature, and flow) and closely observe all process parameters. Then fix problems that cause one or more of these process parameters to be off-design.

If you are going to recover solvent or use continuous emissions monitoring, you need two adsorber beds in parallel with one on-line while the other is off-line being regenerated or waiting to be reused. Stripping chlorinated solvents from the off-line bed produces hydrochloric acid so keep that in mind when choosing materials of construction or deciding on disposal for the stripping solution. Some VOCs build up faster than others, if not totally stripped when the bed was last off-line. Unstripped VOCs build up until they become a fire hazard when the bed is next on-line. Solvents that are immiscible in water are best removed by adsorption. Water-miscible solvents require distillation before the material is reused.

Incineration

Thermal oxidation systems burn up the pollutant. Catalytic incinerators utilize reactions between precious metal and base metal catalysts and the pollutant, generally some species of VOC. Figure 7.29 lists information required to design a catalytic reactor.

Figure 7.29
Catalytic Incinerator Process Requirements

List VOCs and concentrations.
List other contaminants present.
Peak emissions loading (lb/hr) and duration (hr).
Emitting process description.
Airflow (scfm).
Exhaust temperature.
Utilities (power, fuel, pressurized air).

Thermal and catalytic incinerators have high destructive removal efficiencies (DRE), on the order of 95-99 percent. They are simple to use and maintain. Complex incineration is carried out in recuperative and regenerative systems.

Tips for operating incinerators are given in Figure 7.30.

Figure 7.30
Tips for Operating Incinerators

Keep watch on temperatures.
Test inlet periodically for catalyst poisons.

One advantage of incineration is the near complete destruction of VOC. Another is the short residence time which adds little impact to the overall process. A disadvantage is the fuel cost, which can be overcome somewhat by catalytic incineration—effective at lower temperatures than thermal incineration.

Recovery of waste heat from incinerators is governed by an old standard in engineering practice:

$$A = Q / U \Delta t_m \qquad\qquad [7.44]$$

where

Q = heat duty, BTU/hr
ΔT_m = log-mean temperature difference, °F
U = overall heat transfer coefficient, BTU/ft² hr°F

The log-mean temperature difference is taken between the inlet and outlet gas streams and is explained in texts on heat exchanger design.

Determination of fuel usage is an important part of successfully operating an incinerator. The theoretical heating value of unburnt pollutants must be accounted for; however, this value can be ignored assuming 100 percent combustion efficiency, no air available for combustion in the flue gas, and heat losses from the incinerator and heat exchanger are negligible. In this case, fuel consumption may be estimated by:

$$F = \frac{V_i (C_p)_i (T_i - T_o)}{\Delta H_f - \sum_{j=1}^{n} m_j (C_p)_j (T_o - T_f)} \qquad [7.45]$$

In this equation, we have C_{pi} = mean heat capacity effluent, BTU/mol°F

C_{pj} = mean heat capacity product, BTU/mol°F
ΔH_f = gross heating value of fuel, BTU/mol
F = fuel consumption, mol/hr
m_j = moles of combustion product j per mole fuel
T_f = ambient temperature of fuel, °F
T_i = inlet temperature of fuel, °F
T_o = outlet temperature from incinerator, °F
V_i = effluent flowrate to incinerator, mol/hr

The volume of stack gas is many times more than the volume of materials introduced to the incinerator. For one thing, the change in temperature expands the existing gases. For another, the volume of reaction products (or combustion products) is many times more than the volume of reactants.

In the simplest case of burning methane (natural gas):

$$CH_4 + O_2 \rightarrow CO_2 + 2H_2O \qquad [7.46]$$

In this simplest of combustion stoichiometries, three moles of products will be made for every two moles of reactants consumed. However, air is used instead of pure oxygen and the nitrogen goes for a ride through the incinerator (mostly anyway) so for every two moles of reactants consumed, seven moles of products are introduced to the flue. This does not account for excess air or the expansion due to increased temperature in the flue. The general equation used by Vatavuk and Neveril for flue gas volume is

$$V_o = V_i + \sum_{j=1}^{n} m_j \qquad [7.47]$$

As before, the presentation of these equations is intended as an introduction to incinerators, not to make anyone an expert in incinerator technology. However, you should be able to review the work of equipment designers and consultants who prepare estimates for emissions from these devices.

Condensation

A basic technique of separating pollutant gases from air streams is to let the contaminant saturate the stream then cool the stream to the dew point of the contaminant. This is the process of condensation. Another way to get condensation is to increase the pressure to the system until the partial pressure of the contaminant is equal to its vapor pressure at which point condensation occurs. This is a complex removal process when the gas stream has a highly variable concentration of various species. The gas stream must be carefully characterized before using this process.

Surface condensers are essentially shell and tube heat exchangers. Vapors condense on the outside of the tubes while a coolant flows on the inside. Condensed vapor drains to a collection tank for disposal. Cox charts, graphs of vapor pressure against temperature, are used to design condensers. At a given temperature the greatest removal efficiency is proportional to the largest initial concentration of pollutant in the gas. An advantage of condensation is that the contaminant can easily be recovered as a product if it has value.

Toxics

People are keenly aware of cancer as a health threat so the presence of any chemical perceived as a carcinogen in the atmosphere is a highly charged emotional issue. Not everything feared as a carcinogen may ultimately be proven to be one but there are enough certain carcinogens to keep environmental compliance managers busy for decades until new technology can develop substitute raw materials or replace manufacturing processes altogether.

Air toxics (a species of contaminant defined by the 1990 amendments to CAA), as well as other air contaminants, have four avenues into the environment. Many manufacturing processes, in fact nearly all, have emissions from the process. In chemical manufacturing this may be residual in the gaseous state or perhaps vapor phase, which include air toxics. Vapor degreasers are still in use in the metal parts manufacturing business, especially in aerospace and electronics industries, which have some very tough cleaning standards. In minerals and primary metals, furnace emissions contain carcinogenic heavy metals. All these examples are emissions from process vents and that is what we typically envision when we think of smoke stack emissions. Process upsets produce, or tend to produce, emissions contaminated with greater than usual pollutant loads. Many types of equipment also leak process gases and vapors, called fugitive emissions. Finally, from Bhopal, Seveso, and Institute we are all familiar with large accidental releases of contaminated air emissions.

What chemicals are air toxics? Primarily, those chemicals that potentially cause serious health effects such as cancer in an exposed population. Emissions from gasoline filling stations are air toxics. So are everyday industrial emissions such as paint volatiles, welding fumes, primary metal smelter off-gases, dry cleaning vapors, injection molding gases, and vapor degreasing vapors. Even the residential woodburning stove emits air toxics.

What properties make a chemical toxic? Figure 7.31 summarizes properties discussed in a review article by Rich.

Figure 7.31
Toxic Properties of Chemicals

IDLH   Immediately Dangerous to Life or Health: the concentration level to which a healthy male worker can be exposed for 30 minutes without irreversible health effects or impairing symptoms

lc_{lo} Low Lethal Concentration: the lowest concentration observed to cause a fatality in either experimental laboratory animals or humans involved in accidents

LC_{50} 50% Lethal Concentration: the concentration for which 50% of exposed test animals died when exposed for a specified period

PEL   Permissible Exposure Limit: maximum air concentration to which a healthy male worker can be exposed for 8 hr/day, 40 hr/week without adverse effects as determined by OSHA

STEL   Short-term Exposure Limit: the maximum concentration to which workers can be exposed for up to 15 minutes provided no more than 4 such exposures are permitted per work day with at least 60 minutes between exposure periods

---

Other properties of interest when managing air toxics are chemical and physical properties such as boiling point, vapor pressure, heat of vaporization, density, viscosity, reactivity, surface tension, diffusivity, and heat capacities. Particle size is important where solids are concerned as discussed earlier in this chapter. Reactivity includes properties such as flammability, explosivity, exothermicity, and corrosiveness.

VOCs

Organic compounds which readily volatilize (evaporate) are called VOCs (volatile organic compounds). The significance of VOCs as pointed out in earlier chapters is that they react with sunlight to produce ozone in the troposphere where ozone produces smog, a common health threat. One of the largest volume uses of VOCs is in industrial coatings, such as paints, varnishes, and lacquers. Typically, VOC contents of coatings are expressed in grams of solvent per liter of coating or in pounds per gallon. VOCs are also found in gasoline and many consumer products, such as hair spray and charcoal lighter fluid.

Innovative VOC controls include bacteria and membrane separation. European firms have already been using bacteria to remove VOCs. In this control scheme, microorganisms are used to biofilter the gas stream which has been cooled in heat exchangers where

CONTROL SELECTION SUMMARY

In a nutshell, the choices available for control of air pollutants are shown in Figure 7.32 adapted from Farber. Although the design of a control strategy is much more complex than this, it gives an overview of alternatives available.

Figure 7.32 **Air Pollution Control Alternatives**			
Control Technology	PM	Acid Gases	Organics VOC/HAP
Cyclones	Yes	No	No
Electrostatic Precipitators	Yes	No	No
Adsorbers	No	No	Yes
Thermal Oxidizers	No	No	Yes

Control Technology	PM	Acid Gases	Organics VOC/HAP
	Yes		
Wet Scrubbers		Yes	No
Dry Scrubbers	with EP or BH	Yes	No
Baghouses	Yes	with alkali injection	with carbon injection

Figure 7.32
(cont'd)

How Stacks Help and Hurt

Stacks are used to disperse exhaust gases. Otherwise the ground level directly beneath a process discharge or around buildings would be exposed to the residual concentration of pollutants.

Objectives of Stacks

Stacks are about dilution. If the flue gas is distributed high enough into the atmosphere it gets diluted before it reaches groundlevel. All the necessary controls, therefore, have to be upstream from the stack. Since we want to get the gas stream as high into the atmosphere as practical, the exit velocity from the stack needs to be a minimum of 60 ft/sec, or 1.5 times average wind speed, whichever is greater. This adds to the plume rise, giving a higher effective stack height. At this velocity, the gas literally "punches" through an inversion layer, as one writer puts it.

Natural draft in stacks is a function of exit gas temperature, ambient air temperature, and stack height. The temperature and elevation differences create a driving force for moving gas inside the stack by buoyancy. When natural draft is inadequate, a fan is required. Neglecting wind velocity, the draft at the bottom of the stack can be calculated as such:

$$D_r = (\frac{H'}{5.2})(\rho_{ca} - \rho_{HG}) \qquad [7.48]$$

This number must be adjusted for kinetic energy and friction losses in the stack. The temperature drops about 1°F per foot of stack height. The net draft becomes

$$D_r' = D_r - (\frac{12}{\rho_{H_2O}} \rho^{HG})(\frac{v^2}{2g_c})[1 + 4(\frac{L}{D})(\frac{0.04}{N_{Re}^{0.16}})]$$ [7.49]

where

g_c = 32.174 ft lb_m/sec^2 lbf
L = stack height plus length of duct, ft
D = stack diameter, ft
N_{Re} = Reynolds' number, dimensionless
ρ_{H2O} = density of water, lb/ft^3
v = stack exit velocity, ft/sec

The best that natural draft can do is about 10 feet per second. The required stack height with natural draft is

$$H' = 190D_r'$$ [7.50]

However, for fan assisted stacks a typical setup might be as shown in Figure 7.33.

Figure 7.33
Typical Stack Values

Hot Gas Temperature, °F	400-500
Cold Air Temperature, °F	62
Coefficient of Friction	0.016
Hot Gas Density, lb/ft^3 @ 0°F, 1 atm	0.09
Sea Level Pressure, in. Hg	29.92
Exit Gas Velocity, ft/sec	60

Care and feeding of a stack includes draining any moisture which collects at the bottom. Also, insulation may be needed to deliver exit gases into the atmosphere at a sufficient temperature to disperse properly. Under no circumstances should you allow a cool gas (lower than ambient) to flow into the atmosphere.

Basic Issues of Stack Gas Dispersion

Let's examine briefly the basic issues of stack gas dispersion: meteorological, climatological, atmospheric stability, and atmospheric mixing.

Meteorological Principles. The study of atmospheric phenomena, especially of air masses and transportation of heat, pressure and moisture, is the science of meteorology. The chemistry of the atmosphere is highly affected by meteorological phenomena, as we have most recently seen demonstrated in the stratosphere with depletion of the ozone layer. Weather is the collection of short-term variations of temperature, pressure, humidity, wind speed and direction, precipitation type and quantity, cloud cover, and visibility. Climate is the long-term variation and trend of these factors observed in a particular region of the earth.

The driving force for weather and climate is solar energy. Therefore, the moisture content of the atmosphere—including clouds, which are aerosols of fine water droplets—is important for absorbing and reflecting much of that energy. At 300 miles out the thermosphere begins where rarefied gases reach temperatures of 2,200°F! No life—flora or fauna—on this planet if it were not for the atmosphere with its weather activity. The latent heat of vaporization of water uses up enough solar energy to make this rock habitable. Evaporated water moving over land from the oceans at night gives off heat as it condenses, thus warming the dark side of the planet which otherwise would plunge to -453°F (if there were no atmosphere at all).

Water in the atmosphere may be in all its states: vapor, liquid, or ice. Humidity is the term used to express the water vapor content of air as a gas. At any temperature, air will hold a certain amount of moisture, no more. When the air holds 100 percent of the moisture that it is capable of holding at a given temperature; we call that 100 percent relative humidity.

Fifty percent relative humidity, then, means the air only contains half the amount of water it could have held at that particular temperature. Unless the air gives up its moisture somehow, the relative humidity will increase as the bulk air temperature drops until precipitation starts to occur at the dew point. Unless water is taken on somehow, relative humidity drops as the bulk air temperature increases. Drying is the process of flowing hot dry air over a moist bed of solids, at a lower bulk temperature than the air stream, so that the water evaporates and is entrained in the air leaving the system. This same process and its opposite occurs many times daily on our planet. Precipitation can be in the form of rain, snow, sleet, or hail but it will not occur unless some condensation nuclei are also present. Without a seed to form large droplets (0.5-4 mm diameter) the water which condenses will be so fine (0.04-0.2 mm) that clouds will form. A condensation nuclei is a dust grain, salt, sulfuric acid droplet, bacteria, or other organic material which gives the aerosol something to condense onto.

Clouds are formed as warm air rises in the atmosphere. The water that condenses as the air adiabatically cools makes an aerosol or cloud. The three major forms of clouds are cirrus, cumulus, and stratus. Cirrus clouds occur at the highest altitude and have the appearance of feathers. The lumpy, billowy clouds we watched on our backs as children are the cumulus. They also form at high altitudes and have flat bases, usually. An over cast sky, with sheets of clouds, shows us the stratus form. Because they consist of water, clouds are very important in the solar energy balance. Though we tend to think of winds as random air currents flowing here and there they are actually organized and very predictable on the macro-scale (for studying climate) though perhaps not accurate enough for the micro-scale (say for Sunday's picnic). Distinct air masses exist which are uniform and homogeneous, particularly for temperature and moisture content. Figure 7.34 shows the major air masses (generically).

These air masses move around the globe in predictable ways and the boundary of two air masses is referred to as a front where some interesting things happen. Obeying the laws of physics, air masses move from points of high pressure to points of low pressure. Also warm air rises and expands as it cools. If there is little or no energy exchange with the surrounding environment, as the air expands we refer to it as an adiabatic expansion or adiabatic cooling.

Figure 7.34
Major Air Masses

Polar Continental	form over cold land mass.
Polar Maritime	form over cold oceans.
Tropical Continental	form over warm land mass.
Tropical Maritime	form over warm oceans.

The rate of cooling is called the lapse rate and Figure 7.35 gives adiabatic lapse rates for dry and moist air. As moist air cools, it gives up its moisture and condensing water vapor releases heat so moist air does not have the same adiabatic lapse rate as dry air. A common example of the effect of the lapse rate is the Santa Ana Winds in Orange County, south of Los Angeles. As the dry wind descends the 10,000 foot mountains to the east of Orange County, it gains 50°F. Hence, the roaring, dry, 120-130° winds can enkindle thirsty shrubbery and trees.

Figure 7.35
Adiabatic Lapse Rates

Dry Adiabatic Lapse Rate	5°F/1,000 ft
Moist Adiabatic Lapse Rate	3°F/1,000 ft

Air moving horizontally creates winds while that moving vertically creates air currents. Pressure differences are the driving force for wind, while convection currents make air move up or down. The interaction of solar energy, as it is distributed in the atmosphere and into the oceans and land masses with air mass movement, along with the transfer of heat by evaporation and condensation of water, results in weather.

Climatological Principles. Globally, massive transfers of air, moisture, and energy go on in our atmosphere. It is literally a huge reactor where turbulent currents keep things stirred up and chemical reactions take place and where particulate matter can be carried for thousands of miles, even around the world from its origin. Although climate varies by geographical region, certain global phenomena demand our attention first.

We must start with the unequal distribution of solar energy. This unequal distribution is why the poles are cold and the equator is hot. It is also why we have seasons. On the average, solar energy is more nearly normal (that is, perpendicular) to the earth's surface at the equator so that region gets the lion's share of energy per unit area of surface (flux). Northern and southern latitudes receive solar energy at ever increasing angles the more north or south you go, so less energy flux. As hot air rises in the equatorial regions, it cools by expansion and condensation of moisture until eventually it starts sinking again. These patterns are called Hadley cells. The Coriolis effect (the effect of the earth's rotation) causes these air movements to bend into a spiral-shaped pattern which combine with other atmospheric phenomena to produce jet streams. These shifting rivers of air flow several miles deep and tens of miles wide at velocities over 100 mph through discontinuities in the tropopause (the transitional region between the troposphere and the stratosphere) in a general west to east direction.

When two air masses come in contact, they produce a front which is weak or strong depending on their differences in pressure, temperature, and moisture content. A cold air mass moving in to displace a warm air mass produces a cold front, so a warm air mass moving to displace a cold mass produces a warm front. Cold fronts produce massive thunderheads and storms by pushing the warm air high into the troposphere. As the cloud cells push even higher, hail and tornados are the result. In warm fronts, the warm air is also pushed high by the cold air but here the front is much broader (usually) so the effect is a continuous precipitation or drizzle instead of the accumulation of a thunderhead. Rising masses of warm air in low pressure areas produce cyclonic storms such as hurricanes, typhoons, and tornados. The cold air at high elevation and the surface area from where the warm air is being drawn set up a low pressure tube, or cell, which connects the surface and the higher troposphere and the resulting cyclonic air movement builds to super speeds.

Atmospheric Stability. The stability of the atmosphere is affected by many things. Areas of negative lapse rates—increasing temperature with increasing altitude— have an undesirable stabilizing effect on the surface weather beneath them. Donora, Pennsylvania suffers from frequent inversions and this phenomena led to the highly stagnant conditions which locked in the deadly air pollution that killed scores there one Halloween. Less stable conditions than complete stagnation provide more mixing so less pollution has an immediate effect on the human population and the environment. Turbulence is desired from the viewpoint of dispersion. However, unless the air pollution is mitigated somehow other than by mixing, long-term health effects may eventually become a problem as the pollutant continues to accumulate.

The distance from the ground level to the underneath side of the inversion layer is called the inversion height. The inversion layer itself is a layer of warm air sitting atop a cooler mass of air. At the inversion height, the lapse rate reverses from positive (that is, decreasing temperature with height) to negative (increasing temperature with height). Inversions typically exist at night or with overcast weather and persist until broken up by energy radiating from the earth's surface at dawn or when the clouds break.

However, it is not the people who reside underneath the layer who suffer most, as Los Angeles and Donora can attest. Those underneath fair pretty well unless the inversion height is very low, as is the case around London. At Los Angeles and Donora, as well as many other locations around the world, many people live in hills that are actually inside the inversion layer where the pollution is actually at its worst. Then, once these layers break up due to solar energy being absorbed and re-radiated by the earth's surface, the entrapped pollutants are carried many miles downstream in air packets and people at some distant location are cursed with all the undesirable effects of the original pollutant soup. Inversion processes are summarized in Figure 7.36.

Figure 7.36
Inversion Processes

Temperature
Radiation (solar)
Subsidence
Marine

On the other hand, the stability of the atmosphere at the stack on a micro-level is desirable as stability assures the plume will travel far downstream, distributing its effects fairly evenly over a very large territory rather than nearby. This, by the way, is the stability referred to in air pollution modeling. A stable atmosphere produces light winds and very little turbulence. An unstable atmosphere is very turbulent and may distribute large quantities of undiluted pollutants at locations relatively near the stack by virtue of the phenomenon called looping. Rapid changes in wind velocity and direction occur in an unstable atmosphere. A neutral atmosphere will send the plume rising straight up in an ever widening cone as there are less gusts than in a stable situation and less fluctuations in wind direction, too.

Unstable atmospheres occur on strong solar heating days. Neutral atmospheres occur under cloudy skies and windy conditions. In the evenings—when the earth's surface cools faster than the atmosphere does—we observe stable conditions.

Atmospheric Mixing. Atmospheric mixing has two components: average bulk movement and turbulence. The average motion of air mass is generally measured as the average wind velocity, which has turbulence effects included so true velocity varies around the average velocity as you would expect. Turbulence occurs in three directions: vertical, cross-wind and downwind direction of the average wind. Lateral and vertical dispersion from a stack are driven by turbulence. Physical obstacles in the path of wind flow creates mechanical turbulence. Heating of the atmosphere at the surface of the earth creates thermal turbulence and convective winds.

Weather conditions that produce turbulence, and therefore, mixing, are marked by strong solar radiation and high wind speeds. The stronger the heating and the higher the wind speed the more mixing there is and the more dilute the polluting vapor or PM becomes.

Plumes. The concentration of a pollutant in an emissions plume at any point of interest depends on the behavior of the plume which is, in turn, dependent upon discharge rate, atmospheric stability, wind speed, and distance downstream from the stack to our point of interest. Figure 7.37 shows a plume being emitted from a stack according to the Ooms model.

Rise. The vertical distance the plume travels depends on the stack gas temperature, ambient air temperature, relative humidity, wind speed, and atmospheric stability and whether or not an inversion condition exists.

Concentration vs. Time. As a plume travels downstream from a stack the gas stream mixes with more and more clean air so the pollutant concentration is decreasing with time. The concentration will decrease even faster if there is a reaction consuming the pollutant, but on the other hand that usually means new pollutant species to be deal with.

Figure 7.37
Ooms Plume

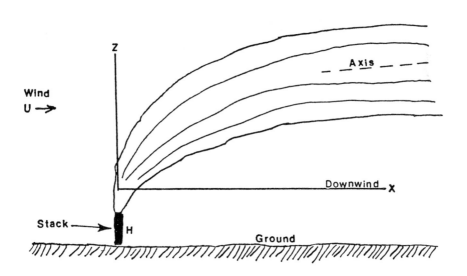

Algorithms and Plume Models

The common engineering practice is to use the Gaussian plume model for fitting concentration of a pollutant being dispersed from a stack. The general equation is often given as:

$$X = \frac{Q}{2\pi\sigma_y\sigma_z u}e^{-y^2/2\sigma_y^2}[e^{-(z-H)^2/2\sigma_z^2} + e^{-(z+H)^2/2\sigma_z^2}]$$ [7.51]

The calculation of X is made for each data point (y, z) from a known source generation rate (Q) at a stack height, H. However, large topographical features such as a large hill or mountain produce curvature in the wind field and in their wake leave a reduced wind speed and thickened boundary layer. Thus, Halitsky includes effective plume centerline height and effective wind speed to improve the accuracy of the basic Gaussian model. He makes these substitutions:

$$X_{ref} = \frac{Q}{2\pi\sigma_y\sigma_z u}e^{-y^2/2\sigma_y^2}$$ [7.52]

$$C = X/X_{ref}$$ [7.53]

$$S = \sigma_z/H$$ [7.54]

$$Z = z/H$$ [7.55]

so,

$$C = e^{-(Z-1)^2/2S^2} + e^{-(Z+1)^2/2S^2}$$ [7.56]

Maximum ground concentrations are indicated where S = 0.75 and at the point where dC/dZ = 0:

$$S = [\frac{2Z_m}{\ln(1+Z_m) - \ln(1-Z_m)}]^{1/2} \qquad [7.57]$$

The contribution of image plumes are negligible where S < 0.3 and the concentration profile is a symmetrical Gaussian plume around the elevation of the stack height. When S lies between 0.3 and 1, the image plume affects the unreflected plume and the maximum concentration in the plume moves groundward.

Industrial Source Complex Algorithm. The EPA developed this steady-state Gaussian plume model (called ISC) which can be used to assess primary pollutant concentrations from a variety of sources. ISC accounts for settling and dry deposition of particulates, downwash, line and volume sources, plume rise as a function of downwind distance, separation of point sources, and limited terrain adjustment. The model can be operated in either long- (ISCLT) or short-term (ISCST) modes. Receptors are assumed to be at ground level, which must be below the stack height. Fumigation is not treated. Vertical wind speed is assumed to equal zero. With rural dispersion coefficients there is no adjustment for surface roughness. Urban dispersion coefficients may be used if appropriate. Chemical transformations are treated by using exponential decay.

Single Source Model. This model, called CRSTER, is a steady state, Gaussian dispersion model designed to calculate concentrations from point sources at a single location in either a rural or urban setting. No terrain can exist above the stack height. CRSTER models primary pollutants but settling and deposition are not accounted for. Although called a single source model, CRSTER treats up to nineteen collocated point sources but no area sources. Receptors are assumed at ground level, which must be beneath the stack height. Neither fumigation nor building downwash are treated by the model. Constant, uniform horizontal winds and no vertical winds are used. Rural dispersion coefficients are used with no adjustment for surface roughness, or urban coefficients can be used. Chemical transformation is decayed exponentially.

Other U.S. EPA Models. Several dozen models are acceptable to EPA as well as to various state air regulating offices, but many are acceptable only under limited conditions. Before purchasing a model for your own use or before paying for a consulting company to make model runs for you, talk to the state or regional EPA and determine what conditions they have for the model under consideration.

Special Considerations

Building and terrain effects are other new feature of plume modeling. Each generation of models adds new features and tools to handle specific problems.

Building Effects. A plume doesn't know a building from a hill or a tall tree. We can visualize a broad urban street lined with high rise buildings as being like a canyon or steep-sided valley, yet the openings among the buildings which create cross flows and eddies destroy the analogy. Most models are now designed to operate in either rural or urban modes. Actually, most industrial sites are located where no terrain features exist above the stack height, and where other buildings, if they exist, are no higher than two or three stories and are the same height as the one with the stack under consideration. Therefore, a great many modeling cases involve simple terrain.

Terrain Effects. Topography also affects plumes. Most older models are based on simple terrain but newer models consider complex terrain. Simple terrain merely means that the model considers any turbulence creating feature to be below the height of the stack, whereas terrain exceeds stack height in a complex terrain model. Bushes and trees create more turbulence than grassy areas but are not typically taken into account. Low momentum plumes that are heavier than air tend to travel around hills rather than go up and over. Four basic complex terrain situations are 1) valley stagnation, 2) valley fumigation, 3) downwash on the leeside of terrain obstacles, and 4) plume impaction conditions. Figure 7.38 summarizes some EPA preferred models for selected applications in simple terrain.

Complex terrain models are typically applied to stationary sources of SO_2 and PM. One problem in complex terrains is the impaction of plumes into an obstacle—causing a local pollutant concentration higher than that predicted by a model. If the model errs, we want it to err on the side of human safety not in the opposite direction. The occurrence of impaction is linked to a critical streamline that separates flow around an obstacle from flow over the obstacle. High concentrations of significant magnitude also occur in the lee of the obstacle.

Figure 7.38
Summary of Simple Terrain Models

Short Term (1-24 hours)	Land Use	Model
Single Source	Rural	CRSTER
	Urban	RAM
Multiple Source	Rural	<
	Urban	RAM
Complicated Sources	Rural/Urban	ISCST
Buoyant Industrial Line Sources	Rural	
Long Term (monthly, seasonal, annual)	Land Use	Model
Single Source	Rural	CRSTER
	Urban	RAM
Multiple Source	Rural	
	Urban	2.0 or RAM
Complicated Sources	Rural/Urban	ISCLT
Buoyant Industrial Line Sources	Rural	

Bent-over Buoyant Plumes. Where buoyant sources are involved, special models must be used or error will be introduced. A typical buoyant source is fossil fuel combustion. The heat in the plume adds to the natural buoyancy as it rises in the atmosphere.

Spill and Emergency Vapor Release. These emissions are emergency and one time situations. Therefore, the critical information for modeling the rate of such releases is release area and released fluid temperature, pressure and composition. From this information, a release rate can be calculated, but instead of an ongoing emission we have a batch emission lasting some finite period of time. The size of the plume will depend on the information just discussed plus percentage of liquid that flashes to vapor (or amount of process gas lost before stopping the spill or leak), liquid entrainment or aerosol formation, degree of containment achieved, weather, and terrain.

The amount of liquid which flashes to vapor depends on the pressure and temperature of the liquid pool at the time of release. The vaporization rate of the liquid is also partly dependent on the surface which holds the spill. For instance, the vaporization rate is constant as long as it lasts if the liquid is floating on water but drops with time if the liquid rests on concrete. Otherwise, the plume travels with air movement and is diluted in time as it mixes with more and more clean air until it is no longer hazardous.

Dew Points

$$Q = 0.8\,E(T_c^4 - T_a^4) + (T_c - T_a)^{1.25}[\frac{V+69}{69}]^{0.5} \qquad [7.58]$$

Calculating the dew point of vapors in a stack gas is important for determining the exit concentration of the vapors but also for preventing corrosion of the stack and drip legs in the flue. Where t_c is the outside wall temperature of a stack underneath insulation and t_a is the ambient temperature of air around the stack, then the heat loss across the insulation is expressed:where $T = t°F + 460$. The emissivity, E, of the stack wall is typically 0.9 for carbon steel. The heat loss, Q, is given in BTU/ft^2 hr.

Wind velocity, V, is given in ft/min. The temperature drop across the gas film on the inside stack wall is

$$t_g - t_{wi} = Q(d_o/d_i)/h \qquad [7.59]$$

The gas temperature is t_g and the inside stack wall is at t_{wi}. The duct inner and outer diameters, in inches, are d_i and d_o, respectively. The gas-film heat transfer coefficient is

$$h = 2.44 W^{0.8} F/d_i^{1.8} \qquad [7.60]$$

in BTU/ft²hr°F. Gas flow rate, W, is given in lb/hr. The factor F is defined as

$$F = (C_p/\mu)^{0.4}/k^{0.6} \qquad [7.61]$$

From this, the duct wall temperature drop is calculated

$$t_{wi} - t_{wo} = Q d_o \ln(d_o/d_i/24 K_m) \qquad [7.62]$$

where K_m is the stack thermal conductivity in BTU/ft hr °F and the temperature drop across the insulation is

$$t_{wo} - t_c = Q L/K_i \qquad [7.63]$$

Here K_i is the thermal conductivity of the insulation. Stacks are typically very large diameter so the curvature can be ignored with respect to having any effect on the heat transfer. Total heat loss from the stack is

$$H_i = \Pi d_o H Q/12 \qquad [7.64]$$

So, the temperature of the gas exiting the stack is

$$t_{g2} = t_{g1} - H_i/W C_p \qquad [7.65]$$

The stack exit temperature must be maintained above the dewpoint of any corrosive gases present in the emissions.

CONCLUSION

Air pollution control devices are hands-off devices that are too easily ignored but permit limitations require vigilance and attention. Understanding how these devices work helps you take care of them and makes compliance that much easier for you and your plant.

REFERENCES

Aerstin, Frank and Gary Street. *Applied Chemical Process Design*. New York: Plenum Press, 1978.

Anderson, Kim E. and Dennis Hussey. "Assessing The Risks of Industrial Air Emissions." *Pollution Engineering*. April 1989.

Ayers, Kenneth W., *et al. Environmental Science and Technology Handbook*. Rockville, MD: Government Institutes, Inc., 1994.

Bains, C.S. "Flue Gas Desulfurization: Economics of FGD in The Refining Industry." *Chemical Engineering Progress*. May 1980.

Bartok, William and Adel F. Sarofim, eds. *Fossil Fuel Combustion: A Source Book*. New York: John Wiley & Sons, 1991.

Baukal, Charles E. and Francis J. Romano. "Reducing NO_x and Particulate." *Pollution Engineering*. September 1, 1992.

Bohn, Hinrich. "Consider Biofiltration for Decontaminating Gases." *Chemical Engineering Progress*. April 1992.

Brady, Jack D. "Particulate and SO_2 Removal with Wet Scrubbers." *Chemical Engineering Progress*. June 1982.

Calvert, Seymour. "How to Choose A Particulate Scrubber." *Chemical Engineering*. August 29, 1977.

----. "Upgrading Existing Particulate Scrubbers." *Chemical Engineering*. October 24, 1977.

Casal, Joaquin and Jose M. Martinez-Benet. "A Better Way to Calculate Cyclone Pressure Drop." *Chemical Engineering*. January 24, 1983.

Chang, S.G. and G.C. Lee. "LBL PhosNOX Process for Combined Removal of SO_2 and NO_x from Flue Gas." *Environmental Progress*. February 1992.

Cheremisinoff, Nicholas P. "Equipment Roundup: Fans, Blowers and Compressors." *The National Environmental Journal*. January/February 1992.

Cheremisinoff, Paul N. "Lime/Limestone Scrubbing of Sulfur Dioxide." *The National Environmental Journal*. November/December 1991.

---. "Solvent Vapor Recovery and VOC Emission Control." *Pollution Engineering*. June 1986.

Chi, C.V., R.E. Peck, F. Tavakoli and D.T. Wasan. "The IIT Flue Gas Desulfurization Process." *Chemical Engineering Progress*. June 1982.

Chicago Blower Corporation. Bulletin EG-1B. *Engineering Guide*.

Chida, Tadashi and Teiriki Tadaki. "Comparison of Rate Expressions for Noncatalytic, Gas-Solid Reactions." *International Chemical Engineering*. July 1982.

Considine, Douglas M., ed.-in-chief. *Chemical and Process Technology Encyclopedia*. "Separation Operations." New York: McGraw-Hill, 1974.

Constantinescu, Serban. "Plant Notebook: Sizing Gas Cyclones." *Chemical Engineering*. February 20, 1984.

Croll-Reynolds Company. *4 Ways to Scrub an Air Stream*. Bulletin FS 76.

Cross, Frank L., Jr. and Joe Howell. "New Technology to Meet Air Toxics Regulations." *Pollution Engineering*. March 15, 1992.

Davenport, Gerald B. "Understand The Air-Pollution Laws That Affect CPI Plants." *Chemical Engineering Progress*. April 1992.

Edwards, Larry and Judy A. Nottoli. "Source Sampling Tests Stack Emissions." *Environmental Protection*. June 1992.

Edwards, W.M. and P. Huang. "The Kellogg-Weir Air Quality Control System." *Chemical Engineering Progress*. August 1977.

EPA 400-K-93-001. *The Plain English Guide to The Clean Air Act*. April 1993.

EPA PB86-245248. *Guideline on Air Quality Models*. Revised. Triangle Park, NC: USEPA, Office of Air Quality Planning and Standard Research. 1986.

Farber, Paul S. "Selecting Systems to Control Emissions." *Environmental Protection*. December 1992.Felsvang, K., K. Gude and S. Kaplan. "SO$_2$ Spray Absorption with Dry Wastes." Niro Atomizer.

Finlayson-Pitts, Barbara J. and James N. Pitts, Jr. *Atmospheric Chemistry: Fundamentals and Experimental Techniques*. New York: John Wiley & Sons, 1986.

Frankel, Irwin. "Plant Notebook: Shortcut Calculation for Fluegas Volume." *Chemical Engineering*. June 1, 1981.

Friedlander, Gordon D., J.C. Yarze and H. Hurwitz. "Scrubbing Gas from High-Sulfur Coal." *Electrical World*. October 15, 1978.

Ganapathy, V. "Plant Notebook: Figure Particulate-Emission Rate Quickly." *Chemical Engineering*. July 26, 1982.

----. "Preventing Corrosion in Stacks and Scrubbers." *Chemical Engineering*. January 1989.

Gilbert, William. "Troubleshooting Wet Scrubbers." *Chemical Engineering*. October 24, 1977.

Gonzalez Valdez, Milton, Isis Garcia and Belkis Beato. "Plant Notebook: Sizing Gas Cyclones for Efficiency." *Chemical Engineering*. April 14, 1986.

Green, Don W. and James O. Maloney, eds. *Perry's Chemical Engineer's Handbook*. 6th Ed. New York: McGraw-Hill Book Company, 1984.

Halitsky, James. "Calculation of σ_z and H for An Observed Vertical Profile of Concentration." *Journal of The Air Pollution Control Association*. December 1986.

Helfritch, Dennis, *et al*. "Combined SO$_2$ and NO$_x$ Removal by Means of Dry Sorbent Injection." *Environmental Progress*. February 1992.

Hernandez, R. J. and T.L. Huurdeman. "Solvent Unit Cleans Synthesis Gas." *Chemical Engineering*. February 1989.

Heumann, William L. "Cyclone Separators: A Family Affair." *Chemical Engineering*. June 1991.

Holmes, T.L., C.F. Meyer and J.L. DeGarmo. "Reversejet Scrubber for Control of Fine Particulates." *Chemical Engineering Progress*. February 1983.

Horzella, Theodore I. "Selecting, Installing Cyclone Dust Collectors." *Chemical Engineering*. January 30, 1978.

Kaplan, Norman and Michael A. Maxwell. "Removal of SO$_2$ from Industrial Waste Gases." *Chemical Engineering*. October 17, 1977.

Kelly, Errol G. and David J. Spottiswood. *Introduction to Mineral Processing*. New York: John Wiley & Sons, 1982.

Khan, Javaid I. and David C. Pei. "Pressure Drop in Vertical Solid-Gas Suspension Flow." *Industrial and Engineering Chemistry, Process Design and Development*. Vol. 12, No. 4, 1973.

Klein, George F. "Tray Spacing Equation." *Chemical Engineering*. May 5, 1980.

Klobucar, Joseph M. and Michael J. Pilat. "Continuous Flow Thermal Desorption of VOC's from Activated Carbon." *Environmental Progress*. February 1992.

Koch Engineering Company. *Koch Engineering Manual: Wet Scrubbing Systems for Air Pollution Control*. Bulletin KPC2.

----. *Koch Scrubbing Systems for Particulate and SO2 Removal*. An undated, unnumbered bulletin.

Kottke, Lee R. "VOC Technology Catches up to Regs." *Environmental Protection*. March 1992.

Lindsey, William E. "Plant Notebook: Obtain Accurate Samples to Determine Scrubber Efficiency." *Chemical Engineering*. October 17, 1983.

Lipfert, Frederick W. *Air Pollution and Community Health: A Critical Review and Data Sourcebook*. New York: Van Nostrand Reinhold, 1994.

Loftus, Peter J. David B. Stickler and Richard C. Diehl. "A Confined Vortex Scrubber for Fine Particulate Removal from Flue Gases." *Environmental Progress*. February 1992.

Lyons, Angus L. "Minimize Dust Erosion when Handling Abrasive Solids." *Chemical Engineering Progress*. December 1990.

Makansi, Jason. "Understanding System Effects when Evaluating Sorbent Injection." *Power*. June 1985.

Manahan, Stanley E. *Environmental Chemistry*. 6th ed. Boca Raton, FL: CRC Press/Lewis Publishers, 1994.

McCabe, Warren L. and Julian C. Smith. *Unit Operations of Chemical Engineering*. New York: McGraw-Hill, 1966.

McCarthy, J.E. "Flue Gas Desulfurization: Scrubber Types and Selection Criteria." *Chemical Engineering Progress*. May 1990.

McInnes, Robert, Kevin Jameson and Dorothy Austin. "Scrubbing Toxic Inorganics." *Chemical Engineering*. September 1990.

McInnes, Robert, Steven Jelinek, and Victoria Putsche. "Cutting Toxic Organics." *Chemical Engineering*. September 1990.

McInnes, Robert and Ross Van Royen. "Desulfurizing Fluegases." *Chemical Engineering*. September 1990.

McInnes, Robert and Mary Van Wormer. "Cleaning up No$_x$ Emissions." *Chemical Engineering*. September 1990.

Mody, Vinit and Raj Jakhete. *Dust Control Handbook*. Park Ridge, NJ: Noyes Data Corporation, 1988.

Newman, Robert P., PE. "Air Pollution Control for Infectious Waste Incineration." *Pollution Engineering*. October 1991.

Nudo, Lori. "Emerging Technologies: Air." *Pollution Engineering*. April 15, 1992.

Ooms, G. "A New Method for The Calculation of The Plume Path of Gases Emitted by A Stack." *Atmospheric Environment*. June 1972.

Pancuska, Vaclav I. "Calculator Program for Designing Packed Towers." *Chemical Engineering*. May 5, 1980.

Patrick, David R. *Toxic Air Pollution Handbook*. New York: Van Nostrand Reinhold, 1994.

Patterson, R.L., L.R. Oquist and A.G. Sassi. "Pacemakers/CORONADO: Weir Scrubber to Start up Soon." *Power Generation Planbook 1979*. McGraw-Hill, 1979.

Pruce, Leslie M. "Why So Few Regenerative Scrubbers?" *Power*. June 1981.

Radian Corporation. *VOC (Volatile Organic Compound) Emission Factors for the NAPAP (National Acid Precipitation Assessment Program) Emission Inventory.* EPA PB87-141040. National Technical Information Service, December 1986.

Rennhack, Rolf. "Dust Extraction from Hot Gases." *International Chemical Engineering.* June 1982.

Rich, Gerald A. *Air Toxics.* Northbrook, IL: Pudvan Publishing Company, 1990.

----. "Air Toxics: Prevention and Mitigation." *Pollution Engineering.* June 1989.

----. "The PM 10 Chart." *Pollution Engineering.* June 1986.

----. *VOC Calculation Manual.* Cahners Publishing Company, 1991.

Riders, Z. V. "VOC Compliance: New Regulations Mean Hard Choices for Industrial Coating Users." *Plant Services.* June 1989.

Robertson, Jospeh L. "New Dravo Lime Plant Is Geared to Growing Scrubber Needs." *Rock Products.* June 1976.

Scholtens, Michael J. "Air Pollution Control: A Comprehensive Look." *Pollution Engineering.* May 1991.

Schwarzkopf, F. "The New 3000 TPD Lime Plant for SO_2 Scrubbing at Maysville, Kentucky." *Zement-Kalk-Gips.* 1/77.

Semrau, Konrad T. "Practical Process Design of Particulate Scrubbers." *Chemical Engineering.* September 26, 1977.

Shah, N.D. "Dry Scrubbing of SO_2." *Chemical Engineering Progress.* June 1982.

Shah, Yatendra M. and Richard T. Price. "Calculator Program Solves Cyclone Efficiency Equations." *Chemical Engineering.* August 28, 1978.

Shreve, R. Norris and Joseph A. Brink, Jr. *Chemical Process Industries.* 4th. ed. New York: McGraw-Hill, 1977.

Sittig, Marshall. *Pollution Control in The Asbestos, Cement, Glass and Allied Mineral Industries.* Park Ridge, NJ: Noyes Data Corporation, 1975.

Sommerlad, Robert E. and Burton T. Otani. "Water Protection under The Clean Air Act." *Pollution Engineering.* September 1991.

Stearn, Enid W. "Scrubber Limestone: A Steady Market for The Stone Man." *Rock Products*. January 1978.

Suhadja, Arthur, Jr. and John Papamarcos. "Catalytic Reactor Controls VOC Emissions." *Plant Services*. July 1989.

Sulphur. No. 153. "Developments in Flue Gas Desulphurization Technology: Improving The Cost Effectiveness of Wet and Dry Scrubbing." March/April 1981.

Tawari, Tulsi D. and Frederick A. Zenz. "Evaluating Cyclone Efficiencies from Stream Compositions." *Chemical Engineering*. April 30, 1984.

Texas, U. of, at Austin. *Hazard Assessment and Risk Analysis Techniques for Process Industries*. Mechanical Engineering Department, September 24-27, 1990.

Thompson, John E. and C. Jack Trickler. "Fans and Fan Systems." *Chemical Engineering*. March 21, 1983.

Treybal, Robert E. *Mass-Transfer Operations*. 3d. ed. New York: McGraw-Hill, 1980.

Truelove, Ronald D. "Control of Benzene Waste NESHAP Emissions from A Petroleum Refinery." *Environmental Progress*. February 1992.

Vatavuk, William M. and Robert B. Nevril. "Costs of Carbon Adsorbers." *Chemical Engineering*. January 24, 1983.

----. "Costs of Flares." *Chemical Engineering*. February 21, 1983.

----. "Costs of Gas Absorbers." *Chemical Engineering*. October 4, 1982.

----. "Costs of Refrigeration Systems for Air-Pollution Control." *Chemical Engineering*. May 16, 1982.

----. "Estimate The Size and Cost of Baghouses." *Chemical Engineering*. March 22, 1982.

----. "Estimate The Size and Cost of Incinerators." *Chemical Engineering*. July 12, 1982.

----. "Estimating Costs of Exhaust Stacks." *Chemical Engineering*. June 15, 1981.

----. "Estimating Costs of Fans and Accessories." *Chemical Engineering.* May 18, 1981.

----. "Estimating The Size and Cost of Ductwork." *Chemical Engineering.* December 29, 1980.

----. "Estimating The Size and Cost of Dust-Removal and Water- Handling Equipment." *Chemical Engineering.* March 23, 1981.

----. "Estimating The Size and Cost of Gas Conditioners." *Chemical Engineering.* January 26, 1981.

----. "Estimating The Size and Cost of Pollutant Capture Hoods." *Chemical Engineering.* December 1, 1980.

----. "Estimating Size and Costs of Venturi Scrubbers." *Chemical Engineering.* November 30, 1981.

----. "Factors for Estimating Capital and Operating Costs of Air-Pollution Control Systems." *Chemical Engineering.* November 3, 1980.

----. "Parameters for Sizing Air-Pollution Control Systems." *Chemical Engineering.* October 6, 1980.

----. "Particle Emissions Control." *Chemical Engineering.* April 2, 1984.

Zanker, Adam. "Determining Air Inlet-Velocity for Cyclones." *Chemical Engineering.* March 19, 1984.

Zenz, Frederick A. "Particulate Solids: The Third Phase in Chemical Engineering." *Chemical Engineering.* November 28,1983.

Zey, A., S. White and D. Johnson. "The ATS Claus Tail Gas Cleanup Process." *Chemical Engineering Progress.* October 1980.

Zinn, C. Dale and Dwight B. Pfenning. "Hazard Assessment and Risk Analysis for Process Industries." A Continuing Education Course presented by University of Texas, Austin. 1988.

8

CONTROLLING WATER POLLUTION

IN-PLANT CONTROL OF WASTEWATER

Before thinking about controlling pollutants in the effluent (wastewater leaving a plant), consider source reduction and conservation. Conduct an in-plant survey of all industrial waste streams, even solid waste. Consider, for instance, metal chips at a machining plant. Usually these are collected in huge metal bins under a shed or in some outbuilding. Look around. Are there not pools of coolant? How do you manage this waste stream presently? Allow it to soak into the ground? The stormwater branch will have some input and the RCRA enforcement office will probably want to see TCLPs of the coolant and the soil. Or take, for instance, that wet scrubber collecting PM over in the corner. Where is the sludge going? What about the dirty water out? You should begin to see all the media under a macroscope. You should begin to see them as parts of an integral whole.

What you need to do now is to conduct a water balance of your plant. This is analogous to an air emissions inventory. The industrial waste survey is your starting point for a good water balance.

The purpose of the survey is fourfold. It identifies waste load quantities: flow rates of waste streams and their pollutant loading, such as BOD, TSS, etc. (More later on the abbreviations.) An industrial waste survey also identifies sources of wastewater, which is critical information for understanding the Big Picture. The three main classes of industrial wastewater are aqueous waste from manufacturing processes, water used as contact coolant in industrial processes, and sanitary wastes. The latter includes kitchen and scullery wastewater, restroom and shower water, and laundry and janitorial water. When industrial wastewater and sanitary wastewater are mixed the resultant waste stream is called combined waste. Untreated combined waste opens up the possibility of contaminant pass through in the treatment system, the accumulation of contaminants in biological sludge, increasing shock loading of biomass, and structural damage of the POTW by the industrial waste portion. Knowing your sources allows you to consider some instant source reductions, which, in turn, reduces treatment chemical requirements, treatment power consumption, and lowers wastewater treatment costs, in general.

Next, the survey allows you the opportunity to discover variations in the flow and loading of the watery waste streams. For instance, scheduled cleanup cycles may be known by everyone but if the wastewater plant operators are not attentive they will experience upsets.

At one plant, every time the president of the company came for a visit, an upset of the wastewater plant resulted in a violation of the permit conditions. An investigation revealed that clean up activities generated unusually heavy wastewater volume containing all sorts of cleaning compounds and solvents not ordinarily experienced.

Finally, a comprehensive waste survey will determine the relative distribution of pollutants under normal operations.

One plant learned the importance of this information the hard way. Under an administrative order to install wastewater pollution control they entertained several treatment ideas presented by representatives of equipment manufacturers. One vendor offered a particularly attractive process and asked for a sample of the wastewater for testing. The unsuspecting plant engineer had someone get five gallons of wastewater from a sump and sent it to the manufacturer's laboratory. A telephone call from the representative asked for another sample because that first sample of wastewater could not possibly be anything like reality. This time the plant engineer went out to the sump several days in a row until he found it fairly clear and sent five gallons of this wastewater to the laboratory. Soon plans, drawings, and a quote were delivered. It was cheaper than the nearest competition by fifty percent so a purchase order was issued. After delivery and installation the wastewater treatment process system took three years to get into compliant operation. Why? Because the first sample was in fact representative of the wastewater the plant generated while the second sample was under unusually clean conditions.

Make sure you know your wastewater streams intimately. Know where every gallon of it comes from, what materials contacted it, what materials were mixed with it, and all its variations during a typical day.

Before ordering a wastewater treatment system, or when taking over an ailing system, consider the internal control strategies of Figure 8.1.

Figure 8.1
Internal Wastewater Control Strategies

1. Maximize recycle and reclamation,
2. Examine dry vs. wet handling of materials,
3. Use high pressure sprays for cleaning and rinsing,
4. Eliminate wasteful, inefficient water usage,
5. Separate process from noncontact cooling water,
6. Minimize water contact with liquid spills,
7. Install automatic hose cutoffs,
8. Use automatic shutoff for water valves where constant flow is not required,
9. Use countercurrent rinses,
10. Minimize tank dragout, and
11. Put a water meter in each department using process water.

PRIMARY WASTEWATER TREATMENT METHODS

Primary treatment consists of equalization, filtration and/or oil removal, precipitation (and coagulation and flocculation), clarification (through sedimentation or flotation), and neutralization. The suggestions in Figure 8.2 are offered as treatment strategy tips to minimize wastewater treatment, though this is far from the sum total of wastewater advice. An infinite number of treatment schemes are available and every strategy has countless exceptions. For the purposes of our discussion, we will examine some wastewater treatment unit operations generically. Among the references below are some books that treat the subject in great technical detail. Here we only want to cover the basic types of treatments, what they do and do not do, and briefly explain how they work.

Figure 8.2
Wastewater Treatment Strategy

1. Equalize flow for all streams.
2. Segregate/treat CN streams before equalization.
3. Segregate/treat Cr VI streams before equalization.
4. Segregate/remove free oil before equalization.
5. Segregate/equalize BOD/COD streams separately.
6. Unless dissolved/emulsified oil streams also bear heavy metals, segregate, and treat separately.
7. Do not treat watery oil as wastewater; treat separately as a used oil stream.
8. After equalization optimize pH for next treatment step.
9. Precipitate heavy metals and other dissolved solids.
10. Coagulate and flocculate.
11. Clarify with sedimentation if heavy metals or refractories predominate.
12. Clarify with flotation if dissolved/emulsified oils predominate.
13. Use polishing unit to eliminate VOCs.
14. Use polishing unit to eliminate toxic compounds.

Before proceeding, let's learn to calculate contaminant mass loads. Because the density of water is roughly 1.0, conversion of concentration to mass loading is relative simple as shown in Equation 8.1.

$$Load = 8.34X_o Q \qquad [8.1]$$

where

X_o = contaminant concentration, mg/l (ppm)
Q = wastewater flow, MGD (million gallons/day).

Mass load is directly proportional to the concentration and flow.

Neutralization

When a wastewater stream is not at optimum pH for treatment or discharging, the pH must be adjusted. Consider these four factors when adjusting the pH of wastewaters: 1) volume of the stream directly affects the size of equipment and quantity of reagents required; 2) the kind of waste being adjusted determines the kind of reagents available for use; 3) the strength of acid or base solution to be neutralized determines the quantity of reagent needed; and 4) overall capital and operating costs can vary widely with your decisions.

Neutralization is a key factor in almost every unit operation of wastewater treatment. It is difficult to operate a neutralization process without understanding logarithms and pH. The pH is the negative log of the concentration of hydrogen ions (called hydronium) $[H^+]$ in solution. The formula for pH is

$$pH = -Log[H^+] \qquad\qquad [8.2]$$

The pH scale ranges from 0 to 14, but lower than 0 and higher than 14 pH is feasible though not practical to discuss here so we will consider 0 to 14 as the range. This is actually a concentration range from 1 mole $[H^+]$ per liter of solution to 1 mole $[OH^-]$ per liter of solution.

$$pH + pOH = 14 \qquad\qquad [8.3]$$

The low end of this scale, which is logarithmic, represents extremely acidic conditions with mostly $[H^+]$ and little $[OH^-]$ present in solution at 0 pH and at the high end, where conditions are alkaline (basic), we have mostly $[OH^-]$ and little $[H]$ present at 14 pH. The midpoint, pH 7, represents neutral pH where an equal number of $[H^+]$ and $[OH^-]$ ions are present.

Example.Calculate the pH of a 1.2% solution of nitric acid (HNO_3) solution.

Convert 1.2% to g/l.

1.2% = 1.2 g HNO₃ per 100 ml solution or 12 g per liter Note: 1 ml weighs 1 gram for water and most aqueous solutions. Determine how many moles of nitric acid we have:

Moles = g/MW = 12/63 = 0.191 mole HNO_3/l.

Determine the number of moles of [H^+]:

HNO_3 ---> H^+ + NO_3^- Since 1 mole of HNO_3 will produce 1 mole of [H^+] and 1 mole of NO_3^-, 0.191 moles of [H^+] will be present.

Calculate pH:

pH = -Log [H^+] = -Log(0.191) = -(-0.719) = 0.719
This is a pretty potent acid solution.

Figure 8.3 is a graph of amphoteric (U-shaped) pH curves for metal ions. Metal ions in laboratory conditions have an optimum pH for precipitation from solution. At other pH's (lower or higher) more and more ions of the metal remain in solution more readily. Even in the laboratory, if you have ions of several different metals in solution it is very difficult to find a pH that they all respond to for precipitation. For heavy metal precipitation in the lab or in the plant, find the optimum pH by doing jar tests with the wastewater. Figure 8.4 gives optimum pH for various metals as determined in the laboratory which are given as a starting point for finding the optimum pH in the field.

Neutralization Example. A highly acidic wastewater flow of 0.12 MGD is to be neutralized to 7.0 pH using lime (CaO). The titration curve prepared by the operations laboratory shows that a two-stage neutralization is required. In the first stage pH raises to 3.8 using 2,800 mg CaO per liter of wastewater. The second stage requires 700 mg CaO per liter of wastewater to continue raising the pH to 7. What is the average lime dosage (lb/day) for each stage? What are the total lime requirements (lb/day)? What is the daily feed rate of chemicals if the lime is commercial grade (90% CaO)?

Figure 8.3
Amphoteric (U-shaped) pH curves for metal ions

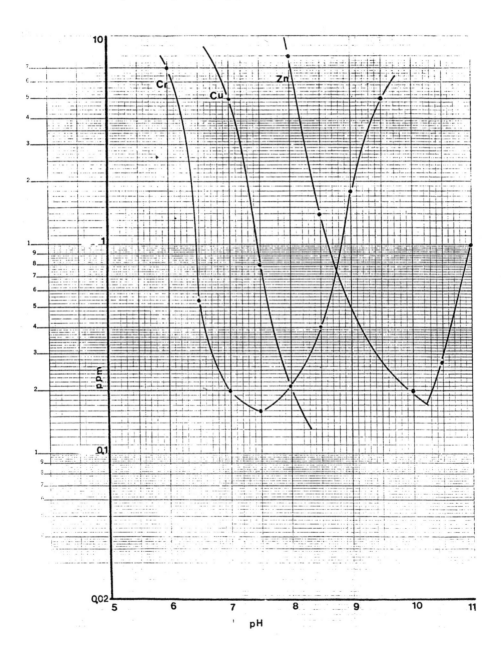

In the first stage the dosage is

$$D = 120,000 \text{ gal ww/day} \times 2,800 \text{ mg CaO/l ww}$$
$$\times 3.785 \text{ l ww/gal ww} /1,000 \text{ mg CaO/g CaO}$$
$$/454 \text{ g CaO/lb CaO} = \underline{2,800 \text{ lb/day}}$$

In the second stage the dosage is

$$D = 120,000 \text{ gpd} \times 700 \text{ mg/l} \times 3.785 \text{ l/gal} /1,000 \text{ mg/g}$$
$$/454 \text{ g/lb} = \underline{700 \text{ lb/day}}$$

Total lime requirements are

$$D_{total} = 2,800 + 700 = 3,500 \text{ lb/day CaO}.$$

The daily feed rate is

$$\text{Feed} = 3,500 \text{ lb CaO/day} /0.9 \text{ lb Cao/lb feed} = \underline{3,890 \text{ lb/day}}.$$

Figure 8.4

Optimum pH for Solubility of Metals

(the pH at which the metal is least soluble)

Metal Ion	pH
Aluminum	5.0
Arsenic	7-12
Barium	6-11.5
Cadmium	9.5-10
Chromium (III)	8.5-9
Copper	8
Iron	5.5-12
Lead	7.5-9
Manganese	7.2
Mercury	7-9
Nickel	10-11

Figure 8.4 *(cont'd)*

Metal Ion	pH
Selenium	7.5-9.5
Silver	11.1
Zinc	9-9.8

Notes:

(1) Optimum pH depends on the precipitating ion used.

(2) The precipitation of arsenic is extremely complex.

Equalization

Before mixing acid and alkaline waste streams together to neutralize them, make sure you have adequate equalization capacity to minimize hour-to-hour fluctuations of flow, composition, and pH. Instead of using mineral acids to neutralize alkaline solutions many plants now use carbon dioxide gas. This scheme has several advantages, such as inability to drive pH lower than 4.5-5 pH, and it is safer to work with than concentrated, strong acids. However, if wastewater treatment includes chromium reduction, some mineral acid will be needed to achieve the low pH required. Aerobic treatment of organic wastes is naturally acidic as it produces carbon dioxide, neutralizing about 0.5 mg of alkalinity as $CaCO_3$ per 1 mg BOD_5 removed.

Do not expect high accuracy of process measurements for pH. The pH is measured as a potential across a glass electrode (probe) as the result of a proton exchange between hydronium [H^+] in the fill and the process solution. The probe has an exterior hydrated gel layer, a dry glass layer, and an interior hydrated gel layer surrounding the fill liquid. The hydrated gel layers are essential for development of the millivolt potentials representing the proportional difference in pH from inside to outside. If the probe remains dry for any length of time or is scratched by abrasive particles in slurries or coated with oil, its response time will be slowed. In unsteady state the pH measurement is like reading last week's stock ticker tape. You might not have seen it before but what good is it now? Take a small sample out of the tank and measure pH with a laboratory instrument or pH strip (litmus paper). If the process unit is in steady state, the problem of the damaged probe is not so terrible but clean and cross check pH probes daily and calibrate pH meters at least once per month. (Calibrate laboratory pH meters daily.)

Equalization is an important concept in industrial wastewater treatment especially where characteristics of wastewater vary widely over time.

In one plant with poor removal efficiencies the influent was determined to change on an hourly basis! O/W emulsion (see discussion below) varied from 1-3% in the morning to 50-60% in the late afternoon. Heavy metals loading ranged from about 200 ppm in the morning to 50 ppm in the afternoon. Oily waste streams were segregated and an equalization basin was installed to make wastewater influent more uniform in characteristics and to lower the overall concentration of the O/W emulsion. Air was injected into the equalization basin to obtain better mixing of the influent, to start chemical oxidation of some metals, and to prevent suspended solids from settling.

This case history is the reason equalization is necessary: it eliminates overloading of downstream treatment process units. Additionally, equalization often reduces the size of equipment needed. Store wastewater during high loading or flow or mass and discharge during low loading to even the situation out. However, a storage tank alone is insufficient for equalization. Each distinct volume of incoming wastewater must be adequately mixed with other wastewater streams by proper distribution, baffling, mechanical agitation, aeration, or any combination of these methods. Distribution and baffling are the most economical method but also least sufficient. Mechanical agitation eliminates most of the need for baffling but provides improved mixing when baffles are used. Aeration is the most effective way of mixing wastewaters but also the most expensive. Small facilities should consider the feasibility of batch treatment of wastewater from an equalization basin. See Figure 8.5 for an equalization examination.

Figure 8.5

Equalization Example

(The flow of wastewater from your plant is as given below:)

Time Period	Flow, gpm	Time Period	Flow, gpm
12-1 A.M.	50	12-1 P.M.	67
1-2	35	1-2	64
2-3	26	2-3	61
3-4	21	3-4	56
4-5	17	4-5	60
5-6	16	5-6	60
6-7	19	6-7	60
7-8	33	7-8	58
8-9	56	8-9	63
9-10	65	9-10	63
10-11	67	10-11	60
11-12	68	11-12	55

If 50 gpm can be treated and discharged, what volume is needed for an equalization basin? Assume contaminant loading is consistent throughout the day. Set up a table as shown in Figure 8.6.

Required equalization volume is 10,980 gallons. Do not be fooled by the minus signs with more effluent than influent. If we had started our table at 8 A.M. the table would have looked different with all positive numbers but would have given the same result. Add 10-25% as a safety margin, say 15% for our example: 10,980 X 1.15 = 12,627 or a nominal 13,000 gallon tank will suffice for our equalization basin.

Figure 8.6

Equalization Table

Storage Time Period	Inflow gal/hr	Outflow gal/hr	(Accumulated Difference) gallons
12-1 A.M.	3,000	3,000	0
1-2	2,100	3,000	- 900
2-3	1,560	3,000	- 2,340
3-4	1,260	3,000	- 4,080
4-5	1,020	3,000	- 6,060
5-6	960	3,000	- 8,100
6-7	1,140	3,000	- 9,960
7-8	1,980	3,000	-10,980
8-9	3,360	3,000	-10,620
9-10	3,900	3,000	- 9,720
10-11	4,020	3,000	- 8,700
11-12	4,080	3,000	- 7,620
12-1 P.M.	4,020	3,000	- 6,600
1-2	3,840	3,000	- 5,760
2-3	3,660	3,000	- 5,100
3-4	3,360	3,000	- 4,740
4-5	3,600	3,000	- 4,140
5-6	3,600	3,000	- 3,540
6-7	3,600	3,000	- 2,940
7-8	3,480	3,000	- 2,460
8-9	3,780	3,000	- 1,680
9-10	3,780	3,000	- 900
10-11	3,600	3,000	- 300
11-12	3,300	3,000	0

Coagulation and Sedimentation

Gross sedimentation involves the removal of grit and floating solids by use of static, rotary drum or vibrating screens, bar racks, grit chambers, and aerated grit chambers. The settling of fine solids from water is called clarification. The simplest example of clarification is a mud puddle. Right after a storm the mud puddle is milky, coffee with cream or brown in color. After a few days, any water remaining is clear because the solids that make water milky or cream color dropped out of suspension.

A simple clarifier is merely a tank that allows solids to drop out of suspension in still water by gravity. This process is also called sedimentation. Clarification, or sedimentation, utilizes the difference in density between water and the solids to effect separation. Clarification is the most common method of removing insoluble particles from wastewater.

To calculate terminal settling velocity of particles in water:

$$v = \sqrt{\frac{4g(\rho_s - \rho_l)D}{3C_d\rho_l}} \qquad [8.4]$$

where

v = terminal settling velocity of the particle
ρ_l = density of the liquid
ρ_s = density of the particle
D = diameter of the particle
C_d = drag coefficient
g = acceleration due to gravity.

The Reynolds number is

$$N_{Re} = \frac{vD\rho_l}{\mu} \qquad [8.5]$$

where μ is the viscosity of the liquid.

With Reynolds' numbers less than 1, viscous forces predominate and the drag coefficient is

$$C_d = \frac{24}{N_{Re}} \qquad [8.6]$$

By substituting equation (8.6) into (8.4) we arrive at Stokes' law:

$$v = \frac{\rho_s - \rho_l}{18\mu} g D^2 \qquad [8.7]$$

As the Reynolds number increases to over 1 but less than 1,000 both viscous and inertia forces are effective in a transition zone and the coefficient of drag becomes:

$$C_d = \frac{18.5}{N_{Re}^{0.6}} \qquad [8.8]$$

As the Reynolds number increases beyond 1,000, viscous forces become insignificant and C_d becomes a constant 0.4.

Finally, the settling velocity is related to tank design by

$$v_o = \frac{Q}{A} \qquad [8.9]$$

where v_o is a cutoff settling velocity. Any particle with a settling velocity greater than the cutoff will be removed by sedimentation while particles with settling velocities less than v_o will be removed in the ratio v/v_o.

Two kinds of clarifiers are currently in vogue. The sludge blanket clarifier introduces the raw waste stream through a blanket of agglomerated particles. Mixing between the raw stream and the sludge blanket promotes particle growth and reduces the concentration of slow-settling, fine particles. A plate clarifier has a series of inclined plates through which the raw, unclarified stream flows from the bottom upward. After only inches of settling, particles impinge on a plate then slide downward to the base of the clarifier.

Clarifier Tip

If the inclined plates are tilted in the direction of water flow, try realigning them in the opposite direction to see if efficiency of the clarifier improves, assuming flow rate remains within the original specifications of the designer.

Either type of clarifier, inclined plate or sludge blanket, requires less maintenance in the circular version rather than the rectangular one.

The solid particles to be removed by a clarifier often form a colloid in water. Colloids have electrical properties which retard agglomeration and settling in the normal sense. In fact, colloids can remain in suspension far beyond your patience or that of the wastewater enforcement authority. Hydrophobic (lyophobic) colloids are relatively easy to destabilize and settle but hydrophilic (lyophilic) colloids require special treatment. Without getting into a technical discussion of *psi (ψ)* and *zeta (ζ)* potentials, realize that modern wastewater treatment polymers can neutralize the charges and overcome these problems. It usually takes some experimentation in jars, though. Figure 8.7 shows the difference between the two types of colloids.

Figure 8.7
Hydrophobic vs. Hydrophilic Colloids

Hydrophobic	Hydrophilic
Suspensoid	Emulsoid
Surface tension like water	Surface tension less than water
Coagulates easily with electrolytes	Not sensitive to electrolytes

---

Two coagulation mechanisms exist. One mechanism, called perikinetic (electrokinetic) coagulation, reduces the electrostatic potential on colloid particles until the molecular *van der Waals forces* are stronger and clumps of the precipitating species begin to form. In orthokinetic coagulation, the micelles—the structural units of the colloid—aggregate and form clumps which agglomerate.

When we assist clarification by adding chemicals to water to speed up precipitation and agglomeration or to improve the efficiency of colloid removal, we are utilizing processes called coagulation and flocculation. Coagulants are aqueous inorganic solutions such as alum, lime, ferric chloride or ferric sulfate which are added to the wastewater before metal ion precipitation and which provide a transition from fine, nonsettling particles called pin-flocs to larger suspended solids that will settle by gravity. Coagulants are used for acidic wastewaters with dilute metal concentrations which precipitate while undergoing neutralization. Flocculants are alum, iron salts, or long-chained organics derived from petroleum that promote the growth of large, dense particles called floc which settle quite rapidly. Flocculants are polyelectrolytes; that is, they have electrical charges that allow coagulated hydroxides to clump together into larger masses. Figure 8.8 compares coagulation and flocculation.

Figure 8.8
Coagulation and Flocculation

Coagulation	Flocculation
Numerous, fine particulates	Scattered, large gels
Coagulant: low molecular weight charge neutralizer	Flocculant: high molecular weight particle binder
Rapid mixing	Slow stirring
High velocity gradient	Low velocity gradient
Process takes seconds	Process takes minutes

after Klemmer.

In coagulation, colloidal particles of different sizes have very measurable differences in settling velocity (high velocity gradient) whereas in flocculation all particles settle about evenly (low velocity gradient), as coagulated particles are aggregated into large, rapidly settling flocs. Chemical treatment experts recommend a shear rate of about 900/sec for coagulation and anywhere from 50/sec to 200/sec for flocculation. Maintain mixing energy low with lower shear rates during flocculation so you do not break up agglomerates, which aid in settling. The shear rate, G sec^{-1}, is calculated:

$$G = \sqrt{\frac{P/V}{\mu}} \qquad\qquad [8.10]$$

where

P = power input, ft lb/sec
V = volume, ft^3 $\quad$ μ = viscosity, lb sec/ft^2

Figure 8.9 lists factors which affect these processes.

Figure 8.9
Factors Affecting Efficiency of Sedimentation

Baffles
Characteristics of Wastewater
"Container-Wall" Effect
Density of Particles
Depth of Tank
Flow Fluctuations
Good Housekeeping
Grit (Large Solid) Removal
Inlet Design
Outlet Design
Overflow Rate
Particle Size
Sludge Removal
Surface Area of Floor
Temperature
Time
Velocity of Particles
Wind Velocity (Large Outdoor Basins)

Crosslinked polymers of the polyacrylamide-acrylate group and polyamines have greatly improved the precipitation-coagulation-flocculation-sedimentation process. Currently available polymers are noted for strong hydrogen bonding, linearity, and ability to form high molecular weight chains. Desired ionic states are obtained by copolymerization or chemical reactions on the amide functional group which can be hydrolyzed to the carboxylate ion. The degree of hydrolysis determines whether the polymer will be anionic, cationic, or neutral. Other polymers include polystyrene sulfonate, acrylamido-sulfonate, polyethylene oxide, polymaleic anhydride, and polyalkylenimines.

Polymer Mixing Tip

Use static mixers—in line—after dosing a feed line to a process unit in order to improve mixing of flocculants.

Filtration

We often think of filtration in relation to sludge dewatering but it can also be used as a primary wastewater treatment process. Generic filtration processes are (from grossest separation to finest): particle filtration, microfiltration, ultrafiltration, and hyperfiltration (reverse osmosis). Inversely, particle filtration requires the least amount of energy while reverse osmosis requires the most (7.5 to 30 kWh/1,000 gallon of wastewater). Countless variations are possible including some unique filtration units under trade names but we will limit this discussion to these four generic filtration processes.

Filtration is labor intensive and—due to technical sophistication—both operating and maintenance personnel require specialized training. Replacement of filter media can also be expensive. Media cost is inversely proportional to fineness of filtration.

Filtration separates solids and liquids. Do not be confused by the designations used for residue solids in water. Total residue is essentially the total of solids in water represented by the amount of material left after water has been evaporated. Filterable and nonfilterable residue are both part of the total residue. Filterable residue is determined by filtering the water then drying the filter paper in gentle heat until the weight no longer changes. The residue on the filter paper is called total suspended solids (TSS) or filterable residue. The water that passes through the filter paper contains the nonfilterable or total dissolved solids (TDS).

Particle Filtration. This solid-liquid separation process is easy to operate and removes particles with diameters of 1.5 microns and coarser. Granular media such as garnet or anthracite are used to remove solids from wastewaters containing 5 to 20 ppm solids; however, these media can handle up to 1,000 ppm (0.1% solids) with ninety percent removal efficiency.

Microfiltration. Particles ranging in size from 0.06 to 2 microns are removed at low pressures by microfiltration. Flow is perpendicular to the filtration media (counter flow). Some macromolecules and dissolved species pass through the semipermeable microfiltration membrane.

Ultrafiltration (UF). Molecular range particles from 0.002 to 0.2 microns can be removed by ultrafiltration. Pressure drops of 20-40 psi or more are required to operate UF units at flux rates of 300 to 400 gallons per ft^2 per day. Flow is parallel with the filtration membrane (cross flow). Water and low molecular weight (less than 1,000 usually) contaminants pass through the membrane. By varying pore size of the membrane at manufacture, the molecular weight separation can be pushed up to 1,000,000. Typically in wastewater treatment we want to go in the other direction. A material balance around the UF unit (this also applies to RO units) can be accomplished to calculate a concentration ratio (CR):

$$CR = \frac{C_b}{C_f} = \frac{F}{B} \tag{8.11}$$

$$F = P\left(\frac{CR}{CR - 1}\right) \tag{8.12}$$

$$CR = \frac{1}{1-R} \qquad\qquad [8.13]$$

for complete rejection of the contaminant to be removed, and

$$CR = \frac{F}{B} \cdot (rejection\,factor) \qquad\qquad [8.14]$$

where less than complete rejection is achieved. The concentration of the contaminant in the bleed is C_b and in the feed is C_f. The feed rate, F, and bleed rate, B, are expressed in gal/min.

Coagulation and flocculation of precipitant followed by neutralization is often performed upstream of a UF unit as pretreatment to preserve the costly membranes. Alternate flushing of UF membranes with fresh water and a mild detergent solution on a regular basis assures best performance on a consistent basis.

Hyperfiltration (Reverse Osmosis or RO). Hyperfiltration removes the finest particles, such as ions, ranging in size from 1 to 20 Angstroms (0.0001 to 0.002 microns) using semipermeable membranes at high pressure. Otherwise, no sharp distinction exists between UF and RO from the particle size removal viewpoint. Important operating parameters for RO are recovery, reflux and rejection. Recovery is the percent feed (40-90 percent is typical) which is converted to permeate (clean water out). Flux is the rate at which the permeate passes through the membrane per unit area of membrane. Reflux is the recycling of the concentrate of dissolved salts for another pass through the RO unit. Rejection is the ability to separate dissolved salts from the permeate. Flow is parallel to the membrane in RO units.

Osmotic pressure, the driving force behind RO, is expressed by the van't Hoff equation:

$$\Pi = (n/v)RT \qquad\qquad [8.15]$$

where, similar to the ideal-gas law,

II = osmotic pressure, atm
n/v = ionic concentration of solution, moles/l
T = absolute temperature, K
R = ideal-gas constant, 0.083 l-atm/mol-K

Although this expression is only an approximation, accuracy is not required. RO applications involve ion concentrations of a few percent or less and working pressures in RO units are many times II (400 to 800 psig in cross flow to thin membranes to overcome the osmotic pressure). When this happens water passes through the membrane and the remaining liquid (called concentrate) has a higher concentration of contaminant salts.

Tubular RO systems require large amounts of floor area and are expensive. The cost of spiral-wound and hollow-fiber RO units are comparable with each other. Hollow-fiber units require less space in the plant and spiral-wound RO systems tolerate more suspended solids without plugging. The performance of all RO membranes gradually drops off as solids plug the openings. Also, as the feedwater becomes concentrated with the contamination and solids are being removed, precipitation could occur which would immediately plug the unit. Therefore, bench scale testing should be performed with typical and extreme samples of the wastewater. These problems can usually, but not always, be overcome with pretreatment of the feedwater by filtration, acidification, bacterial control and selection of the optimum membrane. Cellulose triacetate (CTA) membranes typically reject about 80 percent of dissolved solids. Thin film composite (TFC) membranes are destroyed by chlorine so dechlorination is a necessary pretreatment step. TFC membranes will reject over 90 percent of dissolved solids however.

Flotation

When oil and oil-soaked solids or animal fats cannot be adequately removed by gravitational methods, the secondary treatment is air flotation in which tiny air bubbles are introduced to the wastewater and allowed to rise to the surface as the water enters a quiescent pool called the flotation cell. Two mechanisms separate floating particles from water with air.

Dissolved air flotation (DAF) injects an air-water solution into the DAF cell feedwater. A pump is required to increase the pressure of the dissolved air-water solution into the inlet stream. In *induced air flotation* (IAF) air bubbles and turbulence are provided by rotating mechanical diffusers.

The amount of air dissolved in water is proportional to the pressure and inversely proportional to the temperature of the system. Consequently, expect more DAF problems in the summer and fewer in the winter. If **s** is the amount of dissolved air released from water when the pressure is dropped one atmosphere, it can be estimated by

$$s = s_a \frac{P}{P_a} - s_a \qquad [8.16]$$

where

s_a = air saturation at atmospheric pressure, ft³/1000 gal
P = absolute pressure of system
P_a = atmospheric pressure

Insufficient air causes poor flotation; excess air gains nothing by way of performance. DAF operations rely on the relationship between the air/solids ratio (A:S) and effluent quality and solids concentration in the float.

$$A:S = \frac{s_a R}{S_a Q} (\frac{fP}{P_a} - 1) \qquad [8.17]$$

where

R = pressurized recycle, use same flow units as Q
S_a = influent oil and suspended solids
f = fraction of saturation

Operating in the 20 to 50 psia range gives 30 to 120 micron-sized air bubbles.

Flotation cells are part of the mystique of the black art of wastewater treatment yet experience shows them to be trusty servants when well cared for. Most flotation problems stem from faulty design because the wastewater sample was not typical. A common design problem in DAF cells is placing the pressure regulator valve too far from the vessel, making it hard to achieve the optimum bubble size. Insufficient air supply is a common malady that is easily corrected. This problem is indicated when the pressure tank level control will not control the level or when a tray in the tank plugs. Poor air bubble dispersion in the cell indicates faulty inlet diffuser design.

Floor loading of a flotation cell ranges from 0.5 to 5.0 lb sludge per ft^2 floor per hour. Hydraulic flow rate varies with inlet solids concentration. At a fixed floor load, hydraulic load varies inversely with inlet solids concentration.

Typically, a coagulation step is located upstream of a flotation unit. The feed is injected with a polymeric flocculant to increase the particle size of the pin floc entering the unit as large particles rise faster than smaller ones do. By cutting down the time needed in the flotation cell the throughput can be increased. With fragile floc, however, effluent recycle is necessary. Most flotation cells have some solids carryover, so downstream you usually find some sort of media filter to remove any remaining solids.

Flotation Example. A 60 gpm wastewater stream bears 4000 ppm suspended solids is treated in a DAF unit with an air-to-solids ratio of 0.03 and a rise rate of 0.4 fpm. The recycle pressure is 50 psig, temperature is 77 °F, saturation is 75%, specific gravity is 1.3. Calculate influent suspended solids mass, recycle ratio and hydraulic loading rate.

Calculate mass influent suspended solids.

4000 mg/l X 60 gal/min X 1 lb/454,000 mg X 3.785 l/gal
X 60 min/hr X 24 hr/day = 2881 lb/day

Calculate the recycle ratio.

A:S = 0.03

S_a = 4000 mg/l = 33.3 lb/1,000 gal

Q = 0.0864 MGD

f = 0.75

P = 64.7 psia

For air saturation we have to consult a data source such as Table 3.7 in Eckenfelder where we obtain:

s_a = 2.55 ft³/1,000 gal

Now we solve the following equation for R:

A:S = s_aR/S_aQ (fP/P_a -1)

0.03 = [(2.55/1,000)R]/[(33.3/1,000)(0.0864)]
          * [0.75(64.7)/14.7 -1]

R = 0.0147 MGD

0.00147/0.0864 = 0.17

Calculate the hydraulic loading rate.

V_o = 0.4 ft/min * 1 gal/0.1337 ft³ = 2.99 gal/min-ft²

Ion Exchange

An ion is an atom or molecule that has lost or gained an electron and thereby has an electrical charge. The removal of cations (positively charged ions), such as H^+ and Na^+, or anions (negatively charged ions), such as OH⁻, from wastewater by oppositely charged resin beds is a process called ion exchange(IX). A versatile process, IX has wide use in industry for removal of dilute concentrations of ions from water. This reversible adsorption process uses charged particles on immobile particles to exchange for dilute ions in wastewater.

For cationic exchange we use resins similar to Na_2R and H_2R in a reaction such as:

$$Ca^{++} + Na_2R \rightleftharpoons CaR + 2Na^+ \qquad [8.18]$$

This resin is regenerated with a 5-10% brine solution.

$$CaR + 2NaCl \rightleftharpoons Na_2R + CaCl_2 \qquad [8.19]$$

Or, another route is

$$Ca^{++} + H_2R \rightleftharpoons CaR + 2H^+ \qquad [8.20]$$

Now, regeneration requires 2-10% sulfuric acid.

$$CaR + H_2SO_4 \rightleftharpoons H_2R + CaSO_4 \qquad [8.21]$$

In either case, the calcium salt is the waste stream.

In anionic exchange, $R(OH)_2$ is used.

$$SO_4^= + R(OH)_2 \rightleftharpoons RSO_4 + 2OH^- \qquad [8.22]$$

which is regenerated with a 2-10% solution of NaOH.

$$RSO_4 + 2NaOH \rightleftharpoons R(OH)_2 + Na_2SO_4 \qquad [8.23]$$

Sodium sulfate is discarded as a waste product.

Economic IX depends on capacity vs. cost of the resin, volume of regenerant required, recovery of ions and resin distribution as well as process efficiency. Resin utilization efficiency is the quantity of ions removed compared to the total ions that could be removed. Regeneration efficiency represents the amount of ions removed from resin vs. the total amount of ions in the volume of regenerant used.

Strong acid resins are highly ionized in both the acid (RSO_3H) and salt (RSO_3Na) forms. Weak acid resins use carboxylic acid ($RCOOH$) as the ionizable portion of the resin and have limited exchange capacity when pH is less than 6. Strong base resins are also highly ionized and usable over the entire pH range. Weak base resins are not very effective if the pH is greater than 7. Weak acid and base resins are more easily regenerated than strong acid or base resins. Chelating resins use EDTA to form stable compounds with heavy metals.

Ions are selectively displaced. The order of displacement for ions is shown in Figure 8.10.

Figure 8.10

Order of Ion Displacement

Cations	Anions
La^{3+}	$SO_4^=$
Ba^{3+}	$CrO_4^=$
Sr^{++}	NO_3^-
Ca^{++}	PO_4^{3-}
Mg^{++}	$MnO_4^=$
Cs^{++}	I^-
Rb^+	Cl^-
K^+	F^-
Na^+	OH^-
Ci^+	
H^+	

Ion exchange is used in the plating industry to recover metal ions and for process water production by deionization. Another industrial application is for purifying treated wastewater for reuse. Water softening processes based on IX have been particularly effective where the flow rate is small. The nitrogen fertilizer industry also uses IX to treat wastewaters. Another use is in the treatment of boiler feed water which must be ultra pure. IX typically removes ninety-nine percent of dissolved solids in influent.

In the exchange cycle metal ions are substituted onto the resin, thus in the case of a typical plating bath rinse,

$$[CrO_4^=, Cu^{++}, Zn^{++}, Fe^{++}, Al^{++}] + H_2 R \rightleftharpoons [Cu, Zn, Fe, Al]R + H_2 CrO_4 \quad [8.24]$$

Chromic acid is either recovered or, if too weak, undergoes exchange with an anionic resin, $R(OH)_2$, to give $RCrO_4$ and demineralized water. In the cation regeneration cycle:

$$[Cu, Zn, Fe, Al]R + H_2 SO_4 \rightleftharpoons H_2 R + [Cu, Zn, Fe, Al]SO_4 \quad [8.25]$$

This waste is either discharged to the sewer or, more likely, held for further treatment. The anion regeneration is:

$$RCrO_4 + 3NaOH \rightleftharpoons R(OH)_2 + Na_2 CrO_4 + NaOH \quad [8.26]$$

The waste from this cycle is passed through the cation exchanger for chromium recovery. Operating parameters for a typical IX unit are given in Figure 8.11.

Figure 8.11
Typical Ion Exchange Operating Parameters

Column Depth	24-30 inches
Flow Rate	2-5 gpm/ft³
Rate of Regeneration	1-2 gpm/ft³
Rinse Rate	1-1.5 gpm/ft³
Rinse Volume	100 gal/ft³

An excellent application of IX is as a polishing process for conventional wastewater treatment, perhaps one which was underdesigned or approaching capacity with respect to removal efficiency.

An IX unit can polish off remaining metal ions. The key to effective IX is proper resin selection. Resins that remove ions more effectively can be selected because they are selective for certain ions. Selective resins are particularly useful in recycling processes.

Two IX columns are required in order to be able to operate continuously while a column is being regenerated. Concurrent fixed beds flow untreated wastewater down onto the bed in the loading phase. Backwash is upflow and regeneration is downflow with a downflow rinse. Loading and regeneration are performed as batch operations. This type IX process is used for low loads (200 ppm) and low throughput (1,000 gpm and less). Regeneration flows in the opposite direction to the untreated influent in countercurrent fixed beds. To preserve resin stage heights, backwash is omitted every other regeneration cycle in these beds. Countercurrent beds can handle high loads at moderate throughput (ppm X GPM $\geq$ 40,000). The waste volume is reduced due to less frequent backwashing. Continuous countercurrent units (actually multi-stage countercurrent movement of resin in a closed loop) provides simultaneous treatment, regeneration, backwash, and rinse which is only interrupted for a momentary resin pulse. These units provide high loads with high throughput (ppm X GPD $>>$ 40,000) and are used where constant effluent quality is critical.

An IX system is more sophisticated than precipitation, coagulation, and clarification so operators and maintenance personnel require more focused training in order to operate and maintain an IX system. Be very careful about what your dollar is buying when considering IX.

In order to cut capital outlay for their customers, one company which made IX equipment utilized cheaper materials of construction. This equipment did not persevere in an industrial setting. In fact, the equipment typically lasted for only six to nine months before having to be replaced.

Before committing to buy IX equipment, visit an installed system and talk to the operators and maintenance personnel about it. IX is sound technology and rightly applied can remove a burden from your shoulders but wrongly applied can be a millstone around your neck.

Adsorption

The adsorption of certain pollutants from wastewater is not too different from the adsorption of pollutants from gas streams. Equipment sizing is affected by the noncompressibility of liquids as opposed to the compressibility of gases but otherwise the concept is the same. Adsorbents used for treating wastewaters include a wider range than for gas treatment: activated carbon, synthetic resins, soils, wood chips, saw dust, and alumina. The latter is discussed later.

Activated carbons include granular (GAC) and powdered (PAC) activated carbon forms. Activated carbon is made from wood, coal, or coconut shells heated to around 1,300°F under low oxygen conditions then heated to about 1,800°F under reducing conditions. Activated carbon has ten times as much surface area as it had before heat treatment, thus offering many potential adsorption sites. Biologically activated carbon (BAC) uses aerobic bacteria to continuously consume the organics trapped in the carbon bed.

Adsorption is used to remove biologically resistant substances and to remove taste and odor. Three adsorption processes are in use: physical, chemical, and ion exchange (which has already been discussed). In physical adsorption, the same Van der Waal's forces relied on in gas adsorption are relied on in wastewater treatment to remove undesirable contaminants. Chemical bonding is the basis of chemical adsorption. Electrostatic forces are used in ion exchange as discussed above.

The mechanisms of adsorption start with the transfer of adsorbate to the exterior surfaces of the adsorbent. The amount of exposed surface area is enormous—up to 5,000 ft^2 per ft^3. Next, the adsorbate diffuses into the pore spaces of the adsorbent. The process ends with the adsorption of the adsorbate onto the interior surfaces of the adsorbent. Figure 8.12 shows how the rate of adsorption behaves.

Figure 8.12
Rate of Adsorption

inversely proportional to particle diameter
proportional to concentration of adsorbate
proportional to temperature
inversely proportional to molecular weight
proportional to square root of time of contact
inversely proportional to pH

As with gases the Freundlich empirical formula is used.

$$x/m = KC^{1/n}$$ [8.27]

where x is the weight of adsorbate, m is the dose of adsorbent and C is the remaining concentration of solute. K and n are empirical constants. If the log of $(C_o - C)/m$ is plotted against the log of C, K is the y-intercept and $1/n$ is the slope of the curve called an *isotherm*. Rizzo and Shepherd give some K and $1/n$ values which are summarized in Figure 8.13.

Figure 8.13
Isotherm Constants

Compound	K	1/n
Aniline	25	0.322
Benzene Sulfonic Acid	7	0.169
Benzoic Acid	7	0.237
Butanol	4.4	0.445
Butyraldehyde	3.3	0.570
Butyric Acid	3.1	0.533
Chlorobenzene	40	0.406
Ethyl Acetate	0.6	0.833
Methyl Ethyl Ketone	24	0.183
Nitrobenzene	82	0.237
Phenol	24	0.111
Toluene	30	0.729
Vinyl Chloride	0.37	1.088

Isotherms are specific not only to the compound being adsorbed but also to the adsorbent. Therefore unique isotherms must be developed in the laboratory or pilot plant for each adsorbent used.

In the Langmuir monolayer theory a different equation is used:

$$x/m = \frac{(abC)}{(1 + aC)}$$ [8.28]

where a and b are constants determined in the laboratory.

The Rohart Adams equation is used to design the bed.

$$t = \frac{N_o}{C_o V}[X - \frac{V}{KN_o}\ln(\frac{C_o}{C_B} - 1)]$$ [8.29]

where

t = service time, hours
X = bed depth, column depth, ft
V = flow rate, ft/hr
K = constant, ft^3/lb carbon hr
C_B = concentration of adsorbate in effluent

At time, t = 0

$$X_o = \frac{V}{KN_o}\ln(\frac{C_o}{C_B} - 1)$$ [8.30]

Adsorption columns are designed by selecting an adsorbent and running bench tests with different column heights. Wastewater is flowed through the column and effluent concentration is determined at various times after beginning the test. This is repeated at different flow rates and column heights. A plot of C/C_o is made against time or flow rate. After graphs are drawn, an optimum design is chosen. Typically, columns run ten to twenty feet high and six to ten feet in diameter.

Adsorption Tip

In case of poor column performance, check water temperature and pH against design. Next check flow rate against design. Finally, check to see if loading has increased significantly.

Phenol Tip

The isotherm of phenol is so nearly flat that pretreatment is required to meet tough permit limits. Add 5 ppm ferric chloride to wastewater containing phenol and lower pH to 5. Then add hydrogen peroxide at 5:1 weight ratio with the phenol. Mix for 15 minutes and adjust pH to the permit discharge requirement. Filter to remove suspended solids generated by the pretreatment and pump filtrate to a carbon bed.

Adsorption can also be effected with alumina, a generic name for the oxides and hydroxides of aluminum. Affinity for water on alumina is stronger than most other adsorbents. Initial contact of water with well degassed transition alumina yields surface hydroxyls. A second layer of water is then bound by hydrogen bonding of water molecules to the surface hydroxyls which present a distribution of functionalities (places where contaminants can be adsorbed) ranging from strongly basic to weakly acidic. Specific surface-coordination reactions occur by means of ligand exchange:

$$Al(OH)_3 + 3M^{Z+} \rightleftharpoons Al(OM)^{Z-1} + 3H^+ \qquad [8.31]$$

and

$$2Al(OH)_3 + M^{Z+} \rightleftharpoons \begin{matrix} Al O \\ OM \\ AlO \end{matrix}^{Z-2} + 2H^+ \qquad [8.32]$$

Ligands are the coordinating groups in the alumina that contribute pairs of electrons for coordinating covalent bonds. This is the power of alumina adsorption that permits the capture of some tough ions such as shown in Figure 8.14.

Figure 8.14
Ion Selectivity Series on Transition Alumina

Cations

Th(II), Al(III), U(IV) > Zr(II), Ce(IV) > Fe(III), Ce(III) >
Ti(III) > Hg(II) > UO_2(II) > Pb(II) > Cu(II) > Ag(I) >
Zn(II) > Co(II), Fe(II) > Ni(II) > Tl(I) > Mn(II)

Anions

OH^- > PO_4^{3-} > $C_2O_4^{2-}$ > F^- > SO_3^{2-}, $Fe(CN)_6^{4-}$, CrO_4^{2-} >
$S_2O_3^{2-}$ > SO_4^{2-} > $Fe(CN)_6^{3-}$, $Cr_2O_7^{2-}$ > NO_2^-, CNS^- >
I^- > Br^- > Cl^- > NO_3^- > MnO_4^- > ClO_4^- > CH_3COO^- > S^{2-}

Miscellaneous Treatment Processes

Unique treatment systems that are commercially available for the treatment of specific wastewater streams are mostly proprietary processes. Each has its own particular use and its own set of problems, its own advantages and disadvantages. It is not practical to cover every one of them here even briefly so for this discussion let us examine a few generic processes.

Many manufacturing plants use organic solvents for cleaning, thinning paints, and removing paints. These chemicals are often volatile organic chemicals (VOCs). In refineries and manufacturing plants where VOCs are present, a certain amount ends up in the wastewater. Although these chemicals show up in a TTO (total toxic organic) analysis, the tendency has been to ignore them until recently. Air-stripping of VOCs is a mass transfer process based on Henry's law which says that the vapor pressure of a contaminant in air is directly proportional to the contaminant's solubility in water at equilibrium, or:

$$p = HS \qquad\qquad [8.33]$$

where p is the partial pressure of the VOC contaminant, H is Henry's constant, and S is the VOC's solubility in water. The mass transfer equation for an air-water stripping system is:

$$KLa = \frac{L}{z}\frac{R}{R-1}\ln\left[\frac{(C_i/C_o)(R-1)+1}{R}\right] \qquad\qquad [8.34]$$

where KLa is the mass transfer coefficient, L is the liquid loading rate, z is the packing height, C_i is the influent concentration of the contaminant, C_o is the effluent concentration, and R is the stripping factor.

$$R = HG/LP_a \qquad\qquad [8.35]$$

where G is the gas loading rate and P_a is the operating pressure. With these equations we can solve for packing height to design a stripping tower or check any other variable for troubleshooting. Once the packing height, z, is determined by calculation, add ten percent for safety. Design data needs are summarized in Figure 8.15.

Figure 8.15
Process Information for Air-Stripper Design

Flow Rate (add 20-50% for conceptual design)
Organic Contaminants
Temperature
COD & BOD_5
TSS, pH, FOG

after Okoniewski.

Air-Stripping Tip

tower packing is critical
countercurrent flow: water downward/air upward
loss of airflow
flooding due to fouling

Light organics, hydrogen sulfide, and ammonia can be removed by a variation of air-stripping called steam-stripping. This allows you to recover process condensates, though stripped condensates may need further treatment before reuse.

For light organics which boil at temperatures lower than water, try distillation and recovery. For instance, where isopropyl alcohol (IPA) is used to rinse parts cleaned in aqueous solutions try distilling the IPA which boils at 180°F.

Electrolysis is another treatment available to treat dilute aqueous solutions. A electrolytic cell (EC) is composed of an oxidation reaction at an anode and a reduction reaction at a cathode. EC separators are membranes which allow either cations or anions—but not both—to pass. A simple EC consisting of two electrodes and a cation-permeable membrane can be set up to regenerate spent metal finishing solution (M^+R^-). The reaction at the anode is

$$M^+ + H_2O \rightarrow MO^- + 2H^+ \qquad [8.36]$$

and at the cathode

$$2H^+ \rightarrow H_2 \qquad [8.37]$$

The membrane prevents the reduction of the metal oxide.

Electrodialysis Tip

Ensure that the charge balance is the same everywhere in the system.

If no competing reactions are occurring at the anode, the number of moles, **m,** oxidized is determined from Faraday's law:

$$q = \int i \, dt = m n F \qquad [8.38]$$

where **i** is the current, **t** is time, **n** is the number of electrons involved in the oxidation, and **F** is Faraday's constant. Electron transfer is dependent on the local potential field at the electrode surface which is controlled by the potential applied to the electrode. The local potential field is the driver for the movement of electrons across the electrode-solution interface. The electrode reaction is

$$O + n e^{-} \rightleftharpoons R \qquad [8.39]$$

To drive at a decent rate, this reaction depends on the thermodynamics and kinetics of the couple that are related to the chemistry of O(xidation) and R(eduction) in solution. The Nernst equation is used to determine the equilibrium potential for the electrode reaction.

$$E_e = E_e^0 + [RT/(nF)] \ln (c_O/c_R) \qquad [8.40]$$

where E_e^0 is the formal potential for the couple O/R provided in literature [see Bard], and c_O and c_R are the concentrations of O and R in solution.

At the equilibrium potential, no net transfer takes place between O and R. However, the rate of oxidation-reduction increases exponentially with over potential, so

$$i = i_0 e^{[(\alpha n F/RT)\eta]} \qquad [8.41]$$

The exchange current is i_0 and α is the transfer coefficient. The electrode reaction has a current limit which is expressed

$$i_L = n F A k_m c \qquad [8.42]$$

Figure 8.16 gives some value ranges for typical commercial ECs and Figure 8.17 gives the configuration of electrodes.

Figure 8.16
EC Parameter Value Ranges

Electrode Area, ft^2	2 - 225
Electrode Pairs/Module	1 - 100
Interelectrode Gap, in	0.001 - 0.08
Maximum Current Density, mA/ft^2	20 - 45
Possible Number of Flows	2 - 4

Ultraviolet (UV) wave-length energy has long been used to disinfect wastewater and remove organic pollutants. UV breaks molecular bonds to either induce or catalyze chemical reactions.

Figure 8.17
Electrode Configurations

Static or Solids Electrodes

Porous	Packed Bed
Cloth	Fibers
Felt	Granules or Flakes
Foam	Microspheres
Perforated Plates	Raschig Rings
Stacked Meshes	Rods
	Spheroids

Dynamic or Fluid Electrodes

Fluidized Bed	Moving Bed
Micropsheres	Inclined Beds
Spheroids	Pulsed-flow Beds
	Raschig Rings
	Slurries
	Tumbled Beds
	Vibrated Beds

after Pletcher and Weinberg.

For industrial pretreaters who cannot discharge high chlorine wastewater because of its toxic effect on municipal wastewater plants or who have trouble getting an air permit for an air-stripping tower, UV is an option.

In biological reactions, UV bondbreaking kills the organisms present. UV disinfection of wastewater is a first order reaction. UV also boosts the oxidizing power of chemical oxidants, such as ozone, by exciting the molecules to higher-potential energy states.

Electromagnetic (EM) energy in the wavelength range between 180 and 380 nanometers (nm) is called UV. Visible light has a longer wavelength (starting about 400 nm) and X-ray energy has shorter wavelengths than UV. A photon of UV, or any EM energy, is described by

$$E = h\nu = hc/\lambda \qquad [8.43]$$

where

E = energy
h = Planck's constant
c = speed of light
ν = frequency
λ = wavelength

By converting E to kcal, consider a g-mole (Einstein) of photons

$$E = 28,591/\lambda \qquad [8.44]$$

in kcal/g-mole. Therefore, a UV photon carries 75 to 160 kcal depending on the wavelength. Legan lists dissociation energies required for various chemical bonds and gives examples of several photochemical reactions and their effects.

A high-energy lamp is used to emit UV radiation through a quartz sleeve in a pipe through which contaminated water flows. An oxidation agent such as hydrogen peroxide is activated by the UV energy:

$$H_2O_2 + UV \rightarrow 2(\bullet OH) \qquad\qquad [8.45]$$

These hydroxyl radicals are oxidizing species which destroy any toxic organic compounds in water (TOC). Rate constants for the reaction of •OH radicals and most TOCs are satisfactorily high. Some TOCs such as alcohols and alkanes render up a hydrogen atom to the hydroxyl radical to form water. Others such as the aromatics and olefins bond with the hydroxyl. The simplified general oxidation reaction is:

$$\begin{matrix} Chlorinated \\ Organic \\ Molecule \end{matrix} \begin{matrix} O_2 \\ \dashrightarrow \\ \bullet OH \end{matrix} \begin{matrix} Oxygenated \\ Intermediates \end{matrix} \begin{matrix} O_2 \\ \dashrightarrow \\ \bullet OH \end{matrix} CO_2 + H_2O + Cl^+ \qquad [8.46]$$

In the presence of oxygen, the hydroxyls initiate a series of reactions which end up mineralizing the water as they break down TOCs. Other products besides the ones listed in equation (8.46) are low molecular weight carboxylic acids, which are easily biodegradable and not regulated. Ultraviolet treatment has no air emissions.

Sulfide precipitation can achieve lower concentration levels of metal ions in the effluent than hydroxide precipitation can. This technology is particularly useful in the case of highly chelated wastewaters. Sodium sulfide is used as the treatment chemical in the soluble sulfide process and ferrous sulfide is used in the insoluble process. The sludge generated by either process may be more difficult to deal with and dispose of than hydroxide sludges, however.

The insoluble starch xanthate (ISX) process was developed to achieve low levels of heavy metal ions in treated wastewater using a precipitation method. ISX acts as an ion exchange resin and helps get the metal out of solution.

Sodium borohydride precipitation is another substitute for hydroxide precipitation in order to achieve lower effluent concentrations and also yields less sludge. Some permits require the removal of color from wastewater, for instance, in textile mills where dyes are used. Some authorities do not regulate color but others do, hence the need for color removal treatment. One way to remove color is to bleach it. Actually, this process is chemical oxidation and the electron donors commonly used are chlorine (Cl_2), chlorine dioxide (ClO_2), potassium permanganate ($KMnO_4$) or sodium hypochlorite (NaOCl). Use 1 lb. of bleach per 10,000 gallons of colored water. Color can also be removed by carbon adsorption or by an alum flocculant (then clarified).

BIOLOGICAL TREATMENT METHODS

Generically, two biological processes are available for wastewater treatment: suspended and immobilized growth. Complete mix, plug flow, and step feeding systems are among the schemes used in suspended growth. The complete mix scheme is typically used in anaerobic treatment applications. Packed bed, expanded bed, fluidized bed, and rotating biological contactors (RBC) are some immobilized growth schemes. Upflow sludge blanket and baffled reactor processes are not classified. Finally, the use of artificial wetlands to treat wastewater is also in a class by itself.

Immobilized Growth Systems

Immobilized growth systems are characterized by very long biological solids retention times (SRT) at very short hydraulic retention times (HRT). Therefore, they absorb biological load fluctuations readily but experience upsets of degasification and solids concentration with hydraulic load fluctuations of more than a few percent.

Tip

Maintain design flow by providing flow equalization upstream of the contactor.

Continuous, intimate mixing of raw waste, return sludge, and digester contents is demanded by the short HRT.

Tip

Maintain a velocity of 0.5 feet per second across the bottom of the contactor by good mixing.

Anaerobic contact processes provide the vastly different SRT and HRT by biomass separation in a clarifier with recycling of the settled biomass. Biomass (sludge) recycle rate is three parts sludge to one part raw waste. This type reactor cannot provide the biomass levels that an immobilized growth system can, however.

Generally, in any type biological system, efficiency increases with increasing SRT. A long, safe SRT allows for stressors such as low temperatures and toxics.

Tip

Maintain high biomass level in order to minimize the impact of toxics.

Complete mix reactors without recycle have a long SRT but low biomass level. Immobilized growth reactors provide a high biomass level and long SRT. Upflow blanket reactors and baffled reactors both provide high biomass levels. Figure 8.18 compares aerobic and anaerobic processes generically.

Transient toxicity is caused by a plug-flow-like toxic slug passing through the reactor without washing out biomass. Getting toxic wastewater out of the reactor quickly speeds up recovery. Immobilized growth reactors retain biomass allowing for recovery from toxic slugs and are the best choice where possibility of frequent but transient toxic slugging exists.

Chronic toxicity is another matter. Complete mix reactors allow for gradual exposure of biomass to incoming toxic material which gives the organisms a chance to acclimate to the stress.

Figure 8.18
Aerobic and Anaerobic Systems

Characteristic	Aerobic	Anaerobic
Energy Needs	Large	Low
Removal Efficiency	95% +	60-90%
Sludge	Much	Low
Sensitivity to Toxics	Yes	Some
Startup Period	2-4 weeks	2-4 months
Nutrient Needs	High	Low
Odor	Low	Yes
Alkalinity	Low	High
Biogas	No	Yes

after Eckenfelder,
Argaman, and Miller

Biodegradation

Manufacturing industries discharge wastewaters contaminated with organic materials such as cleaners, defluxing agents, surfactants, defoamers, and photochemical processing solutions such as developers and strippers. Biodegradation of these chemicals is caused by bacteria normally found in process trenches and sumps, sewers, rivers, and streams. Biodegradation is generally an oxidative process in which case it is called aerobic degradation. Oxygen absorbed from air into the wastewater is used by the bacteria to decompose the organic contaminants. A certain amount of time is required in order for microscopic organisms to develop.

Tip

Unaided biodegradation requires an SRT up to 100 days.

BOD_5 is a measure of oxygen depletion caused by bacteria breaking down chemicals in contaminated water which indicates how much biodegradable organic carbon is in the water. Under the right conditions, BOD also reveals how much oxidizable nitrogen is present. High strength organics reduce bacteria efficiency and extremely high strength organics kill bacteria.

COD is a measure of total organic carbon which is easily oxidized in water. Also, sulfides, sulfites, and easily oxidizable compounds such as ferrous iron are reported as part of the COD number. Oxidized compounds will not show up so COD is NOT a measure of the total chemicals in water. COD is related to total organic carbon (TOC) through a carbon-oxygen balance.

Compatibility of the waste stream with biological treatment needs to be demonstrated by a test called electrolytic respirometry. This test shows if and how much of a particular contaminant can be discharged with untreated wastewater. If very little TOC is acceptable, then some other means of treatment and disposal needs to be found.

Another method of determining acceptability of an organic in the sewer is the BOD_5/COD ratio. If the ratio is 0.7 or higher, the waste is essentially biodegradable; partially biodegradable if the ratio is between 0.3 and 0.7; practically nonbiodegradable when the ratio is less than 0.3. However, if the material is very water soluble, do not use this ratio to determine the fate of the waste. (Note: When deciding ultimate fate of a waste stream remember to make RCRA hazardous characteristic/listed waste determinations.)

ROLE OF BIOLOGICAL TREATMENT

An effective way to convert soluble organics to insoluble is called biological oxidation. Aerobic bacteria consume oxygen to metabolize soluble organics to carbon dioxide. On a calm pond surface you have probably noted occasional bubbles rising to the surface. These bubbles are the build up of carbon dioxide released from anaerobic reactions on the bottom, assuming that it is not very deep, where aerobic bacteria are consuming the pond's oxygen and the organic sediments. When a bubble reaches a certain size it breaks off the bottom and plop! This same process can be used to convert industrial oils, fats, and other organics to carbon dioxide in biological contactors. Mechanical aeration can be used to keep the oxygen level up. The process is this:

$$BOD + \underset{microorganisms}{O_2} \xrightarrow{\hspace{1cm}} \underset{microorganisms}{\overset{CO_2}{H_2O}} \qquad [8.47]$$

Each microorganism or microbe is a tiny biochemical reactor, much like a cow is a large biochemical reactor. Imagine zillions of microscopic cows munching away contentedly on BOD silage—that is the process of activated sludge. Microbes from the aerated lagoon are settled out as sludge in a clarifier and returned to the lagoon for another pass. The microbe concentration in the return sludge is called mixed liquor volatile suspended solids (MLVSS). Common bacteria found in sludges are listed in Figure 8.19.

Figure 8.19
Bacteria found in Sludge

Alcaligenes genera
Bacillus genera
Escherichia coli
Flavobacterium genera
Pseudomonas genera
Sphaerotilus natans

Traditional Biological Treatment

Lagoons, ponds, and basins have long been used to treat wastewater. For biological treatment the flow must be equalized. Treatment is either aerobic, facultative, or anaerobic.

Aerobic lagoons are ponds dug in the ground provided with mechanical agitation to aerate the wastewater. HRT is long. BOD in the influent is limited but removal efficiency is high, between 50-70 percent reduction. Sludge production is low in aerated lagoons; effluent solids run about 100 ppm. Cold weather devastates these lagoons and efficiency drops off.

Tip

Aerate at 0.5 scfm/lb BOD-day.
Lagoon depth of 8-10 feet = good oxygen transfer efficiency.

Oxidation ditches are aerobic systems that use an oval race track channel. Trickling filters are towers packed or dumped with plastic media. Wastewater pours into the top of the tower and trickles through the biomass-covered, fixed-film media. Another fixed-film system is the rotating biological contactor (RBC) which is composed of several microorganism-covered plastic discs mounted on a horizontal shaft. As each disc rotates, any specific arc is first submerged in wastewater then rotated into the air where oxidation occurs.

A facultative pond has an aerobic surface, where the oxygen increases during daylight hours due to algal photosynthesis and decreases at night, and an anaerobic bottom where sludge is being decomposed. Facultative ponds run from three to six feet deep. DO is maintained only in the upper portion of the pond without no mixing. If the pond is overloaded, anaerobic conditions will prevail throughout its volume.

Anaerobic ponds are designed with minimum surface area/volume ratio in order to establish and maintain anaerobic conditions and provide maximum heat retention. They can be quite effective if properly designed and operated. Though typically applied to the degradation of concentrated wastes, sludges and slurries anaerobic systems also successfully treat waste streams with COD content as low as 1,000 ppm. They may be acclimated to degrade very difficult, refractive organic compounds left over from aerobic systems. Anaerobic systems process soluble wastes very quickly. Though some anaerobic retention times can be quite lengthy, most of the time they are comparable to aerobic treatment. These systems generate surplus energy when the loading is greater than 3,000 ppm COD and require on 10-20 percent of the amount of nutrients required by aerobic systems, plus alkalinity is controlled by carbon dioxide in the recycle stream.

Oxygen Production. In anaerobic systems, oxygen is produced by photosynthesis of algae. Algae types are shown in Figure 8.20.

Figure 8.20 **Algae Types**	
Green Algae	*Chlamydomonas* *Chlorella* *Euglena* *Oocystis* *Pediastrum*
Blue-green Algae	*Anabaena* *Anacystic* *Aphanizomenon* *Oscillatoria* *Phormidium*

The amount of oxygen produced by photosynthesis is

$$O_2 = CfS \qquad \text{[8.48]}$$

where O_2 is oxygen production in lb/acre day and C is 0.25, a constant. Light conversion efficiency f is given in percent. Light intensity S (BTU/ft^2 day) depends on the latitude of the site and the month of the year. For a single pond

$$\frac{S}{S_o} = \frac{1}{1 + kt} \qquad \text{[8.49]}$$

and for infinite ponds

$$\frac{S}{S_o} = e^{-k_n t_n} \qquad \text{[8.50]}$$

Typical values of k are 0.05/day for anaerobic conditions and 0.5/day for aerobic conditions. Busch makes DO a design parameter of aerated lagoons by this formula:

$$\frac{dO_2}{dt} = R = K_L a (O_2^* - O_2) = K_L a G \qquad [8.51]$$

where O_2 and O_2^* are DO and saturation oxygen concentrations, respectively, in lb/ft³ water, and $K_L a$ is the overall conductance or the reciprocal of overall resistance to the transfer of oxygen from gas to water, hr⁻¹, and

K_L = mass-transfer coefficient, ft⁻²hr⁻¹
a = area of lagoon, ft²
R = transfer rate, lb/ft³ hour
G = driving gradient, lb/ft³.

This equation is often presented as

$$K_L a = \frac{R}{(O_2^* - O_2)} = \frac{R}{G} \qquad [8.52]$$

Since oxygen transfer is affected by several variables, $K_L a$ will have a range of valid values. Temperature affects oxygen transfer which affects saturation concentration (10 mg/l under ideal conditions), transfer rate, and driving gradient. MLSS affects oxygen demand (another expression for R). The rate of air supply and the speed and submergence of mechanical surface aerators affect the size and quantity of air bubbles and water droplets and the intensity of G. Mixing effectiveness depends on the intensity of aeration and affects oxygen consumption efficiency. Surfactants and other organics affect bubble and droplet surface properties and surges in organic loading affect R in biological reactors. Efficiency of aeration is related to oxygen transfer per unit of energy input for aeration. Efficiency generally increases with aeration rate; however, aeration can reach a point where no more dividends may be had and efficiency drops off.

Production of Other Organic Compounds. Odors in biological treatment are almost always associated with sulfides, amines, aldehydes, ketones, and other organic compounds. The rotten egg smell of toxic hydrogen sulfide is produced when bacteria ingest sulfate and metabolize it to the reduced sulfide form.

$$SO_4^= + organic\ matter \xrightarrow{bacteria} H_2S + H_2O + CO_2 \qquad [8.53]$$

The population of sulfate metabolizing bacteria is generally low in fresh wastewater and higher in sludge. Sulfur reducing organisms thrive at low oxidation potential (ORP in the -200 to -300 mv range), 6-9 pH and about 86°F. Sludge deposits and slime growth are the major producers of hydrogen sulfide in tanks and sewers. One way to deal with such odor is to avoid the conditions which favor it. Another, especially once the problem is underway, is to kill the sulfur reducing bacteria with some toxic chemical. This can lead to violations of the wastewater discharge permit so another common method is to oxidize the hydrogen sulfide.

$$3H_2S + 2KMnO_4 \dashrightarrow 3S + 2H_2O + 2KOH + 2MnO_2 \qquad [8.54]$$

and

$$3H_2S + 8KMnO_4 \dashrightarrow 3K_2SO_4 + 2KOH + 2H_2O + 8MnO_2 \qquad [8.55]$$

These two equations are extremes between which any of several reactions may produce various forms of sulfur from elemental sulfur to sulfate, thionate, dithionates, or manganese sulfide.

Figure 8.21 summarizes typical BOD removal efficiencies expected of various biological treatment units and Figure 8.22 summarizes design parameters of lagoons.

Figure 8.21
Biological Treatment Removal Efficiencies

Treatment	BOD Removal %
Aerobic:	
Aerated Lagoon	50-70
Activated Sludge	85-95
Extended Aeration	85-95
Rotating Biolog. Contactor	80-95
Trickling Filter	50-60
Facultative:	
Aerated Lagoon	80-95
Pond	70-95
Anaerobic:	
Anaerobic Pond	50-80
Anaerobic Reactor	70-95

after Eckenfelder, Patoczka and Watkin

Figure 8.22
Lagoon Design Parameters

Lagoon	Retention day	Depth feet	Recycle Sludge, mg/l	Feed BOD, mg/l	Loading lb BOD/ acre-day
Aerobic	0.5-3	8-16	50% BOD in feed	50-750	250-
Anaerobic	0.5-30	8-15	<25	500-2,000	4,000
Facultative	7-50	3-6	<25	50-250	20-50

Biological Treatment Example. Remember the equalization basin we sized earlier? Suppose, besides flow, it had this loading for solids.

Time Period	Flow, gpm	BOD, mg/l
12-1 A.M.	50	150
1-2	35	115
2-3	26	75
3-4	21	50
4-5	17	45
5-6	16	60
6-7	19	90
7-8	33	130
8-9	56	175
9-10	65	200
10-11	67	215
11-12	68	220
12-1 P.M.	67	220
1-2	64	210
2-3	61	200
3-4	56	190
4-5	60	180
5-6	60	170
6-7	60	175
7-8	58	210
8-9	63	280
9-10	63	305
10-11	60	245
11-12	55	180

Let's compute the HRT required to produce an effluent BOD equal to or less than 190 mg/l at least 90% of the time.

First, let's look at the statistics of our data.

Statistic	Flow	BOD
Mean	72.5 gpm	170.4 mg/l
Median	59.0 gpm	180.0 mg/l
Standard Deviation	113.8 gpm	69.5 mg/l
Variation	12,945 (gpm)^2	4,835 (mg/l)^2

50% of BOD values are already less than 190 mg/l. We need to set up another data table. We want to compute the volume of waste in the equalization basin at the end of each current time period. Let's call this value V_{SC}:

$$V_{SC} = V_{SP} + V_{IC} - V_{OC}$$

where:

V_{SP} = volume in basin at the end of previous period,
V_{IC} = inflow volume, current time period,
V_{OC} = outflow volume, current time period.

and the BOD in the effluent during any current period is

$$x_{OC} = [(V_{IC}\, x_{IC}) + (V_{SP}\, x_{SP})]/(V_{IC} + V_{OC})$$

where:

x_{OC} = BOD in effluent, current period,
x_{IC} = BOD in waste, current period, and
x_{SP} = BOD in effluent, end of previous period.

Period	V_{IC}, gal	V_{OC}, gal	V_{SP}, gal	V_{SC}, gal	x_{IC}, mg/l	x_{SP}, mg/l	x_{OC} mg/l
12-1 A.M.	3,000	3,000	0	0	150	0	150
1-2	2,100	2,100	0	0	115	150	115
2-3	1,560	1,560	0	0	75	115	75
3-4	1,260	1,260	0	0	50	75	50
4-5	1,020	1,020	0	0	45	50	45
5-6	960	960	0	0	60	45	60
6-7	1,140	1,140	0	0	90	60	90
7-8	1,980	1,980	0	0	130	90	130
8-9	3,360	3,000	0	0	175	130	175
9-10	3,900	3,000	360	1,260	200	175	198
10-11	4,020	3,000	1,260	2,280	215	198	211
11-12	4,080	3,000	2,280	3,360	220	211	217
12-1 P.M.	4,020	3,000	3,360	4,380	220	217	219
1-2	3,840	3,000	4,380	5,220	210	219	215
2-3	3,660	3,000	5,220	5,880	200	215	202
3-4	3,360	3,000	5,880	6,240	190	202	198
4-5	3,600	3,000	6,240	6,840	180	198	191
5-6	3,600	3,000	6,840	7,440	170	191	184
6-7	3,600	3,000	7,440	8,040	175	184	181
7-8	3,480	3,000	8,040	8,520	210	181	190
8-9	3,780	3,000	8,520	9,300	280	190	218
9-10	3,780	3,000	9,300	10,080	305	218	243
10-11	3,600	3,000	10,080	10,680	245	243	244
11-12	3,300	3,000	10,680	10,980	180	244	229

Notice how much flatter the variation of x_{OC} is than x_{IC}.

Statistically, we have

$$y = (x_{e, max} - x_{avg})/\sigma_e$$

where y is the number of standard deviations σ that lie within the mean BOD and 190. The value of y is 1.28, so

$$1.28 = (190\text{-}170.4)/\sigma_e$$

We calculate the standard deviation of the effluent as

$$\sigma_e = 15.31$$

∴ the variance is

$$S_e = (15.31)^2 = 234.4$$

From the statistics table we prepared above, S_i is known, so

$$t = \Delta t S_i / 2 S_e$$

$$t = (1hr)(4,835mg^2/l^2)/2(234.4mg^2/l^2) = 10.31 \text{ hrs}$$

Alternative Biological Treatment

Some facilities use the trickling filter technique which consists of flowing wastewater over a cascading bed of rocks covered with slime (bacteria colonies), performing the same job as bacteria does in a lagoon. Slime sloughs off (breaks off) and flows with the wastewater out of the trickling bed to be clarified and returned to the trickling bed. The trickling bed is not a very effective process and most industrial plants are under permit limits too tight for such inefficiency.

A more effective alternative treatment is the anaerobic lagoon. Sometimes these are used in series with aerobic lagoons. Anaerobic lagoons are deeper and flow is strictly laminar to prevent turbulence. Anaerobic bacteria convert organics to methane, nitrogen, and hydrogen sulfide.

How to Remove Metal Ions from Wastewater

The treatment of wastewater containing heavy metals as the pollutants of primary interest involves equalization followed by neutralization, plus segregation of streams which must be treated specially (such as cyanide or hexavalent chromium bearing waters) and one of three treatment schemes—ion exchange, membrane processes, or chemical precipitation—are used to remove heavy metal ions. Heavy metal removal is controlled by the thermodynamics of dilute aqueous solutions.

Typically, the equalization basin receives wastewater bearing a few hundred ppm of heavy metal ions and the treatment scheme must remove all but ten or less ppm. For individual metal ions, we may have to remove all but a fraction of one ppm.

Take, for instance, the reduction of hexavalent chromium to trivalent followed by precipitation. The reduction is expressed

$$Cr^{6+} + 3e^- ---\rightarrow Cr^{3+} \qquad\qquad [8.56]$$

$$CrO_3 + H_2O \rightleftharpoons H_2CrO_4 \qquad\qquad [8.57]$$

and Chromium is reduced by treating with ferric sulfate around 2 to 2.5 pH:

$$H_2CrO_7 + 6FeSO_4 + 6H_2SO_4 \rightleftharpoons Cr_2(SO_4)_3 + 3Fe_2(SO_4)_3 + 7H_2O \qquad [8.58]$$

and then by adding slaked lime

$$\begin{aligned}
Cr_2(SO_4)_3 + 3Ca(OH)_2 &\rightleftharpoons 2Cr(OH)_3\downarrow + 3CaSO_4\downarrow \\
Fe_2(SO_4)_3 + 3Ca(OH)_2 &\rightleftharpoons 2Fe(OH)_3\downarrow + 3CaSO_4\downarrow
\end{aligned} \qquad [8.59]$$

For each 1 mg/l Cr (1 ppm) we need

16.03 mg/l $FeSO_4 \cdot 7H_2O$
6.01 mg/l H_2SO_4
9.48 mg/l 90% lime (CaO).

This aqueous mixture produces 6.09 mg/l $Fe(OH)_3$ sludge, 11.06 mg/l $CaSo_4$ sludge, and 1.98 mg/l $Cr(OH)_3$ sludge for every mg/l Cr in solution which is precipitated. Figures 8.23 and 8.24, respectively, give a metabisulfite and sulfur dioxide reduction scheme for hexavalent chromium.

Figure 8.23
Metabisulfite Reduction of Chromium

$Na_2S_2O_5 + H_2O <===> 2NaHSO_3 <===> H_2SO_3 + NaOH$
if pH > 2 ---> $Cr_2(SO_4)_3$
if pH around 3 ---> $4Cr_4(OH)_6(SO_4)_3$
if pH around 6.5 ---> $Cr(OH)_3$
$2H_2CrO_4 + 3NaHSO_3 + 3H_2SO_4 <===> Cr_2(SO_4)_3 + NaHSO_4 + 5H_2O$

Figure 8.24
Sulfur Dioxide Reduction of Chromium

$SO_2 + H_2O <===> H_2SO_3$
$2H_2CrO_4 + 3H_2SO_3 <===> Cr_2(SO_4)_3 + 5H_2O$

The reduction of chromium is pH driven and the rate of the reaction is faster at lower pH's. Figure 8.25 shows rates of reaction as a function of pH.

Other metals are precipitated from solution as follows where M represents a generic metal ion:

$$M^+X^- + NaOH ---\rightarrow MOH + NaX \qquad [8.60]$$

or

$$M^{++}X^= + Ca(OH)_2 ---\rightarrow M(OH)_2 + CaX \qquad [8.61]$$

Figure 8.25
Time to Complete Reduction of Chromium

Time (minutes)	pH
0.1	1.0
0.5	1.5
5.0	2.0
30.0	3.0
60.0	4.0
200.0	5.0

Caustic soda (NaOH) or slaked-lime ($Ca(OH)_2$) can be used in either reaction. Magnesium hydroxide is another alternative and it produces less sludge. This chemistry can only precipitate metals to a certain residual concentration, so low concentration levels, such as required by permit limitations, cannot be achieved if a chelating compound is present. Some metals are amphoteric meaning the metal has a minimum concentration in water at a specific pH and if pH is increased or decreased from that optimum pH the metal ions redissolve. That is why, along with chemistry of dilute solutions, undeservedly, wastewater treatment has a black art reputation. Science is science, and it works.

Tip

Metal hydroxide precipitation requires a close eye on pH.
Watch the water chemistry closely.
Learn how to conduct jar tests.
Make the process behave as in the jars.

If one or two metals give you fits, try *cementation* which is the electrochemical reduction of metal ions by contact with a metal of higher oxidation potential. Add scrap iron to the precipitation reactor to assist in the removal of cadmium, cobalt, nickel, tin, lead, copper, mercury and/or silver. If you need help with zinc or chromium add aluminum or magnesium. You can add magnesium for help with aluminum but the pH will have to be around 10. Ions from added metal with low EMF potential go into solution and help precipitate ions higher on the EMF series. Cementation is usually not affected by the presence of chelating agents discussed below. The process increases pH of the solution as the target metal is removed.

Complexing agents called *chelate* compounds (from the Greek word meaning claw) cause much grief in wastewater treatment as mentioned earlier. Ammonia, citrate, tartrate, and EDTA are some chelating agents found in many industrial plants. All cleaning solutions contain chelating agents as well as surface active agents such as detergents which also upset wastewater treatment plants.

In the hydroxide precipitation process, the extent of precipitation is dependent on the solubility product K_{sp} of the metal hydroxide and the ionization equilibrium constant K_i of any metal-hydroxyl complex. The effectiveness of the process depends on the size, density, and other physical properties of the metal hydroxide precipitates. Complexing agents increase the solubility of metal ions and significantly change particle size and shape of metal hydroxide precipitates. Most complexing agents hinder and inhibit growth of the precipitates making it very difficult to separate these particles from solution. Today we have at our disposal several polymeric treatment products to help overcome problems caused by chelating agents. The chemical vendor should be able to work this out by performing jar tests.

Tip

Pretreat liquid from mop buckets, floor cleaning machines, industrial laundry, and janitorial sumps:

Mix a 100 lb. bag of Epsom salt (magnesium sulfate) into a 55-gallon drum (not quite full to allow room for mixing) of spent cleaning solution and mix well for 30 minutes. Now you can dump this mixture to the wastewater equalization basin without fear of upsets in your wastewater treatment system.

Metal hydroxide sludges from treating electroplating wastewater are listed as hazardous waste and must be so disposed. Metal hydroxide sludges from other processes must be characterized with respect to hazardous waste regulations and may or may not be hazardous depending on the analytical reports.

Figure 8.26
Tips for Precipitation/Coagulation of Metals

Aim for high metal concentrations in the floc.
Avoid silicates and phosphates.
$Ca(OH)_2$ gives a fast settling sludge.
$Mg(OH)_2$ sludge has less volume.
Mix-mix-mix! during neutralization.
Provide 5-10 minutes between neutralization and floc.
Use chemical floc with same charge as floc particles.
You cannot jar test too often when troubleshooting.

Heavy Metal Example. An unbuffered influent to the wastewater plant contains 200 ppm chromium (trivalent) and 150 ppm zinc at 3.0 pH. The treatment system consists of three reactors in series. How much sodium hydroxide is required to minimize chromium (0.17 ppm at 7.5 pH) and leave no more than 1 ppm zinc dissolved (8.9 pH)? How much sulfuric acid is required to discharge the treated wastewater to 7.0 pH?

$$pH = -\log[H^+] = 7.5 \rightarrow \log[H^+] = -7.5 = 0.5 - 8.0$$

$$[H^+] = 10^{0.5} \times 10^{-8.0} = 3.16 \times 10^{-8}$$

$$H^+ + OH^- \rightleftharpoons H_2O \rightarrow K_w = [H^+][OH^-] = 1.0 \times 10^{-14} \text{ at } 77°F.$$

At 7.0 pH $[H^+] = [OH^-]$, so for the pH's required in this example problem:

$$3.0 \text{ pH} \rightarrow [H^+] = 1 \times 10^{-3} \text{ moles} \rightarrow pOH = 11 \rightarrow [OH^-] = 1 \times 10^{-11}$$

7.0 pH $\rightarrow$ [H$^+$] = 1 x 10^{-7} moles $\rightarrow$ pOH = 7 $\rightarrow$ [OH$^-$] = 1 x 10^{-7}

7.5 pH $\rightarrow$ [H$^+$] = 3.16 x 10^{-8} moles $\rightarrow$ pOH = 6.5
$\qquad\qquad\qquad\rightarrow$ [OH$^-$] = 3.16 x 10^{-7}

8.9 pH $\rightarrow$ [H$^+$] = 1.25 x 10^{-9} moles $\rightarrow$ pOH = 5.1
$\qquad\qquad\qquad\rightarrow$ [OH$^-$] = 1.25 x 10^{-6}

In the first reactor precipitate chromium (and any zinc that falls out). First, adjust pH to 7.5:

[H$_1$][OH$_1$] = [H$_2$][OH$_2$] = 1 x 10^{-14} $\rightarrow$ [OH$_2$] - [OH$_1$] = [OH$_A$]

but ([OH$_A$] - [H$_1$])[H$_2$] = 1 x 10^{-14}

[OH$_A$] = (1 x 10^{-14})/(3.16 x 10^{-8}) + 1 X 10^{-3}
$\qquad$ = 3.16 x 10^{-7} + 1 X 10^{-3} $\approx$ 1 X 10^{-3} = 0.001 mole

For the chromium removal:

Cr^{3+} + 3OH$^-$ $\rightleftharpoons$ Cr(OH)$_3$↓

So we need 3 moles of NaOH per mole of Cr removed.

Cr removed/l = (200mg-0.17mg)/(52mg/mg-mole) = 3.84 mg-mole

NaOH = 3 x 3.84 = 11.5 mg-mole

For zinc removal (at 7.5 pH 28 mg/l of zinc will remain dissolved):

Zn^{++} + 2OH$^-$ $\rightleftharpoons$ Zn(OH)$_2$↓, 2 moles of NaoH/mole Zn.

Zn = (150-28)/65 = 1.88 mg-mole

NaOH = 2 x 1.88 = 3.76 mg-mole

The total NaOH required for this first stage is

$$0.001 + 0.0115 + 0.00376 = 0.050 \text{ g-moles NaOH/liter}$$

Notice that the removal of the heavy metals requires more sodium hydroxide than the pH adjustment does. This situation could reverse itself under other circumstances such as lower metal loading or pH-buffered water.

In the second reactor we complete the zinc precipitation.

$$[OH_A - H_1][H_2] = 1 \times 10^{-14}$$

$$[OH_A] = (1 \times 10^{-14})/(1.25 \times 10^{-9}) + 3.16 \times 10^{-8}$$

$$[OH_A] = 8.0 \times 10^{-6} + 3.16 \times 10^{-8} = 8.03 \times 10^{-6}$$

$$Zn^{++} + 2OH^- \rightleftharpoons Zn(OH)_2\downarrow$$

$$\text{Zn removal} = (28\text{-}1)/65 = 0.415 \text{ mg-moles}$$

Total second stage NaOH requirement is

$$8.03 \times 10^{-6} + 0.415 \times 10^{-3} = 4.23 \times 10^{-4} \text{ g-mole/liter}$$

In the final stage we will neutralize the pH for discharge into the environment or POTW sewer whichever our permit allows:

$$[OH_1 - H_A][OH_2] = 1 \times 10^{-14} \ -[H_A] = (1 \times 10^{-14})/(1 \times 10^{-7}) - (7.95 \times 10^{-6})$$

$$[H_A] = 7.95 \times 10^{-6} - 1 \times 10^{-7} = 7.85 \times 10^{-6} \text{ g-mole/l}$$

BE CAREFUL! One g-mole sulfuric acid contains 2 g-moles $[H^+]$:

$$H_2SO_4 \rightleftharpoons 2H^+ + SO_4^=, \text{ so the sulfuric acid required is}$$

$$1/2 \ (7.85 \times 10^{-6}) = 3.93 \times 10^{-6} \text{ g-mole/liter.}$$

How to Make Oil Separations

Wastewater may contain oil in three forms: emulsified, free, or dissolved. *Emulsified oil* is made when fine oil droplets of the 1-10 micron diameter are introduced to water. This occurs as water and oil are mixed while passing through a centrifugal pump, for example. Fine oil droplets form an extremely stable suspension in water and will not separate by gravity. *Free oil* forms droplets of oil with sufficiently large size that buoyant forces cause them to rise to the surface of water. Finally, that fraction of petroleum which forms a true solution with water is called *dissolved oil*.

Conventional skimmers and gravity oil-water separators remove only the free oil from water. Acidic coagulation with neutralization followed by flocculation then by flotation must be used to remove emulsified and dissolved oil. Filtration can handle the high solids from oil removal by flotation but frequent backwashing is required. Biological removal of soluble oils is another alternative but is subject to upsets and high solids carryover. Carbon has a great affinity for oil which tends to plug the beds, therefore adsorption is best used as an oil removal polishing unitA related aqueous waste stream comes from waterfall curtain paint spray booths. Before discharging the sump of one of these paint booths to the wastewater treatment system, deaden it with an alkali and detackify it with sodium carbonate. Synthetic polymers are available to do the job also. Detackified paint releases its solids to float to the top (generally but sometimes the solids sink). The liquid is ready for treatment.

An oil-water separator is nothing more than a container that provides quiescent flow. This gives gravity and buoyant forces time to separate the free oil from the water. Ideally, an oil-water separator has no short-circuits, eddies, or turbulence. The rise rate of free oil globules is predicted by the Stokes' equation (8.7). Oil globules greater than or equal to 0.015 cm in diameter are removed quite handily in oil-water separators. Fixing D at 0.015 cm allows the simplification of the design equation to calculate rise rate v ft/min in terms of specific gravity:

$$v = 0.0241 \frac{S_w - S_o}{\mu} \qquad\qquad [8.62]$$

where

S_w = specific gravity of wastewater, dimensionless
S_o = specific gravity of oil, dimensionless.

The chief purpose of the oil-water separator is to remove the gross quantity of free oil which interferes with subsequent treatment processes. The separator also serves as a sedimentation basin to remove coarse particles suspended in wastewater.

Inadequate performance of oil-water separators has two chief causes. Should the characteristics of the influent wastewater change, all bets are off concerning the design of the oil-water separator. Secondly, if the initial characterization was not typical you will have a poor performing unit on your hands, too.

Tip

If oil/water separator performance is a problem:

1. determine average and peak flow rates,
2. take temperature of wastewater influent,
3. determine specific gravity of densest oil stream,
4. analyze influent loading for free and total oil,
5. measure length, width and depth of the unit.

With this information in hand one must go through a design exercise in order to troubleshoot the current problem.

If total oil differs greatly from free oil a large amount of emulsified and dissolved oil is present and needs further treatment.

Emulsions are intimate mixtures of two liquid phases like oil and water. Oily wastewater is oil emulsified in wastewater, called O/W emulsion. Waste oil emulsions are water emulsified in oil, called W/O emulsion. O/W emulsion looks like dirty water while W/O emulsion is thick and viscous, even tarry. Types of emulsified oils are animal fat, vegetable fat, lubricants, hydraulic fluids, cutting fluids, machine coolants, tars, greases, crude oils, diesel oils, gasoline, kerosene, and jet fuel, in parts per million concentrations up to 10 percent by volume. Even 30-60 percent is seen, though rarely. These emulsions are broken by either chemical, electrolytic, or physical methods or a combination of any of the three. When the emulsion is broken, the mixture ideally forms an oil layer over a water layer but in reality a troublesome rag layer often exists. This is a transition layer that is neither oil nor water and which lies between the two layers.

HOW TO SIMULTANEOUSLY REMOVE OIL AND METALS

When fats, oils and greases (FOG) are present in wastewater in significant concentration they obstruct piping and sewers, interfere with the removal of metals, interfere with aerobic processes, and in general cause untold grief. Of particular interest is the interference with removal of heavy metal because, after all, the little bugs will chomp on the large FOG molecules just like other organics, it just takes longer. However metal removal and FOG treatment are apparently not compatible.

They are apparently not compatible because it turns out that after upstream removal of floating fats, free oil, and other light oils by gravity separation we are left with an emulsion-breaking chore not unlike chemical precipitation of heavy metals. Simultaneously with emulsion breaking we can perform the precipitation/coagulation of metal hydroxides, add a polymeric flocculant and send this soup to a DAF cell. Set the air to solids (A:S) ratio to:

$$A:S = [15,600 A_s (fP-1)R]/QS_a \qquad [8.63]$$

where

A_s = air saturation, ft^3/gal
f = fraction of air dissolved at P, use 0.8
P = operating pressure, atm
R = recycle flow, gpm
Q = influent flow, gpm
S_a = influent suspended solids, mg/L

How to Deal with Cyanide

Wastewater contaminated with cyanide must be dealt with separately before mixing with other waste streams. Cyanides are toxic to bacteria which are the backbone of the POTW. Significant presence of cyanide can interfere with other treatment steps as well as present an acute toxicity hazard to personnel working in the plant. Remember, most wastewater treatment plants have inorganic acids in large quantities and acid and cyanide compounds are a lethal combination.

As a pollutant, cyanide comes in three general forms: HCN, NaCN, and MCN where M represents a metal ion or metal complex ionically bonded with the CN⁻ ion. Typically, a segregated cyanide-bearing waste stream is subjected to alkaline chlorination in two steps to oxidize the CN to the cyanate form.

$$NaCN + 3/2\,Cl_2 + NaOH ---\!\rightarrow CNCl + 2NaCl + OH^-$$ [8.64]

$$CNCl + 2NaOH ---\!\rightarrow NaCNO + H_2O + NaCl$$ [8.65]

In this reaction, 2.73 mg/l Cl_2 is required per each mg/l of CN⁻. Process control is provided by pH and ORP (oxidation-reduction potential) controllers and the excess hydroxyl ions assure an alkaline pH. After chlorination the CN salt is oxidized to the cyanate. Here 1.125 mg/l NaOH is needed per mg/l CN, however, the pH must be 10 or greater to keep the reaction driving, so excess NaOH is justified. To completely oxidize the cyanate, additional chlorine and sodium hydroxide are added:

$$2NaCNO + 4NaOH + 3Cl_2 \rightleftharpoons 2CO_2\uparrow + 6NaCl + N_2\uparrow + 2H_2O$$ [8.66]

which uses 4.09 mg/l Cl_2 and 3.08 mg/l NaOH per mg/l cyanate. In practice it is wise to use excess chemicals—especially NaOH—to maintain the reaction tank at a pH around 8.5.

An alternative to additional chlorination of the cyanate is the acid hydrolysis process. In either case, the result is carbon dioxide and sodium salt or ammonium salt.

Figure 8.27
Tips for Cyanide Oxidation

Maintain first stage at 10 pH or higher.
Maintain second stage at 8.5 pH.
Add excess chlorine.
Use a well-designed ORP control system.

Ozone can also destroy cyanide by oxidation and with reduced operating costs. It is generated at the process site but the equipment is costlier. Thermal oxidation is another cyanide destruction technology but is energy intensive.

$$NO_3^- + BOD \xrightarrow{bacteria} reducedBOD + N_2 \uparrow \qquad [8.67]$$

HOW TO REMOVE NITROGEN

Denitrification requires mixing raw organic matter with wastewater bearing nitrogen compounds. The combined waste streams are allowed to flow through an anoxic zone (where oxygen is low). The process is represented as Bacterial floc in a clarifier will consume nitrate by extracting the oxygen from it but the real work is done in the anoxic zone.

Bacteria first decompose organic nitrogen compounds to ammonia which is oxidized to NO_3^- in the aerobic zone (aerobic nitrification) which is then reduced to N_2 in the anoxic zone (anaerobic denitrification). The key to good nitrogen removal is SRT (solids retention time) which is dependent on the nature of the wastewater and the temperature of the system.

Nitrogen compounds, especially ammonia, can also be air stripped or chlorinated if there is no other reason to use biological methods as lagoons require considerable real estate. Stripping towers for ammonia are induced-draft, that is they have the blower downstream of the tower pulling gas toward the tower. The wastewater must be raised to a pH of 10.8 or more in order to get the ammonia into the dissolved gas form. The equilibrium relationship for ammonia dissolved in water follows Henry's law, p = HS. Cheremisinoff calculates the gas-to-liquid ratio as

$$\frac{G}{L} = \frac{1}{Y_2/X_2}$$ [8.68]

where Y_2 is the ammonia concentration in the gas leaving the stripper and X_2 is the ammonia concentration in the wastewater entering the stripper. The ammonia concentrations in the liquid effluent and gas influent are zero. According to Cheremisinoff (1995), the Henry's law constant for ammonia in water at 77°F is 0.0074.

Ion exchange is the treatment of choice for denitrification at facilities where nitrogen concentration is high in wastewater such as fertilizer and munitions plants.

How to Remove Phosphorus

Polyphosphates and organic phosphorus are easily adsorbed in floc particles. For instance, aluminum ions will remove phosphate ions in this manner:

$$Al_2(SO_4)_3 \cdot 14.3H_2O + 2PO_4^{=} \dashrightarrow 2AlPO_4 \downarrow + 3SO_4^{=} + 14.3H_2O$$ [8.69]

Excess aluminum ions are needed to effectively precipitate phosphorus partly due to this competing reaction:

$$Al_2(SO_4)_3 \cdot 14.3H_2O + 6HCO_3^{-} \dashrightarrow 2AL(OH)_3 \downarrow + 3SO_4^{\wedge=} + CO_2 \uparrow + 14.3H_2O$$

[8.70]

Process efficiencies are shown in Figure 8.28.

Iron salts can be used to precipitate orthophosphate and, just as with the alum, an excess is required. After the chemistry has played its role, biology takes over and completes the treatment in a trickle bed or rotating bed contactor.

Figure 8.28	
Phosphorus Removal Efficiencies	
Alum/Phosphorus Weight Ratio	% Phosphorus Removal
13 to 1	75
16 to 1	85
22 to 1	95

HOW TO MANAGE WASTEWATER SLUDGE

Sludges from clarifiers usually range 0.5 to 3 percent solids. If retention time is increased, the metal hydroxide sludges can be thickened to 3-5 percent solids in the clarifier. This is still too much water to be hauling around the country and the land disposal ban enacted by Congress prohibits bulk liquids from being managed in landfills.

Dewatering

Before filtering sludge to remove water, a process called gravity thickening is used. The water removed in this process saves filtration energy later.

A thickener is a settling basin that allows the sludge to naturally dewater before expending energy to finish the job. Sludges that only reluctantly settle may be pumped straight to a filter or centrifuge without going through a thickener but when large volumes of normal sludges are being dewatered a thickener will quickly pay for itself. The key to good thickener design is that its diameter must exceed its depth. The terminal velocity V_t of particles in ft/sec is the overflow rate or surface hydraulic loading of the thickener.

$$V_t = 1.55 \frac{Q}{A} \qquad [8.71]$$

where Q is the flow rate (MGD) and A is the surface area of the thickener (ft²).

In a free settling system the basin height is irrelevant but this is rarely the case as settling is often hindered by some factor or another. Therefore the height of the thickener is

$$V_t = \frac{H}{t}$$

[8.72]

where H is in feet and t is time in seconds.

After thickening, the sludge is typically filtered to increase the solids concentration. Specific resistance to filtration is the quantification of sludge dewaterability. Decreasing specific resistance indicates increasing dewaterability. Mechanical dewatering requires a specific resistance of less than 3×10^{12} ft/lb. Sludges with a specific resistance greater than that value require a chemical conditioner to bring the specific resistance down.

To determine specific resistance, mount a Buchner funnel with filter paper on top of a graduated cylinder and apply vacuum. Pour a mixed sample of sludge into the filter and record volume of filtrate as a function of time at a constant vacuum. After the test, plot time/filtrate volume vs. filtrate volume. Three distinct sections of the plotted curve have meaning. A straight line section will extend some distance from zero and the general laws of filtration apply here. The slope of this segment of the curve is used to calculate specific resistance. The intermediate segment of the curve is where the cake begins to compress. The final, asymptotic section shows that increase in filtration gives little or no increase in filtrate volume. Using the slope of the straight line section:

$$r = \frac{2PA^2b}{\mu w}$$

[8.73]

where

r = specific resistance, ft/lb
P = vacuum, psia
A = filter area, ft²
b = slope of filtration curve, sec/ft⁶

μ = filtrate viscosity, $lb_f\text{-sec}/ft^2$
w = suspended solids, lb/ft^3

Once we know specific resistance, we can design a filter to dewater the sludge. Specific resistance can be lowered by using filtration aids such as potassium permanganate or a cationic polymer.

Plate and frame filter presses or rotary filter drums are the common equipment for dewatering sludge. Advanced dewatering filter presses produce filter cakes having solids concentrations in excess of 65 percent. Sometimes drying is used. Vacuum filters and centrifuges are also used to dewater. Rotary vacuum filters are used with difficult sludges. They are precoated with diatomaceous earth to aid the filter media. These filters achieve 25-40 percent cake solids. Solid-bowl or decanter centrifuges operate in a continuous mode and provide a discharge with 26-28 percent solids. Belt filters provide gravitational drainage from a traveling belt followed by several compression rolls which compress the slurry between two cloths until it discharges sludge having a solids content of 18-25 percent from the end roll.   The plate and frame filter dewaters in a batch operation and is very labor intensive during the operation. An operator must load the filter by pumping the watery sludge into the spaces between the plates. Preparation of the filter media (cloth) on the plates is required. Also the operator may have to add a chemical as a filtering aid. For instance, alum sludges are very hard to dewater without chemical filtration aids. Under vacuum a porous media allows the filtrate (water) to pass but retains the solids as filter cake. Synthetic polymers are also used in the vacuum filter to aid the dewatering process. Filtering rates from 2 to 10 lb/ft^2 hr are achievable.

Centrifuges can also be used to dewater batches of sludge. This method is very energy intensive but usually not as labor intensive as filters. Large 20 h.p. centrifuges concentrate 3,000-4,000 gallons per hour of wastewater sludge bearing 0.5-0.75 percent solids to about five percent solids. Centrifuge design is based on equation 8.74 for tubular-bowl centrifuges and on equation 8.75 for disc-types centrifuges.

$$\Sigma = \frac{\Pi/\omega^2}{g} \frac{r_2^2 - r_1^2}{\ln[2r_2^2/(r_2^2 - r_1^2)]} \qquad [8.74]$$

where

Σ = equivalent area of the centrifuge
ω = angular velocity, rad/sec
r = radius from axis of rotation

$$\Sigma = \frac{2 \Pi n \omega^2 (r_2^3 - r_1^3)}{3 g C \tan \theta}$$

[8.75]

r_1 = radius to inner surface
r_2 = radius to outer surface
l = light-phase discharge radius
g = gravitational constant
n = number of spaces between discs
C = concentration of solute
θ = half-included angle of the disc.

To get an appropriately designed dewatering device, provide the potential vendor with a sample of the sludge for a bench test or provide this process information: solids concentration, particle size analysis, compressibility, volume of sludge, and disposal requirements.

Sludge Disposal

Electroplating wastewater treatment produces a sludge that is listed as hazardous by EPA. Other metal finishers must conduct the TCLP analysis on their sludge to determine whether it is hazardous or not. One way or another, dewatering decreases the amount to be disposed of. The filtrate must be recycled through the wastewater plant unless it is acceptable for reuse in a process.

The activated sludge process clarifies valuable bacteria from the effluent of a biological treatment unit, such as an aerobic lagoon, and recycles it. One scfm air per pound of BOD per day is introduced to the sludge with extended aeration. The MLVSS in the sludge is maintained around 4,500-6,500 ppm (mg/kg). The feedrate of the activated sludge is 0.4 lb SS per lb BOD in the influent to the lagoon. Activated sludge systems allow high strength wastewaters to be treated with high removal efficiency in a limited space.

Extended aeration systems are a variation on the activated sludge system where longer HRTs must be maintained. Less sludge is generated in these systems and they are less susceptible to upset. Extended aeration requires much space but the suspended solids level is higher in the effluent.

The sequencing batch reactor (SBR) is another variation on activated sludge which uses a tank to serve as an equalization basin, aeration tank, and clarifier in one vessel in a semi-continuous fashion. SBR can handle more variation in the influent and eliminates the need for other pieces of equipment.

Other sludges are not as useful and must be disposed in some other way. Be sure to check the hazardous waste regulations carefully. For instance, certain petroleum refinery sludges are also listed as hazardous wastes. Other sludges may not be listed but the generator is obligated to analyze for toxic characteristics in the leachate of the sludge after an acid treatment specified in the regulations. Also, the generator is obligated to determine whether the sludge has other hazardous characteristics or not.

Stabilization. The food industry uses lime stabilization plus aerobic and anaerobic digestion to treat sludges. The stabilization step limits the petrification and odor generating processes and the digestion step reduces biomass. If solids are removed from aerated lagoons in early Fall or late Summer the sludge will be self-stabilized.

Land Treatment. Sludge is typically landfilled or landfarmed. Congress has banned bulk liquids in landfills so the sludge must be dewatered to the point of not dripping in the paint filter test, (see SW-846). Where a large hole can be dug without intersecting the water table a trench landfill can be used for nonhazardous sludge. More often, stabilized sludge is applied in the open landfill where municipal trash and garbage have been stored for centuries.

A better disposal application is the use of sludge as a fertilizer on landfarms. Biosolids are applied to the soil as either liquid (2-5% solids) or dewatered cake (18-25% solid). A special tanker truck pulls a tiller behind it with knife injectors between the tiller blades to apply the sludge several inches deep into the soil as it tills. The sludge must go through a reduction process for pathogens and vector attractors before it is deemed suitable for landfarming. Aerobic digestion must hold solids for an average of 40 days at 68 °F or 60 days at 60° F in order to say that the pathogen reduction requirements are met.

Plant-Soil Assimilative Capacity. The suitability of a sludge for landfarm application depends on the heavy metals content of the sludge, the maximum allowable accumulation of heavy metals at the site, and the nitrogen balance of the site. Plants can take up a certain amount of heavy metals but this will be bioaccumulated in the food chain as food animals consume the plants or humans consume them directly. Landfarming is only allowed for grazing plants, not for food crops intended for direct human consumption.

Loading rates. The nitrogen balance of the soil determines how much sludge per acre must be applied to the land as fertilizer. However, the metal loading rates must also be taken into account. These are restricted by permit, so the required application rate for nitrogen cannot cause any of the metal loading rates to be exceeded. If any are exceeded then the landfarming project is infeasible.

DEALING WITH THE "BLACK ART"

Wastewater treatment processes have a reputation for being black art. The implication is that they do not follow the laws of science and physics and that it takes an adept to deal with them. Nothing could be further from the truth. In fact, these processes precisely follow physical and chemical laws so rigidly that troubleshooting is a dream because the problem is as plain as the nose on your face. Sometimes the obvious is harder to see and understand than the not-so-obvious.

For example: A manufacturing plant asked an expert to look at their wastewater treatment system. It was not efficient at removing zinc and their attorney advised them to retain someone who understood wastewater systems to gather performance data in preparation for a lawsuit. After observing the process equipment and controls for twenty minutes the problem was obvious to the expert.

"Why do you operate this pH controller at 8.0 pH?" the expert asked, pointing to a controller on the side of the precipitation and coagulation tank.

"We have always operated at 8," came the reply.

"Does your operating manual tell you to do that?"

"No."

"Did the vendor representative tell you to use that pH?"

"No."

The expert adjusted the pH to 10 and took samples of the tank's influent and effluent. Residence time in the tank was ten minutes so he took another sample of influent and effluent 30 minutes later. Zinc in the influent was around 500 ppm. The effluent contained 30 ppm zinc when the control change was made. Thirty minutes later it was 1.0 ppm. Zinc is an amphoteric ion which means that it precipitates at an optimum pH range and outside that range it dissolves again. The pH setting of 8 was much too low and zinc precipitation was inefficient.

Another example: A chemical vendor and a wastewater expert were trying to get a new wastewater plant under control. One or the other of them ran a jar test every hour and made dose changes but the plant was not responding. They were so frustrated that "black art" was beginning to sound like a compliment for wastewater treatment. On the fourth day they were still getting nowhere. Each dose change did not work or else made the situation worse. Yet they were getting terrific results in the jars!

Rather than give up the expert drew a schematic of a successful jar test completed earlier in the day. The first thing he did was to check proportioning pump settings for proper doses. The settings were correct.

So why wasn't the process working?

As he stood there wishing he did something else for a living he saw the problem.

"If it had been a rattlesnake it would have bit me!" he yelled over the noise of the machinery.

The wastewater system was not like his schematic! The reason the plant was not working was because it was set up to do something else! He found the maintenance foreman and got help to arrange pipes and pumps to set the plant up exactly like the schematic.

Bingo! Science works. The plant was discharging compliant wastewater within two hours.

The problem is that we tend to give up and live with our problems or buy some flashy new technology that tends itself or do any number of things except solve the real problem. Wastewater treatment is about the thermodynamics of dilute aqueous solutions. It is a science; it is not black art. Understand what is happening and your problem will suggest its own solution. Or you can call the expensive guy with the Master of Black Arts degree from the College of Wastewater Knowledge. It's your nickel.

These comments presume the design of the plant was based on sound engineering. The second biggest problem in wastewater treatment is that unwary managers buy treatment systems from either the first person through the door who talks a good game or from the lowest quote from a fistful of quotes for dissimilar equipment.

Wastewater treatment systems must be designed to do a specific job. This means two things to the environmental manager. One, we cannot buy wastewater treatment systems from catalogs. Your plant is identical to no one else's. Bank on it. Every industrial wastewater treatment problem is unique and should be treated as such. Two, because each industrial wastewater stream is unique we must take time and money to characterize it. The EPA calls this Baseline Monitoring but the EPA requirements are only a start. We must get to know the wastewater stream's idiosyncrasies, its secrets, moods, and upsets. Only then can we design a treatment system intelligently.

STORMWATER MANAGEMENT

EPA issued stormwater management regulations in May 1973 which exempted uncontaminated stormwater from permitting unless the source was one specifically designated by a permitting authority. These rules were almost immediately challenged by the Natural Resources Defense Council (NRDC). In March 1976, due to a court case that ruled in favor of NRDC, the rules were revised to provide coverage of all stormwater discharges except uncontaminated rural runoff. After several more lawsuits by trade associations and environmental groups, EPA revised the regulations in June 1979 and again in May 1980 to require testing for toxic pollutants as defined by the 1977 CWA. July 1982 marked a settlement agreement with industry petitioners who got a narrowed definition of stormwater point source and reduced application requirements by defining two different groups of applicants (Group I and Group II). Meanwhile EPA agreed not to enforce certain discharges.

In November of the same year, EPA proposed a new rule based on the recent settlement agreements which was issued in final form in September 1984 and which defined stormwater point source in the same broad terms of the 1976 and 1980 rules. This rule also established a six month deadline for applications. Once again EPA braced for mountains of applications and proposed a rule in March 1985 which again referred to Groups I and II but reduced the data requirements in applications for Group I filers in an attempt to lighten the work load. Application deadlines were again extended for both Groups. Then on August 12, 1985, EPA reopened the comment period on the rule proposed in March of that year and during this period the group application was proposed. EPA also placed industrial pretreaters discharging to POTWs into Group I. The final rule was issued on August 29th and applications were due on December 31, 1987 for Group I and June 30, 1989 for Group II. In February of 1987, Congress passed the Water Quality Act of 1987 clarifying its own policy of stormwater management. But in December, before the application deadline, a court remanded the regulations. In a final rule issued in February 1988, EPA deleted the stormwater regulations.

A new proposed stormwater rule was issued in December 1988 and this time proposed application requirements were based on Congress' wishes stated in the WQA of 1987. November 1990 was when the rule that we have today was finalized. Though stormwater management has a colorful history in our country, the rules are needed to eliminate major sources of contaminated surface water. The best management of stormwater follows the requirements spelled out in your permit exactly. However, you must understand why the requirements exist and what they are trying to accomplish. Although the same could be said for any environmental program enforced by EPA and the states (air, wastewater, hazardous waste), it is ever so more true of stormwater since there is not a plethora of stormwater rules to guide you. So what do you do? You write a Stormwater Pollution Prevention Plan (SPPP) in which you tell the world how you are going to manage stormwater on your property. At least stormwater that is or could be exposed to industrial pollutants.

Pollutant Source Assessment

In order to effectively manage stormwater you must know the actual conditions of your site. This calls for regular, frequent inspections or walk-arounds to determine potential sources of contamination, signs of actual contamination and changing conditions.

To understand flow patterns you need to obtain a topographical map of the area where your plant is located. This will give you a general feel for the pattern of flows in the area during a storm. Typically, however, a topographical map will not give sufficient detail to know how stormwater will run off your property so you need to have a special site map, or storm layout, developed which shows facility drainage. This may require an engineer to shoot elevations on the property in order to develop the runoff map.

After understanding the flow patterns of stormwater, the next step is to understand the history of contamination. This involves developing a list of significant spills and leaks of materials which potentially contaminate stormwater. Has everything been done to prevent recurrence and to mitigate the original problem?

Next, understand what is going on right now. Describe significant materials that are used, handled, stored, or disposed of on-site in a manner allowing contact with stormwater. What are the specific procedures to use, handle, store, or dispose of these materials? How can these methods be changed or substituted in order to prevent or mitigate stormwater contamination? What management practices are in place to prevent or mitigate stormwater pollution? What management practices are needed? Where are the material loading and unloading areas on-site? Is stormwater being contaminated from these areas? What are the existing structural (collection basins, etc.) or non-structural control methods for reducing stormwater contact with potential pollutants? Finally, describe any treatment of stormwater already provided.

Where a reasonable potential for contamination of stormwater from current industrial activity exists, list the following information in Figure 8.29 for each such area:

Figure 8.29
Data Requirements for Stormwater Contamination Areas

1. the direction of flow,
2. the types of pollution likely to be present,
3. sampling and analytical data for runoff from these areas.

Selection of Best Management Practices

Some management practices are listed in the permit, others are hinted at by language in the permit or in other written materials provided in connection with getting the permit. An EPA guidance document lists best management practices and discusses them in detail.

Stormwater Pollution Prevention Committee. This management practice is required by permit. A committee is expected to be established at each facility holding a permit. Managers and supervisors within the plant staff who will be implementing the provisions of the SWPPP or who are responsible for areas it covers should be on the committee.

Risk Identification, Assessment, and Material Inventory (RIAMI).
One of the first action items is to identify potential sources of stormwater pollution. Some areas to consider are loading and unloading operations, outdoor storage, outdoor processing, particulate sources, and on-site waste management units. For each such area, inventory the quantities of chemicals used, produced, or stored there. Also consider the toxicity of each chemical.

What is the likelihood of any of these materials contacting stormwater? If not very likely, so state in the RIAMI document, you need not contemplate any action. However, with increasing probability of stormwater contact you need an increasing level of effort to prevent such an event. Beware of too easily assigning "not very likely" to a particular situation.

Part of the RIAMI document is a history of significant leaks and spills of pollutants at the facility. If your plant has a spill or leak history, can you say truthfully there is no likelihood in the future? You might be able to do so but be sure to document your logic. The compatibility of chemicals with tankage and container materials of construction as well as the compatibility of materials stored in close proximity to each other figure into the likelihood of stormwater contact and must also be documented in the RIAMI.

Preventive Maintenance. What procedures and practices do you have or can you implement to maintain stormwater control devices such as collection systems, oil/water separators, diversion structures, detention ponds, and catch basins? How will you maintain outdoor processing equipment to assure no stormwater contact?

Good Housekeeping. Describe how you will maintain cleanliness around the outside of the plant and inside, too, if that can affect stormwater in any way. It is hard to imagine poor housekeeping until you visit a plant where it is the rule not the exception. As stated in an earlier chapter, cleanliness of the plant area, inside and out, also goes a long way during compliance inspections.

Spill Prevention and Response. Expand the oil SPCC or rewrite one to cover just the hazardous substances.

Sediment and Erosion Prevention. Whenever earth moving activities are underway, implement EPA guidelines for sediment and erosion control.

Employee Training. Spill response, housekeeping and good material handling, and storage practices are the minimum required training under stormwater rules.

Visual Inspection. On a regular basis, inspect areas where stormwater contacts processes and materials. Quarterly inspections (or more often) is recommended depending on the size of the stormwater contact area, amount of outdoor activity, and toxicity of chemicals handled. A tracking procedure for corrective action is required. Inspection records are part of the SPPP.

Traditional gravity-flow storm sewers consist of sand-trap catch basins and a network of 0.6 to 0.8% sloping underground pipelines that flow to a collection sump at the system's lowest point. Designers size these lines to flow three-quarters full with the design rainfall. Process areas should be curbed to prevent contaminated stormwater from entering these catch basins and sewer lines. The catch basins have a liquid seal to give a minimum degree of fire safety but if flammable liquids enter a storm sewer the potential for fire and explosion are high. Manholes provide access for inspection, cleaning, and maintenance of the system. Maintenance will be performed by others if the municipality owns the system but you should make frequent inspections anyway. If your plant has installed and owns the storm sewer, whether it has a connection to the municipal storm sewer or flows directly to some surface water body, maintenance is fully your responsibility.

With this kind of storm system it is necessary to catch and treat only the first part of a storm flow. After that, the water will be clean. At least so diluted that treatment will be impractical. A contaminated stormwater sump will fill up early in the storm and additional water will flow straight through it. At the end of the storm, the water in the contaminated sump can be analyzed and treated as necessary.

Should you consider installing a contaminated stormwater sump? What is the mobility of liquid chemicals handled at your facility? If the fluids are miscible with water, the stormwater must be treated in some manner to remove the contamination. Catch basins and contaminated water sumps will do no good. If immiscible, what is the specific gravity? If heavier than water, the liquid will collect in the contaminated stormwater sump and catch basins and can be pumped out after the storm. If lighter than water, some of it may be caught in the sump but downstream containment such as a detention pond or decanting vessel may be required. Is flammability a consideration? If yes, a flooded stormwater sewer is indicated. If not, a traditional gravity flow system is all that is necessary. Are ambient temperatures extreme? Especially extremely cold? If freezing temperatures are expected, a flooded system must be buried well below the frost line. The amount of soil moisture may limit the depth of the lowest point in the system, which cannot be located below the water table. The frequency and density of precipitation must also be considered during sizing of a stormwater system. Clogging of basins and sewer pipes by sediments and debris is a frustrating problem with traditional gravity systems but which totally rules out a flooded system. Expansion and contraction of the system by movement of clays shifting during earthquakes or for other reasons is another consideration.

Rainfall events are described in terms of intensity and duration at some probability of occurrence on *isopluvial* maps distributed by the National Weather Service. Equations for accumulated rainfall volume per unit area must be calculated for specific locations using isopluvial maps. This allows for calculation of maximum storage volume based on the maximum achievable withdrawal rate of the stormwater sewer and the time at which the maximum impoundment volume will be reached for a particular rainfall.

Recordkeeping and Reporting. Management is to be informed of stormwater management status by a report which is maintained as part of the SPPP.

Nonstorm Discharges. Stormwater discharge systems must be inspected and tested for non-storm discharges. A certification that no nonstorm discharges are present in the stormwater must be signed and submitted to the permitting authority each year.

Development and Implementation of SWPPP

EPA requires the development of Stormwater Pollution Prevention Plans (SWPPP or SPPP) to insure that permitted facilities are taking steps to identify sources of pollution and promptly implementing management practices to minimize pollutants in stormwater discharged from the property. Consequently, each document that is made part of the SPPP should focus on either identification of potential stormwater pollutants or management techniques to be used to eliminate or mitigate stormwater pollution.

Inspection and Evaluation

Good management of stormwater requires that we make regular inspections of our property, especially wherever an outdoor activity or material storage exists. Only by keeping up to date on what is going on outside can we make suitable judgements about preventing the contamination of stormwater. Timely decisions and action are the way we meet the goal of the stormwater regulations.

CONCLUSION

Controlling water pollution is not too dissimilar to controlling air pollution. Some of the same unit operations are involved. In other ways, wastewater treatment is so much more complex than air pollution control is. For one thing, air pollution control equipment tends to be in the form of black boxes that we inspect and maintain but spend precious little time operating. Wastewater treatment systems require almost constant operator attention as well as a great deal of maintenance. Actually this is not surprising. Water is not compressible whereas gas streams are. Much more momentum impacts equipment, piping, fittings, and instrumentation. Also, water is much more erosive and corrosive than air. Finally, more chemistry happens in wastewater treatment than in air pollution control and biology is nearly unheard of as a control option in air pollution.

REFERENCES

Albertson, Orris E., *Chair, et al. Sludge Thickening: Manual of Practice No. FD-1*. Washington, D.C.: Water Pollution Control Federation (now Water Environment Federation), 1980.

API Publication 421. *Monographs on Refinery Environmental Control—Management of Wastewater Discharges: Design and Operation of Oil-Water Separators*. Washington, D.C.: American Petroleum Institute. February 1990.

Avery, Larry. "The Filter Press Maintains Its Reign." *Pollution Engineering*. October 1993.

Bard, A.J., R. Parsons and J. Jordan. eds. *Standard Potentials in Aqueous Solution*. New York: Marcel Dekker, 1985.

BETZ Laboratories, Inc. *Handbook of Industrial Water Conditioning*. 8th ed. Trevose, PA: Betz, 1980.

Boynton, Marge. "Casebook: Filtration System Reduces Chemical Usage/Waste Disposal in Paint Spray Booths." *Pollution Engineering*. February 1986.

Brinigar, Stephen C., Patrick Keating and Timothy S. Simpson. "Complying with Storm Water Permits." *Pollution Engineering*. February 15, 1992.

Busch, Arthur W. "A Practical Approach to Designing Aeration Systems." *Chemical Engineering*. January 10, 1983.

Cheremisinoff, Paul N. "Ammonia Removal." *The National Environmental Journal*. July/August 1995.

---. "Update on Wastewater Treatment." *Pollution Engineering*. September 1986.

Crittenden, John C., David W. Hand, Harish Arora and Benjamin W. Lykins, Jr. "Design Considerations for GAC Treatment of Organic Chemicals." *Journal of The American Water Works Association*. January 1987.

Cushnie, George C., Jr. *Electroplating Wastewater Pollution Control Technology*. Park Ridge, NJ: Noyes Publications, 1985.

----. *Removal of Metals from Wastewater: Neutralization and Precipitation*. Park Ridge, NJ: Noyes Publications, 1984.

Dietz, Jess C., Paul W. Clinebell and A.L. Strub. "Design Considerations for Anaerobic Contact Systems." *Journal of The Water Pollution Control Federation.* April 1966.

Eckenfelder, W. Wesley, Jr. *Industrial Water Pollution Control.* 2d. ed. New York: McGraw-Hill Book Company, 1989.

----, Y. Argaman and E. Miller. "Process Selection Criteria for The Biological Treatment of Industrial Wastewaters." *Environmental Progress.* February 1989.

----, Jerzy Patoczka and Andrew T. Watkin. "Wastewater Treatment." *Chemical Engineering.* September 2, 1985.

Elton, Richard L. III. "Designing Stormwater Handling Systems." *Chemical Engineering.* June 12, 1980.

EPA 625/3-73-002. *Waste Treatment: Upgrading Metal-Finishing Facilities to Reduce Pollution.* July 1973.

EPA 625/5-79-016. *Environmental Pollution Control Alternatives: Economics of Wastewater Treatment Alternatives for The Electroplating Industry.* June 1979.

Eysenbach, Elin, *Chair, et al. Pretreatment of Industrial Wastes: Manual of Practice No. FD-3.* Alexandria, VA: Water Environment Federation, 1994.

Farmer, J. Kevin. "Wastewater Treatment Technologies." *Pollution Engineering.* September 1991.

Fleming, Hubert L. "Application of Alumina in Water Treatment." *Environmental Progress.* August 1986.

Fosberg, T.M., D. Mukhopadhyay, T.M. O'Neail and R.C. Whalen. "Selecting Energy-Efficient Wastewater Treatment Systems." *Chemical Engineering Progress.* October 1981.

Goronszy, Mervyn C., W. Wesley Eckenfelder and Emory Froelich. "Waste Water Part 2." *Chemical Engineering.* June 1992.

Hammer, Mark J. *Water and Wastewater Technology.* 2d. ed. New York: John Wiley & Sons, 1986.

Heilshorn, Elyse D. "Removing VOCs from Contaminated Water." *Chemical Engineering.* February 1992.

Holiday, Allan D. "Conserving and Reusing Water." *Chemical Engineering*. April 19, 1982.

Kemmer, Frank N. *The NALCO Water Handbook*. 2d. ed. New York: McGraw-Hill Book Company, 1988.

Ku, Young and Robert W. Peters. "The Effect of Weak Chelating Agents on The Removal of Heavy Metals by Precipitation Processes." *Environmental Progress*. August 1986.

Legan, Robert W. "Ultraviolet Light Takes on CPI Role." *Chemical Engineering*. January 25, 1982.

Louchart, Gary and John Papamarcos. "Magnesium Hydroxide Improves Acidic Wastewater Treatment." *Plant Services*. July 1988.

Mason, Geoffrey S. and Craig Arnold. "Contain Liquid Spills and Improve Safety with A Flooded Stormwater Sewer." *Chemical Engineering*. September 17, 1984.

McDonald, George J. "Applying Sludge to Agricultural Land -within The Rules." *WATER/Engineering & Management*. February 1995.

Michal, Jaroslav. "Air Stripping of Organic Compounds." *Pollution Equipment News*. August 1988.

Mishra, Surendra K. "Polymer Flocculation of Fine Particles, Part I: Theoretical Developments." *Pollution Engineering*. March 1989.

---. "Polymer Flocculation of Fine Particulates, Part II: Synthetic Polymers." *Pollution Engineering*. April 1989.

Mutsakis, Michael and Robert Rader. "Static Mixers Bring Benefits to Water/Wastewater Operations." *WATER/Engineering and Management*. November 1986.

Nemerow, Nelson L. *Industrial Water Pollution: Origins, Characteristics and Treatment*. Reading, MA: Addison-Wesley Publishing Company, 1978.

Newton, James J. "Special Report: Chemicals for Wastewater Treatment." *Pollution Engineering*. November 1985.

Okoniewski, Bradley A. "Remove VOCs from Wastewater by Air Stripping." *Chemical Engineering Progress*. February 1992.

Olthof, Meint and Jan Oleskiewicz. "Anaerobic Treatment of Industrial Wastewaters." *Chemical Engineering*. November 15, 1982.

Parkin, Gene F. and R.E. Speece. "Anaerobic Biological Waste Treatment." *Chemical Engineering Progress*. December 1984.

Patterson, James W. *Industrial Wastewater Treatment Technology*. 2d. ed. Boston: Butterworth Publishers, 1985.

Perrich, Jerry R. "Implementing Storm Water Plans." *Pollution Engineering*. May 15, 1993.

Pisarczyk, Kenneth S. and Laurie A. Rossi. "Sludge Odor Control and Improved Dewatering with Potassium Permanganate." 55th Annual Conference of the Water Pollution Control Federation. St. Louis, MO. October 5, 1982.

Pletcher, Derek and Norman L. Weinberg. "The Green Potential of Electrochemistry. Part 1: The Fundamentals." *Chemical Engineering*. August 1992.

Rich, Linvil G. "Designing Aerated Lagoons to Improve Effluent Quality." *Chemical Engineering*. May 30, 1983.

Rizzo, Joseph L. and Austin R. Shepherd. "Treating Industrial Wastewater with Activated Carbon." *Chemical Engineering*. January 3, 1977.

Severin, Blaine F. and Makram T. Suidan. "Ultraviolet Disinfection for Municipal Wastewater." *Chemical Engineering Progress*. April 1985.

Strilko, Peter S. "Responsible Effluent Disposal." *Pollution Engineering*. January 1, 1992.

"Technical Talk." *Environmental Protection News*. September 22, 1991.

Toy, David A. "Selecting The Right Method for Wastewater Treatment Problems." *Chemical Processing*. June 1985.

Van Gils, Gerald J. and Massoud Pirbazari. "Development of a Combined Ultrafiltration and Carbon Adsorption System for Industrial Wastewater Reuse and Priority Pollutant Removal." *Environmental Progress*. August 1986.

"Waste Reduction." *The National Environmental Journal*. September/October 1994.

"Waste Reduction Q & A. "*The National Environmental Journal.* January/ February 1992.

"----." *The National Environmental Journal.* July/August 1992.

9

MANAGING HAZARDOUS WASTE ON-SITE

You may be an inexperienced manager of hazardous waste; if you work in a generator facility, chances are that your duties are not voluntary. Even if you have little preparation for these responsibilities, you want to do well, so we will now discuss the basics of hazardous waste management from a generator's viewpoint. The fundamental principles of TSDF management are covered, but if you are a new manager at a TSDF, you will eventually be expected to become a specialist with operational knowledge far beyond the scope of this chapter. Here, you will find a good baseline, though.

Chovit and Rhodes point out five good business reasons to manage hazardous wastes well (*see* Figure 9.1).

Figure 9.1
Business Advantages of Effective Hazardous Waste Management

Avoid spills/releases and cleanup costs.
Generate less hazardous waste.
Avoid generator, transportation, disposal fees.
Avoid increase in pollution liability premiums.
Cut operating costs by using less raw materials.

Effective management of hazardous waste makes sense for another reason, too—good stewardship of the environment. Most of us genuinely do not want to spoil our natural environment. Ownership of any parcel of land on this planet is only meaningful for a few years, to a handful of people who themselves will soon be gone. When we render a piece of land unusable due to toxicity, we potentially affect future generations. The track record of some industrial facilities is evidence that their managers do not give two hoots about how they leave a piece of land or what damage they might do to future generations. RCRA and its attendant regulations were written especially for those who could care less.

RCRA establishes *cradle-to-grave accountability* for hazardous waste, meaning your company is accountable for its hazardous waste from the time it is created (cradle) until the time it is destroyed or rendered harmless (grave). No one can relieve you of this responsibility, so long as the waste you generated is in existence as the unique waste you created, even if it is mixed with someone else's waste. No contract can assign your responsibility to someone else. You, the generator, have a strict duty to take care of your waste. No one assumes your liability.

A related concept is *cradle-to-grave management*. EPA developed regulations that not only restrict the activities of generators of hazardous waste, but of transporters and TSDFs as well. So Congress assigned strict responsibility from cradle-to-grave and EPA placed management restrictions on various parties from cradle-to-grave.

Generators who choose to manage hazardous waste in permitted facilities, as opposed to managing generator accumulation and storage areas, are required to meet full RCRA management standards. If unpermitted generators subsequently cause significant contamination because of their hazardous waste management activities, they too have to meet these standards, though retroactively (summarized in Figure 9.2 .)

Figure 9.2
General Technical Requirements

Take corrective action if groundwater contamination is detected.
Design management units to prevent the release of hazardous waste.

You have already identified your waste streams, properly classified them as to hazardous or nonhazardous, made proper notification to EPA and/or your state, and kept your paperwork as discussed earlier. The next chapter discusses manifests and land ban notifications as well as other shipping requirements. What do you have to do in the meantime, until the transporter's truck arrives?

How to Manage the Storage of Hazardous Waste Containers

Storage Periods

The most common method of accumulating and storing hazardous waste is the 55-gallon drum. The amount of time allowed for the storage of hazardous waste in drums depends on the status of the facility. A permitted storage facility can store containerized waste for as long as the permit allows, which in some cases is indefinitely. Most industrial facilities opt for generator status, however, in order to avoid the RCRA permitting process and because experience has shown that hazardous waste containers can be transported at least once during the ninety day period allowed for (large quantity) generators. The only time problems arise with the time restriction is when a new waste stream has to be characterized and profiled. Sometimes laboratory analyses and contracting paperwork push the 90-day limit. In this case, a brief one-page explanatory letter to the hazardous waste office of the state—before the ninety days expire—earns an automatic thirty day storage extension (you will not necessarily receive a timely reply but the extension is yours for the asking). Once your extended storage time runs out, the paperwork must have cleared and the hazardous waste must have been shipped off-site. No more extensions are available. The extension reply letter typically asks for documentation (a copy of the manifest) showing the waste was shipped within the extended storage period.

Small quantity generators (SQG), which generate less than 2,200 pounds (1,000 Kg) per month, are allowed to accumulate waste for 180 days, without a permit. This time is automatically extended to 270 days, if the waste must be shipped 200 miles or more, so long as the total hazardous waste accumulated does not exceed 13,200 lbs. (6,000 Kg). Some states do not allow this SQG accumulation period extension.

Conditionally exempt SQGs, which generate less than 220 pounds (100 Kg) per month, have no specific time limit for accumulation, though the accumulated storage may never exceed 13,200 lbs.

However, anyone who generates more than 2.2 pounds (1 Kg) of *acutely hazardous waste* (the P-List) per month is a generator regardless how much other hazardous waste is generated. Even though you generate less than 220 pounds per month of hazardous waste, you cannot claim conditionally exempt SQG status, if you also generate as much as one quart (assuming this waste has the same density as water) of a P-List waste. The P-List refers to wastes which are commercial chemical products—not process wastes—which are to be discarded. The waste may be discarded because it has no further use, it is off-spec, it is the residue of a spill (in which case the P-number applies even to soil and cleanup materials), or to the empty container of the product. Take every precaution not to have P-waste.

Hazardous Waste Management Tip

Do not order materials which are on the P-List. If you must, use all of it. Guard against spills vigilantly. If you spill any, clean it up with as little absorbent as you can.

Handling and Treatment of Containers

Hazardous wastes must be kept in closed containers except when actually adding waste to the container. Some compliance inspectors take a strict interpretation of this rule, as the following example shows.

A RCRA compliance inspector was touring a plant with the facility's environmental coordinator. They stopped to observe a paint booth where a satellite accumulation station was located. As they reviewed the operations, an employee at a work bench opened several one-gallon cans of paint with an expired shelf-life. After opening the cans, he removed the lid from the hazardous waste accumulation container and walked back to the bench to get a gallon of paint, which he immediately poured into the waste container. He continued walking the twenty feet from the work bench to the accumulation container until he had poured all of the out-of-date paint into the waste container. Then he closed the lid and fastened it. The compliance inspector held that a violation existed each time the employee left the accumulation container open and walked the forty feet round trip to the workbench and back with another can of expired paint. The facility subsequently paid a negotiated $1,000 penalty for this violation.

Perhaps this compliance inspector was too "nitpicky," but he was technically correct and this is not an isolated incident. What can you do, except quibble?

Hazardous Waste Management Tip

The best way to keep a container closed, when frequent additions will be made to it, is to install a bung-funnel with a normally-closed spring-loaded lid. The lid must be opened, and held open, while adding to the contents of the drum. As soon as you quit pouring, and let go of the lid, the spring-loaded lid snaps shut. Several versions of this type of device are available at industrial equipment suppliers.

A related requirement: the treatment of the container while opening and closing it, or otherwise handling or storing it, must not rupture it or cause it to leak.

Probably the most common drum leak is caused when transporting drums on forklift tines. The rim of a drum head is two pieces of very thin metal crimped together: the head and the cylindrical wall. If the rim scrapes on concrete or another abrasive surface, a tiny, but effective, weeper is opened, allowing the drum to leak its contents. The barest contact between the rim and an abrasive surface will open the weeper.

Have you ever seen a forklift driver zipping around at dizzying speed with a drum lying between the tines? A common accident is the impalement of the head of the drum on a sharp corner, a protruding pipe or rail, or some other fixed spear. This is probably the second most common drum handling accident.

Discuss these kinds of incidents with your hazardous waste handlers as part of their annual training. Awareness is the best preventive measure for careless handling. Also, try rewarding correct behavior of employees in the presence of their colleagues. For that rare employee who is aware but cavalier about her responsibilities, take swift and just disciplinary action. Administer negative forms of discipline in private.

Contingency Plans and Personnel Training

Besides the accumulation, storage and shipment requirements generators are required to 1) have a contingency plan and emergency procedures to use in case of fire, explosion, spill, leak, or other emergency, and to 2) train personnel who handle hazardous waste. Disaster preparedness requires fire protection equipment and alarms for starters.

The facility must also have either 1) an internal communications system, such as a PA (public announcement) system, or 2) an alarm system to provide immediate emergency instructions by voice or signal to facility employees. Any signal understood by all employees may be used. The important thing is that everyone knows what the problem is and their role in response. This requirement applies to the entire facility, not just the area where hazardous waste is stored.

Either a telephone or two-way radio must be available where hazardous waste is handled and stored, so that hazardous waste handlers can summon help in case of emergency. Preferably, this communication device is capable of directly summoning outside help, but at many facilities it rings to a guardhouse or central reception, where someone else summons outside help.

The response to an incident involving hazardous waste cannot be taken for granted. Generators and TSDFs are expected to arrange for coordination with local authorities who may respond to an emergency. The purpose of the arrangements is to make authorities familiar with the operations, so they are not just learning about it during an emergency. The usual way to do this is to send them a copy of your contingency plan (discussed below), but you should also invite them for a tour of the facility. Keep copies of letters to and from authorities. Some may not respond to your communication. Make a note of telephone conversations and keep letters that were returned to you marked "Return to Sender" or those letters from authorities making negative replies. In situations where more than one authority has jurisdiction, or where the same jurisdiction may send responders from any of several locations, attempt to get an agreement as to primary and backup responders. Although it is a very rare thing, you do not want a jurisdictional dispute going on while your plant burns down.

Also, try to work out in advance primary and backup triage facilities at local hospitals. Invite the triage doctors and nurses to tour your facility. Share any applicable MSDSs or hazardous waste profiles, or any information which may help them make decisions about patient care during an emergency.

Make advance agreements with emergency response and remedial action contractors, too. If you need 4-tons of sawdust to soak up a spill, where will you get it from? How long will it take to get it? Or if you need to use a bulldozer to move soil to soak up a large spill, where will you get it? Can the equipment dealer get the bulldozer to you in, say, an hour's time? Work these details out before a disaster. A disaster planning committee is not a requirement but a good idea.

Contingency plans are written action plans used in an emergency to control losses and minimize the impact of sundry hazards on victims, rescuers, emergency responders, and property. The contingency plan must designate the *facility emergency coordinator* whose name ought to exactly coincide with the designated coordinator reported under SARA Title III (see Chapter 10). The emergency coordinator is a 24-hour per day, year round responsibility, so you will need to designate alternates for when the primary emergency coordinator is not available. This list should include name, home address, and internal and home telephone numbers. The contingency plan should include a summary of the arrangements made with police, fire officials, and hazardous materials and medical responders. Attach a list of emergency equipment available: permanent fire extinguishing systems, portable fire extinguishers, spill control equipment and supplies, communications equipment, internal and external alarm devices, and decontamination equipment. The list should also tell where this equipment is located. A physical description of each item and a brief outline of its capabilities is required. A copy of the facility evacuation plan should also be attached.

Training is covered in a previous chapter; however, keep this in mind: you wouldn't teach your child how to prepare cookie dough for baking and expect him or her to intuit the necessity for protection against extreme heat and instinctively take other safety precautions, would you? Nor would you merely tell him or her, "Be careful." We both know you would somehow impress a safe attitude on your child as well as safety precautions for self-preservation. Prudent management of any hazardous material, but hazardous waste in particular, requires that we impress on our employees safe attitudes and precautions for self-preservation. These attitudes and precautions are not usually intuitive, so we cannot assume that employees will somehow be infused with them just by working around hazardous waste or that the employees will induce these attitudes and precautions on their own. In a nutshell, RCRA training is all about safety of human handlers from exposure to the waste and the waste from the mismanagement of handlers. The details are left to the regulations and our previous discussions about training.

Accumulation Points

Knowing the difference between *accumulation point* and *satellite accumulation point* is vitally important. An accumulation point is a place where material, under the control of no specific person, is collected in containers of unlimited size and number, while a satellite accumulation area is under the control of the operator of the process generating the waste and collection capacity is limited to one 55-gallon drum at a time. The importance of this distinction is that the accumulation start date begins as soon as the first drop of waste enters an accumulation container at the accumulation point.

At an accumulation point, containers must be labeled hazardous waste, or at least have their contents clearly labeled and visible. Bungs and covers must be closed tightly unless someone is in the act of adding waste. Funnels with spring-loaded covers are recommended at accumulation points where frequent but intermittent additions of waste are made to the container.

Satellite Accumulation Areas

A valid way to extend accumulation time is to establish satellite accumulation areas at strategic places within your facility. Containers may remain here as long as it takes to fill them, plus three days, without the accumulation start date being initiated. Some very strict rules apply, however. The satellite accumulation area must be near (compliance inspectors read "at") a process line and under the direct control of *the* (one) process operator. If more than one person can operate the process—such as a vapor degreaser where anyone can bring a basket of parts to be cleaned—the satellite accumulation area is not a valid one. Carefully think through the requirements for a satellite accumulation area; don't get into a semantics game with the enforcement authority. Be careful not to set yourself up for failure; lay your groundwork well and follow the regulation as closely as possible.

Just as anywhere else, hazardous waste at a satellite accumulation area must be stored in containers that are in good condition and compatible with the waste. Also, only one container of each waste stream may be located at the satellite accumulation area. As soon as two containers of the same waste are present, with any amount in them, or more than 55-gallons, the accumulation start date applies to both containers, regardless of whether they are full or not (cf. 262.34(c)(2)).

Hazardous Waste Storage Areas

Two types of hazardous waste storage areas (HWSA) are designated for containers: generator storage where hazardous waste containers are stored for up to ninety days and permitted storage where containers are stored for periods specified in a RCRA Storage Facility Permit. Operations in generator HWSAs are required to meet packaging, marking, and labeling regulations and to date the receipt of hazardous waste containers from satellite accumulation areas. The accumulation start date of containers from accumulation points was the day the first drop of waste was added. Requirements for generator HWSAs are given in 40 CFR 262.20 and 262.34. Permitted facilities are subject to the requirements of 40 CFR Parts 264 and 265 and permit requirements in Part 270.

Consider using existing storage, which conforms to the rules, before considering the construction of a new HWSA; however, if necessary, a properly constructed HWSA minimizes future liabilities, if not present capital outlay. In other words, if you have a well-built facility already, make minor improvements as necessary and use it, but, if not, do not hesitate to spend money to get into compliance.

Hazardous Waste Management Tip

A good management strategy for generators is not to apply for a RCRA Storage Permit, but to store minimum quantities of hazardous waste for 90 days or less.

An alternative HWSA, a free standing storage unit with built in containment and safety features, is being offered by several companies. These units can also be moved if structurally designed for mobility.

Hazardous waste must be stored in an area with restricted access. Guidelines for the site of a permitted HWSA are given in 40 CFR 264.18. A buffer zone of 50 feet (15 meters) is required between the HWSA and the nearest inhabited area (not on your property), stream, or body of water. An inhabited area would be someone's residential property, a street or highway, public park, school, etc. Larger buffer zones may be required by some states or local ordinances or in the case of petroleum, oils, lubricants, explosives, or flammable stores.

Restrict access to the HWSA to those people who need access to handle and manage hazardous waste. Make sure no other activities take place there and that all other employees stay out. This minimizes your training requirements and helps reduce the possibility of spills and other mishaps. When the HWSA is not manned, even if the entire factory is fully operational, lock it. Post a sign that is visible and readable (with 20/20 vision) from 25 feet (8 meters) away and that has this legend:

Danger - Unauthorized Personnel Keep Out

A security fence is required, either around the HWSA itself or around the entire facility it serves. However, since you want to restrict access to all except those who have business there, some sort of walled structure or fence is suggested for the HWSA itself. A natural barrier such as a cliff may be relied on in lieu of a security fence. Chain-link fences that are at least 6 feet high are recommended. Standard fence fabric should be 9-gauge (3.8 mm) zinc or aluminum-coated steel wire chain link, with openings not larger than two inches (50 mm) and a twisted and barbed selvage at top and bottom. Use 9-gauge steel fabric ties on the fence. If the ties are coated or painted, make sure they are electrolytically compatible with the fence fabric in order to inhibit corrosion. Fastening and hinge hardware should be secured in place by peening or welding. Locate posts and structural supports on the inside of the fence (away from a potential intruder). Secure posts positively into the soil with concrete. Install and make taut reinforcing wires by interweaving or affixing with fabric ties along the top and bottom of the fence. Make sure the bottom of the fence fabric is less than 2-inches from firm soil or is buried in soft soil. Culverts under or through the fence must be no larger than 10 inches in diameter. Clusters of culverts can be used in lieu of larger diameters.

A fenced in yard should be illuminated to the level of 0.1 foot-candle or greater. Lighting inside the HWSA should generally meet illumination levels for good occupational health; however, the lighting must at all times be sufficient, when containers are stored in the HWSA, to ensure immediate detection of leaks and spills.

The container HWSA must have provisions for handling leaks, spills and accumulated precipitation as required by 40 CFR 264.175. Containment for flammable storage must also comply with NFPA 30. The containment system chosen must be capable of holding 10 percent of either the volume of all containers or the volume of the largest tank, whichever is a greater containment volume. The base of the containment must be kept free of cracks or gaps. As soon as these are noted, during routine inspection or otherwise, patch them. When containers are closed—anytime, but especially when being placed into the storage area awaiting transportation—all hazardous wastes and residues must be removed from the outside of the container. Any equipment or soil contaminated as a result of handling, accumulating, or storing hazardous wastes must be decontaminated or removed and disposed as hazardous waste. If the residue was contaminated by characteristic waste only the alternative is to TCLP it to prove it is nonhazardous. Maintain an adequate supply of compatible sorbent material for use in cleaning up liquid spills and leaks. Inspect hazardous waste containers weekly for leaks and evidence of corrosion.

Maintain grounding strap connections between drums of ignitable wastes and electrical ground. Eliminate potential for fire or explosion by removing sources of ignition. Drums of ignitable and reactive wastes must be more than 50 feet (15 m) from your property line. Provide fire protection such as a sprinkler system or a liberal number of portable fire extinguishers. Reactive wastes that have violent reactions with water require a gaseous fire suppression system such as carbon dioxide or authorized HCFCs. Sprinkler density for a HWSA is 0.35 gpm/ft^2, unless your insurance carrier or fire protection authority says otherwise. Use sprinkler heads suitable for a corrosive environment. Water lines supplying sprinkler water must have a positive backflow preventer (check valve).   A standard 4-hour fire rated wall is suggested in order to meet fire codes for liquid storage areas. If your HWSA is located in one corner of a warehouse or shed used for storage of other liquid materials, fire codes do not allow for the subdivision of a liquid storage area to change its fire classification. Therefore, whatever fire protection you provide to the HWSA proper must also be installed for the remainder of the liquid storage area. *Separate hazardous waste storage area* means separated from all other types of occupancies. The best way to minimize the requirement is to have a stand alone HWSA.

If you store hazardous waste liquids classified I-A by NFPA in containers greater than 1 gallon, either the exterior wall or roof requires explosion venting features such as a lightweight wall section, an explosion dome mounted in the wall or roof, or roof hatches or windows of the explosion venting type.

Keep drums under roof or raised off the ground to prevent contact with storm water. If outside, the storage area must be inside a secondary containment area.

Determine the quantity and direction of groundwater flow. Evaluate the consequences of a spill or release from the HWSA and take steps to assure that the HWSA is designed to prevent spilled wastes from contaminating groundwater or surface water. Groundwater monitoring sufficient to establish background levels of selected contaminants may be required when applying for permitted storage. The site must also be protected from flooding. Therefore, evaluate surface water hydrological data and insurance company or FEMA floodplain maps. Floodplains are low, relatively flat lands adjoining coastal waters and inland streams. At a minimum, floodplains include areas subject to a one percent (0.010) or greater chance of flooding in any given year. This area is designated the *100-year floodplain*. The *500-year floodplain* is the area which has the probability of 0.2% (0.002) of flooding in any given year. A permitted HWSA is not allowed within a 100-year or more frequent (more probable in any given year) floodplain.

The permit application process may require that soil conditions be determined and reported, but for generator HWSAs this requirement would be a rarity. If required, a minimum of two points must be sampled on the site, in order to determine the fate of spilled contaminants. Also, the facility will have to submit geological information, if located within 200 feet (61 meters) of a fault that has had displacement in the Holocene time (approximately the last 11,000 years).

Though not specifically required for generator HWSAs it is a good practice to know the prevailing wind direction for your site. Permitted facilities must report this information in the application.

Provide an eyewash/deluge shower within 10 seconds (100 feet) of travel from the HWSA. Each person involved in hazardous waste operations should have an assigned locker with two sets of protective clothing and personal protective equipment suitable to the hazards involved.

Maintain negative-pressure ventilation (air leaks inward) in an enclosed HWSA. Adjacent administration areas that are normally occupied should have positive pressure ventilation (air leaks outward). If containers of water-reactive material are present, or if corrosive vapors are a problem, provide dehumidification of the air in the HWSA and ventilate it to the outside. This means storage ventilation will have to be positive instead of negative pressure.

Divide the storage area into areas of compatibility, unless your wastes have no incompatibilities. EPA suggests this scheme for storage: determine which waste streams fit into the compatibility categories shown in Figure 9.3.

Figure 9.3
Categories of Compatibility

Acid Wastes   Inorganic acids with pH $\leq$ 4.

Caustic Wastes   Inorganic bases with pH $\geq$ 9.

Organic Wastes   Nonreactive organic materials.

Oxidizer Wastes   Oxidizing inorganic compounds.

Reactive Wastes   Wastes that react violently with water.

General Wastes   Wastes that are not chemically reactive and not primarily organic in nature.

after EPA.

Figure 9.4 shows how these categories can be stored.

Figure 9.4
Storage Compatibility

	Acid	Caustic	Organic	Oxidiz.	React.	Gen'l
Acid	--	NC	NC	NC	NC	NC
Caustic	NC	--	NC	C	NC	NC
Organic	NC	NC	--	NC	NC	NC
Oxidiz.	NC	C	NC	--	NC	C
React.	NC	NC	NC	NC	--	NC
General	NC	NC	NC	C	NC	--

after EPA. C-Compatible, NC-Not Compatible

The wastes may be compatible by generic type, but not compatible within that type. Diligence requires that each waste stream be reviewed individually regarding compatibility. Also, individually regarding compatibility. Also, be careful about confusing generic categories of compatibility with hazardous waste characteristics. Compatibility categories and characteristics are not related.

Telephone, or wireless, communication must be available to the operators/handlers anytime the HWSA is active. In large facilities, a master/remote receive/talk system should be installed at various locations if internal telephones are not available. Emergency alarms must have the capability of being activated inside the HWSA. The fire protection sprinkler system must have a flow alarm to indicate it is activated. This signal should be transmitted to a fire station or some suitable local station such as a continuously manned guardhouse. Twenty-four hour surveillance by either television monitoring or guards is required for permitted facilities.

Container Requirements

Hazardous materials containers are not themselves considered hazardous wastes, if empty. Containers are empty when the residue is less than 1 in. of material in the bottom. A container of 110 gallon or less capacity is also considered empty if no more than three percent of the weight of material remains. If less than 0.3 percent of the weight of material remains in containers having more than 110 gallon capacity, they can be considered empty.

A container is in good condition if it is not caved in, bulging on top or bottom, chimes are not seriously dented, open tops are closed tightly, gaskets are in place, and bung caps are tightly closed. If a container is not in good condition, either transfer its contents to a new container or place the entire container into a salvage drum or overpack.

Hazardous waste must be compatible with the container that holds it. Also, if the container is reused and contains residue, the hazardous waste must be compatible with the residue.

If stored in racks, the containers may not exceed 25 feet in height where a material handling system that elevates the operator with the container is used. This is the *operator-up* system. The *operator-down* system is when the operator handles all containers from the ground or floor level, in which case the stack of containers may not exceed 18 feet.

As long as they are not going on the road, the containers may be any that are compatible with the waste contained, and which are not leaking.

Hazardous Waste Management Tip

In order to avoid frequent transfer of hazardous waste from one container to another, use only roadworthy (DOT-rated) containers from the first drop of waste material.

Marking and labeling containers for shipment will be discussed in the next chapter, but containers held in 90-day storage have some minimum label requirements. Each container awaiting transportation must have the words "Hazardous Waste" clearly visible for inspection. Unless the container is legitimately located in a satellite accumulation area, it must also bear the accumulation start date as either 1) the date the first drop of waste entered the drum at an accumulation point, or 2) the date the container was moved from a satellite accumulation area to the HWSA. That is all that is required to be on the drum, as long as it is in 90-day storage. A good practice, however, is to have the complete hazardous waste label suitable for shipment, less manifest document number, but this is not a requirement until the container is offered for transportation.

EPA recently streamlined some regulations in response to President Clinton's plan to reinvent environmental regulations. The new regulations make it easier to manage a new category of solid waste called *universal waste*, while ensuring safe collection, recycling, handling, and treatment. Universal waste (UW) is defined as hazardous waste batteries (containing nickel, cadmium, mercury), certain hazardous waste pesticides, and mercury-containing thermostats. Any battery not regulated by Part 266 is UW. Pesticides that are part of a voluntary or mandatory recall under FIFRA 19(b) or voluntarily recalled by the registrant are UW. Also, stocks of unused products that are part of a waste pesticide collection program are UW. Mercury thermostats are UW, when discarded or sent for reclamation. Household and conditionally exempt SQG hazardous wastes become UW if mixed with UW.

A UW generator is one that has accumulated more than 11,000 pounds (5,000 Kg) of the material and a UW SQG, then, is one that has accumulated less than that amount. A UW handler is a generator of UW, or a facility that receives UW from other handlers for accumulation and subsequent treatment or disposal. Treaters, disposers, recyclers, and transporters are not UW handlers by definition. A UW destination facility is a TSDF which treats, disposes, or recycles any of the UW category wastes. A UW transfer facility is a transportation-related facility where UW is held, during the normal course of transportation, for ten days or less.

SQG UW handlers cannot dispose, dilute, or treat UW, with the exception of spill cleanup materials. They can perform certain operations on batteries and thermostats to make them more amenable to efficient packaging and handling. Batteries can be discharged, regenerated, sorted, removed from consumer product access, or the electrolyte can be removed, without jeopardizing SQG status. Ampules can be removed from thermostats, but this must be performed over a tray and a mercury cleanup kit must be handy. The employer must monitor the ampule removal work area for compliance with the OSHA mercury exposure limit. Employees performing the task of removing ampules from thermostats must be trained on mercury safety and handling procedures. Ampules must be packed to prevent breakage.

Storage of UW must comply with Part 265 rules. UW may be accumulated for 1 year, from time of generation, or receipt from another handler. The accumulation time can be exceeded, if the handler can show that additional time is necessary for treatment, recovery, or disposal. As a UW handler, you should date containers of UW with the earliest date waste was put into the container, unless you want to mark each item added to the container. Alternatively, you may maintain an inventory of the UW container, with the date each item was placed there.

Material generated from a cleanup of UW releases is subject to full hazardous waste regulations.

Inspections

A written schedule of weekly inspections should be maintained, with a list of monitoring equipment, safety and emergency equipment, security devices, operating and structural equipment, and any other equipment which ought to be accounted for, on a regular basis. Inspections should also look for problems, such as equipment malfunctions, operator error, and potential for discharge or release.

Hazardous waste containers, whether they are in an accumulation point or satellite accumulation area or 90-day storage, must be clean and free of corrosion. Hazardous waste is required to be in a container of some sort, so any leakage or spillage is a violation.

Hazardous Waste Management Tip

Keep containers clean. Have employees, who add waste to containers or who otherwise handle hazardous waste, clean up dribbles and spills immediately. Ensure that bung plugs are in place and better than hand tight.

To avoid HAZWOPER training, make sure container inspectors and handlers have received hazard communication training for the hazardous waste. If a container is damaged, you have two options: overpack or new container. Transfer of hazardous waste liquids from a damaged drum to a good drum, without exposing the handlers to questionable levels of vapors, is very difficult, but not impossible. Therefore, make sure to train drum handlers to minimize spillage and to provide them with adequate ventilation and protective equipment. Containers awaiting shipment should be stored as discussed earlier. Material handling equipment and emergency responders should be able to operate between pallets of drums, which may be stacked no higher than two pallets.

The most effective way to manage the inspection requirement is to write a brief inspection procedure which tells the person(s) responsible when and how to inspect. This employee is expected to assess the status of the storage facility and accumulation areas and to detect potential problem areas. Observations made by the inspector are to be recorded in the operating log and filed for three years. Figure 9.5 lists the information about inspections to be kept in the operating log.

The log should also record timely correction of the problems noted. Malfunctions or other deficiencies that cannot be corrected in a timely manner should be explained in the log.

Figure 9.5
Inspection Information to Be Logged

Date and time of inspection.
Name of inspector.
Observations.
Date and nature of corrective action.
Identification of potential problems.

How to Manage Tanks of Hazardous Waste

Tanks are merely permanent containers for accumulating materials. Do not take any tank available and put hazardous waste into it indiscriminantly. If you use a tank to store or treat hazardous wastes, you must manage it in such a way as to avoid leaks, ruptures, and spills—starting with the design and materials of construction, which must take into account the service. Therefore, protect all design records carefully. You must also provide corrosion prevention for ongoing protection. Make sure that the initial shell thickness of each tank follows prescribed design standards exactly. Tankage freeboard must be maintained, or a containment structure such as a dike or trench must be provided, to prevent waste from spilling over the top and escaping. Secondary containment for tanks must hold one hundred percent of the design capacity of the largest tank, plus any bulky equipment including the tank itself located inside the spilled liquid volume, and a 25-year, 24-hour rainfall.

> **Example**. A hazardous waste containment area holds three 5,000 gallon vertical tanks and one 2,000 gallon horizontal tank mounted on a saddle, about 30" off the ground. The tanks sit on a concrete pad. A one foot high dike has been built around the perimeter of this pad, which measures 50' X 20' according to a drawing you found, but when you measured it with a steel tape the inside corners were 48' X 17.5'. National Weather Service data for your city reveals that the 25-year 24-hour rainfall is 9 inches.

Is this adequate containment for the hazardous waste tankage?

The entire pad is not available for containment, three vertical tanks rest on it, which reduces the containment volume. You use your steel tape again to find that the diameters of the vertical tanks are 8, 9, and 10 feet, respectively.

You have this amount of containment:

Area = $(48 \text{ X } 17.5) - \pi/4 \ (8^2 + 9^2 + 10^2) = 647 \ ft^2$

Volume = $647 \text{ X } 1 = 647 \ ft^3$

You need this amount of containment:

Containment = 5,000 gallons ÷ 7.47 gallons/ft^3 = 668 ft^3

Rainfall = $647 \ ft^2 \text{ X } 9/12 \ ft = 485 \ ft^3$

Total = C + R = 668 + 485 = 1,153 ft^3

Inadequate containment capacity is available as built. How much would you have to add to the wall in order to bring this containment up to par? $(1,153 - 647) \ ft^3 \div 647 \ ft^2 = 0.782$ ft or 10 inches (always round up in order to add safety)

You are not in compliance with RCRA. What should you do?

Your options are:

1. do nothing and hope no one ever finds out,
2. add to the dike,
3. tear down the dike and build a new one with correct dimensions, or
4. attempt to get the dike approved (by the RCRA compliance authority) as built.

What would you do? Before we leave the subject: be careful about getting a good seal whenever you add a dike onto a concrete pad or when adding to the height of a dike wall. Make sure a structural engineer approves the design and materials.

Provide a positive method for shutting off flow to the tank or bypassing it. You must operate in such a manner as to avoid overfilling or be able to quickly cease filling in the event of a spill or leak. Level detection devices can provide a warning alarm at one level and provide a signal to a solenoid valve to shut off a fill line at a higher level. High level alarms and shutoff controls should be maintained vigilantly so they are always operational.

Spill prevention controls also include check valves which prevent the flow from backing up. Dry disconnect couplings cut down on spillage when adding or removing liquids between the tank and a tanker truck. If the tank is open topped and in the weather, sufficient freeboard should be allowed to prevent stormwater from overfilling it or wind from blowing liquid over the top. Liquid detection devices can be used in an unattended area to alert remote personnel that a leak or spill is occurring. For highly volatile liquids, gas detectors can be installed to provide warning of a spill or leak in progress.

An enclosed atmospheric storage tank will collapse, if it is drained with a blockage of the vent. Drainage calculations are only accurate as long as pressure is constant. If draining is rapid, the head space vapors, inside the tank, follow an adiabatic expansion. The vacuum on a tank draining by pump and that is not vented is

$$P = 2.036 P_o [1 - \{V_o / (V_o + \pi R^2 h_o)\}^\gamma] \qquad [9.1]$$

where

P = final tank vacuum, in. Hg,
P_o = atmospheric pressure, lb_f/in^2,
V_o = initial air space volume, ft^3,
R = tank radius, ft,
h_o = initial fluid height, ft, and
γ = ratio of molar specific heats, C_p/C_v (1.4 is used for diatomic gases).

The final height, h_f, of the liquid will be

$$h_f = NPSH + F_l + VP - h_i - \frac{144 P_o \{V_o / [V_o + \pi R^2 (h_o - h_f)]\}}{\rho g / g_c}$$ [9.2]

where

NPSH = net positive suction head, ft,
F_l = friction loss, ft,
VP = vapor pressure, ft,
h_i = height difference between tank base and centerline
    of pump, ft,
ρ = liquid density, lb_m/ft^3,
g = acceleration due to gravity, ft/sec^2, and
g_c = conversion factor, $ft\ lb_m/ft\ lb_f\ sec^2$.

Where draining is by gravity flow,

$$P = \frac{29.92 h_f \rho g}{144 P_o g_c}$$ [9.3]

and

$$h_f = \frac{144 P_o (1 - \{V_o / [V_o + \pi R^2 (h_o - h_f)]\}^Y)}{\rho g / g_c}$$ [9.4]

Realistically, you need to consider the questions in Figure 9.6.

Often secondary containment is thrown up around a tank without much thought given to design. A common mistake is to place a dike wall on an existing concrete pad. How was the wall-to-pad seal made? Many such dikes leak under any amount of head (pressure due to the force of gravity acting on a column of liquid). Ideally, the secondary containment structure (base and walls) is a monolithic pour. That is, the concrete for the walls and floor is poured all at once—the structure has no seams. Sometimes seams are necessary, for thermal expansion or because of the sheer size of the containment structure. In this case, the joint between wall and floor should have a leak proof design with a vapor barrier placed between wall and floor. Consider the nature of the chemical hazard to be contained: acid dissolves concrete, for example. Also, consider the movement of material handling equipment, such as forklifts or front-end loaders. Can they come and go without allowing storm run-on to enter the containment area? Can they operate with minimum tracking of leaked material? Did you consider the effects of solar energy on the tanks and containment? Temperature? Windage?

Figure 9.6
Tank Spillage Checklist

1. If the tank is damaged or fails, what will be the consequences?
2. How likely is a blocked vent?
3. If not unlikely, how often might a blocked event occur?
4. Was the tank designed to withstand maximum possible vacuum?
5. Do location and surroundings allow for easy access to repair or replace the tank?
6. Do location and surroundings allow for easy access to clean up spillage/leakage?

Liquids collected in secondary containment must be removed daily. Keep a log of how much liquid was removed, what it was and where it was disposed. Hazardous waste liquids which spill over into the containment area must be disposed as hazardous waste. Precipitation that falls into the containment area must be presumed to be contaminated unless you have never had a spill or leak in the area. Presumed contamination should give you some incentive to safeguard the pristine condition of your containment areas. That is not to say that you cannot clean up a spill or leak well enough not to contaminate future precipitation or that chemical analysis of otherwise presumed contamination might not prove differently.

Tanks require annual tests for integrity as well as engineering inspection for corrosion. Figure 9.7 lists tests methods commonly used.

Feed system, safety cutoff, bypass system, and pressure controls must also be assessed annually.

Figure 9.7

Tests for Tank Integrity and Corrosion

Test	To Detect
Acoustic Emission	cracks, friction wear, plastic deformation
Acoustic Impact	delamination, loose rivets
Dry Magnetic Particle	surface cracks or flaws
Dye Penetrant	surface cracks or discontinuities
Eddy Current	surface/subsurface cracks/wall thickness and coating thickness
Hydrostatic	gross flaws, flange leaks
Radiographic	subsurface discontinuities
Spark	lining holidays
Ultrasonic	subsurface discontinuities
Wet Magnetic Particle	surface cracks or flaws

The inspection includes looking for weld breaks, punctures, scrapes on protective coating, cracks, corrosion, and signs of damage or inadequate construction. Daily inspect all aboveground, straight piping which is not protected by secondary containment. Carefully examine welded flanges, joints, and connections. Also, inspect sealless or magnetically coupled pumps and automatic shutoff devices. The tank should have a corrosion potential assessment, prepared by a NACE (National Association of Corrosion Engineers) *corrosion expert*. Did a corrosion expert supervise or inspect the installation of field-fabricated corrosion protection? Do you have a written record of it? Are sources of impressed current for cathodic protection inspected bimonthly? Figure 9.8 lists some common tank deficiencies. Figure 9.9 covers piping and 9.10 covers deficiencies of other ancillary equipment. Double-walled tanks need corrosion protection between the walls. Concrete containment vaults and sumps need liners or coatings.

Figure 9.8
Common Tank Deficiencies

Metal Tanks
gross leakage
major corroded areas
metal blisters
discolored paint
flaking paint
cracks in nozzle connections
cracks in welded seams
cracks under rivets
buckles and bulges
defective manhole gaskets
corrosion on roof
corrosion around nozzles and valves
foundation erosion
cracks in curbing and ringwall
rotting of wooden supports

Fiberglass-Reinforced Tanks
gross leakage
bending, curving, flexing
longitudinal cracks in horizontal tank
vertical crack in vertical tank

Concrete Tank
gross leaks
cracks
wet spots
discoloration of coating
lifting of coating

Figure 9.9
Common Piping Deficiencies

leaks
external corrosion or rust spots
metal blisters
discolored paint
deteriorated orifice plates
broken stems/missing handles on valves
worn/torn flexible hoses
traffic passing over hoses
vibrating/swaying pipes while pumping

Figure 9.10
Common Deficiencies in Other Ancillary Equipment

Pumps and Compressors
foundation cracks
excessive vibration
cavitation of pump
leaky pump seals
missing anchor bolts
excessive dirt
burning odors
smoke
depleted lube oil reservoir

Heat Exchangers or Vapor Controls
rust spots or blisters

Miscellaneous Ancillaries
level sensors nonoperational
alarms do not function
spill proof couplings not used
safety cutoff or bypass nonoperational
pressure relief vents nonoperational

HOW TO MANAGE WASTE PILES

Waste piles used for treatment or storage of non-containerized accumulation of solid, non-flowing hazardous waste may comply with either the requirements for waste piles or landfills. If used for disposal, or to treat or store containerized accumulations or flowing waste, the waste pile must follow landfill requirements.

The requirements for managing storage or treatment waste piles is aimed at protecting the pile from wind dispersion. Control systems must be installed to collect hazardous leachate or storm runoff. Stormwater needs to be diverted to avoid storm run-on. Current requirements include a liner for waste piles, so that the waste cannot migrate to nearby soils and water courses. The leachate collection system must be installed immediately above the liner, unless the pile is covered or otherwise protected in such a manner that neither stormwater runoff nor leachate is generated.

During construction, the liners and covers must be inspected for damage. The waste pile must be inspected weekly, during operation, for deterioration, runon and runoff controls, wind dispersion control, and leachate collection system.

If ignitable or reactive wastes are disposed in the pile, their addition to the pile must either result in a mixture which is no longer ignitable or reactive, or the waste must be protected from sources of ignition. Separation and confinement procedures must be written to protect the waste in the latter case. At the very least, you need to inventory and maintain a list of sources of ignition. Do not forget lightning.

Where incompatible wastes are placed together in a waste pile, they must be separated by a dike, berm, wall, or other protective structure. Storage of F020, F021, F022, F023, F026, and F027 wastes in waste piles requires an approved management plan.

HOW TO MANAGE SURFACE IMPOUNDMENTS

A surface impoundment is a pond, lagoon, depression, pit, or diked area used to store, treat, or dispose of hazardous waste. The surface is open to the atmosphere and it contains accumulated liquid or semi-solid waste. The difference between a wastewater lagoon and a hazardous waste surface impoundment can be a matter of semantics, except that one is regulated under CWA and the other under RCRA.

The chief problem with managing hazardous wastes in surface impoundments is that the wastes tend to escape, thus defeating the goals of RCRA. The pooled liquids exert pressure on the bottom materials and the contents flow down into the surrounding soils. This potentially leads to contamination of surface water and/or groundwater. Therefore, unless the impoundment meets some strict design requirements specified in regulations written under the authority of HSWA, these hazardous waste management units (HWMU) are prohibited by Congress.

Monofill impoundments (having only one liner) are restricted to certain waste types. Waste from foundry furnace air emission controls or metal casting molding sand are two waste types that may be placed in monofills; however, the impoundment must have a good, nonleaking liner. The monofill must be designed, located and operated so that contaminants do not migrate into groundwater or surface water.

As the operator of a surface impoundment, you must prevent overfilling. This can be managed procedurally or structurally or by control instrumentation. Rainfall can be prevented from overfilling the impoundment by strictly maintaining a minimum of 2 ft (60 cm) freeboard. Divert runon from other areas of your property by berms and diversion dikes. Inspect and test level controllers and high level alarms frequently. Conduct training to minimize human error, the most common cause of overfilling. At least two feet of freeboard must be maintained in surface impoundments, in order to prevent overtopping. Dikes are required to have protective exterior covers, such as grass, shale or riprap, to preserve structural integrity. Double liners are required to prevent leakage from the bottom and internal sides. During construction and installation, the liners and cover systems must be inspected for uniformity, signs of damage, and imperfections. Groundwater monitoring provides assurance that the leachate collection system installed between liners is doing its job. Variances may be granted, if the nearest drinking water well is over 1/4 mile away, and at least one non-clay liner is installed, and not leaking.

While operational, surface impoundments must be inspected weekly for maintenance of unit integrity and signs of the development of potentially disastrous situations. For instance, if the liquid level in the impoundment suddenly drops, what caused it? Or what if a dike starts leaking, even just a trickle? The impoundment must be taken out of service while the problem is repaired. Then the liquid inventory must be moved elsewhere, at least temporarily, if the leak cannot be stopped by external dike repairs.

When closed, a surface impoundment cannot just be left in place. Simple logic tells us that soon the impoundment would reach its inventory limit, with a mixture of stormwater and waste, and not too long after that the waste/water mixture would be sloshing all over the ground, heading for the nearest body of surface water. All waste residues must be removed from the impoundment or else the impoundment must be decontaminated, upon closure. A properly designed cover, pre-approved by the permitting authority, must be applied to the closed impoundment, and it must be maintained for the agreed upon amount of time.

LANDFILL MANAGEMENT

The state-of-the art method of disposing of hazardous waste in the mid-1970s was epitomized by the Love Canal landfill, located in Niagara Falls, New York. Landfills are the oldest—and still cheapest—method of waste disposal, although many tough restrictions now apply to this hazardous waste management device.

The problem is that the waste lies forever buried in the landfill, just as potent as the day it was put there—in most cases, anyway. Corroding containers in unlined landfills result in contaminated water somewhere else. At Love Canal, the only place liquids could go to was the surface, once the containment structure was saturated with liquids.

Today, we operate under modified rules aimed at preventing future Love Canals. Unstabilized liquid wastes are prohibited. Bulk or noncontainerized liquids are strictly prohibited. Untreated wastes are prohibited in many cases.

New requirements include two or more liners, two leachate collection systems, with one located above and one between the liners, and groundwater monitoring. The only exemption from groundwater monitoring is for those structures engineered to exclude liquids anyway and also built to prevent migration of liquids.

The landfill operator has recordkeeping requirements which are not common to other HWMUs. The operator must maintain a map, showing the exact location and dimensions (length, width, depth) of each cell (a subdivision of this type HWMU). The contents of each cell must be recorded on the map. Also, the exact location of specific kinds of waste within the cell must be noted. Placement of F020, F021, F022, F023, F024, F026, and F027 wastes in a landfill requires explicit approval of the Regional EPA Administrator.

INCINERATION OF HAZARDOUS WASTE

Incineration of waste is the second oldest methodology of waste management. Presumably, our ancestors tossed their waste a few feet away from their resting places long before they learned to build fires to warm the place up, and, consequently, to burn the waste. While you may lament the fact that those long-gone relatives of ours had no RCRA regulations to contend with, surely you do not want to live like that.

The role of an incinerator is to destroy hazardous waste using flame combustion. Therefore, the waste must be principally organic. This does not mean that inorganics cannot be incinerated. Inorganics are destroyed in incinerators all the time, but supplemental fuel is required. Normal, steady-state combustion must be achieved before waste is introduced to the incinerator feed. Continuous combustion and emission monitoring are also required.

The chemical reaction taking place in incineration is oxidation, primarily of organics. The reaction products are combustion gases and ash or solid residue as shown in the combustion of methane.

$$CH_4 + 2O_2 \dashrightarrow CO_2 + 2H_2O \qquad [9.5]$$

This means that 2 moles (or volumes) of oxygen are needed for every mole of methane burned in order to produce one mole of carbon dioxide and 2 moles of water vapor. This is called the *stoichiometric volume*. In practice, we burn with air, not pure oxygen, and incineration typically requires excess air. Air is about 20% oxygen and 70% nitrogen (not exactly but close enough). Therefore,

$$CH_4 + 2O_2 + 7N_2 \dashrightarrow CO_2 + 2H_2O + 7N_2 \qquad [9.6]$$

The nitrogen is inert—it does not enter into combustion—but in this chemical equation we account for its presence. Now, let's say we are incinerating with 50% excess air (that makes the numbers easier to follow):

$$CH_4 + 3O_2 + \frac{21}{2}N_2 \dashrightarrow CO_2 + 2H_2O + O_2 + \frac{21}{2}N_2 \qquad [9.7]$$

The practicality of this chemical equation is this: for every cubic foot of methane burned, 14.5 cubic feet of flue gas is produced! Plus, we have not accounted for the moisture in the combustion air, not to mention the fact that the volume of gas expands as the temperature rises. The 14.5 cubic feet at standard engineering temperature (77°F) becomes more than 66 cubic feet at 2,000°F. [Be careful about standard temperature and pressures: *STP scientific* is 1 atmosphere and 60°F while *STP engineering* is 1 atmosphere at 77°F!]

Efficiency of combustion depends on conditions in the combustion zone, the status of which can be inferred from the nature of gases exiting the incinerator: percent excess oxygen and carbon dioxide. Controlling conditions in the combustion zone are temperature; residence time; percent oxygen; and turbulence. Adequate mixing of oxygen and the waste material is assured by a high Reynolds number (gas flow turbulence indicator.)

All materials in the incinerator—gas, liquid, and solid—move in the same direction, from the feed end to the exit, which drives phase equilibrium toward the gaseous side, thus increasing the pollutant load in the stack gas. Pollutants such as heavy metals. The critical factor is vapor pressure, which is highly dependent on temperature. An incinerator has a relatively low thermal capacity and thus thermal stability, so process upsets can occur within a matter of minutes, or sometimes even within seconds of time.

Not too long ago, a RCRA inspector entered the control room of an incinerator permitted to burn hazardous waste. She was unannounced. The operator had been experiencing difficulty controlling combustion and the feed that evening contained some solvents that were rather potent anesthetic agents. Due to the poor combustion efficiency of the incinerator at the moment, solvent vapors were heavy in the air of the control room. Consequently, the operator was intoxicated and almost comatose when the inspector entered the door. She smelled the solvent, saw the lethargic operator, walked straight to the emergency stop button and pushed it. Then she walked to the administrative office and announced that the facility was shut down, until a team of inspectors could review the situation.

This case history is mostly based on hearsay. The point is, this was no fly-by-night outfit, but a professionally operated, highly technical waste disposal company. The uninitiated have a mistaken idea that high temperature incinerators burn the stew out of everything, and leave nothing in the wake of the combustion process. Not so. The reaction kinetics of combustion can take several minutes if operating conditions are just a little off and far too long if operating conditions slip just a little more. Operating an incinerator is no easy task, which ought to explain why it is so hard to get one permitted. On the other hand, if the conditions are just right, the incinerator does burn the stew out of most waste. Many incinerator operating companies opt for an afterburner to take up the slack, though.

RCRA on Design and Operation of Incinerators

Hydrogen chloride emissions (HCl) must be minimized, by scrubbing if necessary. Particulate emissions must be eliminated. Regulations require that 99.99% (four-nines) of each principal organic hazardous constituent (POHC) specified in the permit must either be destroyed or removed in the incinerator. This is called the destruction and removal efficiency (DRE).

The permit will specify the composition of waste feed that may be fed to the incinerator. A new or modified permit is required in order to incinerate any other feed composition. Normal operating conditions (fuel flow, temperatures, pressures, stack gas composition) must be achieved before introducing the hazardous waste feed. Figure 9.11 gives a very rough composition of municipal solid waste (MSW) streams.

Figure 9.11
Municipal Waste Composition

40%	paper
8.5%	metal
8%	plastics
7.5%	food scraps
7%	glass
21%	other

TSCA on PCB Management

Many electrical transformers still contain polychlorinated biphenyls (PCBs). Any *PCB-transformer* (transformer oil contains 500 ppm PCBs or more) was to have been removed or replaced by October 1, 1990. Why? A PCB fire produces dioxins and furans, two of the most toxic compounds known to humanity according to some scientists.

Many facilities logically opted to have PCB fluids removed from their transformers, in a process called drain-flush-refill. After removing the PCB oil, the transformer is flushed with clean non-PCB oil, and drained again. Finally, the transformer is refilled with new, non-PCB oil. After a period of time, however, the PCB molecules, which attached to metal bonding sites or lodged in metal pores or crevices and among the electrical windings, let go and disperse into the new oil. If the level of PCB exceeds 50 ppm, the transformer is *PCB contaminated.*

PCBs can be destroyed at approved incinerators. The PCB liquids must be retained in the fire box for at least two seconds, between 2,000 and 2,400°F, with a minimum of three percent excess air, or, alternatively, for at least 1.5 seconds between 2,700 and 3,100°F with two percent excess air. PCB DRE must be equal to or greater than six-nines ($\geq 99.9999\%$)! Combustion efficiency must be a minimum of 99.99%, based on the concentration of carbon dioxide and carbon monoxide, as determined by this equation:

$$\eta = \frac{C_{CO_2}}{C_{CO_2} + C_{CO}} \times 100 \qquad\qquad [9.8]$$

The PCB feedrate to the incinerator must be measured and recorded at least once per quarter hour. Process temperatures must be continuously measured and recorded as determined by either pyrometer, or wall thermocouple-pyrometer correlation. Anytime temperature drops below the specified operating temperature, the flow of PCBs in the feed must be ceased by automatic controller.

Figure 9.12 lists the stack parameters that must be monitored routinely. When a monitoring device fails, or PCB rate and quantity measurement and recording device fails, or excess oxygen falls below the specified concentration, PCB feed must halt automatically.

Hydrochloric acid emissions must be scrubbed continuously, during operations of the PCB incinerator. When PCB solids are incinerated, the air emissions are limited to one mg HCl/Kg PCB introduced (1 ppm) and DRE must be at least six-nines.

Figure 9.12
Stack Parameters for PCB Incineration

Carbon Monoxide (CO)
Hydrogen Chloride (HCl)
Nitrogen Oxides (NO_x)
Oxygen (O_2)
PCBs
Total Chlorinated Organics
Total Particulate Matter

Incineration Engineering

The minimum allowed hazardous waste DRE is four-nines (99.99%) for each POHC introduced as determined by:

$$DRE = \frac{(m_i - m_o)}{m_i} \times 100 \qquad\qquad [9.9]$$

where

m_i = mass feed rate for a POHC, lb/hr,
m_o = mass emission rate for the same POHC, lb/hr.

Based on the result of the trial burn, submitted with the RCRA Part B permit application, some, or all, of the operating criteria listed in Figure 9.13 may be specified in the permit. Understanding the incineration process requires a mass balance to determine amounts of various products formed by the reactants of the combustion equation. This requires thorough characterization of both waste and fuel feeds. Next, perform an energy balance to determine the energy transferred during the process, how much supplemental fuel is required, and how much energy, if any, comes from waste.

Figure 9.13
Typical Permit Parameters - Incineration

air feed	maximum rate
ash content in waste feed	maximum
carbon monoxide in stack gas	maximum concentration
chloride in feed	maximum concentration
combustion temperature	minimum
feed POHCs	maximum concentration
flue gas	maximum velocity
waste feed	maximum rate

The goal is to maintain a minimum operating temperature. A thermodynamic analysis reveals the changes of the chemical components of the combustion system and a kinetic analysis indicates how rapidly these changes can occur. Analyzing heat transfer mechanisms determines the temperature distribution within the system and allows completion of the energy balance. Analysis of mixing conditions determines whether the waste and other reaction compounds undergo enough turbulence to react completely. Results of all these analyses, and the volume of the combustor, lead to the calculation of residence time.

The incinerator stack must be equipped with continuous sampling and analysis devices, where technically achievable. At a minimum, routine sampling of the stack must be conducted with immediate analysis. The four fundamental components of combustion are fuel, oxidizer, diluent, and waste. Chemical potential energy is provided to the process by the carbon-carbon or carbon-hydrogen bonds of the fuel. The fuel requirement can be offset, to the extent that the waste contains chemical potential energy. Air is the usual source of the oxidizer, although the use of pure oxygen has advantages. Dry air parameters are shown in Figure 9.14.

Figure 9.14
Dry Air

Molecular Weight   28.84 lb/mole

Volumetric Analysis
 Oxygen   21% or 0.21 mole/mole air
 Nitrogen   79% or 0.79 mole/mole air

$$0.21O_2 + 0.79N_2 \rightarrow Air$$
$$O_2 + 3.76N_2 \rightarrow 4.76\ Air$$

Gravimetric Analysis
 Oxygen   23% or 0.23 lb/lb air
 Nitrogen   77% or 0.77 lb/lb air

$$0.23\ lb\ O_2 + 0.77\ lb\ N_2 = 1\ lb\ Air$$
$$1\ lb\ O_2 + 3.35\ lb\ N_2 = 4.35\ lb\ Air$$

Air Density   0.0808 lb/ft^3

Standard Volume (any gas)   1 mole $\rightarrow$ 359 ft^3 @ 25°C/760 mmHg
              (77°F/29.92 inHg)

Any substance in the waste, or fuel, or air that does not participate chemically in the combustion reaction is a diluent. Nitrogen in air is a diluent. Moisture is a diluent, usually. Excess oxygen is a diluent. Any compound that becomes ash after combustion is a diluent. Trace metals are diluents. All these materials act as temperature sinks—requiring additional fuel in order to sustain combustion efficiency. Presence of diluent gases can offset the equilibrium of the reacting gas mixture, and thus throw off the reaction kinetics—requiring additional residence time.

Three simultaneous chemical reactions take place in the fire box. *Strong oxidation* is the reaction generally understood as combustion, in which a (hazardous) material is completely disintegrated into harmless products. The generalized strong oxidation equation is:

$$C_xH_yCl_z + [x + (y-z)/4](O_2 + 3.76N_2) \rightarrow$$
$$xCO_2 + zHCl + (y-z)/2 H_2O + 3.76[x + (y-z)/4]N_2$$

[9.10]

where x, y, and z are the moles of carbon, hydrogen, and chlorine, respectively. Strong oxidation requires 50-150 percent excess air to ensure that enough oxygen is available for the reaction to go to completion.

Pyrolysis is the thermal degradation of carbonaceous material in the absence of oxygen, caused by breaking the bonds of the organic compound with thermal energy. Small waste fractions, which can be retained at high temperature long enough, may undergo pyrolysis and be destroyed, even when oxygen concentration is inadequate to support complete strong oxidation. Products of pyrolyzed waste typically contain some fuel value (C, CO, H_2, CH_4) and give back some energy, if subsequently oxidized.

A *weak radical attack* reaction takes place in the gaseous phase where radicals of atomic hydrogen (H), atomic oxygen (O), atomic chlorine (Cl), hydroxyl (OH⁻), methyl (CH_3⁻), and chloroxy (ClO⁻) attack the waste and facilitate its complete destruction. Incinerator operation, as you can see, is not a matter of throwing some waste material into a fire, and, presto, that's that! Very complex thermodynamic processes are at work, and proper conditions must be carefully preserved and protected. No wonder, then, that the environmentalists protest the use of incinerators to manage hazardous waste. Either the waste is effectively destroyed by these reactions, or some is not destroyed, or else incompletely destroyed (high POHC), or intermediate compounds are produced which present hazards in their own right (high PIC or products of incomplete combustion). Figure 9.15 lists the assumed products of complete incineration for various waste elements.

Figure 9.15
Assumed Products of Complete Incineration

Waste Element	Product of Incineration
Carbon, C	CO_2
Chloride, Cl	HCl or Cl_2
Copper, Cu	CuO
Fluoride, F	HF or F_2
Hydrogen, H	H_2O
Iron, Fe	Fe_2O_3
Metals, alkali	metal hydroxide
Metals, non-alkali	metal oxide
Nitrogen, N	N_2
Potassium, K	KOH
Sodium, Na	NaOH
Sulfur, S	SO_2

Complete incineration is a hypothetical concept, so far as technology can support, and typical PICs include CO, soot, and any number of organic compounds. A critical factor in complete combustion is the air/fuel ratio, which is defined either on a mole or weight basis. The former definition is:

$$AF_m = 4.76 n_a / n_f \qquad [9.11]$$

and the latter definition is:

$$AF_w = 137.3 \frac{n_a}{n_f + M_f} \qquad [9.12]$$

where:

n_a = moles of oxygen,
n_f = moles of fuel,
M_a = molecular weight of air, 28.84 lb/lb-mole, and
M_f = molecular weight of fuel, lb/lb-mole.

Maximum achievable temperature in the fire box is the *adiabatic flame temperature*, assuming no work is performed and no change in kinetic or potential energy. Any given fuel, at stoichiometric air/fuel ratio, yields a specific adiabatic flame temperature (shown in Figure 9.16 for some common fuels). Many factors prevent the achievement of this ideal temperature.

Figure 9.16
Adiabatic Flame Temperature

Fuel	Adiabatic Flame Temperature, °F
Acetylene, C_2H_2	4,778
Benzene, C_6H_6	4,058
Butane, C_4H_{10}	3,860
Carbon Monoxide, CO	4,328
Ethane, C_2H_6	3,824
Ethanol (Ethyl Alcohol), C_2H_5OH	3,716
Ethylene, C_2H_4	4,157
Hydrogen, H_2	4,085
Methane, CH_4	3,725
Nitric Oxide, NO	4,670
Octane, C_8H_{18}	3,878
Propane, C_3H_8	3,842
Propylene, C_3H_6	4,049

The required residence time in an incinerator is 2 seconds minimum, but the typical is 0-3 seconds. If the incinerator is a rotary kiln, the residence time θ is calculated as follows:

$$\theta = \frac{0.19L}{NDS} \qquad [9.13]$$

where θ is in minutes and

D = diameter of kiln, ft
L = length of kiln, ft,
N = rotational velocity of kiln, min^{-1}, and
S = slope of kiln, ft/ft.

The coefficient 0.19 is empirically derived. The ratio L/D should fall between 2 and 8. Slow rotating kilns with high L/D provide long residence times for wastes that need it. Rotational velocities from 0.2 to 1 in/sec are common, but the rotational velocity used in equation 9.13 is:

$$N(min^{-1}) = 5n(inch/sec) \times \pi D \qquad [9.14]$$

Nitrogen, chlorine, and sulfur in the hazardous waste produce NO_x, HCl, and SO_2 when burned. These acid gases must be scrubbed in wet caustic units, though other possibilities exist as discussed in the chapter on air emission control. HCl is limited to 4 lb/hr or 1% of the stack gas, whichever is less. CO and PM are also problem contaminants. PM can be scrubbed, but the CO is best managed by burning it up in an afterburner. PM is limited to 0.08 grains per dry standard cubic foot (180 mg/m^3, dry, STP). The amount of PM, corrected for excess oxygen, is calculated

$$P_c = P_m \frac{14}{21 - y} \qquad [9.15]$$

where

P_c = PM concentration, corrected,
P_m = PM concentration, measured, and
Y = oxygen concentration, measured by Orsat method.

Heavy metals, especially mercury, are difficult to remove from exhaust gas. Separation of batteries from MSW reduces the mercury content of the overall waste stream. Incineration of industrial hazardous waste containing mercury is restricted, if not prohibited, locally. The best demonstrated technology (BDT) for MSW is to run the flue gas through a spray dryer, then a dry venturi, on the way to a baghouse. An induced-draft fan provides the momentum for this scheme. Medical waste is quenched in a caustic venturi scrubber, then fed to a wet (water tower) scrubber out of which an induced-draft fan pushes the exhaust up the stack.

Hazardous waste incinerator flue gas is quenched to prevent the post-combustion formation of dioxins and furans (a process called *Denovo synthesis*). The cooled gas is fed to a caustic tower scrubber and an ID fan moves the gases. Unburned POHC and CO can be handled in an afterburner, but are best destroyed by assuring effective operation of the combustion zone. Dioxin and furan emissions are especially hard to control. Incinerators must be certified by the Assistant EPA Administrator for Solid Waste and Emergency Response in order to burn F020, F021, F022, F023, F024, F026, or F027 wastes.

Incineration Process Equipment

Other, unconventional types of thermal destruction equipment other than incinerators are shown in Figure 9.17.

Figure 9.17
Innovative Thermal Destruction Processes

Advanced Electrical Reactor (AER)
Circulating Bed Combustor (CBC)
Fluidized Bed Combustor (FBC)
Infrared Destructor
Microwave Destructor
Molten Salt Pyrolyzer
Multiple Hearth Furnace
Oxygen-Enriched Incineration
Plasma Arc Reactor
Supercritical Water
Westinghouse/O'Connor Water-cooled Rotary Combustor
Wet Air Oxidation

These miscellaneous processes, especially the more common ones discussed below, must be operated under the same requirements as incinerators, with one major exception. Miscellaneous thermal treatment devices are prohibited from open burning of hazardous waste—not counting the detonation of explosives.

One generic type of miscellaneous incinerator is the mobile unit. These HWMUs can be used on Superfund, RCRA corrective action, and underground storage tank (UST) corrective action sites. Mobile incinerators will be discussed in detail in Chapter 11 on cleaning up the environment.

The advanced electric reactor is a vertical hot tube, operated around 5,000°F, using technology developed in the space program. As material falls through the reactor tube, it is first dried, then heated up and, finally, combusted. An additional free fall, underneath the hot tube, allows time for quenching, before the residue drops into a catch (quench) pan. This marvelous device may some day replace huge rotary kilns, but much more technical development of the AER is required in the meantime. For one thing, if too much waste material is poured into the AER, particles of the material near the hot walls act to *shade* other particles in the center, causing incomplete reaction to take place. Obviously, EPA will not tolerate this situation, if the material is a hazardous waste. Also, the EPA has been reluctant to issue operating permits for these devices, due to the millisecond (90-150 msec) residence times. A thorough kinetic analysis is a strict requirement for permitting this reactor. Current technology only allows a working diameter of one foot, so the throughput of this reactor is limited, even if other problems are solved. Citizens of the 21st century will use this device a lot, but right now, take your waste elsewhere (except for experimentation). The most promising potential use for the AER is the destruction of wastes with fuel value. As fuel ignites within the hot zone, shading may be effectively eliminated.

The circulating bed combustor (CBC) uses lower temperatures than convention incinerators (1,000-1,500°F) to achieve similar DREs, yet with relatively higher throughput. The need for afterburners and scrubbers is eliminated. A high-velocity air stream entrains solids or liquids in a turbulent combustion loop. These are huge devices with thirty-foot-high combustion chambers and twelve inch thick ceramic liners. Solids are fed into hot recirculating solids leaving the hot cyclone. Liquids are injected directly into the combustion zone. Gases remain in the combustion zone for about two seconds but particles up to one inch in size may remain for thirty minutes or longer. Hydrocarbons are completely converted to carbon dioxide and water. Organosulfur compounds release SO_2, which is oxidized in the presence of anhydrous lime to make gypsum ($CaSO_4$) and CO_2. Organochlorides form hydrochloric acid, which is oxidized along with lime into $CaCl_2$ and water. The CBC can efficiently destroy a wide range of hazardous waste types with a minimum of five-nines (99.999%) efficiency and some compounds are destroyed with greater than six-nines (99.9999%) effectiveness. Disposal of the inert residual bed is the chief disadvantage of the CBC.

Fluidized bed combustors consist of a vertical, cylindrical, refractory-lined vessel with a windbox that receives the fluidizing/combustion air, an air-distribution plate that transports air from the windbox to fluidize the bed of inert but fluid material, such as sand or ash, and freeboard over the bed. Upcoming air fluidizes the bed—makes it float. The suspended-solid/gas mixture has a rolling boil action that mixes bed material, incoming fuel, air, combustion gases, and wastes with residence times of 5-8 seconds.

The waste is literally injected into very hot inert fluidized material providing an extremely large heat transfer area and acting as a liquid. This is, at one time, an advantage and a disadvantage. Fluid beds provide excellent conditions for destruction of waste material but the drawback is that the waste must be able to be fluidized. Large solids sink to the bottom and interfere with the combustion process. Destruction efficiencies in excess of four-nines (99.99%) are common, five-nines (99.999%) are achievable, and six-nines (99.9999%) are not rare. Figure 9.18 shows some of the POHCs which are successfully destroyed in fluidized bed incinerators.

A chemically active fluid-bed is operated at a temperature just below the melting point of the ash constituents, or of any eutectic which may be formed. The maximum operating temperature of a bed is determined by feed constituents or compounds with eutectic that may be formed. The operating temperature may not exceed the melting point of the solids or you will lose the fluid-bed and gain a pool of molten liquid in the windbox.

The chief advantages of a fluid-bed incinerator over an ordinary hazardous waste incinerator are the more efficient combustion available, ease of control, variable feed acceptability, and cyclic operation capability. For the fluid-bed operator the possibility of fuel savings is attractive, as many hazardous wastes have fuel value, lower NO_x emissions due to lower operating temperatures, and lower metal emissions due to operating at a higher temperature than ordinary incineration.

Figure 9.18
Wastes Destroyed in Fluid-Bed Reactors

Aniline
Carbon Tetrachloride
Chlorobenzene
Chloroform
Cresol
p-Dichlorobenzene
Methyl Methacrylate
Naphthalene
Perchloroethylene
Phenol
Tetrachloroethane
1,1,1-Trichloroethane
Trichloroethylene
Toluene

Fluid-bed incinerators are sized according to the stack exhaust volume, which is minimized by dewatering the feed. If very much steam will be generated in the feed, the operating temperature of the incinerator must be raised to account for the heat of vaporization, and this also increases the size of the bed required. *Subautogenous* waste has a heating value too low to sustain combustion and thus requires supplemental fuel. *Overautogenous* waste has such a high heating value that some sort of temperature control is required in order to avoid melting the feed and bed materials. An *autogenous* waste, then, is one which has sufficient heating value to burn without supplemental fuel, but also presents no control problems.

Hazardous waste with the specific feed characteristic (SFC) of 4,000 Btu/lb water is exactly autogenous in a cold (not preheated) windbox unit. With a hot windbox, an SFC of 2,600 Btu/lb water is required to be autogenous, but the windbox must be preheated to 1,000°F. The autogenous SFC is lowered to 2,400 Btu/lb water at 1,200°F preheat. The waste is overautogenous if the SFC is greater than 4,000 Btu/lb water. Temperature is controlled by using either excess air to absorb heat, or by injecting water into the bed to absorb heat. Either way increases the exhaust volume. Another alternative is to lace the bed with steam coils so that the water flashed to steam does not enter the process. This also has the advantage of recovering the heat for potentially useful purposes, such as preheating the windbox or driving a feed pump or the main fan.

Hazardous waste with SFCs less than 2,600 (at 1,000°F preheat) or 2,400 (at 1,200°F) is subautogenous and therefore requires supplemental fuel, even if heat is recovered from the fluid-bed. Industrial sludges have a moisture content that is too high to be autogenous, for example. If the SFC lies between 2,600 (2,400) and 4,000, the waste feed is subautogenous, but can be made autogenous by recovering heat. The operator may chose to use supplemental fuel instead, which has the advantage of lower capital cost, but the distinct disadvantage of higher operating costs.

Fluid-Bed Combustor Example. Suppose you have an oily wastewater sludge, from a refinery, that has a higher heating value (HHV) of 4,500 Btu/lb solids. As fluid-bed feed, the sludge is to be destroyed at the rate of 4 TPH, dewatered to 25% solids. What is the SFC?

SFC = 4,500 Btu/lb solids X 25% solids/75% water
     = 1,500 Btu/lb water

This is a very definite subautogenous waste. A hot windbox and supplemental fuel are required in order to destroy this waste material.

With a windbox temperature of 1,000°F what amount of supplemental fuel is required?

Water = 8,000 lb wet feed/hr X 75 lb water/100 lb wet feed
= 6,000 lb water

$FUEL_{supp}$ = 6,000 lb water/hr X (2,600-1,500)Btu/lb water
= 6.6 MMBtu/hr

Controlled-air incinerators are starved-air modular incinerators having either two- or three-stage combustion chambers. The primary chamber is the site of partial combustion of the waste, with production of a low-energy flue gas. The combustion air is starved in this chamber, so the amount of flue gas is less than with excess air, but combustible. The gases are completely burned in the secondary chamber, where a waste heat boiler recovers the energy of combustion. This limits the contamination of flue gas.

The infrared destructor system consists of a primary combustion chamber (PCC), secondary combustion chamber (SCC), air pollution control equipment (APCE), and a process monitoring and control center. The PCC is powered by electricity. Waste is fed to the PCC on a high-temperature-alloy wire-mesh conveyor belt. Inside the PCC, temperatures range from 1,500-2,000°F. Horizontal rows of electric silicon carbide rods provide the IR energy. The SCC is gas-fired and raises the temperature to 2,300°F. APCE includes a venturi scrubber for particulates, a packed tower for vapors and an induced draft blower that draws clean gas to a free-standing stack. This is now the most used technology on Superfund sites for thermal destruction.

The microwave destructor is another new device with a promising future. This equipment is ahead of the AER in the development process, so more and more permitted microwave facilities can be expected within ten years. The molten salt pyrolyzer utilizes a bath of liquid salt. Multiple hearth furnaces offer more contact time, thus higher DREs.

Oxygen-enriched incineration is another highly effective alternative to conventional technology. In order to meet EPA burn parameters, conventional incinerators have to use 150 percent excess air. Most of this excess air —which is 79 percent nitrogen—does not contribute to the combustion process, and extra fuel is required to heat all that nitrogen up to combustion temperature. In oxygen-enriched incineration, high-purity oxygen replaces excess combustion air, which keeps nitrogen content low and reduces the gas flow rate significantly. Operating temperatures between 1,500 to 2,000°F are achievable. In tests, a mobile incinerator designed for 2,000 lb/hr, but which was achieving a little less than 1,500 lb/hr due to excess air requirements, successfully burned 4,000 lb/hr with 0.14 ton O_2/ton waste. Use of pure oxygen instead of excess air saves 50 MMBtu fuel/ton O_2.

Plasma arc technology is about to come into its own. Electrical energy is used to achieve an 18,000°F plasma—a conductive gas flow, consisting of both charged and neutral particles. Waste materials are decomposed to atoms by ionization and pyrolysis, effectively destroying them with respect to their hazardous characteristics. The equipment has a liquid feed system, a plasma torch, a reaction chamber, and a caustic scrubber. On-line instrumentation is used to monitor and control the operation. A flare burns off 5-6 m^3/min of simple organic materials, such as methane. A plasma reactor can process about 4 kg/min (55 gallons per hour). After the flare, the emissions are about 30-40 m^3/min at standard conditions.

High temperatures, with long residence times desirable for destroying hazardous waste, are available in rotary kilns, such as those used in the cement industry, or as gypsum dryers in the gypsum mines. Many flammable hazardous wastes, such as solvents and other petroleum derivatives, can be used as fuel. The need to destroy such waste materials is a natural match for rotary kilns. Recent technology developments in filter press media and drying technologies, make it possible to pneumatically introduce organic sludges to kilns, improving the efficiency. Cement kilns have four distinct process steps in the long, hot tube. The first step, called dehydration, is where free moisture (or unbound water) is evaporated. The combustion gases, which supply the heat for evaporation, lose sensible heat and pick up water vapor. In the calcination step, the bound water is removed from the solids. This step takes place closer to the firing hood, so the combustion gases are hotter than in the dehydration step. Besides a little water vapor, the solids release carbon dioxide in this zone. The hottest part of the kiln is where clinkerization occurs. Here the dehydrated lime formed in the last step is combined with various silicate species to make tricalcium silicate (abbreviated C_3S in the cement industry—do not confuse this with a chemical formula). Belite (C_2S), tricalcium alumina (C_3A) and dicalcium ferrous oxide (C_2F) are also formed from various desirable mineral impurities in the kiln feed. The final process step inside the kiln, located underneath and behind the firing hood, is called the cooling, or clinker quenching, step.

With all these processes occurring in the cement kiln, it may seem to be a wonder that hazardous waste gets destroyed, but keep in mind that each of the process steps, except the latter one (clinker cooling), requires reaction temperatures exceeding 1,800°F. Also, the weight ratio of process solids to hazardous waste is about 1,000:1 yielding an enormous thermal stability, unlike the situation in the incinerator where the weight of hazardous waste can sometimes exceed the weight of combustion gases. Because of the large amount of process solids, an upset can take hours to correct, but impact on product is slight, so the combustion process can receive priority attention in the meantime. This assures destruction of waste rather than upsetting this function. Critical combustion factors are percent excess oxygen and correct draft fan operation. Combustion zone conditions are given in Figure 9.19.

Figure 9.19
Typical Kiln Conditions

Maximum Gas Temperature	4,000°F
Maximum Solid Temperature	2,700°F
Gas Retention $\geq$ 2,000°F	6-10 sec
Solid Retention $\geq$ 2,000°F	20-30 min
Atmosphere	Oxidizing
Reynolds' Number	> 100,000

Therefore, cement kilns can destroy a wide variety of wastes safely. For instance, they can incinerate inorganic liquids and sludges that are blended into wet process slurries, which are not suitable for incinerators. Inorganic solids can be blended directly into the raw feed material. Mixtures of organics and water are fed to the kiln, as they would be into an incinerator. Liquid hazardous waste fuels can be burned in the kiln as fuel, or used to supplement fuel. Sludges of hazardous waste fuels, though difficult to handle, can be blended with liquid fuel and fed to the kiln. Solids and sludges contaminated with organics, such as soils and filter cake, have to undergo some sort of thermal separation before being fed to the cement kiln. The kiln cannot be operated at temperatures that will melt the process feed, lest the material pour out the low, cool end in a puddle. Otherwise, the cement kiln has no restrictions on what it can destroy thermally.

The Westinghouse/O'Connor combustor is a unique incinerator consisting of a water-cooled rotary barrel made of alternating longitudinal water tubes and flat, perforated steel plates. The barrel is inclined and rotates like a kiln with combustion air distributed through the plate perforations. Water cooling maintains the barrel wall at a safe temperature. Incoming waste is first dried, then combusted. The underfire air allows for better mixing of hot waste and oxygen, thus improving combustion efficiency.

Figure 9.20 offers some tips for burning waste materials.

Figure 9.20
Tips for Waste Combustion

Maintain a minimum of 1,800°F in the furnace.
Control underfire air with plenums under the drying and burnout zones
   and two separate plenums under the burning zone.
Maintain overfire air at 40% of total air.
Have sufficient supplemental fuel to meet start-up requirements and
   maintain 1,800°F.
Maintain 6-12% excess combustion oxygen on a dry basis.
Restrict turndown to 80% unless specifically designed to operate at lower
   rates.
Use supplemental fuel to correct prolonged high CO or low furnace
temperature.
Maintain 6-12% oxygen in flue gas.
Maintain a maximum 50 ppm CO in flue gas on a 4-hr avg.

CONCLUSION

While some aspects of hazardous waste compliance has more to do with good management practices than science and technology, a rhyme and reason does exist. If you understand the basics, you will cope well with compliance.

REFERENCES

Allawi, Ahmed J. "Designing A Trial Burn Plan." *Pollution Engineering.* November 1991.

Bartok, William and Adel F. Sarofim. eds. *Fossil Fuel Combustion: A Sourcebook.* New York: John Wiley & Sons, Inc., 1991.

Bawkon, Bruce. "Incineration Technologies for Managing Solid Waste." *Pollution Engineering.* September 1991.

Brunner, Calvin R. "Industrial Sludge Waste Incineration." *Environmental Progress.* August 1989.

Chovit, Kathleen and Douglas Rhodes. "Effective Hazardous Waste Management Helps Generators Reduce Costs." *Occupational Health & Safety.*

Daugherty, Jack E. "Fundamentals for New Hazardous Waste Managers." *Occupational Hazards.* January 1993.

Ecology and Environment, Inc. and Whitman, Requardt and Associates. *Toxic Substance Storage Tank Containment.* Park Ridge, NJ: Noyes Publications, 1985.

EPA 530-F-95-011. *Environmental Fact Sheet: Final Streamlined Regulations for Collecting and Managing Universal Wastes.* EPA Office of Solid Waste, May 1995.

Gossman, David. "The Reuse of Petroleum and Petrochemical Waste in Cement Kilns." *Environmental Progress.* February 1992.

Heffner, Dale and John J. Oransky. "Five Steps to Effective Secondary Containment." *Pollution Engineering.* July 1, 1992.

King, John A. "Waste Handling and Storage: Onsite Practices." *The National Environmental Journal.* March/April 1992.

Lee, C.C. and George L. Huffman. "Incineration of Solid Waste." *Environmental Progress.* August 1989.

----. "Innovative Thermal Destruction Technologies." *Environmental Progress.* August 1989.

McGowan, Thomas and Richard Ross. "Hazardous Waste Incineration Is Going Mobile." *Chemical Engineering.* October 1991.

Motter, Marla Jeane and Rick Batyko. "PCB Removal and Handling." *Plant Services*. January 1990.

Mullen, John F. "Consider Fluid-Bed Incineration for Hazardous Waste Destruction." *Chemical Engineering Progress*. June 1992.

Naval Facility Command. *Military Handbook: Hazardous Waste Storage Facilities*. Unclassified. NAVFAC DM-5.1, 30 April 1989.

Seigies, Joern and Morris Trichon. "Waste to Burn: Controlling Incinerator Emissions." *Pollution Engineering*. February 15, 1993.

Van Valkenburgh, Gary. "Storing Hazardous Wastes Safely." *Chemical Engineering*. September 1991.

Wentz, Charles A. *Hazardous Waste Management*. New York: McGraw-Hill Publishing Company, 1989.

Wintner, Barry. "Check the Vacuum Rating of Your Tanks." *Chemical Engineering*. February 1991.

Woznicki, Michael J. and John Molnar. "Hazardous Waste Management Program Insures Compliance with State, Federal Regulations." *Plant Services*. July 1989.

10

Shipping Environmentally Hazardous Materials

Concern about the safe transportation of hazardous materials is neither an isolated nor a recent phenomenon. Untrained emergency responders in Aberdeen, South Dakota were at a loss to know how to dispose of hazardous materials containers which rolled off a truck bed. A tank car full of white phosphorus derailed and exploded in Miamisburg, Ohio, making a large cloud of dangerous smoke and forcing authorities to evacuate 25,000 residents from their homes. A gasoline truck overturned in a tunnel in Oakland, California and exploded. The fireball killed seven people. A gasoline truck in Memphis, Tennessee overturned and exploded on a freeway cloverleaf ramp and the resulting fireball killed nine people. Getting hazardous materials, hazardous waste included, from point A to point B is no easy matter and do not think it is not your concern. If tort litigation alone were not enough to convince you, EPA and DOT have plenty of regulations which should.

This chapter was written primarily for unpermitted generators who are limited to 90-day storage and have to ship hazardous waste off-site for disposal, treatment, or storage elsewhere. To some degree, the information herein applies to treatment, storage, or disposal (TSD) facilities as well. This chapter is intended to cover more than the shipment of hazardous wastes, however. From time to time, you may ship nonwaste material, for one reason or another, so any shipment of hazardous materials is included in our discussion, implicitly if not explicitly. One thing this chapter will not do: it will not set you up in the transportation business—there are so many other things you need to know which are outside the scope of this chapter and indeed of this book.

Both EPA and DOT require you to present hazardous waste or materials to be shipped in sound containment with proper paperwork and markings/labels. This is not the carrier's responsibility, but yours. That waste is forever your concern. Think of a container of hazardous waste as a child whom you are putting on a school bus. Certainly you hold the bus driver accountable for the safety and welfare of your child during the trip and you hold someone else accountable for the safety and well being of your child at the destination, but the child is always yours, never theirs. Once you create hazardous waste, it is always yours, always your responsibility, never anyone else's. Just as the condition of your child when he or she gets onto the bus is your responsibility, not the driver's, so the condition of your hazardous waste containers when being presented for shipment is your responsibility, not the carrier's.

RCRA PAPERWORK MANAGEMENT

If you ship hazardous waste off-site for treatment, storage, or disposal—or for any reason (it had better be a good reason if not one of the three mentioned)—you must use a hazardous waste manifest. The federal Uniform Hazardous Waste Manifest is used in many cases, but some states have their own form, which is typically very much like the federal manifest. Some states require the use of their special manifest if you ship waste to them. Others require instate generators to use a state form. How do you know whose manifests to use? Figure 10.1 gives the accepted pecking order for manifest usage.

Figure 10.1
Which Manifest to Use

1. the "ship to" state: where the TSDF is located
2. the "ship from" state: where the generator is located
3. the federal UHWM: the generic form

If the state you ship to requires the use of its own state manifest, use that. If not, use your own state's manifest. If your state does not have a state manifest either, use the federal manifest. Another thing about manifests. TSDF states that have their own manifest typically require that the generator and the TSDF each mail a copy of the manifest to them.

Generator states that have their own manifest typically require the generator to mail a copy of the manifest to them. If you are not clear on the requirements of your state, call them. If you are not clear about the requirements of your TSDF's state, call either the TSDF or their state hazardous waste division. We'll cover the manifest, line-by-line, below, under Shipping Papers.

PREPARING FOR SHIPMENT

Although some carriers help you prepare for shipment, you are held accountable for improper preparations.

Shipper vs. Carrier Duties

Because some carriers are more helpful than others, the duties of the generator/shipper sometimes gets blurry for novices and nonexpert managers. Both EPA and DOT hold you—the generator/shipper —accountable, not the carrier, for four things you have to prepare for shipment: containers, marking/labeling of containers, placarding of the vehicle, and shipping papers. Diligent drivers will not accept damaged or leaking or even doubtful containers, nor will they prepare containers with markings and labels (but they do inspect), and not to prepare manifests (but they do review them). Even if a carrier offers you a computer generated manifest, as a service, your responsibility is to see that it is correctly filled out. Figure 10.2 reiterates the generator/shipper's responsibilities.

Performance Packaging

Hazardous waste must be packaged in accordance with DOT regulations during transportation. You have called the TSDF or carrier or broker and the time for the shipment has been arranged. Before the truck arrives, make a final inspection of the Hazardous Waste Storage Area, count the number of containers of each waste stream, and confirm the condition of each container. Containers offered for transportation cannot be leaking or corroding.

Figure 10.2
Generator/Shipper's Responsibilities

Container	not leaking
	clean of residues
	tight head/bungs
	no damage
Marking/Labeling	HAZARDOUS WASTE
	DOT Shipping Name
	Generator Name/Address
	Generator EPA Identification
	Number
	EPA Waste Stream Number
	Accumulation Start Date
	DOT Hazard Class Label
Shipping Papers	EPA/State Uniform Hazardous
	Waste Manifest
Placarding	DOT Hazard Class Placard

If any are leaking, either transfer the waste to an intact container or place the entire leaking container of waste into an oversized Salvage Drum. If any have residual materials on the heads or sides, have them cleaned up. Make sure that none of the chimes have been flattened for greater than two inches running. The chime—the raised ring on the drum wall—gives the drum strength. Closed-top drums have two chimes. Open-top drums have three chimes. If you find an open-top, two-chimed drum, it has been reclaimed and the original closed-head was cut out. Make sure that the bungs are better than hand tight with a bung wrench.

As for corrosion, obviously we are speaking of visible corrosion, as corrosion cannot be seen by naked eye in its earliest stages. However, DOT performance packaging regulations are intended to prevent corrosion of packaging. Also, there should be no evidence of heat generation due to reactions of incompatible materials inside the containers. Verify this by touching the side of the drum with your bare palm.

How do you select performance oriented packaging? The old DOT hazardous materials table specified a particular container to go with each material in the table. Everyone was confused. That was then. With the recent revision of regulations, DOT introduced packaging groups I, II, and III and now everyone is positively, thoroughly confused. Well, not exactly. As far as actually shipping hazardous waste, or any hazardous material, you can always opt to upgrade packaging. For hazardous waste, ship in 1A1 or 1B1 steel drums, except for strong mineral acids which should be in 1A1 plastic drums. The former, 1A1 drums, are closed-top, bung drums for liquids (old DOT 17E specification) and the latter, 1B1, are open-topped drums for solids and sludges (old DOT 17H specification). These drums meet packaging group I performance requirements in all hazard classes and take the guess work out of choosing packaging, so you are always in compliance as far as packaging goes.

However, even though you use the best drum available, you must still determine which packing group rightfully applies to your hazardous waste/material. That is because the packaging group serves two purposes: 1) it establishes the performance specification for the packaging, but 2) it also communicates hazard information. Packaging group I materials are more dangerous than packaging group II, which are more dangerous than packaging group III. Therefore, even though you upgrade the package, you must specify the correct packaging group as part of the DOT shipping name.

What do you do if the hazardous materials table assigns more than one packing group?

How long can you continue to use old specification containers? Until October 1, 1996. That's when packaging must conform to the new standards.

Figure 10.3
Requirements for Container Reuse without Reconditioning

packaging is otherwise according to DOT
shipment is by truck
shipment is within 24 hours of filling container
each reused container is found to be leak free at loading
reused container is loaded by shipper or carrier
reused container is unloaded by carrier or consignee
each container is reused only once

If you reuse containers for hazardous waste shipments, make sure the requirements in Figure 10.3 are met.

Figure 10.4 lists requirements for reconditioned containers.

Figure 10.4
Requirements for Reconditioned Containers

conform to all DOT specifications
be free of incompatible residue
show no signs of rupture
show no signs of other damage that might reduce structural integrity

---

Marking vs. Labeling

The DOT terms *marking* and *labeling* can be confusing to someone who is not involved in the transportation business. Compliance with EPA regulations requires that we place a label on a hazardous waste drum which contains the words *HAZARDOUS WASTE* and other information such as generator name and address, EPA I.D. number, DOT proper shipping name, EPA waste codes, and the accumulation start date. This EPA label is a DOT marking. DOT labels are those diamond-shaped symbolic labels that define the hazard class of the material being shipped. EPA regulations specify that this label (DOT marking) be placed on hazardous waste containers of less than 110 gallons:

HAZARDOUS WASTE

Federal Law Prohibits Improper Disposal.
If found, contact the nearest policy or public safety authority or the U.S. Environmental Protection Agency.

Generator name and address_____

_____

Manifest document no._____

Universal waste must be marked as follows:

BATTERIES

Universal Waste—Batteries
or
Waste Batteries
or
Used Batteries

---

and

THERMOSTATS

Universal Waste—Mercury Thermostats
or
Waste Mercury Thermostats
or
Used Mercury Thermostats

Hazardous waste containers must be labeled (per EPA; marked and labeled per DOT) *when they are offered for shipment*. This means when you are about to load them onto the truck or rail car. In storage, hazardous waste containers must have the words HAZARDOUS WASTE or else the specific contents clearly marked and visible on the container, as well as the accumulation start date, but the rest of the information does not have to be added until time of shipment.

How do you select the appropriate DOT label? Simple. The precise label required is specified in column 6 of the DOT Hazardous Materials Table (*49 CFR 172.101*). No other label will do. Buy them by the roll from label and sign supply catalogs. Apply one near the marking and place one on the opposite side of the drum, too.

If the contents of a container meet the definition of more than one hazard class, additional labels, called *subsidiary labels*, are placed next to the original label. In this case, the subsidiary labels must not bear the number of their hazard class. This is a rare situation and most of the time you will need only one hazard class label per drum. Bulk marking requirements are slightly different. On tank trucks and rail tanks the placard and the shipping papers serve as the marking. Do not remove, deface, destroy, or tamper with marking or labels or placards.

Shipping Papers

The EPA universal hazardous waste manifest, or state equivalent, satisfies the DOT requirement for shipping papers. Each hazardous waste manifest must have a unique five digit manifest document number. There are any number of ways to do this. Figure 10.5 offers a few suggestions, but not the end of the possibilities.

The most common method is the first one described, because of its simplicity. Many people get confused trying to figure out Julian dates or trying to figure which digits to drop from the standard date to get a five digit number. The advantage of the latter two schemes, though, is that if you have a consistent system of arriving at a unique five-digit number based on the date, you can always tell when the shipment was made without looking it up. However, this advantage is meaningless if your employees are confused by date schemes, and mistakes can be costly.

Although there would appear to be no excuse for getting the generator name, address, telephone number, and EPA I.D. number incorrect, these are common manifest mistakes. Double check, especially if others have prepared the manifest for you.

Also, double check the transporter's name and EPA I.D. number. Do not fill in transporter data beforehand. Sometimes, the TSDF does not select a contract carrier to send for your shipment until the last minute. A lot of manifests get ripped up because a different transporter showed up.

Double check the TSDF name, street address, telephone number, and EPA I.D. number. This information had better not change. Changing transporters at the last minute is one thing, but changing the TSDF is quite another.

You may list an alternate TSDF, but you must also state that the waste is to be returned to your facility, if undeliverable. The carrier may not haul your waste around the country looking for a home for it. He can only haul it to a specified location. Also, he can only hand it over to another carrier one time (which must be so indicated on the manifest) and that carrier must deliver to the TSDF specified on the manifest or return the waste to you.

Figure 10.5
Manifest Document Number

1. Use a sequential number from 1 to....

2. Use the date of shipment: for instance, a shipment date of March 4, 1997 would be 30471, while a shipment date of October 10, 2000 would be 10101. Occasionally these numbers could recur so change the last digit to a 2 if this should happen.

3. Use the Julian date for shipment: for instance the Julian date is the last digit of the year and the three digit number of the day of the year from 001 for January 1 to 365 for December 31 except in leap years. So, February 29, 1996 would give 60601 for instance. Like the last scheme this one repeats every ten years so make the last digit change by one. Of course manifest records only have to be kept for three years so does it matter?

New DOT regulations require that you list an emergency telephone number on the manifest. Some facilities, out of ignorance, are not taking this seriously. The emergency telephone number is supposed to ring to a place where emergency response authorities can get more information about a waste material involved in a transportation accident. As long as the waste shipment is between your facility and the TSDF, that telephone number must be a direct communication link with someone with specific knowledge about the waste.

Is your plant telephone number answered by a live person (no taped messages, voice mail, or pagers) 24-hours per day, 7-days per week?

If not, then do not list it as the emergency number.

If it is, are you or some other knowledgeable person available to answer questions at all times, until that waste is received at the TSDF?

If not, do not list it.

Unless you answer yes to both of these questions, you must find some other way to take care of the emergency telephone number listing.

Some facilities use the CHEMTREC number. This is not a number just anyone may use, however. It is not a number to some free government service. CHEMTREC is a private, fee paid service. You pay the fee; CHEMTREC provides the service. If you do not pay the fee, but use the number, they will deny knowing anything about your waste should the number be called by emergency officials. Therefore, you must contract your emergency telephone number, and, in order to answer questions about your waste during shipment, any emergency telephone service will need to receive a profile of each of your waste streams as well as any MSDSs associated with the waste or raw materials from which the waste is derived. Besides contract emergency numbers such as CHEMTREC, many TSDFs also provide emergency telephone service to their customers. They already have all the necessary information on their customers' waste streams, and they must provide emergency numbers for their own vehicles. So it is natural they would extend this emergency answering service to cover their customers, usually for an additional fee, but some even offer it as a free service.

Each time you or someone in your company signs a manifest, you certify that the materials being shipped have been properly classified, described, packaged, marked and labeled, and are in good condition for shipment, as each of these things are defined by EPA and DOT regulations. You are also certifying that you are making reasonable efforts to minimize the generation of these wastes. Just a reminder—you cannot claim ignorance when the inspector is at the door.

You must maintain manifests for three years (see the discussion on recordkeeping in Chapter 2). A complete manifest set should have one copy of the manifest signed by generator and transporter and another copy (the first page), which is the returned copy, signed by generator, transporter(s), and TSD facility operator who received the waste shipment. If you wish to save certificates of destruction or disposal and/or TSDF shipping papers/documents in addition to the required manifest, staple those documents behind the completed manifest set. Also, staple your landban documents for the shipment behind the manifest so they can be examined at the same time the manifests are.

If you ship universal waste or used oil, keep a record of each shipment sent off-site, in the form of a log, invoice, manifest or bill of lading. It need not be on a UHWM. In fact, never use a UWHM to ship only nonhazardous wastes or used oil. No regulation requires this; it is just bad form. However, the documentation used for universal waste and used oil must include the name and address of the originating facility, name and address of the destination facility, quantity of each type UW or used oil, and the dates shipped and received.

Do you ship hazardous waste to a foreign country? If you do, have you filed a notice of this activity with your state and the regional EPA administrator? This waste, too, must be manifested and signed by the foreign TSDF's designated cosignee, usually the exporting agent. However, besides getting the closure copy of the manifest returned to you, you should also receive a confirmation of delivered shipment from the TSDF, and attach this to your manifest record set. Exported waste must have a copy of the consent agreement sent with *each* shipment.

Placarding

You are responsible for offering the driver placards for over-the-road transportation. He or she does not have to accept them, but you must offer them. Companies that sell labels, markings, and signs from catalogs usually offer a set of disposable placards for a reasonable price. Typically, the truck has its own flip-placards which the driver can arrange for any placarding need. However, if he leaves your plant without proper placarding, the onus is on your company. Therefore, get a set of disposable cardboard placards and keep them in the hazardous waste storage or shipping dock, whichever is the more logical place in your situation. Some companies make the driver sign a form that she accepted or refused placards and which ones were offered/accepted. For rail shipments, placarding is the responsibility of the rail line.

A good idea, but not an absolute requirement, is to visit the transporter, if different from your TSDF, and observe operations at his or her transshipment point. Also, audit how she tracks your waste, from the time it leaves your plant to arrival and storage at the transshipment point, to ultimate delivery at the TSDF. Find out if he interlines—transfers shipments to other carrier lines—in order to make shipments more cost efficient. Remember, transporters can only interline once per manifested shipment. Preferably, your waste will not be interlined at all. Also, remember that transporters can only keep the waste for ten days at the transshipment terminal. Transporters cannot dispose, dilute, or treat hazardous waste, and must comply fully with DOT hazardous materials regulations.

DOT Hazardous Materials

The Hazardous Materials Transportation Uniform Safety Act (HMTUSA) of 1990 (P.L. 101-615) amended the Hazardous Materials Transportation Act (HMTA), which authorizes DOT to regulate the transportation of hazardous materials on the nations highways, rails, and seaways. A *hazardous material* is any substance or material that has been determined by DOT to be capable of posing an unreasonable risk to health, safety, and property when transported in commerce. The universe of DOT hazardous materials includes EPA hazardous wastes, but not all hazardous materials, as defined by DOT, are hazardous waste. For one thing, the hazardous material may not be a waste at all. Universal waste (UW)—the most recent waste category defined by EPA—is not recognized as hazardous waste under DOT regulations, but they are DOT hazardous materials.

A *hazardous material (hazmat) employer* is one who transports or causes hazardous materials to be transported in commerce. Hazardous waste generators are therefore hazmat employers. Drum reconditioners, and companies that test containers offered for transportation, are also defined as hazmat employers.

Hazmat employees are employed by hazmat employers and perform duties that directly affect the transportation safety of hazardous materials such as described in Figure 10.6:

Figure 10.6
Duties of HazMat Employees

load, unload or handle hazardous materials
recondition or test containers used in hazmat transportation
operate a hazmat transportation vehicle
prepare hazardous materials for transportation
oversee safety of hazardous materials transportation

Proper Shipping Names

Select proper shipping names from the DOT Hazardous Materials Table at 49 CFR 172.202, which gives the exact order of the proper shipping name string for the manifest. Do not use italicized words under the proper shipping name column in the table. The string is as follows: proper shipping name (technical or chemical group names in parentheses), hazard class as an Arabic numeral (1-9), UN/NA (United Nations/North American) number, and packing group as a Roman numeral (I-III). The technical or chemical group name, if applicable, may be included at the end of the string as an option. If one container holds a reportable quantity, then you should begin the string with the designation "RQ." Always separate each of the elements of the proper shipping name string by a comma.

Two things about proper shipping names. First, the DOT Hazardous Materials Table does not include every possibility, but it has enough generic categories to cover anything you might ship (with technical or chemical group name in parentheses). So, do not make up a proper shipping name because you cannot find your specific material in the table. The name must come from the table and be worded and punctuated *exactly as in the table*. Second, and this is extremely important, the choosing of the proper shipping name is your responsibility. Do not let anyone else choose it (someone else may give you advice) and *NEVER, EVER* let anyone change a proper shipping name on a manifest after you have shipped the hazardous waste. Some TSDFs think they know more about hazardous waste than their customers and are given to making changes. Change TSDFs instead!

Why? Do you ever claim *generator knowledge* concerning profiling or characterizing waste streams? Yes? Then no one but you is qualified to choose that proper shipping name. If you have manifests in your files with proper shipping names struck through and changed by someone at a TSDF, even if you agreed and made the changes on the generator copy, that is tantamount to saying you do not know your waste and now you must have TCLP and other necessary analyticals on file because your generator knowledge is definitely suspect, *tainted* as the attorneys would say. Secondly, DOT requires the shipper to choose the appropriate proper shipping name and part of DOT training is being able to fulfill all DOT requirements. If someone else chooses the proper shipping name, that is tantamount to saying your DOT training is inadequate, so now you must get to a DOT training course immediately to rectify the situation. Third, do not let TSDFs treat you in this manner. It is unprofessional and, in my opinion, calls their training and capabilities into serious question. Why did the TSDF not catch the problem during the profiling process? Fire them and get a new TSDF.

DOT Training

Hazmat employers must conduct DOT training and certify that their hazmat employees, as that term is defined by DOT, have been tested in one or more of the subject areas listed in Figure 10.7.

Who must be trained? DOT defines three training levels: 1) shipping supervisors, purchasing managers/agents, traffic managers, and plant managers; 2) shipping clerks, dispatchers, and distribution clerks; and 3) drivers, compliance managers, and packaging clerks.

The required scope of training depends on the degree with which the employee has direct contact with hazardous materials and shipping duties. Training must be repeated annually. Chapter 2 discussed how to document training.

Figure 10.7
DOT Training Topics

recognition and understanding of DOT hazmat classification
use and limitations of DOT placards, labels, markings
general hazmat handling to prevent incidents
health, safety, and risk associated with hazmat transportation
emergency response to hazmat incidents
emergency response communications procedures
use and limitations of DOT Emergency Response Guidebook
emergency response information resources
hazardous materials transportation regulations
personal protection techniques
preparation of shipping documents

SORTING THROUGH LAND DISPOSAL RESTRICTION NOTIFICATIONS

Perhaps one of the least understood aspects of hazardous waste management is the land disposal restrictions (LDR) or land bans. Everyone should understand, by now, that Congress intends that certain wastes shall not be managed in land units such as landfills, landfarms, and surface impoundments. The land bans were established by the Hazardous and Solid Waste Amendments (HSWA) of 1984. Congress required EPA to set treatment standards for all wastes, below which land disposal is authorized, and above which treatment to achieve the standards is required. Yet confusion reigns in the regulated community. Part of the misunderstanding derives from the "hammers" that Congress built into the law. In the past, Congress passed laws and EPA developed regulations to help the regulated community to apply the law to varying circumstances. Often, it takes EPA years to catch up to the intention of Congress, as stated in any particular law. In the LDR's of HSWA, Congress recognized EPA's backlog of work, and set compliance dates for the regulated community, irrespective of the status of EPA regulations. Figure 10.8 summarizes these hammer dates.

Figure 10.8
Land Ban Hammer Dates

dioxin/solvent wastes - 11/7/86
California list - 7/8/87
first-third wastes - 8/17/88
second-third wastes - 6/23/89
third-third wastes - 6/1/90

With the promulgation of treatment standards for the third-third wastes, nearly all hazardous wastes are now restricted and require treatment before land disposal. Since commercial TSDFs must also comply with LDRs, most provide notification and certification forms to their customers and assist them in determining which restrictions apply to which waste. Nevertheless, you should have a working understanding of the regulations yourself, since your company is always responsible for its wastes.

A generator must make a notification—and in two cases a certification —to the TSDF, regarding land disposal restrictions (LDR), with each shipment of hazardous waste. Not only must the notification accompany the shipment, but it must also contain information about the treatment standards for each waste in the shipment. If hazardous waste cannot be placed in a hole in the ground and forgotten about, what else can be done with it? Well, we can treat it somehow, so that it is safe to place in a hole in the ground. That is why we have LDR treatment standards.

If the waste offered to a TSDF has hazardous constituents at low enough concentration, or meets the measurements of certain characteristics, it is permissible to land dispose the waste without any treatment. Otherwise, we must destroy it, reuse it, recycle it, or render it land disposable by some treatment method. However, even though we may ship to a recycler or someone who will reuse the waste, we must make the LDR notification, because the constituents of concern could be passed on to a land unit in the residuals from the treatment or handling of the waste, and it is *your* duty to notify all subsequent handlers of those constituents and restrictions. The generator is responsible for the selection of treatment and disposal methods, which must follow all federal/state requirements for treatment, storage, and disposal. EPA established two forms of treatment standards: technology-based and concentration-based.

If your waste is hazardous at the initial point of generation, and appears in Table 2 at 40 CFR 268.42, a specific technology must be used as designated by a five letter acronym in the table. These wastes carry a treatment standard of a specified technology and, here, no analysis is required. As long as the waste was treated as specified, it is deemed suitable for land disposal.

Concentration-based standards work differently. Once your waste has been treated, the results from a TCLP must be less than the values in the constituent concentration in the waste extract (CCWE) table at Part 268.41 or, alternatively, the results from a toxicity characteristics analysis must be performed on the treatment residuals and compared to the values in the constituent concentration in the waste (CCW) table at Part 268.43. Waste codes, with treatment standards found in the CCW table, usually require some form of destruction as waste treatment. Waste codes, with treatment standards found in the CCWE table, typically require some form of immobilization. CCW and CCWE values represent performance-based treatment standards. This means that you can choose to treat the waste by any method so long as the residual, or the extract of the residual, yields an analytical value lower than the standard.

EPA chose these concentration limits based on the best demonstrated achievable technology (BDAT). However, any treatment suitable for a waste stream, not just the specific treatment technology that was deemed BDAT, can be used, so long as the end results are the same. Hence, a performance standard.

Two situations require you to complete an LDR certification, to accompany the manifest for your hazardous waste shipment. If your waste is a lab pack, managed under the exemption found at 40 CFR 268.42(c), and, if you choose to have the waste incinerated, you must sign a certification that the lab pack contains only organics or organometallic waste, as defined in the appendices of Part 268. If your hazardous waste already meets the LDR treatment standards, you must sign a certification to this effect.

Treatment technologies, whether BDAT or some other technology, generate some sort of residue. The residue may be in the form of a wastewater or some nonwastewater residue. Regardless, residues from RCRA listed wastes must meet the same treatment requirements, prior to land disposal, as the original waste did. Residue of characteristics waste is no longer hazardous, unless it exhibits a characteristic (ignitability, corrosivity, reactivity, or toxicity).

Figure 10.9 lists BDAT for ignitable wastes. Some of these technologies are discussed briefly below.

Incineration was discussed at length in Chapter 9 on hazardous waste management. Recycling and recovery hardly needs discussion. Ignitable liquids with sufficient BTU value can replace fuel (fuel substitution) in combustion operations. Certain restrictions apply, of course, on chlorine, sulfur, heavy metals, and other potential air pollutant precursors in the liquid. Deactivation of ignitable waste involves reducing the volatility of the liquid to the point that ignition occurs at a temperature greater than 140°F.

Figure 10.9
BDAT v. Ignitable Characteristic

Part 261.x Subcategory	BDAT
Ignitable Liquid [21(a)(1)]	Incineration Fuel Substitution Recovery (no dilution)
Ignitable Reactive [21(a)(2)]	Deactivation (no stabilization)
Ignitable Compressed Gas [21(a)(3)	Incineration Recycle
Oxidizer	Deactivation

BDAT for corrosive waste is given in Figure 10.10 and discussed below.

Neutralization of aqueous wastes to produce insoluble salts is no strange technology to you if you have a wastewater plant. Recovery of valuable products such as heavy metals can then be accomplished by a cascade of ever finer filters. Deactivation can be any process that renders the corrosion rate less than 6.34 mpy.

Figure 10.10
BDAT v. Corrosivity Characteristic

Part 261.x Subcategory	BDAT
Aqueous Acid Waste [22(a)(1)]	Neutralization/insoluble salts Recovery
Aqueous Alkaline Waste [22(a)(1)]	Neutralization/insoluble salts Recovery
Non-aqueous Corrosives [22(a)(2)]	Deactivation [meet SAE 1020] steel corrosion rate <6.34 mpy

Treatment standards for the reactive characteristic are listed in Figure 10.11. The treatment of cyanides and sulfides is the same as discussed in Chapter 8 on wastewater treatment. Wet air oxidation is the aqueous phase oxidation of material at elevated temperature and pressure, to maintain water in the liquid phase. Electrolytic oxidation takes place at a higher temperature and is followed by alkaline chlorination with chlorinated hydrocarbons. Deactivation of reactives usually involves explosion or reaction, after which the material is safe.

Figure 10.11
BDAT v. Reactive Characteristic

Part 261.x Subcategory	BDAT
Reactive Cyanides [23(a)(5)]	Electrolytic Oxidation plus Alkaline Chlorination
	Wet-air Oxidation
Reactive Sulfides [23(a)(5)]	Alkaline Chlorination plus precipitation of insoluble sulfides
	Chemical Oxidation + precip.
	Incineration
Explosives [23]	Deactivation
Water Reactives	Deactivation
Other Reactives	Deactivation
Organics/Hydrazine	Thermal Destruction (non-wastewater)
	Incineration
	Chemical Oxidation + precip. (wastewater)
Metallics	Recovery
Fluorine Compounds	Recovery

Treatment of toxic metals, as listed in Figure 10.12, uses processes similar to wastewater treatment for liquid waste streams. Alternatively, some metals may be immobilized.

Immobilization is the rendering of a hazardous constituent unleachable, or at least, less leachable. Therefore, immobilization techniques reduce the rate of release of the metal into the environment. Two techniques commonly used are solidification and stabilization which render a liquid or sludge into a solid, reduce the solubility of the contaminant(s), and/or decrease the surface area of the waste (thus decreasing the mass transfer area). Solidification may be accomplished by microencapsulation of fine particles or macroencapsulation of large blocks of waste material.

Figure 10.12
BDAT v. Toxic Metals

Part 261.24 Subcategory	BDAT
Arsenic	Alkaline Precipitation (wastewater)
	Chemical Oxidation (organoarsenicals)
Barium	Acidified Precipitation
Cadmium	Chemical Precipitation (wastewater)
	Stabilization (non-wastewater)
	Recovery (non-wastewater)
Chromium	Reduction plus Precipitation
	Sludge Dewatering
Lead	Reduction + Precipitation (wastewater)
	Sludge Dewatering (non-wastewater)
	Incineration + Stabilization ($\geq 2.5\%$)
	Stabilization
	Thermal Recovery ($\leq 2.5\%$)
	Direct Encapsulation ($\leq 2.5\%$)
	Surface Deactivation ($\leq 2.5\%$)
	Surface Removal ($\leq 2.5\%$)

Figure 10.12 *(cont'd)*

Part 261.24 Subcategory	BDAT

Mercury
: Chemical Precipitation
Roasted + Retorted (non-wastewater)
Incineration
Acid Leaching (< 16 mg/kg)
Chemical Oxidation + Dewatering
Amalgamation with Zinc

Selenium
: Alkaline Precipitation (wastewater)
Chemical Oxidation (organoseleniums)

Silver
: Chemical Precipitation (wastewater)
Stabilization (nonwastewater)

The BDAT for pesticides, as shown in Figure 10.13, is incineration.

Figure 10.13
BDAT v. Toxic Pesticides

Part 261.24 Subcategories	BDAT
Endrin	Incineration
Lindane	Incineration
Methoxychlor	Incineration
Toxaphene	Incineration
2,4-D	Incineration
2,4,5-TP (silvex)	Incineration

CONCLUSION

If you learn one lesson about shipping hazardous waste from this chapter, it is hopefully this: the shipment of hazardous waste from your door to its final resting place is a joint venture between you, the transporter, and the TSDF and the three of you bear a great responsibility for protecting the public welfare, *ad infinitum*.

REFERENCES

Daugherty, Jack E. "Shipping Hazardous Materials without Fear." *Occupational Hazards*. January 1995.

Min, Muang, Richard Barbour and Jou Hwang. "Land Ban Technologies, Impacts and Implications." *Pollution Engineering*. July 1991.

----. "Treating Land Ban Waste." *Pollution Engineering*. August 1991.

Schenk, John P. "Transportation of Hazardous Materials Requires Compliance with P.L. 101-615." *Occupational Health & Safety*. November 1991.

Tidwell, John. "Waste Wise: Focus on Land Disposal Restrictions." *Texas Engineering Extension Service EnviroLetter*. Edition 94-1. January 1994.

11

PREVENTING ENVIRONMENTAL DISASTERS

In this chapter we will discuss some of the regulations and laws aimed at protecting the public from environmental disasters of an imminently dangerous nature. In the next chapter we will discuss cleaning up chronic problems (Superfund cleanups for instance), but here we will concern ourselves with those situations that rivet the public to the news media for days or weeks.

TOXIC SUBSTANCE CONTROL ACT

The President's Council on Environmental Quality offered a bill to Congress in 1971 to deal with the increasing problem of toxic substances that present a risk of significant harm to the public. For instance, tens of millions of pounds of PCBs (polychlorinated biphenyls) had been produced and released to the environment before anyone knew they were both persistent and potentially toxic. Suddenly, PCBs were found in human bodies and in the milk of nursing mothers. Congress held endless public hearings and debates on the issue. The Toxic Substances Control Act (TSCA) was passed into law in 1976 and is found at 15 U.S.C. 2601-71 as amended. TSCA gives EPA broad authority to regulate the manufacture, use in manufacture, importation, distribution, end use, and disposal of chemical substances that present substantial risk of injury to public health or the environment and to levy criminal and civil sanctions. This law gives EPA authority to gather basic information on chemical risks from those who would offer them for distribution in commerce and includes the authority to place bans and restrictions on use or production of a chemical substance. Restrictions include requiring hazard-warning labels right up to a complete ban on the manufacture of the substance. EPA may regulate any stage in the life of a chemical substance from manufacture to end use. The Asbestos Hazard Emergency Response Act

(AHERA) amended TSCA in 1986 adding a title which dealt with asbestos in schools. Another amendment was the Deadline Deferral of Asbestos Plans in 1988. Also in 1988 the Indoor Radon Abatement Act added a title to the law. The Asbestos School Hazard Abatement Reauthorization Act of 1990 (ASHARA) updated the asbestos title of TSCA and a new title was again added by the Lead Exposure Reduction Act of 1992 (LERA). As amended, the titles of TSCA are summarized in Figure 11.1.

Figure 11.1
Toxic Substance Control Act

Title I - Control of Toxic Substances
Title II - Asbestos Hazard Emergency Response
Title III - Indoor Radon Abatement
Title IV - Lead Exposure Reduction

TSCA, with respect to other environmental laws, closes the loop on the regulation on control of contaminations in the environment. Figure 11.2 illustrates in a simple way how each major law pertains to protection of the environment.

The impact of TSCA is far reaching, much farther reaching than many compliance managers realize. If you take a poll at any gathering of environmental professionals, with the possible exception of a TSCA or chemical health effects symposium, you will most likely find fewer than a handful who know anything about TSCA, other than its name. Of those who claim to know something, chances are that they will discuss PCBs or asbestos or lead or radon or a combination of these, but it is doubtful that they will otherwise consider themselves regulated under this law. In fact, TSCA pertains to almost every single industrial facility in one way or another and besides the huge fines that any environmental law can boast of, TSCA has the teeth to shut down your operations.

Figure 11.2
Closing the Loop on Chemicals

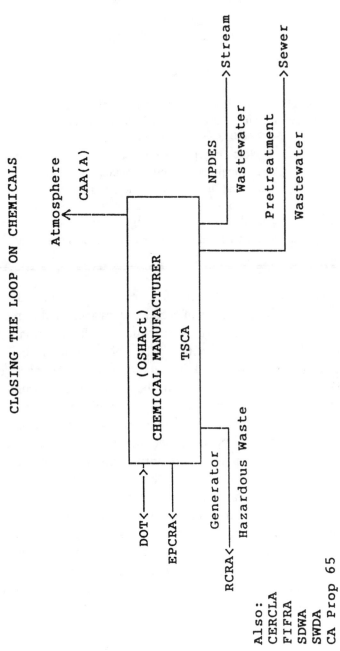

Figure 11.3 summarizes the major provisions of Title I.

Figure 11.3
Major Provisions of TSCA Title I

(Section - Subject)

4 - Testing for health and environmental effects.
5 - Establishment of chemical substance inventory.
6 - Regulate existing toxic chemicals.
8 - Recordkeeping and reporting.
8(c) - Significant adverse reactions.
8(d) - EPA call in health and safety studies.
8(e) - Substantial risk notification.
12 - Export notification and testing requirements.
13 - Import certification requirements and exclusions.

TSCA authorizes EPA to obtain data from industry regarding the production, use, and health effects of chemical substances and to regulate the manufacture, processing, and distribution of those substances to protect the public health and welfare. The objective of the law is to characterize and understand the risks posed by chemical substances before they are introduced into commerce. All the other major environmental laws are after the fact. They deal with controlling air emissions, wastewater discharges, solid waste, or releases of hazardous substances. TSCA pertains to what is happening, not only in your processes, but in your research and development laboratory. This law allows EPA to balance the common good (through evaluation of economic and social benefits of a chemical substance and its known risks) against your desire to produce, use, import, distribute, or dispose of the substance.

A chemical substance, according to TSCA, is any organic or inorganic substance or any combination of such substances, whether anthropogenic or natural, whether elemental or uncombined radical or complex molecule. Pesticides are not included as they are controlled by the Federal Insecticide, Fungicide, and Rodenticide Act (FIFRA). Tobacco and tobacco products are not included. Nuclear material is excluded as it is already controlled by the Nuclear Regulatory Agency (NRA). Firearms and ammunition are regulated by the Internal Revenue Service (IRS) and the Alcohol, Tobacco, and Firearms Agency (ATF). Any food, food additive, drug, drug additive, cosmetic or cosmetic additive or cosmetic device is the bailiwick of the Federal Food, Drug, and Cosmetic Act (FFDCA). Only those chemical substances that pose an *unreasonable* risk are subject to regulatory action by EPA; however, EPA, not the manufacturer or user of the substance, decides what unreasonable means.

TSCA covers not only the manufacturing of chemicals—as most people probably visualize when they think of TSCA—but also covers processors and distributors, including importers and exporters. The *processing* of chemicals is a jurisdiction of TSCA that is hard to understand. Processing is the repackaging, preparing or otherwise processing of a chemical substance. Many industrial plants—including those that manufacture metal parts or consumer goods—do not see themselves as chemical processors. They see themselves as machinists or bottlers or sewing plants, or anything other than a chemical processor. Let's take a closer look at processing as defined by TSCA.

Any person who receives a chemical substance, from manufacturer, distributor, or importer and distributes it in the same form as received is a *repackager*. If he distributes the chemical substance in a different form as received he has *prepared* the chemical substance. An industry would *otherwise process* a chemical substance if it distributes it as part of an article.

EPA Processor Example 1. Suppose a person reacts chemicals X and Y to produce a new chemical Z. She is a processor of X and Y and a manufacturer of Z.

EPA Processor Example 2. A person who purchases or manufactures chemicals and then mixes or reacts them is a processor of each chemical, if the mixtures or compounds are distributed in commerce. Some real life processors, which come under this example, are blenders of paints, antifreeze, oil additives, specialty cleaning compounds, and floor wax preparations.

EPA Processor Example 3. A person who heats and mixes powdered resins, fillers, pigments, and plasticizers to form a homogeneous mix, which is then formed into sheets of a desired thickness, would be a processor of each component because the components are distributed in commerce as part of an article. In real life, tire manufacturers, and manufacturers of rubber and plastic articles are processors.

EPA Processor Example 4. A person who purchases steel cans and then coats the cans with a resin would be a processor of the resin, since the resin is now part of an article, which is distributed in commerce. Canneries, textile mills, furniture plants, tanneries, or others who apply urethanes or other resin coatings onto substrates are TSCA processors. A person who purchases printing ink and then applies the ink to paper or boxes would then be a processor of the ink, which has become part of an article distributed in commerce. Newspaper and magazine printers are among the persons regulated.

EPA was required by TSCA to develop a chemical inventory, which it did in May 1979. Anything meeting the definition of a chemical substance, newly manufactured, processed, or distributed since then, or newly reported since then, even if it was already manufactured, processed, or distributed, is considered new. As of July 1, 1979, new chemical substances are subject to a process called Premanufacture Notification (PMN). New chemicals are added to the inventory only when the PMN is complete and manufacturing begins. EPA has the authority to prohibit the manufacturing, processing, or distribution of a chemical substance it deems unsafe from a public health and welfare viewpoint. Besides the chemical substances exempted because they are regulated elsewhere, Figure 11.4 lists some PMN exemptions.

Figure 11.4
PMN Exemptions

byproducts not used commercially
reaction products resulting from incidental contact
reaction products incidental to storage and disposal
reaction products resulting from end use
reaction products formed while manufacturing an article
reaction products from physical actions
nonisolated intermediates

Figure 11.5 illustrates the PMN procedure. The PMN must be complete and approved by EPA before manufacturing may begin. The PMN itself is a standard EPA form (7710-25) which for purposes of discussion has three sections to be completed by the applicant. Part I contains general information such as identification of the submitter, chemical substance identity information and production, import and use information.

Figure 11.5
Premanufacturing Notice Procedure

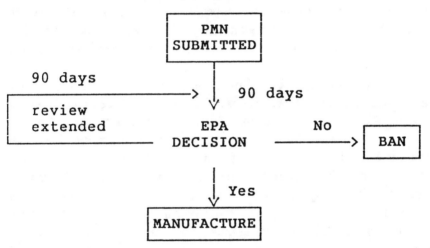

Part II requires the reporting of human exposure and environmental release information. This means a complete description of the planned operation, its physical location, production rates, flow diagram of production, identity and quantity of each feedstock material, and identity of points of release to the environment. You must identify to workers any activities which would expose them to the chemical substance, including how many workers will be in this situation, and list any protective equipment they will be wearing and how long the exposure will last. You must estimate and report the amount of material released into each media (air, water, soil) and what control technology, if any, you plan to use. You must include a description of efforts taken or planned to reduce or minimize potential risks associated with manufacturing, processing, using, and disposing of the PMN substance. This includes pollution prevention activities, recycling, etc. The narrative should include the expected net benefits of these activities such as an overall reduction in risk to human health or the environment, reduction in volume manufactured, a reduction in the generation of waste materials, a reduction in the potential toxicity or human exposure or environmental release, an increase in product performance, an increase in operational efficiency compared to the operational efficiency of some similar production unit, etc. Part II is completed for sites controlled by the submitter and sites controlled by others.

Part III is a list of attachments such as chemical and physical property information or test data, health aspects, and any other information the submitter feels is pertinent to the application to list this chemical substance on the inventory. EPA has ninety days to review PMNs for new chemicals and significant new uses, but this period can be extended for an additional 90 days for good cause.

What is substantial risk to human health? According to EPA it is a risk of considerable concern because of the seriousness of the potential effect and the fact or probability of its occurrence. Any risk that is potentially serious to human health is considered by EPA to be significant enough that possible human exposure factors are assumed to be relatively insignificant. That means that the burden of proof is on industry— according to EPA, the mere fact that a dangerous chemical is in commerce is sufficient proof of risk of exposure on their part. The serious health effects EPA is considering under TSCA are cancer, mutagenicity, teratogenicity, birth defects, neurotoxicity, serious or prolonged incapacitation, and death.

What is substantial risk to the environment? Here, at least, EPA looks at more than whether the chemical substance is in commerce. It attempts to determine whether there can be a significant level of exposure to the environment. What are the production levels of the chemical substance? Is it persistent in the environment or biodegradable? How will it be used? Where? By whom? What means of disposal is anticipated?

When EPA identifies a chemical substance that warrants close scrutiny, but does not warrant prohibition based on available information it issues a significant new use rule (SNUR) for the chemical substance in which it specifies prohibited activities if needed based on anticipated extent and type of exposure to humans and the environment, and delineates approved activities and data requirements before new activities with the chemical substance can be approved. Any person intending to manufacture, import, or process a chemical for such a significant new use must notify EPA no earlier than 90 days before the planned activity, even if the chemical is already on the inventory and went through PMN review, so EPA can evaluate the situation. Figure 11.6 lists chemical substances with SNURs. You are referred to the regulations for further definition of the terms used in this figure.

Figure 11.6
SNUR Chemicals

Disubstituted Diamino Unusual
Substituted Polyglycidyl Benzeneamine
1,2-Benzenediamine-4-Ethoxy Sulfate
Benzoic Acid 3,3'-Methylenebis[6 Amino Di-2-Propenyl] Ester
Dicarboxylic Acid Monoester
Hexachloronorbornadiene
Hexamethylphosphoramide
Isopropylamine Distillation Residues
Ethylamine Distillation Residues
Potassium N,N-bis (Hydroxyethyl) Cocoamine Oxide Phosphate
Potassium N,N-bis (Hydroxyethyl) Tallowamine Oxide Phosphate
Substituted Methylpyridine
Substituted 2-Phenoxypyridine
Derivative of Tetrachloroethylene
Urethane
Metalworking Fluids
Polychlorinated Biphenyls (PCB)
Fully Halogenated Chlorofluoroalkanes (CFC)
Asbestos

EPA has the authority under TSCA to require the submission of data from any or all of the tests summarized in Figure 11.7. It is unusual for EPA to require all these tests, though over period of time any of these requirements may be called in by EPA, for one reason or another. TSCA allows companies to cooperate in conducting the tests and companies that actually perform the tests (which may run into the millions of dollars worth of scientific research and testing) may expect remuneration from companies that would like to use the data in order to avoid remuneration.

Figure 11.7
TSCA Testing Requirements

Environmental Fate Data
Spectra (UV, visible, infrared)
density of liquids and solids
water solubility
melting point/range
boiling point/range
vapor pressure
partition coefficient, n-octanol/water
biodegradation
hydrolysis v. pH
photochemical degradation
adsorption/desorption to soil types
dissociation constant
other chemical/physical properties

Health Effects Data
Mutagenicity
Carcinogenicity
Teratogenicity
Acute Toxicity
Repeated Dose Toxicity
Metabolism Studies
Sensitization
Irritation of Skin/Eyes

Environmental Effects Data
Microbial and Algal Toxicity
Terrestrial Vascular Plant Toxicity
(seed germination, growth inhibition, etc.)
Acute and Chronic Toxicity to Animals
(fish, birds, mammals, invertebrates)

Figure 11.7 *(cont'd)*

Risk Assessment

Structure/Activity Relationships

Test Data Not in Possession or Control of Submitter

Miscellaneous Tests
Behavior Modification
Synergisms
Hematoxicity
Hepatotoxicity
Nephrotoxicity testing

If EPA determines, for instance, that a PMN has insufficient information to evaluate potential risk, it may prohibit the manufacture or importation of the chemical until adequate data are developed. The submitter has no deadlines to meet but cannot ignore EPA's ban until it has submitted the required data and EPA has used its 180 day extended review period without comment. Any data that is available in specified scientific literature or EPA reports is acceptable but must be photocopied and submitted with the PMN, not merely cited. Specific testing requirements are imposed after a rulemaking proceeding which gives both sides the opportunity to state its case in oral presentation, but which also allows public input on the issue.

TSCA Section 4 also gives EPA authority to require other reports from regulated industries. The PMN application and its supporting documentation is a given, as is SNUR documentation. EPA can also make a general data collection from all manufacturers, processors, and distributors of a chemical substance when adding it to the inventory. This is called a *general data call in* and anyone who wants to do anything with this chemical substance is now obligated to respond to EPA before proceeding. EPA has used its TSCA reporting authority to obtain production, use, release, and exposure data on a number of chemicals. EPA can also call in specific health and safety studies from manufacturers or research laboratories. TSCA also puts some reporting and recordkeeping obligations other than PMN and SNUR on the regulated community. For instance, whenever any evidence of a substantial risk to workers, the public, or the environment is identified in connection with a chemical substance, a Substantial Risk Notification, Section 8(e), must be filed with EPA. A file documenting discovery of the risk and supporting information from the investigation and report preparation must be maintained by the report filer. A general data call in is usually triggered by a Substantial Risk Notification. If not a general call in then a specific call in for sure.

A manufacturer, processor, or distributor who identifies a potential significant adverse reaction to health or the environment caused by a chemical substance is required to maintain records on the discovery and any subsequent incidents and supporting documentation for 30 years. This is a recordkeeping requirement only, not a report. What is a significant adverse reaction? It is any long-lasting or irreversible damage to human health. EPA has inspection rights under TSCA which are not unlike those of OSHA and if one of the employees should mention that he has been complaining to the company for some time about these health problems he has been having the employer had better be able to produce a Significant Adverse Reaction file. EPA's TSCA authority overlaps with OSHA jurisdiction but EPA and OSHA have a memorandum of understanding that OSHA will handle the compliance issue with respect to the workers. EPA will still want to see that file. OSHA requires that the adverse effects on the health of an employee be documented in his or her personal medical record. So being in compliance with the TSCA requirement will not be enough to be in compliance with OSHAct, and vice versa, although it is a simple matter of making copies of information for two different files.

Under TSCA, EPA has the authority to prohibit the manufacture, processing, and distribution of any chemical substance which poses an unreasonable risk or substantial threat to public health and welfare or to the environment. Over the years EPA has issued just six such prohibitions which are listed in Figure 11.8.

One writer on the subject of TSCA made a statement not unlike one attributed to a Japanese admiral right after the infamous attack on Pearl Harbor, who said, "I fear we have awakened the giant."

Figure 11.8
Banned Chemical Substances

Pose An Unreasonable Risk

- Asbestos in schools and recently in public buildings
- TCDD - TetraChloroDibenzoDioxin or just Dioxin
- CFC - ChloroFluoroCarbons such as FREON ® 113
- PCB - PolyChlorinated Biphenyls such as AROCHLOR ®
- Indoor Radon which is a naturally occurring radioactive gas
- Lead in paint

COMMUNITY RIGHT-TO-KNOW

Despite the fact that TSCA enforcement penalties reach new heights each year, industry has largely been blissfully ignorant of the sleeping TSCA giant for two decades. In the mid-eighties, media coverage of the Bhopal, India incident rattled some cages and industry, especially the one involved, responded slowly and in a disorganized fashion. Then, to add insult to injury, a near miss occurred with the same deadly chemical in Institute, West Virginia! Congress let down its biggest hammer yet by adding the Emergency Planning and Community Right-to-know Act (EPCRA) to the Superfund amendments it had under consideration at the time. EPCRA is Title III of the Superfund Amendments and Reauthorization Act (SARA) of 1986.

SARA TITLE III OVERVIEW

Whatever you think about SARA Title III (EPCRA), keep in mind that people (you too, if you are honest with yourself) do not want a secret time bomb in their community, especially in mixed industrial/residential neighborhoods. Some industrial managers buried their heads in the sand and blamed the Bhopal incident on the lack of training and competence at a foreign operation. Wholesale defamation of the Indian nation in general and the Indian chemical industry in particular occurred in trade journals. It will never happen in the United States "where process safety is practiced as well as preached," the articles claimed. The Institute Incident totally destroyed that argument, did it not? At the very least, the incident lowered the credibility of the American chemical process industry. Although EPA already had all the authority it needed to deal with the problem under TSCA, Congress was in a tampering mood—so, we have SARA III, or EPCRA if you would prefer. However, as you will see below, SARA III does much more than regulate industry—it requires communities to prepare themselves for chemical disaster in the factory or on the highway, railway or seaway by advanced planning.

Section 311

Congress wanted to ensure that emergency planning bodies called for in EPCRA had the cooperation of industry, so it required each facility in any of twenty Standard Industrial Classification (SIC) codes to designate an Emergency Coordinator whose functions include cooperating with the local emergency planning committee. Section 311 requires each facility to name this person in writing in a letter to the committee. Also, the committee, the local fire department, and the state emergency response commission were to have received a list of materials for which a Section 312 report would be due, by October 17, 1987. Many of these organizations requested copies of the Material Safety Data Sheets (MSDSs), not just a list.

Section 312

Each year, on March 1, every facility is required to submit a Section 312 report, called a Tier I or Tier II, depending on the exact form used. The Tier I/II goes to the local emergency planning committee, the local fire department, and the state emergency response commission. The report lists chemical products stored on-site in greater than threshold quantities listed in EPA regulations.

Section 313

Each year, on July 1, every facility is required to submit Section 313 reports, called Form Rs, to the EPA and state emergency response commission. These reports quantify the annual emissions of certain hazardous materials (listed in EPA regulations) to all media.

PROCESS SAFETY MANAGEMENT AND ACCIDENTAL RELEASE PREVENTION

An industrial facility is accountable to the public for its operations. Some states have a less litigious climate but nowhere in these United States would the citizenry turn the other cheek after a serious incident. In fact, you and your management might want to consider retiring to the Mediterranean or Caribbean if you can make it to a portal of exit before the EPA enforcement officer finds you.

Suffice it to say the American public demands safe industrial neighbors. They have a right to expect you to be reasonably safe and responsible. For the most part, American industry *is* safe and responsible but there have been, are, and will be some who, for expediency's sake, will cut safety corners to save dollars. They're a very rare breed nowadays but some are still out there. Because they are, the rest of us must abide by the laws that were written to force them to act responsibly. The *Emergency Planning and Community Right-to-Know Act* (EPCRA) was passed into law as Title III of the Superfund Amendments and Reauthorization Act (SARA) of 1986. The Clean Air Act Amendments of 1990 put some more process safety requirements on us as an OSHA standard on Process Safety had earlier.

Safety Techniques and Control Methods

The probability of explosion is minimized by venting or isolation. An explosion vent relieves the buildup of pressure by blowing out to the atmosphere. Explosion isolation arrests, diverts, or extinguishes flames to prevent the pressure wave from spreading. Flame arresters are used in process lines and vessels to prevent flames, once formed, from traveling in a direction which would lead to a worsened situation. For instance, flame arresters are installed on the atmosphere side of vents on atmospheric-pressure storage vessels in order to prevent a flame, caused by the leak through the vent of an ignitable vapor, from traveling back through the vent and igniting the vapor inside, thus turning the vessel into a huge bomb. Anywhere there is a possible discharge of ignitable vapor through a pipe or vent leading back to a pool of liquid supplying more ignitable vapor, a flame arrestor is indicated. The gas environment in which the flame arrestor is located in critical and materials of construction must be selected for the worst case with respect to corrosivity. A short pipe (less than five pipe diameters in length) may be added to the flame arrestor on the side away from the vessel being protected in order to divert burning vapors away from the side of the vessel. These arresters can stop a deflagration but not a detonation. A *deflagration* is an explosion that has a flame speed something less than the speed of sound whereas a *detonation* flame has a speed exceeding the speed of sound. In-line flame arresters must be capable of stopping both deflagrations and detonations. Therefore these devices are built with considerable structural strength.

The worst case condition for combustible mixtures of air and ignitable vapor is a concentration which is 10-20 percent richer than stoichiometric. Near stoichiometry, a flame can be either a deflagration or a detonation. Some flame properties are given in Figure 11.9.

Figure 11.9
Flame Properties of Various Gases

Gas	Burning Velocity, cm/sec	Quench Diameter, mm
Hydrogen	312	
Methane	40	3.5
Propane	46	2.5
Butane	45	2.5
Ethylene	80	
Propylene	52	

Electrical equipment rooms located inside areas where flammable materials are present should be constructed with a vapor-tight solid wall with a preference to precast concrete. Openings in walls, floor, and ceiling should be sealed to prevent air infiltration. Door closers should be able to operate against positive room pressure. Ventilation for electrical equipment rooms in high fire hazard areas should maintain a minimum of

0.1 iwg positive room pressure. The capture velocity of the ventilation system should be 60 fpm with air ducted from outside the hazard area with a twenty-five foot high intake where heavier-than-air flammables are in use and at ground level if lighter-than-air flammables are in use. Use good engineering judgment where both heavier- and lighter-than-air flammables are present. A continuous combustible gas monitoring system is recommended with one sensor placed at the fresh air intake port.

Characterizing Accidental Releases

When a pool of flammable liquid burns, it does so at a predictable rate:

$$\dot{y} = \dot{y}_{max}(1 - e^{-kd}) \qquad [11.1]$$

where

    $\dot{y}$ = burn-down rate, ft/sec,
    $\dot{y}_{max}$ = burning velocity, ft/sec,
    d = diameter of pool, ft, and
    k = extinction coefficient, ft^{-1}.

Burn-down can also be calculated in mass terms.

$$\dot{y}\rho = \dot{m} = (\Delta h_c / \Delta h_v) \times 10^{-3} \qquad [11.2]$$

Here, Δh_c is the lower heat of combustion and Δh_v is the latent heat of evaporization. This equation applies when the boiling point of the liquid is less than ambient temperature. When the boiling point is greater than ambient,

$$\dot{m} = [\Delta h_c / (\Delta h_v + \Delta T C_p)] \times 10^{-3} \qquad [11.3]$$

where

    ΔT = temperature difference between that of the liquid and its boiling point, and

C_p = heat capacity.

The burning rate of a liquid will be greater on water than on a solid surface such as concrete or soil. The reason is that water readily transfers heat back to the pool, increasing the rate. Total heat from a fire is calculated as

$$Q = \dot{m} A_{pool} \Delta h_c \qquad\qquad [11.4]$$

with five to ten percent deducted for incomplete combustion.

For an uncontained spill, the diameter of the pool that is formed will increase until the burning rate matches the release rate and equilibrium is established. At this condition, the release rate will be:

$$\dot{v}_L = \frac{\pi d 2 \dot{y}}{4} \qquad\qquad [11.5]$$

assuming the predominant source of heat is from the flame and not from the land or water. Therefore, it is inaccurate for spills of liquefied gases on water. A transient inaccuracy, for the first few minutes, may be expected for spills of liquefied gases on land.

Assuming the fire is circular, the height of the flame that will be reached is

$$H/d = 42 \left[\frac{\dot{m}}{\rho_a \sqrt{gd}} \right]^{0.61} \qquad\qquad [11.6]$$

The angle of flame tilt from the vertical in relationship to the wind velocity is

$$\cos\theta = 1, for U^* < 1$$
$$\cos\theta = \frac{1}{\sqrt{U^*}}, for U^* \geq 1 \qquad\qquad [11.7]$$

where

$$U^* = \frac{U_w}{[(g \dot{m} d)/\rho_a]^{1/3}} \qquad [11.8]$$

U_w is the actual wind velocity and U^* is a nondimensional velocity. Flame drag is the extension of the base of the flame downwind from the pool with the upwind edge and the body of the flame intact. As you might imagine, flame drag is highly dependent on wind speed as seen in this model:

$$\frac{d'}{d} = [\frac{U_w^2}{gd}]^{0.069} [\frac{\rho_a}{\rho_b}]^{0.48} \qquad [11.9]$$

Radiant heat transfer is limited by the view factor but for planning purposes, assume the view factor is 1 (100% of radiant heat is transfer in the direction of observation). The transfer of heat by the radiation mechanism is also limited by the emissivity of the flame. Fortunately, emissivities are almost always one or close to it. Bagster and Pitblado have calculated the energy released from a flame based on its temperature allowing for emissivity and found.

Flame Temperature, R	Heat, kW/m³
1,150	99.2
1,450	250

In fact, Mudan found that the energy release is pretty constant for some hydrocarbons, being about 42 kW/m² for JP-4, JP-5 and gasoline fires where the flame is 80 percent obscured by black smoke.

Estimating Dispersion

When a release to the environment occurs, the potential hazardous events, in sequence, are:

- vapor generation
- vapor dispersion
- explosion/BLEVE/fire

The potential for vapor generation exists when any liquid is released from a container. Whether or not a significantly dangerous vapor cloud will develop depends on these factors:

- amount and type of fluid
- pressure and temperature of fluid just prior to release
- percent of liquid that flashes to vapor
- liquid entrainment or aerosol formation
- degree of spill confinement
- weather conditions during release
- local terrain

Vapor may be generated from a single-phase release of gas or liquid or from a two-phase release of a liquid flashing to vapor. The rate of generation for a single-phase gas-phase release is merely the gas release rate. How many cubic feet per minute are exiting containment? For a liquid-phase release below its boiling point, the vapor pressure, which is temperature dependent, indicates the release rate.

If a liquid that is hotter than its boiling point is released, some of it will flash to vapor, resulting in a high vaporization rate and two-phase flow. Liquid that does not flash will cool to its equilibrium temperature at atmospheric pressure. Pressure/enthalpy characteristics and the temperature of the liquid just prior to release determine the fraction that is flashed to vapor. However, rapid formation and expansion of vapor causes some of the liquid to atomize and the entrainment of these droplets in the vapor results in an increase in the flash fraction.

Accumulated liquid from a release immediately starts to vaporize due to the transfer of heat from the surroundings (soil, water, structures) and mass transfer. The rate of vaporization depends on properties such as the latent heat of vaporization, the surface conditions, and the weather. While a liquid is being heated and vaporized, the spill surface is being cooled, decreasing the rate of heat transfer. Therefore, most of the vapor generation is at the beginning of the spill, assuming no flame or other heat source is present. This is why the vaporization rate is strongly dependent on surface type. A spill on water is very different than a spill on concrete. A spill on a wood floor is different than a spill on concrete is different than a spill on soil.

Convective heat transfer from the wind and radiative transfer from the sun add to the vaporization potential though the contribution is typically minimal compared to the conductive heat input from the spill surface. These heat inputs become dominant, however, once the spill surface has been chilled by evaporation. For liquefied gases the spill may remain at boiling temperature until the spill completely boils away or, if the heat input is very low, the spill will evaporate by virtue of mass transfer. Mass transfer is the usual and prime driving force for ordinary flammable liquids, such as gasoline.

Two components of atmospheric motion are important in dispersion of vapor clouds: average bulk movement (average wind velocity) and turbulence. These factors are not completely separable. Turbulence is the chief driving force for the lateral and vertical dispersion of vapor. The rate of dispersion is directly proportional to the degree of turbulence. Physical obstructions in the path of wind flow (buildings, hills, tree lines) cause *mechanical turbulence. Thermal turbulence* is caused by heating of the atmosphere at the earth's surface by the sun.

Another important atmospheric factor is the adiabatic lapse rate. See the chapter on Air Pollution Control for a complete discussion. Vapor cloud modeling is the same for emergencies as it is for routine emissions. However, some companies offer real time models that allow you to plug in observed weather conditions, release rate, and release material to get a printout of the predicted vapor cloud. These models are very expensive and not necessary for many industries, though large chemical manufacturing complexes ought to have the capability. Certainly, local emergency planning committees and emergency response authorities ought to have a real time model.

Relief Valves

Pressure safety valves protect equipment and piping from buildup of pressures exceeding maximum allowable working pressure. Equipment that can be completely isolated by cutoff valves need relief valves to protect them from external fires or runaway exothermic reactions. This is the root cause of the Seveso incident. Where the open vent or overflow of a vessel is of such size or length to cause pressure buildup in a runaway exothermic reaction, a relief valve is needed. When the cold side of a heat exchanger can be isolated while the hot side continues to flow, a pressure safety valve is required. Place a relief valve after each pressure-reduction valve in a piping system. Also use one where the maximum discharge pressure of a pump or compressor exceeds the maximum allowed working pressure of the next vessel it is feeding into. Use safety vents in parallel pairs anytime fouling by solids or gummy substances may prevent the valve from reseating properly. Also add these valves to your process inspection checklist.

Vents for Deflagrations

The American Petroleum Institute (API), American Society of Mechanical Engineers (ASME) and National Fire Protection Association (NFPA) issue consensus standards governing design and installation of relief valves and rupture disks. NFPA 30 gives these equations to determine the heat absorbed by a vessel in a fire:

$$Q = 20,000 A_R, \text{for} A_R < 200$$
$$Q = 199,300 A_R^{0.566}, \text{for} 200 < A_R < 1,000 \qquad [11.10]$$
$$Q = 963,400 A_R^{0.338}, \text{for} A_R \geq 1,000$$

A_R is the wetted area of the vessel. For a sphere, 55 percent of the total exposed area is used. Seventy-five percent of the total exposed area of a horizontal tank is used. Only the first 30 feet above grade is used for vertical tanks. The required relief capacity is

$$W = \frac{Q}{\Delta H_v} \qquad [11.11]$$

where Q is the total heat absorbed in BTU/lb, W is the vent flowrate in pounds per hour, and ΔH_v is the latent heat of vaporization in BTU/lb. Latent heat is temperature dependent and you must have the value for the temperature of interest. If your data sources do not provide that value, use the Watson correlation provided by Reid, Prausnitz, and Poling:

$$\Delta H_{v2} = \Delta H_{v1} \left(\frac{1 - T_{r2}}{1 - T_{r1}} \right)^{0.38} \qquad [11.12]$$

Temperatures are in Rankine. T_r is reduced temperature computed from the critical temperature for the material, T_c

$$T_r = \frac{T}{T_c} \qquad [11.13]$$

Another important consideration is the protection factor (F), which NFPA provides in NFPA 30:

for drainage   F = 0.5
for approved water spray   F = 0.3
for approved insulation   F = 0.3
for approved water spray with
approved insulation   F = 0.15

Applied to the total heat calculated as above, the protection factor tells us how much of that heat will actually reach the vessel. Obviously, if we take more preventive measures, less heat reaches the vessel. Compare F for approved water spray with approved insulation, for instance, with F for water spray alone. Approved means constructed and installed exactly as defined in NFPA 30.

Example. A horizontal tank is insulated for fire protection. The wetted area is 600 square feet. The exposure temperature is 471°F. How much heat could be absorbed from the fire by the tank and how much relief capacity is required?

A_R = 600 ft² X 0.75 = 450 ft², the middle range heat equation applies.

$Q = 199,300(A_R)^{0.566} = 199,300 (450)^{0.566} = 6.33$ X 10^6 BTU/hr (Toasty!)

FQ = 0.3 X 6.33 X 10^6 = 1.90 X 10^6 BTU/hr (still pretty toasty)

T_c = 967 R, see Perry, Fig. 3-9, which also provides the latent heat by nomograph. Call it 115 BTU/lb at 931 R.

W = $Q/\Delta H_V$ = 1,900,000 BTU/hr ÷ 115BTU/lb = 17,000 lb/hr

Deflagrations vs. Detonations

A flame is a low-velocity subsonic decomposition wave. The difference between combustion and explosion is one of pressure and volume, and the velocity of the decomposition wave. As explained above, the difference between the two types of explosions is one of flame (decomposition wave) speed. Subsonic decomposition yields deflagrations while detonations are caused as the decomposition velocity approaches a certain supersonic level. Once the wave reaches that supersonic velocity, called the *upper Chapman-Jouguet point*, a self-sustaining detonation is produced. These are called *strong* or *over driven detonations*. Weak detonations, velocity less than the C-J point, amount to supersonic combustion.

Explosions in vessels are well studied and documented and the simplest model is a detonation in a spherical process vessel. As aerosols (finely divided dusts or mists) explode, a flame develops spherically around the point of ignition. Flames will spread through ducts and piping. However, certain dynamic effects can complicate the explosion process. Flame-generated flow past obstacles located ahead of the flame causes turbulence and large eddies in the wave propagation. When the flame front accelerates toward the hot reaction products, a phenomenon called the Taylor instability is introduced. A Kelvin-Helmholtz instability is produced when the flame impulsively accelerates perpendicular to the direction of propagation. Combustion instability arises when heat released by the flame couples with the acoustics of the chamber. The two processes that cause deflagration waves (flames) under confinement to transition into detonation waves (explosions) are the heating of a portion of the gas to autoignition temperature by shock compression and either 1) hot gas-cold-gas mixing which triggers rapid exothermic processes, or 2) severe flame folding which causes a rapid increase in flame area, increasing the rate of heat release. So, temperature, as well as pressure, is very important in a detonation.

Inerting

Sometimes the quickest way to make a potentially explosive vessel safe is to inert it. This technique depends on the materials involved and the reason for inerting. For instance, a tank can be permanently inerted, after cleaning, with sand, gravel, or concrete. For emergency response, nitrogen is a good inerting material, if you can get your hands on enough. Remember, with nitrogen in use as an inerting agent, each person who enters the inerted space must have self-contained breathing apparatus.

Static Electricity

When looking for sources of ignition, don't forget static electricity. Clothing, shoes, moving equipment, or flowing liquids can generate static electricity. Many people conscientiously bond metal containers but ignore plastic containers. A liquid pouring from a plastic container can build up a static charge, too. Ever rub a balloon through your hair and stick it to a wall?

Finely divided solids (dusts, meals, powders, etc.) can be ignited by static electricity. Figure 11.10 summarizes the steps Dahn sets forth to identify and prevent these hazards. Electrostatic charging of solid particles can be prevented by keeping particle diameters relatively large, greater than 60 mesh. Under the right conditions, the charge density of a particulate aerosol can be 10^{-3} coulombs/kg. You can also reduce the velocity of the flowing particles to decrease charge. Round particles have a low surface area to volume ratio and are therefore less likely to be detonated by a static discharge. Do not introduce volatiles to the particles, such as fumigants, and if you do already because you must, reduce the amount. Increasing the moisture content of the particles also helps to reduce detonation potential. Another way to prevent these problems is to change the particle size distribution if you can shift to less fines.

Figure 11.10
Procedure for Identifying Electrostatic Discharge
to Finely Divided Solid Particles

- Identify particle chemical & physical properties.
- Determine electrostatic charging properties of particles relative to adjacent materials.
- Identify charge drainoff properties by test or analysis.
- Locate areas where PM clouds could be ignited.
- Identify how this can occur.
- Identify ways to prevent occurrence.

You can increase the drain off of charge by wetting the particles, adding conductive particles or adding antistatic material. The latter two options are not always available with food products.

A voltage field in a pneumatic conveyance can be reduced by decreasing power to the air flow rate. Anything you do to reduce electrostatic charging will have a proportional effect on the voltage field it is associated with. Smaller vessel diameters limit the size of voltage fields.

Ground all conductive material, reduce voltage fields, and use large, round particles to reduce the potential of electrostatic discharge by sparking. Reduce propagating brush discharges by reducing vessel diameter, using smaller particles and reducing voltage fields.

Minimize the potential for dust explosion by eliminating—or at least reducing—60 mesh particles (fines) and reducing electrostatic discharge potential.

Some nonpolar (nonconducting) liquids can be charged by static electricity while flowing through pipelines, across a surface or through a narrow opening and if a suitable vapor/air mixture is formed the mixture could detonate. Adding highly polar solvents or water to these liquids, if that is feasible, will reduce the potential for electrostatic ignition. A spark will not likely contain enough energy to raise the bulk temperature of a flammable liquid, which is cooler than its flash point—high enough to sustain a fire. Aerosols, on the other hand, can be ignited easily, even when bulk temperature is below flashpoint. Kerosene mists have been ignited as low as 40 degrees (F) below the flashpoint. Even mists of hydraulic oil have ignited and, generically, this material's flashpoint is 600-700°F.

$$I = k \times 10^{-6}(Vd)^n \qquad [11.14]$$

The charging rate is related to the equivalent electrical current, called streaming current (I), associated with charge being transported past a point per unit time, where I is in amps and

V = average velocity, m/sec
d = inside pipe diameter, m
n = exponential constant, 2 for hydrocarbon fuels, and
k = constant, 3.75 for hydrocarbon fuels.

When emptying or filling a drum or other small container electrostatic charges have an opportunity to build. For instance, as a liquid flows over the inner, nonconductive surface of a plastic container high charges accumulate due to friction and liquid/plastic separation processes. As a conductive object is approached—such as a metal funnel or container—a brush discharge may occur. This is also called corona discharge. Spark discharge may occur on the conductive surface such as between the funnel and metal container or between the human attendant and container.

Anytime two immiscible liquids are present in a nonconductive container the conductive liquid will cause the nonconductive liquid to form an isolated, conductive, and chargeable layer. Use conductive containers only and interconnect them and ground when transferring liquids from one container to another. Conductive containers, nozzles, funnels, and pouring tubes must all be interconnected between themselves and ground. Flammable liquids should always be stored in metal containers connected to ground. Similarly, connect drum pumps conductively to the container being emptied and to the container being filled.

Electrostatic sparks inside a fuel container are related to the charge density of the incoming fuel. Bonding and grounding requirements are related to streaming current. Micro filters in fuel handling systems can produce charge densities of 10^{-3} coulombs/m³ at the filter outlet.

BLEVEs

An interesting phenomena occurs as a container of a flammable liquid heats up in a fire. A container of a flammable liquid will have some *head room* or *ullage space* in which some amount of vapor will be in equilibrium with the liquid depending on its vapor pressure, which is temperature dependent. When subjected to the high heat flux of a flame, the bulk temperature will start to increase, which increases the pressure in the container due to more vapor being in the ullage space. If the container has a pressure relief vent, it will open when the proper pressure is reached and start venting vapor to the atmosphere. At the same time, the liquid level drops, more ullage space is created, and the temperature of the container shell that is not in contact with liquid jumps up dramatically. The remaining bulk of liquid is now superheated (hotter than the boiling point) since it is under pressure and not at atmospheric pressure. The vent cannot handle all the vapor that needs to escape to prevent pressure from rising. Heat weakens the container shell around the ullage space, inducing thermal stresses in the shell at the liquid/vapor interface. Finally, the thermally induced stresses, heat weakened shell, and high ullage space pressure combine to create a sudden and violent rupture of the container. Fragments of the shell are propelled at great distances with considerable force. Most of the superheated liquid vapors nearly instantaneously due to the sudden decrease in pressure and some is atomized into small droplets by the explosion, creating a fireball of burning vapor and atomized liquid. This spectacular and awesome event is a BLEVE (boiling liquid—expanding vapor explosion) and if you ever witness one you will know fear first hand.

The explosion is spectacular in its own right but the fireball is the event that does most of the damage by means of intense thermal radiation. Large fragments of the container will be propelled up to six-tenths of a mile away but, fortunately, they will be few in number. On the other hand, expect fatalities from burns for those within a few hundred feet of a fireball of any size and nonfatal burns on persons up to twelve hundred feet away! That's a quarter of a mile away! Is there anywhere on your property that is safe if your plant is unfortunate enough to have a BLEVE occur? Expect walls to tumble to overpressures greater than 0.5 psi. Process equipment will be mangled if overpressures greater than two psi develop. Second degree burns will develop on skin exposed to 5,000 BTU/hr-ft^2 for five seconds or more.

If more than ten percent of the liquid contents of a container will vaporize when depressurized from the design pressure or safety relief valve setpoint, the container has the potential for a BLEVE. Most containers of hydrocarbons do have BLEVE potential. The fireball radiation is calculated

$$Q_f = \frac{[818.2 R h_{LV} M_f^{2/3}]}{L^2} \qquad [11.15]$$

where

Q_f = radiant heat, BTU/hr-ft^2

R = radiative fraction of combustion energy
  use 0.3 if burst pressure < PRV setpoint
  use 0.4 if burst pressure $\geq$ PRV setpoint

h_{LV} = net heat of combustion for liquid, BTU/lb

M_f = material in the fireball, lb
  use maximum contents of the container

L = distance from fireball center to point where Q_f is
  being calculated.

Evacuate personnel for three thousand feet from the ends of horizontal pressure vessels. All other evacuation zones should be about two thousand feet from a potential BLEVE. Evacuate all buildings—do not consider them as shelter—within this zone unless they are designed for eight psi overpressure. BLEVEs do not occur instantaneously but take several minutes to develop and explode.

Attention Emergency Response Teams

Evacuate IMMEDIATELY if a container involved in a fire begins to deform or noticeable bulges appear in the wall. RUN like your life depends on it. IT DOES.

Risk Assessments

Title III of the Clean Air Act Amended (not to be confused with SARA III), dealing with hazardous air pollutants (HAPs), requires risk management plans for regulated HAPs present in a process in quantities greater than a regulatory *threshold release quantity*. See Section 112(r)(7) of the CAAA. An acronym for this plan is Chemical Accidental Release Prevention (CARP) plan. These requirements do for the community what the OSHA Process Safety Standards do for the employee relative to chemical process safety. In fact, similarities exist between the two sets of requirements that make it easy to combine efforts. Bear in mind that some of the thresholds are different between the EPA and OSHA list of chemicals and that the goals of the two rules are different.

Analysis of the risk of a particular accident includes determining the probability of it happening and the magnitude of the resultant damage. Accident risk is three-dimensional: scenario, occurrence frequency, and consequence. Mathematically, accident risk is:

$$R = \sum_{1}^{n} f \times E \qquad [11.16]$$

for n scenarios, where

f = frequency, or probability of occurrence, and
E = consequence of each scenario.

A *scenario* is simply any chain of events leading to a disaster. The first event in the scenario is the *initiating event*, which may also be an *external event* (flood, hurricane, earthquake) if it is beyond the control of the facility to do anything about it.

Process Reviews

The OSHA required Process Safety Plan and the EPA required Chemical Accidental Release Plan are based on a wide body of systematic methods of identifying potential hazards and characterizing accident scenarios. The American Institute of Chemical Engineers (AIChE) Center for Chemical Process Safety (CCPS) has reviewed alternative methods for conducting process reviews and lists these.

Figure 11.11
Process Review Methods

- "What-If" analysis
- Checklist analysis
- Safety review (PSR)
- Hazard and operability analysis (HazOp)
- Failure mode and effects analysis (FMEA)
- Fault-tree analysis (FTA)
- Event-tree analysis (ETA)
- Cause and effect analysis
- Human reliability analysis

HazOp (hazard and operability) studies have been used extensively by the chemical industry for many years. A team composed of several professional disciplines studies plant drawings and examines process equipment first hand to determine how possible deviations from normal operating conditions might occur. Although they work reasonably well for complex chemical manufacturing facilities, these studies are not well suited for other manufacturing industries such as metal parts manufacturers.

The latter manufacturers might benefit more from a Preliminary Hazard Analysis (PHA), which was developed for the military. A PHA identifies and evaluates hazards associated witheach subsystem of high-technology equipment or systems. This is well suited for machine shops where there might be several hundred machines of many different kinds, employing hydraulics, pneumatics, electrical, and electronic circuits.

Event trees are the most widely used means of evaluating the consequences of natural disasters such as earthquakes, hurricanes, tornados, floods, and winter storms. On the other hand, fault trees are usually used to evaluate the potential failure of an individual component or subsystem, as opposed to the entire system or a scenario involving multiple systems.

Analysis of failures that occur involve discipline and logic. As a investigative team member, be careful not to draw conclusions and then hunt for proof. Also, be careful about limiting investigation objectives and too narrow a focus. First, characterize the problem in its broadest terms in order to consider all possibilities. Next, document observations, conversations, and mental impressions. Training on admissibility of evidence should be given to the team if litigation is pending. Now, identify, collect, and preserve evidence. Examine the evidence, remembering to record observations on paper. Hypothesize a scenario and see if you can reconstruct what may have happened. Start simple and add complexity only as necessary to explain unanswered questions. Determine why it happened. What is the first cause accounting for facts and evidence and which logically and reasonably explains inconsistencies? Now formulate conclusions and recommendations and report the results of your investigation.

Many plants that are marginally regulated by either the OSHA Process Safety Standard or the EPA Chemical Accidental Release Plan rule will be able to make do with a what-if analysis or a checklist review of their operation. The best strategy is to have an experienced system safety engineering firm come in and train and facilitate your staff, which then does the data collection and analysis.

Process Area Inspections

An important aspect of providing process safety is the process area inspection, to be done frequently. Some plants have roving inspectors with radios, who check valves, flanges, vents, and process equipment and communicate to an operator in the control room. These inspections are done frequently or continually. Not all plants require this diligence. The laws capture a great many plants that can tolerate daily process area inspections. Machining plants, for instance. Perhaps flammable storage is the only reason they are under the rules. Weekly inspection is the bare minimum. Anything less frequent than weekly is unacceptable as good engineering practice.

Spill and Release Response and Reporting

A confusing matter to newcomers in the profession is when and to whom to make spill or release reports. We will consider laws that require release reporting, the substances covered, when to report and to whom.

Four laws require release reporting as shown in Figure 11.12 below. More about the conditions requiring release reporting below.

Figure 11.12
Hazardous Substances Release Reporting Laws
Hazardous Materials Transportation Uniform Safety Act (HMTUSA) of 1990   applies to materials released in transportation.
Emergency Planning and Community Right-to-Know Act (EPCRA)   applies to materials released or potentially about to be re-leased into the community from a functioning facility. Permitted releases are exempted.
Clean Water Act   applies to materials released or potentially about to be re-leased into the waters of the U.S. from a functioning facility. Permitted releases are exempted.
Comprehensive Emergency Response, Compensation, and Liability Act (CERCLA or Superfund)   applies to ongoing or imminent releases from abandoned facilities but also covers releases from functioning facilities if the release is outside the purview of OSHA (leaves building).

First, we must consider the question of which materials must be reported if released? Figure 11.13 has been prepared to illustrate the requirements.

Also, who is notified of the release? HMTUSA, CWA, and CERCLA releases must be reported to the National Response Center, a 24-hour emergency operations center run by the federal government. The number is 1-800-424-8802. CWA and CERCLA releases should also be reported to the state water, air, and RCRA divisions as appropriate. If the release passes the plant boundary, notify the state emergency response commission (SERC) and the local emergency planning committee (LEPC).

Figure 11.13
Materials That Must Be Reported When Released

HMTUSA release situations: materials in the appendix to 49 CFR 172.101 (see EPA list at 40 CFR 302.4).

CWA release situations: petroleum products + list at 40 CFR 110.

CERCLA release situations: list at 40 CFR 302.4 + characteristic hazardous wastes (RCRA) + Hazardous Air Pollutants (CAAA).

EPCRA (SARA III) release situations: list at 40 CFR 355 + 302.4.

HMTUSA Release Situation

Reportable quantity released from one container.

CWA Release Situation

Petroleum or RQ of a listed substance released to "navigable" waters, AND a sheen is created OR a sludge is deposited OR a Water Quality Standard is violated.

CERCLA Release Situation

RQ of a listed substance released within 24-hour period out-side the building. Actual property boundary does not matter.

EPCRA Release Situation

RQ of a listed substance released beyond property boundaries.

DISASTER PREPAREDNESS

The operation and maintenance of any industrial facility requires a minimal level of preparedness and common sense prevention measures to minimize the possibility of fire, explosion, or release of hazardous substances to the four environmental compartments (air, water, soil/sediments, and biota). The purpose of such prudence is to minimize threats to human health and the environment. These goals are laudable but also required of hazardous waste generators and permitted hazardous waste facilities (see Chapter 9). OSHA, likewise, uses the *general duty clause* (of OSHAct) and 29 CFR 1910.38(a)(1), *Emergency Action Plan*, to ensure that employers provide for employee safety from fire and other emergencies. EPCRA requires planning and reporting of chemicals that may be involved in chemical emergencies. No matter who requires what, think of this: your employees are your most precious resource and any emergency that requires involvement of the community or governmental agencies in your business is probably going to put you out of business, anyway. Your financial survival as a company requires prudent planning and prevention regarding potential emergencies. In other words, 1) no set of regulations should be needed to get you to do what common sense and survival instinct require anyway, and 2) no set of rules or codes are good enough; you should exceed all outside requirements as far as planning and prevention of emergency situations go.

Therefore, the facility needs some internal communications system or alarm system to alert employees when disaster is imminent or the emergency situation is underway. Such systems can be voice (telephone, public announcement, radio) or signal (sirens, flashing lights, flags). A telephone or two-way radio is needed for immediate communication with police, fire, state emergency response commission, local emergency planning committee, and other authorities as needed, such as the National Response Center. Portable fire extinguishers, spill control equipment and supplies and decontamination equipment must be provided and personnel trained with regard to their use. Where water sprinkler systems are in use, an adequate water supply must be assured.

Communications, alarm systems, fire protection equipment, spill control equipment and decontamination equipment must be periodically tested to ensure proper operation during an emergency. Inspect portable fire extinguishers monthly for proper location and weight (unless the extinguisher has a gauge to indicate content) and make a full maintenance check annually. Maintenance procedures for other equipment should be included in the OSHA EAP, RCRA Contingency Plan or Preparedness and Prevention Plan, CWA Spill Prevention, Control and Countermeasures Plan, or some other readily available written plan.

Any plan for disaster preparedness and prevention requires careful consideration of all possibilities beforehand. Many facilities find that a committee effort is required to brainstorm all potentialities and then to itemize preparations and response actions. The end result will be a plan whatever its name might be. Some facilities write one plan to cover all requirements by various laws and regulations while others write a specific plan to cover each law/regulation individually. Which should you do?

One Plan Fits All

Use when the same or very similar hazards, emergencies, and disasters are the issue with each major required plans.

Separate Plans

When different hazards, emergencies, and disasters are the issue with the requirements.

You are referred to the specific requirements of the laws and regulations for the contents of specific plans but here are some generics.

Who will coordinate activities and provide leadership for facility personnel responding to an emergency situation? The plant manager should designate an Emergency Coordinator in writing (required by EPCRA, RCRA anyway). The plan should include a page on which the Emergency Coordinator is named, with his or her address, off-site telephone number, on-site extension and pager number, if one is worn. Unless this person will remain on-site at all times, two or three secondary emergency coordinators should also be designated. The names and job titles of other responsible personnel who have a role to play in emergency action/emergency response should also be listed.

Tip

Post this list of names, responsibilities, and numbers at the reception desk, guard house, and on several bulletin boards around the plant.

Response personnel, especially emergency response leaders and most especially the facility emergency coordinator, should be familiar with the plan, plant operations, and hazards that may be encountered. The facility emergency coordinator must have the authority to commit any resources necessary to abate a release, control a disastrous situation, evacuate the plant, or take any other action necessary to salvage property and protect human life.

Next, the plan should list hazards that may be encountered in the workplace during an emergency situation. Actually, several lists must be compiled, depending on the specific plan. Figure 11.14 lists some of the lists that may be required.

Figure 11.14
Emergency Situation "Hazard" Lists

Electrical Cutoffs
Hazardous Waste Streams/Storage Areas
Natural Gas Shutoffs
Post Indicator Valves—Sprinkler System
Tanks of Hazardous Substances
Workplace Fire Hazards

Next, list resources indicated in Figure 11.15.

Figure 11.15
Resources for Emergencies

Alarm Systems (Internal and External)
Communications Equipment/Systems
Containment Structures
Decontamination Equipment/Supplies
Fire Extinguishers (Fixed Systems)
Fire Extinguishers (Portable)
Neutralization Supplies
Spill Control Equipment

Keep an adequate supply of soda ash or bicarbonate of soda around to neutralize acid spills. Instruct spill responders to expect carbon dioxide to be generated in the form of a white smoke cloud when this material is spread over acid. In the open, this is no concern, but in a closed room have someone outside measuring the oxygen content of the room while the responders are inside. You can use an existing local exhaust hood in the room to prevent buildup of CO_2 concentration or use a smoke blower exhausting the room. For caustic (alkaline materials) spills, use three percent acetic acid (commercial grade vinegar) to neutralize the spill. During any neutralization process be aware of fluid temperatures. The purpose of using a weak acid and base for neutralization is to minimize heat generation and provide some degree of protection to spill responders.

Next, in the Plan, list and describe any arrangements made with police and fire departments, hospitals, emergency response contractors, or state and local emergency response teams. In fact, each of these organizations should have a file copy of the Plan. Do not forget to send them a copy when the Plan is amended due to changes in regulations, failure of the Plan in action, facility changes, emergency coordinator changes, or emergency equipment changes.

The flagship procedure in any of these plans is evacuation of the facility. Knowing when to fight an incipient (newly started) fire and when to abandon a structural fire is a key survival factor. Unless your emergency responders attend the state fire academy once per year for intensive firefighting training and are fully equipped as a fire brigade ought to be and also conduct routine drills and maintain their equipment diligently, do not even pretend to be a fire brigade.

Incipient fire responders should be trained on two acronyms: RICE and PASS. At the sound of a fire alarm, they should rush to the scene and Rescue any victims who are not ambulatory. When victims are clear, the fire responders should investigate and report to the facility emergency coordinator who assesses the situation and begins other appropriate responses including calling for outside help if it is not already on the way. The first responders, meanwhile, are Controlling the incipient stage fire by the DEFENSIVE use of portable fire extinguishers (not hoses). As soon as smoke covers more than the upper one-third of the room or the fire spreads to the walls and/or ceiling, the responders Evacuate. To summarize:

R - RESCUE
I - INVESTIGATE
C - CONTROL
E - EVACUATE

To use a portable fire extinguisher:

P - Pull the safety pin.
A - Aim the nozzle.
S - Squeeze the trigger handle.
S- Sweep the nozzle at the base of the fire.

An evacuation plan must include evacuation signals and routes of evacuation. Primary and alternate routes of egress should be drawn on an easy-to-understand layout of the plant and posted at several locations for easy reference by employees and visitors. Provide an area for departments to gather in and take role so that absentees can be reported to the emergency coordinator.

The emergency coordinator must not fail to act promptly to activate internal alarms when an emergency is imminent, but especially when an emergency is in progress.

Emergency Coordinator

Do not fail to act for fear of doing the wrong thing.

The "wrongest" thing you can do is to do nothing!

Practice, practice, practice and you will do all right when the real thing happens.

Notify emergency agencies early. Do not worry about being premature. If you call the authorities too early, everyone will soon forget, but if you call them too late, you will forever be the known as the fool who called them too late! Be prepared to give a brief summary of situation: hazardous substance release, fire, explosion, amount of material involved, hazardous characteristics, injuries, fatalities, evacuation status, your resources to defend in place until help arrives, your assessment of possible hazards to human health, and the environment outside the facility boundaries. Above all, take any action necessary to achieve your basic goal as an emergency response team to relieve the fire, explosion, hazardous material release, or other emergency condition.

When the emergency has been dealt with, provide for treatment, storage, and disposal of decontamination materials, spilled materials, neutralization residue, contaminated materials such as soil, sludges, and water. Some materials may have to be characterized if hazardous wastes were involved in the emergency. (*See* Chapter 12 for dealing with these materials.)

Training is the key to successful mitigation of emergencies. Not just any training. Ongoing, repetitive training with drills, drills, drills. Each one of us has a tendency to panic during a fire, explosion, or other emergency. Very few have a propensity for setting aside their natural panic and doing what needs to be done, on the spur of the moment. The way the rest of us deal with such matters is to walk through our potential actions and decisions in non-threatening, nonemergency conditions.

Repetitious drills make these actions and decisions second nature so that the chances of panic robbing us of sanity, even momentarily, is greatly reduced. The day you stand and survey a leveled plant, you will understand the need for drilling. Right now it seems to be too costly to lose all those productive man-hours to drilling. As you stand among the rubble the cost will seem insignificant. Do not let it happen to you!

Drills also give you a chance to see if your action plans will work. Therefore, it is important to have all responders come to a debriefing session after each drill in order to share experiences and learn where potential glitches may be.

In the classroom or on-the-job give all personnel the emergency training they need for their role in the Plan. Tell them how to implement the Plan. Tell them how to respond to a fire or explosion. That is, tell each individual what his or her role is in the emergency. Explain how the communications and alarm systems will be operated. Review this information annually, at a minimum.

Train a sufficient number of employees to implement the plan and take defensive actions, such as using portable fire extinguishers.

If you expect a person to use any piece of equipment during an emergency: 1) show them step-by-step how to use it; 2) let them use the equipment under your direct guidance in the classroom or shop; 3) let them use it in a drill situation where performance is measured under near or simulated emergency conditions; and 4) let them explain how to use the equipment to another person.

If you expect a person to use a portable fire extinguisher, let them put out a waste basket or oil pan fire (under controlled conditions). Don, wear, and doff respirators and protective clothing under timed conditions. Work with respirator and protective clothing on, doing whatever would be required during an actual emergency. Both EPA and OSHA require hands-on experience. Recovery operations are critical. Smoldering embers can flash up into a new fire. This event is called *flash back*. Flammable vapors can be present in explosive concentrations. Toxic gases can be present in lethal or harmful concentrations. The purpose of recovery is to eliminate hazards caused by the disaster and prevent further losses of personnel and property.

Figure 11.16 gives a recovery checklist that you can build on and customize to your plant.

Figure 11.16
Recovery Operations Checklist

1. Define/control HOT ZONE (where specific personal protective equipment is required).
2. Define/control BUFFER ZONE (where decontamination of personnel and equipment take place upon exiting and donning of PPE takes place upon entrance).
3. Check for oxygen level ($\geq$ 19.5% required).
4. Check for combustible gases (<20% LEL required).
5. Check for toxic gases, vapors, mists, dusts (<50% PEL required).
   NOTE: PPE for these three hazards may be relaxed if these conditions are met.
6. Inspect ceiling. Shore up or remove if necessary.
7. Inspect roof. Shore up as necessary.
8. Drain excess fire water from roof, ceiling, light fixtures.
9. Shore up walls if necessary.
10. Remove or wrap damaged equipment.
11. Shut off/lock out broken supply lines.
12. Shut off/lock out exposed circuits.
13. Prioritize a list of circuits to be repaired and restored.
14. Shut off/lock out gas handling systems until repaired.
15. Shut off/lock out material handling systems until repaired.
16. Conduct a hazardous materials inventory.
17. Collect waste-like material for characterization.
18. Call in waste/debris handling contractor.

after Langerman.

CONCLUSION

Well-planned emergency procedures and well-trained personnel are the best way to prepare for disaster. Also check and recheck process designs for safety and inspect and audit often.

REFERENCES

Aerstin, Frank and Gary Street. *Applied Chemical Process Design*. New York: Plenum Press, 1978.

Bagster, D. F. and R. M. Pitblado. "Thermal Hazards in The Process Industry." *Chemical Engineering Progress*. July 1989.

Barsell, Arthur, Uday K. Singh and Douglas Jordan. "Use of Military and Utility Power Plant Risk Methodologies for Industry Risk Assessments." *Proceedings of HAZTECH International Waste Conference*. Houston, Texas: May 8-10, 1990.

Bartok, William and Adel F. Sarofim (eds.). *Fossil Fuel Combustion: A Source Book*. New York: John Wiley & Sons, Inc., 1991.

Burk, Arthur F. "Strengthen Process Hazards Reviews." *Chemical Engineering Progress*. June 1992.

Chatrathi, Kris. "Analysis of Vent Area Estimation Methods for Non-nomograph Gases." *Plant/Operations Progress*. July 1992.

----. "Explosion-Isolation Systems." *Chemical Engineering*. October 1991.

Cheremisinoff, Paul N. "Working with Hazardous Materials." *Pollution Engineering*. May 1991.

Cockerham, Lorris G. and Barbara S. Shane. *Basic Environmental Toxicology*. Boca Raton, FL: CRC Press, 1994.

Dahn, C. James. "Electrostatic Hazards of Pneumatic Conveying of Powders." *Plant/Operations Progress*. July 1992.

Daugherty, Jack E. "TSCA." *Certified Hazardous Materials Managers Review Course*. Mississippi State University.

DeGood, Robert. "Isolation: Another Way to Take The Bang out of Explosions." Periodical Unknown.

EPA 560/1-87-011. *The Layman's Guide to the Toxic Substances Control Act.* Washington, DC: Office of Toxic Substances, June 1987.

EPA TSCA Hotline. *EPA TSCA Processor Examples.*

Expert Commission for Safety in The Swiss Chemical Industry (ESCIS). "Static Electricity: Rules for Plant Safety." *Plant/Operations Progress.* January 1988.

Green, Don W. and James O. Maloney. *Perry's Chemical Engineers' Handbook.* 6th ed. New York: McGraw-Hill Book Company, 1984.

Griffin, Roger D. *Principles of Air Quality Management.* Boca Raton, FL: Lewis Publishers, 1994.

Hearn, Graham. "Coping with Electrostatic Hazards." *Chemical Engineering.* November 1991.

Howard, Walter B. "Use Precaution in Selection, Installation, and Operation of Flame Arresters." *Chemical Engineering Progress.* April 1992.

Langerman, Neal. "Fire Clean-up Operations Lead to Second Emergency at Laboratory." *Occupational Health & Safety.* August 1988.

Lesso, William G., C. Dale Zinn, and Dwight B. Pfenning. *Hazard Assessment and Risk Analysis Techniques for Process Industries.* A short course sponsored by Mechanical Engineering Department, administered by Continuing Engineering Studies at The University of Texas at Austin, College of Engineering, September 24-27, 1990.

Mancini, Robert A. "The Use (and Misuse) of Bonding for Control of Static Ignition Hazards." *Plant/Operations Progress.* January 1988.

Nazario, Francisco N. "Preventing or Surviving Explosions." *Chemical Engineering.* August 15, 1988.

Patrick, David R. ed. *Toxic Air Pollution Handbook.* New York: Van Nostrand Reinhold, 1994.

Reid, Robert J., John M. Prausnitz, and Bruce E. Poling. *The Properties of Gases & Liquids.* 4th ed. New York: McGraw-Hill Book Company, 1987.

Rekus, John F. "Disaster Drills Identify Potential for Problems in Real Emergencies." *Occupational Health & Safety*. October 1989.

Sandler, Henry J. and Edward T. Luckiewicz. *Practical Process Engineering*. New York: McGraw-Hill, 1987.

Steinway, Daniel M. "TSCA: Will EPA Enforcement Increase?" *Pollution Engineering*. December 1990.

Wiemhoff, John. "TSCA: The Bump under The Carpet." *The National Environmental Journal*. July/August 1992.

Witherell, Charles E. "Forestalling Failure in the Plant." *Chemical Engineering*. October 1991.

Woods, J. T. "Preventing Flammable Atmosphere in Electrical Equipment Rooms." *Chemical Engineering Progress*. November 1980.

12

CLEANING UP ENVIRONMENTAL HAZARDS

Remediation is the cleaning up of a contaminated environmental site. You may have heard horror stories about environmental remediation. No doubt, certain remedial actions have been hell on earth for those involved. However, when the Big Picture is understood, it is clear the horror stories have contributed unjustifiably to a myth. In this introductory chapter we cannot solve all the remediation problems of the world nor dispel all of the myths that need correction, but it is prudent to briefly examine the problem of cleaning up. A colleague who had to clean up several acres of petroleum saturated soil said, "Cleaning up to the regional EPA's satisfaction is like shooting at a moving elephant with a BB-gun, blindfolded!"

HOW TO CLOSE A HAZARDOUS WASTE MANAGEMENT UNIT

When closing a RCRA regulated land-based solid waste management unit (SWMU), you have two options. You may make a clean closure by removing or decontaminating all waste residues, contaminated containment system components, contaminated subsoils, and any structures or equipment that may be contaminated with either waste or leachate. Or, if contaminated materials are to be left in place, thirty year post-closure care must be planned and preapproved, typically when the RCRA Part B permit is applied for.

Closure Strategy

The best strategy in the long-term, but the most expensive in the short-term, is clean closure. Do what is necessary to remove or decontaminate materials and equipment now, at time of closure. The post-closure care option is cheaper up front but you tie up money for thirty years at best, and are still open for costly litigation at worst.

Closure Investigation

Somehow, you must identify and inventory contaminated materials and equipment which must be removed and/or decontaminated. Those items that typically must be removed or decontaminated *in situ* are: standing liquids, waste and waste residues, liners, underlying and surrounding contaminated soils, subsoils, contaminated process system components, structures, and other contaminated equipment. Obviously, in order to know about the need to remove or decontaminate some of these items, you will have to take some samples, using statistical sampling techniques, and have analyses performed as necessary.

Closure Design

Negotiations with the RCRA permit enforcement authority is necessary because the regulations do not clearly tell us how to manage contaminated subsoils and other environmental media that must be removed in order to achieve clean closure. RCRA closure rules do not distinguish between contaminated media, which is not a solid waste, and other contaminated materials which can be solid waste. Other rules state that removed contaminated soils must be managed as hazardous waste unless a delisting petition is made and you demonstrate the absence of any hazardous waste characteristic. Even though soils and groundwater are not solid waste, EPA may extend the delisting and demonstration of absence of characteristic to your environmental media. While the contaminated media is not a solid waste, EPA holds that the contamination within the media is solid waste, therefore, contaminated media from RCRA closures must be managed as if they were hazardous waste and must meet hazardous waste requirements until they no longer contain a listed waste or exhibit a hazardous waste characteristic. Where treatment of a contaminated medium yields a decontaminated component and one or more waste components, EPA has taken the position that the decontaminated medium component is not subject to RCRA hazardous waste rules but that the waste component is.

Investigation and design of closure and post-closure care lead to a written Closure Plan, which is typically reviewed and approved as part of the Part B application of a facility. Figure 12.1 lists the requirements for a closure plan.

Figure 12.1
Closure Plan

- technical description of the closure
- estimated maximum amount of waste handled at closure
- description of decontamination
- estimated year of closure
- closure schedule

Closure plans submitted as part of a permit application and approved by EPA may be amended at any time during the active life of the TSDF. When changes to the TSDF or its operation occur, which affect the closure plan, it must be amended. The public is given time to review and comment on the closure plan before the EPA approves it.

Closure Implementation

Closure activities must proceed exactly as described and when scheduled in the Closure Plan. The EPA administrator can make changes to the plan, after public review and comment, but you are bound by it. Of course, you may apply to have it amended. All hazardous wastes must be treated, removed from the site, or disposed of on-site, in accordance with the approved plan.

When the Closure Plan has been executed exactly as approved by EPA, a registered, professional engineer who witnessed the closure and who is qualified in such matters, must send a certification of closure, bearing his or her official PE stamp, to the appropriate administrator. A survey plat indicating the location and dimensions of landfill cells or other disposal areas, if any, must be submitted to local land use authorities and the EPA Regional Administrator. A notation on the deed to the property is required, too. The deed notation warns potential purchasers of the property that the land was previously used to manage hazardous waste.

CORRECTIVE ACTION AT A RCRA HWMU

Superfund addresses contamination at abandoned sites. What law and set of regulations pertain to cleanup at active sites? The corrective action measures of RCRA do. Any site that threatens human health and the environment, yet is not abandoned, is subject to corrective action under RCRA. One EPA estimate puts the number of RCRA TSDFs at 5,700 with up to 80,000 solid waste management units (remember HWMUs in Chapter 9?)

How is corrective action ordered? One way is through the RCRA operating permit application process. If the site is contaminated when a permit is applied for, the permit authority may require that a cleanup be completed before it will issue the permit. Another way in which corrective action is forced on an industry is when a post-closure care permit is applied for. When a permitted HWMU is shut down, a post-closure management plan must be strictly followed for thirty years. Typically, any pre-existing contamination must be cleaned up before the post-closure care permit is valid. The enforcement authority can cause a corrective action to be implemented. Finally, if an unpermitted generator stores hazardous waste for more than ninety days, the issue of corrective action is automatically put on the table. An SMWU is anyplace where solid waste has ever been managed. RCRA enforcement agents can inspect any SMWU they wish, but they can also inspect any *area of concern (AOC)*, that is, anyplace where they even suspect contamination, without first proving contamination exists.

A RCRA facility assessment (RFA) is roughly the same as preliminary assessment/site investigation (PA/SI) conducted at Superfund sites. The EPA regional office reviews state and federal regulatory files on the site and make a site visit to document information summarized in Figure 12.2.

Figure 12.2
RCRA Facility Assessment

1. identify regulatory file discrepancies,
2. document site environmental history, and
3. locate visual evidence of need for corrective action.

No, EPA does not take samples to prove contamination. If the assessment comes back unfavorable, you will have to collect samples and conduct analyses to prove or disprove contamination. This action on your part is called a RCRA Facility Investigation (RFI). Wait until you receive the RFA from EPA and use it to prioritize your expenses. No need to spend money on areas about which the EPA is unconcerned. When you present your RFI to the EPA, two outcomes are possible. They may require no further action or require a corrective measures study (CMS).

Alternative Corrective Action Selection

In those cases where the RFI reveals excessive contamination, EPA will request a CMS which is like a Superfund feasibility study. The goal of the CMS is to identify a method of removing or reducing the contamination to a level everyone will agree to, at a cost you can live with. Some screening decisions are recommended to eliminate corrective actions which are obviously economically or technically infeasible. This is the point at which you absolutely must have legal and engineering assistance. It would have been better to have had counsel from the beginning, but proceed without counsel at your own peril. Look for legal and engineering firms that are not only technically competent at what they do, but also have good reputations for negotiating tough cases with EPA.

Determine Remedial Costs

Once potential corrective action methods are identified, gather the cost of capital, installation, and operation for each process. Bench or pilot scale studies may be necessary to show technical feasibility or to tie down operating costs or to gather design data. Minimize the number of alternatives as early as possible. Most corrective actions suggest their own remedy, already proven and acceptable to EPA, so do not go too far afield without a good (cost savings) reason. If you offer too many alternatives, EPA may choose one you would not have, given your druthers. Figure 12.3 lists acceptable criteria for a corrective action. Cost is the acceptable factor to you, not necessarily to EPA. Be prepared to negotiate.

Figure 12.3
Acceptable Corrective Action

protects human health and the environment
attains cleanup standards
is reliable
reduces toxicity &/or mobility &/or volume
has short-term effectiveness
is doable

Allocate Responsibilities. This is easy. All the costly responsibility is yours. All the oversight and approval is the EPA's.

Design Remedial Action. RCRA corrective action is similar to CERCLA remediation except that you are still there when the job is complete but this does not lessen the requirements. EPA will review your action plan to determine whether it meets rules and standards. You want it to minimize future liabilities.

Implement Design. Once approved, follow your plan or get approval to make changes. One question that often comes up in remediation: is contaminated groundwater a hazardous waste? The EPA's contained-in policy states:

> ...groundwater in an aquifer is not a solid waste and thus not a hazardous waste, but...groundwater contaminated with hazardous waste leachate is subject to RCRA Subtitle C regulations because it contains a hazardous waste and therefore must be managed as if the groundwater itself was [sic] hazardous. However, if groundwater is

treated such that it no longer contains a hazardous waste, the groundwater would no longer be subject to regulation under Subtitle C of RCRA.[1]

EPA also applies the contained-in policy to contaminated soil, debris, and leachate. Further, EPA maintains that the mixture rule and derived-from rule do not pertain to contaminated environmental media:

> Under our regulations, contaminated media are not considered solid wastes in the sense of being abandoned, recycled, or inherently waste-like as those terms are defined in the regulations. Therefore, contaminated environmental media cannot be considered a hazardous waste via the mixture rule (*i.e.*, to have a hazardous waste mixture, a hazardous waste must be mixed with a solid waste per 40 CFR §261.3(a)(2) (iv)). Similarly, the derived-from rule does not apply to contaminated media. Our basis for stating that contaminated environmental media must be managed as hazardous waste is that they contain listed hazardous waste. These environmental media must be managed as hazardous waste because and only so long as, they contain a listed hazardous waste (*i.e.*, until decontaminated).

This contained-in policy applies to environmental media known to be contaminated with listed hazardous waste, but does not address contamination from characteristic hazardous waste. Both EPA and remediation engineers know that the typical situation in the field is that no one knows for sure if the environmental media was contaminated by either listed or characteristic hazardous waste. At SWMUs it is usually both which contaminate. So, what criteria can be used to determine whether contaminated media required controlled management? Here is Region IV's policy:

> ...the criteria...is based upon human health and environmental risk. By definition a medium is contaminated if one or more hazardous constituents, as identified in 40 CFR Part 261 Appendix VIII, are present above levels of human health or environmental concern and

---

[1] EPA Region IV RCRA Guidance, TSC-92-02.

above naturally occurring (background) levels (this is specifically for areas where there are naturally occurring high levels of Appendix VIII constituents). Contaminated environmental media should either be managed in accordance with RCRA Subtitle C requirements or best management practices... However, if a contaminated medium is treated to at or below risk-based standards (or to naturally occurring background levels), it can be rendered decontaminated. Anytime you would like to rely on an EPA or state policy as opposed to regulation or standard, get confirmation in writing that the policy applies to your situation because neither EPA nor the state are obligated to be consistent in applying policies whereas they must be tirelessly consistent in applying regulations.

What material, then, from a RCRA corrective action is to be treated as hazardous waste? Figure 12.4 summarizes.

Contaminated medium containing a listed hazardous waste from a RCRA corrective action is subject to hazardous waste rules. Also, any process units (equipment and structures) used for treatment, storage, or disposal of the medium are to be treated as hazardous waste. Medium that exhibits a hazardous waste characteristic, and its process units, is subject to Subtitle C.

POST-CLOSURE CARE OF A RCRA HWMU

The requirement for providing post-closure care implies that waste and waste residues have been left in place in the SWMU. Post-closure care should be *the* incentive for any generator not to apply for a RCRA storage permit. Sometimes getting hazardous waste shipped out every 90 days gets to be a scheduling nightmare. But, it is not that difficult when the alternative is a RCRA permit and all that entails, including post-closure. The purpose of post-closure is to ensure the integrity of any containment system and detect contamination by monitoring the closure for thirty years. That should be long enough, the EPA thinks, to tell whether there will ever be any trouble in the future, without unduly burdening the permittee.

Figure 12.4
Environmental Media from RCRA Corrective Action

Subject to hazardous waste rules:

    medium contaminated with a listed hazardous waste
    units used for treatment, storage or disposal of medium

    medium contaminated with a characteristic hazardous waste
        (if the medium exhibits hazardous characteristic)
    units used for treatment, storage or disposal of medium

    waste from decontamination of media
        (which contained listed hazardous waste) or
        (waste exhibits a hazardous waste characteristic)

Subject to best management practices:

    medium contaminated with a characteristic hazardous waste
        (if the medium does not exhibit hazardous characteristic)
    units used for treatment, storage or disposal of medium

May be subject to best management practices, state and local
requirements, and RCRA Subtitle D:

    decontaminated media components
    waste from decontamination of media
        (which did not contain listed hazardous waste) and
        (waste does not exhibit hazardous waste characteristic)

Post-closure care is cut and dry. Do it exactly as specified in your RCRA Part B Permit. The time to negotiate was when the Part B was filed as an application. Once it is approved and made into a permit, negotiations are over. Typically, you will be required to provide a minimum of 30 years of care, sometimes more—unless you opted for clean closure. Sometimes, as in the case of a storage facility, clean closure may eliminate the need for post-closure care, but only if that is how your approved Part B reads.

Figure 12.5 lists the minimum post-closure requirements when at least some hazardous waste or contamination is left in place.

Figure 12.5
Post-Closure Care

groundwater monitoring/reporting
inspection/maintenance of containment systems
security

A groundwater detection monitoring grid must be established to determine if hazardous waste or contamination from hazardous waste is leaking from the closure containment. Background and semiannual monitoring for indicator patterns are required. Monitoring at a compliance point specified in the permit is conducted and compared to background using the Student's T-test, to determine if a statistically significant change has occurred. The compliance point will be just downstream of the closure containment at an imaginary boundary with the rest of the world. If leakage is detected, the owner is required to implement compliance monitoring and corrective action.

UNRAVELING THE SUPERFUND MYTH

The Comprehensive Emergency Response, Compensation, and Liability Act (CERCLA), also known as Superfund, was enacted in Congress in 1980—the same year RCRA took effect for many facilities—as the direct result of public outcry following several highly publicized environmental disasters, most notably Love Canal. The intent of Congress is to address actual or potential uncontrolled releases of hazardous substances to the environment, with stiff regulatory requirements. If a release is controlled, it is regulated by either the Clean Air Act (CAA), the Clean Water Act (CWA), or the Resource Conservation and Recovery Act (RCRA), depending on its nature and characteristics. Therefore, CERCLA primarily covers inactive (that is, abandoned) sites, but in some cases it also covers actively managed sites that are not covered by RCRA. CERCLA applies to both land-based facilities and vessels at sea and to all environmental media: air, surface water, groundwater, and soil. Unlike RCRA and other basic regulatory programs, CERCLA is self-implementing with regulations issued only as guidance documents that define policy, as opposed to being rules to be followed.

CERCLA is not about compliance. Nor is it about justice. CERCLA establishes a mechanism of response for the *immediate* clean up of hazardous substance contamination from accidental spills or from abandoned (uncontrolled) hazardous waste sites that *may* result in long-term environmental damage or imminent threat to human health. The language of this law makes certain parties strictly liable for response costs incurred as the result of a release of a threatened release of hazardous substances. Fault or blame are not issues here. No one is interested in a party's guilt or innocence. By virtue of having a specified relationship with the scene of the CERCLA action, you may be liable for the clean up.

"Wait!" you stormily protest. "That's not fair!"

True, but you are required to clean up anyway. At Love Canal, one of the delays was caused by the fact that Hooker Chemical was not clearly at fault. Even today Hooker is not clearly to blame. So, in CERCLA Congress said, in effect, let's not hassle over blame—it takes too long—let's clean up, then the legal battles can begin.

Yes, you are right. The lawyers jumped on that fanciful idea in a hurry. Despite the CERCLA action timetable explained below, most CERCLA sites take forever to clean up, due to court battles. What Congress wanted to avoid has happened in spite of CERCLA because the lawyers keep trying to play by the old *who's to blame* rules. And aren't you and I for all that, given the huge invoice we may have to sign off on? You bet we are! Strict liability is fine and dandy but our stockholders do not understand why such a large chunk of profits go bye-bye if we are not to blame.

Adding insult to injury, Congress made the strict liability joint and several. That is, the responsibility—but not liability—is shared equally by anyone who had a business relationship with the site—not just any business relationship, but one that directly dealt with the hazardous substances causing the real or pending contamination. Yet, by making the liability several, EPA can send a bill to all parties or just some of the parties. That way, if one or more entities no longer exists, EPA can still collect all moneys from the remaining parties. They do not have to subtract out the part belonging to the missing parties. We'll examine this joint and several notion in more detail below.

What strict liability and joint and several means to you is this: call your attorney as soon as you even suspect you might be party to a CERCLA action and especially if you receive a PRP letter.

As is the case with most of Congress' intentions, as outlined in any of various environmental laws, the original version of CERCLA contained so many ambiguities and inconsistencies that putting its novel but complex requirements into practice proved extremely difficult. Since 1980, roughly 200 sites have been identified for CERCLA action (to have occurred within 180 days of identification) yet only a handful have been successfully closed from an environmental clean up standpoint and none have been closed legally or financially. Even Love Canal still has some legal activity ongoing after 25-plus years. Hence, the Superfund Amendments and Reauthorization Act of 1986 (SARA), but the closure record for uncontrolled sites is still dismal at best, scandalous at worst.

Focusing on the engineering and managerial aspects of Superfund, it concerns the release of hazardous substances into the environment from facilities, the remediation and clean up of those releases, and the reimbursement of the government by potentially responsible parties (PRPs) for response costs.

A *release* is any spilling, leaking, pumping, pouring, emitting, emptying, discharging, injecting, escaping, leaching, dumping, or disposing of hazardous substances into the environment. SARA added the abandonment or discarding of barrels, containers, or other closed containers holding hazardous substances. Exposures regulated by other laws are excluded from coverage.

May people use the terms hazardous materials, hazardous chemicals, hazardous substances, and hazardous wastes interchangeably, but they are not. For the purposes of CERCLA, which deals with uncontrolled releases into the environment, *hazardous substance* means almost every possible material, specifically those substances designated as *hazardous discharges* or *toxic pollutants* under CWA, *hazardous wastes* under RCRA, *hazardous air pollutants* under CAAA, and *imminently hazardous chemical substances* or *mixtures* under TSCA. Just in case any material slipped through the cracks of this definition, Congress added section 102 [paraphrased here]:

any other unlisted substance which will or may reasonably be anticipated to cause any type of adverse effects in organisms and/or their offspring.

Petroleum and natural gas are excluded from CERCLA. While this encompassing definition of a hazardous substance includes the entire universe of chemical substances, including those present at the Big Bang, keep in mind the definition only applies to those substances that are being released from an unmanaged facility into the environment.

A facility subject to CERCLA is any structure, installation, equipment, landfill impoundment, storage vessel, vehicle, or any site or area where hazardous substances have been deposited or otherwise have come to be located. *The simple presence of a hazardous substance at an unmanaged site qualifies that site as a*
"facility" under CERCLA.

However, Congress did not intend for the nation to have to deal with minute quantities of hazardous substances, so CERCLA instructs EPA to establish a list of *Reportable Quantities, RQ*. An RQ is a specifically listed amount of a particular hazardous substance that, if released within a 24-hour period, requires an oral report to the National Response Center.

Example 1. A chromate conversion bath containing 40 gallons of fluid consists of 45% nitric acid, 45% water, 5% chromic acid and 5% other materials dissolved in the acid solution. Assume for our example that the other materials are not of interest. Friday afternoon, before going home for the weekend, you instruct the second shift to empty the bath into a drum—this is a routine practice for them—and to label the drum HAZARDOUS WASTE, put Friday's date on it and remove it to the hazardous waste container storage area.

On Monday you return to work to find that your instructions were followed but apparently the drum handler scraped the bottom rim on a concrete floor and shaved off some metal. The entire contents, forty gallons, leaked out over the weekend. The acidic waste dissolved a weak area in the concrete curb and poured out of the building onto the community playground next door (no ignitables are stored inside the drum storage area, so it is located alongside the property line). Do you have to report this spill?

Quick answer: you ought to because of the nature of the adjoining property.

Suppose for interest's sake that the adjoining property is someone's undeveloped lot and you are in an industrial park. Do you have to report?

This is an aqueous solution so let's assume that the specific gravity is 1.0, or in other words, the density of the solution is about 8.34 lb/gal.

40 gal X 8.34 lb/gal = 333.6 lb.

You look in 302.4 and find the RQs:

Chromic acid   10 lb.
Nitric acid   1,000 lb.

You do not have to report it due to the nitric acid content, even if it were 100% nitric acid.

0.05 X 333.6 lb. = 16.68 lb. chromic acid

If the liquid were spilled in one twenty-four hour period, it would be reportable due to its chromic acid content. However, it spilled from Friday evening to Monday morning, a minimum of two twenty-four hour periods, going on three. Therefore the spill is not reportable. You may report it if you have reason to believe that reporting is in your best interests, but you do not have to report.

What should you do, if anything? Clean up the soil and debris that may be contaminated by the acid spill. This is a minor event as these things go. Recover enough soil and other debris so that corrosivity will not be an issue for handlers. If the original waste material were hazardous for any reason other than corrosivity, have a sample of soil and debris analyzed (TCLP) for those parameters (probably chromium, lead and cadmium at a minimum). If the material fails TCLP, it is hazardous waste. Otherwise it is a nonhazardous solid waste and you should arrange for proper disposal by a contractor who is aware of its history and TCLP analysis.

Example 2. On a recent trip our plane was easing up to the terminal when we saw the plane parked next to us had been involved in a fuel spill. Crash crews stood by to douse any incipient fire as a cleanup crew, dressed in protective clothing applied absorbent beads, blankets, pillows, and other shapes to the jet fuel on the tarmac. Part of the spill was already recovered when we pulled up but I imagine that 150 gallons or more were spilled. Is this reportable as a CERCLA spill? No. 1) It involves petroleum, and 2) it did not leave the property and enter the environment except the little bit that evaporated.

Example 3. You are the swing shift foreman at a small specialty chemical. Right after your two o'clock rounds one of the control room operators radios that a reactor is getting away from him. You run toward the control room but before you reach it an explosion knocks you off your feet. When you come to, the operator tells you that a breach has occurred in the hydrazine reactor. About 1,500 pounds of reactants and product have been sprayed out into the atmosphere before he could get valve shut off and the reactor under control. He wants to know if the spill has to be reported.

A no-brainer. Hydrazine is a dangerous chemical with an RQ = 1 pound. You would know this as the swing shift foreman. You had better know it, anyway. Do not worry about the math right now. Report the spill. If the fire department was not called in while you were passed out, call them right now and get them on the way.

A question I hear often has to do with calculating spill volumes and weights in an emergency when it is hard enough to think, much less compute. The answer is simple. You know the material on hand at your facility. You have an inventory for OSHA, one for SARA III, one for your air permit, one for RCRA. How much information do you need?

Take these inventories and for each stream determine in your quiet, calm office the RQ, where appropriate. Make a spill reporting list for yourself and post it in several places: your office, the reception desk, the guardhouse, the plant manager's office, the nurse's station. Make it like Figure 12.6, for instance. This example list has values for some pure chemicals. Most commercial chemical products have additives, inhibitors, stabilizers, and other impurities that make the reportable quantity for the mixture more than for the pure chemical. For instance, if the hydrochloric acid product on your list were at 50% strength, then reporting is not required unless 1,200 gallons or more are spilled. The weight RQ always remains the same for the reportable substance. That is set by force of law. The reportable volume (number of gallons) changes depending on the purity of the substance. Always have the RQ in pounds handy because that is the required reporting threshold. I suggest that you calculate for your own purposes reportable volume because that is how your personnel are probably used to handling liquids, by gallons rather than by weight.

Figure 12.6
Example List

Spilled Substance	RQ, lb.	RQ, gal.
Chromic Acid	10	1
Hydrazine	1	<1
Hydrochloric Acid	5,000	600
Nitric Acid	1,000	120
Toluene	1,000	138
Trichloroethylene	100	8

CERCLA established that any individual or company is a *potentially responsible party* (PRP) if he or she or they contributed to the contamination problems or even potentially were responsible. Any owner, operator, transporter, generator, or other entity ruled on by the courts can be a PRP. On more than one occasion, banks and other lending institutions have been included (but not necessarily in every case). The key issue is whether such lending PRPs participated in the management of the facility through the loan. Whenever possible, EPA requires the PRPs to clean up the site directly and promptly through committee action. A PRP committee is formed to manage the remedial design and the remediation.

When EPA has to take over the cleanup operation because of PRP committee foot dragging or because sufficient PRPs cannot be located or the PRPs among them have inadequate financial resources, it performs the cleanup then takes the PRPs to court to recover the response costs. All costs associated with the cleanup, removal, emergency response, remedial action, and related enforcement activities are fully recoverable, per CERCLA.

Under section 107, CERCLA designates four categories of persons liable for response costs and other damages arising from releases or threatened releases of hazardous substances to the environment. The current owner and operator of a facility is logically the first party to go to in order to recover costs, but if the site is abandoned (as they so often are), the last owner and operator may be included. State and local governments are excluded as PRPs if they acquired ownership through bankruptcy or some other involuntary circumstance. The owner and operator at the time the release occurred are PRPs without question. Anyone who arranged for disposal of hazardous waste at the facility is liable as a PRP too. This is how generators get pulled into CERCLA actions. Even transporters of hazardous wastes for treatment and disposal are PRPs. Much of this law deals with compensation and liability (the second CEE and ELL in CERCLA). As mentioned earlier, three types of costs are retrievable by the government under CERCLA: 1) response costs and removal or remedial action costs incurred; 2) response costs incurred by others (but not PRPs); and 3) damages to natural resources owned or controlled by the government. Liability is retroactive for releases that occurred before the law was passed in 1980. Strict liability means you cannot claim a defense due to ignorance. Liability is also joint (shared by all PRPs) and several (the EPA can come after any or all PRPs).

Section 113(f)(1) of SARA allows PRPs to resolve their liability and be immune from contribution actions. This means they may make a settlement with the government for the cleanup. Common law governs contribution actions, through which courts determine how to allocate response costs. PRPs not joining in the settlement can benefit through claim reduction, but remain liable for any costs in excess of the settlement. Liability is limited to the response costs plus a maximum of $50 million for natural resources damages, except where the release was willful, or caused by a violation of a regulation. If the release was an approved one, such as by permit, no cost damages are sought for actual damage to natural resources.

Five defenses are allowed for liability. You need a lawyer to explain them well and to apply them, if appropriate, to your situation, but in a layman's nutshell here they are for discussion starters: 1) Act of God; 2) act of war; 3) third party defense; 4) innocent purchaser (a.k.a. innocent landowner); and 5) involuntary acquisition (by state or local government). *Causation* generally does not have to shown by the EPA to collect from you. While the costs of cleaning up a federally permitted release are not recoverable per CERCLA and SARA, other laws do allow recovery.

CERCLA authorizes the federal government to respond to the release or substantial threat of a release into the environment of hazardous substances or pollutants or contaminants that may present an imminent or substantial danger to public health or welfare. SARA additionally authorizes EPA to determine whether private parties can conduct the cleanup directly. EPA can subpoena, enter, inspect, take remedial actions, and acquire property for remedial action if the state will accept the property immediately afterwards. EPA may also prepare toxicological profiles of health-threatening substances and conduct health assessments at National Priority List sites.

EPA can take two basic types of action in order to get a site cleaned up: removal or remediation. *Removal actions* are short term actions taken to protect the public from imminent threats. They include temporary evacuation, installing a fence, providing alternative water supplies, and removing waste and contaminated material. Ongoing actions such as monitoring groundwater are also included. Most of these activities were learned the hard way at Love Canal. *Remedial actions* are longer term or more permanent actions that require extensive study to implement effectively. Dredging, excavating, and groundwater treatment are remedial actions. CERCLA limits remedial actions to National Priority List sites. No limits are placed on cost or duration of these activities.

The National Contingency Plan (NCP) is our national plan for responding to oil and hazardous substance spills beyond regional response capabilities. Each EPA region is required to have its own contingency plan with designated response teams and coordinators. All government responses under CERCLA are required to follow NCP procedures. Releases in excess of a reportable quantity in a 24-hour period must be reported immediately to the National Response Center.

The NCP provides the response methodology for dealing with releases of hazardous substances and oil (which is not covered by CERCLA). The NCP method has three elements, which may be divided into four phases. The elements of response are site identification, site listing, and site cleanup.

After an uncontrolled release site is identified (Element 1), the first phase, called Preliminary Assessment/Site Investigation (PA/SI) is begun. During this phase, information is gathered off-site (PA) and on-site (SI), if adequate off-site information is not available. All that can be answered at the end of the PA/SI is: does the site need thorough investigation or not? If not, the matter is dropped or an immediate removal of contamination is begun, as appropriate.

If further investigation is prudent or an immediate cleanup is infeasible, the second phase, called Remedial Investigation/ Feasibility Study (RI/FS), is begun in order to answer these questions: 1) how bad is the problem; 2) does the site get listed on the National Priorities List (NPL); and 3) what are the technical alternatives for cleanup? The purpose of the RI is to obtain enough information to characterize site conditions such as 1) source and extent of contamination; 2) potential pathways; and 3) extent of human exposure. The RI is a comprehensive evaluation of contamination in the soil, groundwater, or surface water and specific site characteristics, such as geology and hydrology. The extent of human exposure is estimated by conducting an exposure assessment. The FS presents cleanup alternatives based on information gathered during the RI and verified, sometimes by laboratory experiments. The process of selecting a suitable remediation method is immortalized as the *record of decision* or ROD. This is a public record and public input is invited by EPA.

The second element of response is based on the RI/FS report or ROD. If appropriate, the site is placed on the NPL and the third phase, called Remedial Design/Remedial Action (RD/RA), begins. Implementation of this phase through the operation and maintenance of a remediation process may take years or decades. Remediation processes run the full gamut of devices and equipment discussed in chapters in air and water pollution control and hazardous waste management and then some. The feasibility study performed in the RI/FS phase provides the data needed to select and design the most appropriate process from an economic and technical feasibility viewpoint. EPA prefers that a specific hierarchy of choices be examined.

Destruction or treatment-based technologies are given priority. Experimental or unproven technologies can be approved where feasibility is demonstrated, especially conventional technology is infeasible. The remedy selected must meet the requirements of other laws (CWA, CAAA, TSCA, SDWA, and RCRA). State and local criteria must also be met, if applicable, and not just laws and formal regulations, but informal criteria such as policy and guidance statements as well. The latter are negotiable, especially if they have not been through a public scrutiny and hearing. SDWA Maximum Contaminant Levels (MCL) are used when drinking water is involved. Alternate Contaminant Levels (ACL) can only be used within a site owner's property boundaries. If the owner is an innocent third party, his or her approval would be necessary, but innocent third parties are rare in CERCLA actions. Where ACLs cannot be met, then RCRA groundwater standards must be met by meeting SDWA standards or showing no excess above background. Unless the cleanup is total, EPA will review the site every five years and require additional action as warranted. EPA reports to Congress on all that are not clean closed.

The Hazardous Substance Response Trust Fund, called Superfund, is a sink of $8.5 billion used to compensate for injury or damage to natural resources. Claims are honored only after having failed to recover damages from PRPs. Private parties can be forced to clean up a site if even a threat of imminent and substantial endangerment exists to natural resources or human welfare. Common law may also provide a basis for injunctive relief against parties to a release.

How does a CERCLA action progress? After identifying a site, EPA give PRPs notice of an anticipated remedial action and solicits their voluntary participation, usually to their advantage. After the notification, a sixty-day moratorium on the RI/FS phase and enforcement action begins, to see if the PRPs will form a committee and finance the RI/FS directly. If no agreement among PRPs is reached within the sixty days allotted, EPA initiates the RI/FS after 30 more days pass, or 90 days total, and remedial action is begun 60 days after the moratorium, or 120 days total. If PRPs do reach agreement among themselves, they have the same 90 and 120 periods to begin their RI/FS and RD/RA phases, respectively. Congress allowed no room for piddling around in CERCLA. That is why the legal settlements were supposed to happen after the cleanup.

As we all know, only too painfully, that is not the way CERCLA actions do progress. Immediately after the PRP notification, hearings for all sorts of legal maneuvering begin and even if the PRPs want to cooperate their legal staffs tie up the process, sometimes *ad nauseam*. Some CERCLA actions have taken more than a decade and are still on the NPL. Some do progress just as originally envisioned by Congress and at those times we can all be thankful the system works. All is not lost, however. Several good things have come out of the legal dueling that takes place with many CERCLA actions.

For one thing, the legal and financial horror stories have prompted a more fiscally conservative Congress to threaten drastic measures, and, as a consequence, EPA is being more selective of sites placed on the NPL. Truly, some NPL sites presented little in the way of obvious imminent threats to human welfare or the environment. In fairness to EPA though, not many occurred.

Other outcomes of legal wrangling were *de minimis* and *de micromis* settlements. Early on, small volume PRPs were allowed to take *de minimis* settlements in which they agree to pay, up front, a set fee for the cleanup. Payment of the fee releases the *de minimis* PRP from further enforcement actions, though they are not exempt from citizen lawsuits. Settlements over $500,000 require the Attorney General's approval.

EPA uses volume of waste shipped to a site as the criteria for distributing charges among PRPs. The cleanup costs are allocated in what is referred to as a Non-Binding Preliminary Allocation of Responsibility (NBAR). Mixed funding arrangements are encouraged, as well as covenants not to sue. Obviously, mixed funding and covenants speed up the process. Mixed funding is the process of one of the PRPs getting funds from third parties, such as partners, insurance policies, and any other creative ideas you may have (that are legal).

Insurance coverage for activities that impact the environment is generally a good idea and in some cases required. For instance, insurance is required for a RCRA Permit, unless you arrange for some other method of financial assurance. Pollution exclusion clauses in comprehensive general liability (CGL) insurance policies are not always effective, either, so you may be able to get relief in the event of an environmental disaster (sudden or nonsudden). Risk retention groups are authorized under CERCLA as a way to facilitate self-insuring.

CONCLUSION

Operate your plant cleanly and in compliance at all times and you will avoid RCRA or CERCLA actions. Choose TSDFs and transporters wisely and avoid RCRA/CERCLA cleanups. If your worst nightmare happens, obtain an attorney and a remediation engineer immediately. Hire by credentials not by hourly charges.

REFERENCES

Abbasi, Rafat A. "RCRA Corrective Action—A Practical Guide." *Environmental Solutions*. October 1995.

EPA Region IV. *RCRA Guidance: Management of Contaminated Media*. Guidance Number TSC-92-02. August 1992.

Hamper, Martin. "Corrective Action's Impact on Business." *Pollution Engineering*. September 1, 1992.

INDEX

Environmental and Health/Safety References

Total Quality for Safety and Health Professionals

F. David Pierce, a CSP and a CIH, shows you how to apply concepts - proven and successful - to your safety management program to achieve increased productivity, lowered costs, reduced inventories, improved quality, increased profits, and raised employee morale.
Hardcover, 244 pages, June '95, ISBN: 0-86587-462-X **$59**

Pollution Prevention Strategies and Technologies

This book is an indispensible guide to understanding pollution prevention policies and regulatory initiatives designed to reduce wastes. *Hardcover, Index, 484 pages, Oct '95, ISBN: 0-86587-480-8* **$79**

Environmental Audits, 7th Edition

This is the most comprehensive manual available on environmental audits! Completely updated, it provides you with all the step-by-step guidance you need on how to begin - and manage - a successful audit program for your facility. Includes over 50 pages of exercises that cover Audit Verification, Interviewing Skills, Management Assessments, Report Writing, and Audit Conferences.
Softcover, approx. 500 pages, Mar '96, ISBN: 0-86587-525-1 **$79**

Toxicology Handbook

Get a basic, non-technical understanding of toxicological principles and have the relevant EPA Key Guidance and Implementation Documents highlighted throughout.
Softcover, 180 pages, Sept '86, ISBN: 0-86587-142-6 (Code 714) **$65**

Environmental Law Handbook, 13th Edition

Includes changes in major federal environmental laws. Details how those laws affect the regulated community.
Hardcover, Index, 550 pages, Mar '95, ISBN: 0-86587-450-6 **$79**

"So You're the Safety Director!" *An Introduction to Loss Control and Safety Management*

This book concentrates on your role in evaluating, managing, and controlling your company's losses and handling the OSHA compliance process.
Softcover, Index, 186 pages, Oct '95, ISBN: 0-86587-481-6 **$45**

Safety Made Easy: A Checklist Approach to OSHA Compliance

This new book provides a simple way of understanding your requirements under the complex maze of the Occupational Safety and Health Administration regulations. The authors have created safety and health checklists for compliance organized alphabetically by topic.
Softcover, 192 pages, June '95, ISBN: 0-86587-463-8 **$45**

Understanding Workers' Compensation: A Guide for Safety and Health Professionals

This book is designed to help you understand how the workers' comp system works, and provides a basic understanding of injury prevention, types of injuries, and cost containment strategies.
Softcover, 250 pages, July '95, ISBN: 0-86587-464-6 **$45**

Government Institutes • 4 Research Place • Rockville, MD 20850 • USA • (301) 921-2355

Environmental and Health/Safety References

Chemical Information Manual, 3rd Edition (Book and Disk Format)
This database contains essential data for over 1,400 chemical substances. The following information is available to you: proper identification synonyms, OSHA exposure limits, description and physical properties; carcinogenic status, health effects and toxicology, sampling and analysis.
Softcover, 400 pages, Aug '95, ISBN: 0-86587-469-7 **$99**
Also available on disk!
3.5" Floppy Disk for Windows, #4070 **$99**

Occupational Safety and Health Administration Technical Manual, 4th Edition

This inspection manual is used nationwide by the U.S. Occupational Safety and Health Administration's inspectors in checking industry compliance with OSHA requirements. *Softcover, 400 pages, Feb '96, ISBN: 0-86587-511-1* **$85**

Exposure Factors Handbook, Review Draft
The U.S. Environmental Protection Agency uses this document to develop pesticide tolerance levels, assess industrial chemical risks, and to undertake Superfund site assessments and drinking water health assessments.
Softcover, 866 pages, Nov '95, ISBN: 0-86587-509-X **$125**

Ergonomic Problems in the Workplace: A Guide to Effective Management
The valuable insights you'll gain from this new book will help you develop and implement your own successful ergonomics program.
Softcover, 256 pages, Sept '95, ISBN: 0-86587-474-3 **$59**

Product Side of Pollution Prevention: Evaluating the Potential for Safe Substitutes
This report focuses on safe substitutes for products that contain or use toxic chemicals in their manufacturing process.
Softcover, 240 pages, Sept '95, ISBN: 0-86587-479-4 **$69**

Sampling, Analysis & Monitoring Methods: A Guide to EPA Requirements
This book provides a guide for determining which chemicals have sampling, analysis, and monitoring requirements under U.S. environmental laws and regulations, and where those testing and sampling methods can be found.
Softcover, 256 pages, Sept '95, ISBN: 0-86587-477-8 **$65**

Emergency Planning & Management: *Ensuring Your Company's Survival in the Event of a Disaster*
This book will help you assess your exposure to disasters and prepare emergency response, preparedness, and recovery plans for your facilities, both to comply with OSHA and EPA requirements and to reduce the risk of losses to your company.
Softcover, 192 pages, Nov '95, ISBN: 0-86587-505-7 **$59**

Environmental, Health & Safety CFRs on CD ROM
Now you can scan EPA, OSHA and Hazmat regulations in seconds. Search on a regulation number, word, or phrase, and print or save the results!
Single Issue (most recent quarterly release) #4018 **$395** + **$5** shipping & handling

One-Year Subscription (receive an updated CD quarterly, beginning with the most recent release) #4000 **$998**

Government Institutes • 4 Research Place • Rockville, MD 20850 • USA • (301) 921-2355